7th Workshop on Technologies for Machine Translation of Low Resource Languages (LoResMT 2024)

Bangkok, Thailand
15 August 2024

ISBN: 979-8-3313-0169-9

Printed from e-media with permission by:

Curran Associates, Inc.
57 Morehouse Lane
Red Hook, NY 12571

CURRAN ASSOCIATES INC. proceedings .com

Some format issues inherent in the e-media version may also appear in this print version.

Association for Computational Linguistics
209 N. Eighth Street
Stroudsburg, Pennsylvania 18360

Phone: 1-570-476-8006
Fax: 1-570-476-0860

acl@aclweb.org

Additional copies of this publication are available from:

Curran Associates, Inc.
57 Morehouse Lane
Red Hook, NY 12571 USA
Phone: 845-758-0400
Fax: 845-758-2633
Email: curran@proceedings.com
Web: www.proceedings.com

LoResMT 2024

The Seventh Workshop on Technologies for Machine Translation of Low-Resource Languages (LoResMT 2024)

Proceedings of the Workshop

August 15, 2024

The LoResMT organizers gratefully acknowledge the support from the following organizations.

In cooperation with

Association for Computational Linguistics (ACL)
209 N. Eighth Street
Stroudsburg, PA 18360
USA
Tel: +1-570-476-8006
Fax: +1-570-476-0860
acl@aclweb.org

Preface

Based on the success of past low-resource machine translation (MT) workshops at AMTA 2018, MT Summit 2019, AACL-IJCNLP 2020, AMTA 2021, COLING-2022 & EACL-2023, we introduce seventh LoResMT workshop at ACL 2024 (https://2024.aclweb.org/). In the past few years, machine translation (MT) performance has improved significantly. With the development of new techniques such as multilingual translation and transfer learning, the use of MT is no longer a privilege for users of popular languages. However, the goal of expanding MT coverage to more diverse languages is hindered by the fact that MT methods require large amounts of data to train quality systems. This has made developing MT systems for low-resource languages challenging. Therefore, the need for developing comparable MT systems with relatively small datasets remains highly desirable.

Despite the advancements in MT technologies, creating an MT system for a new language or enhancing an existing one still requires a significant amount of effort to gather the necessary resources. The data-intensive nature of neural machine translation (NMT) approaches necessitates parallel and monolingual corpora in various domains, which are always in high demand. Developing MT systems also require dependable evaluation benchmarks and test sets. Furthermore, MT systems rely on numerous natural language processing (NLP) tools to pre-process human-generated texts into the required input format and post-process MT output into the appropriate textual forms in the target language. These tools include word tokenizers/de-tokenizers, word segmenters, and morphological analyzers, among others. The quality of these tools significantly impacts the translation output, yet there is a limited discourse on their methods, their role in training different MT systems, and their support coverage in different languages.

LoResMT is a platform that aims to facilitate discussions among researchers who are working on machine translation (MT) systems and methods for low-resource, under-represented, ethnic, and endangered languages. The goal of the platform is to address the challenges associated with the development of MT systems for languages that have limited resources or are at risk of being lost.

This year, LoResMT received research papers covering many languages spoken worldwide. The workshop received many papers on large language model (LLM) methods for MT. The acceptance rate of LoResMT this year is 51.28%. Aside from the research papers, LoResMT also featured two invited talks. These talks allowed participants to hear from experts in the field of MT and learn about the latest developments and challenges in MT for low-resource languages.

The program committee members play a crucial role in ensuring the success of the workshop. They review the submissions and provide constructive feedback to help the authors refine their papers and ensure they meet the set standards. Without their dedication, expertise, and hard work, the workshop would not be possible. The authors who submitted their work to LoResMT are also an integral part of the workshop's success. Their research and contributions offer new insights into the field of machine translation for low-resource languages, and their participation enriches the discussions and fosters collaboration. We are sincerely grateful to both the program committee members and the authors for their invaluable contributions and for making LoResMT a success.

Kat, Valentin, Nathaniel, Atul, Chao
(On behalf of the LoResMT chairs)

Organizing Committee

Workshop Chairs

Atul Kr. Ojha, Atul Kr. Ojha, Data Science Institute, Insight SFI Research Centre for Data Analytics, University of Galway
Chao-hong Liu, Potamu Research Ltd
Ekaterina Vylomova, University of Melbourne, Australia
Flammie Pirinen, UiT Norgga árktalaš universitehta
Jade Abbott, Retro Rabbit
Jonathan Washington, Swarthmore College
Nathaniel Oco, De La Salle University
Valentin Malykh, Huawei Noah's Ark lab and Kazan Federal University
Varvara Logacheva Skolkovo, Institute of Science and Technology
Xiaobing Zhao, Minzu University of China

Program Committee

Abigail Walsh, ADAPT Centre, Dublin City University, Ireland
Alberto Poncelas, Rakuten, Singapore
Ali Hatami, University of Galway
Alina Karakanta, Fondazione Bruno Kessler (FBK), University of Trento
Anna Currey, AWS AI Labs
Aswarth Abhilash Dara, Walmart Global Technology
Atul Kr. Ojha, University of Galway & Panlingua Language Processing LLP
Bogdan Babych, Heidelberg University
Chao-hong Liu, Potamu Research Ltd
Constantine Lignos, Brandeis University, USA
Daan van Esch, Google
Dana Moukheiber, Massachusetts Institute of Technology
Ekaterina Vylomova, University of Melbourne, Australia
Eleni Metheniti, CLLE-CNRS and IRIT-CNRS
Flammie Pirinen, UiT Norgga árktalaš universitehta
Jinliang Lu, Institute of automation, Chinese Academy of Sciences
John Philip McCrae, University of Galway
Jonathan Washington, Swarthmore College
Koel Dutta Chowdhury, Saarland University
Majid Latifi, UPC University
Maria Art Antonette Clariño, University of the Philippines Los Baños
Milind Agarwal, George Mason University
Nathaniel Oco, De La Salle University
Pavel Rychlý, Masaryk University and Lexical Computing
Pengwei Li, Meta
Rashid Ahmad, International Institute of Information Technology, Hyderabad
Santanu Pal, Wipro
Sangjee Dondrub, Qinghai Normal University
Sardana Ivanova, University of Helsinki
Sourabrata Mukherjee, Charles University
Thepchai Supnithi, National Electronics and Computer Technology Center
Timothee Mickus, University of Helsinki

Valentin Malykh, Huawei Noah's Ark lab and Kazan Federal University
Wen Lai, LMU Munich
Xuebo Liu, Harbin Institute of Technolgy, Shenzhen
Yalemisew Abgaz, Dublin City University
Yasmin Moslem, Bering Lab
Zhanibek Kozhirbayev, National Laboratory Astana, Nazarbayev University

Secondary Reviewers

Gaurav Negi, University of Galway

Keynote Talk: Hyperparameter Optimization for Low-Resource Machine Translation

Kevin Duh
Johns Hopkins University, USA

Abstract: Neural Machine Translation models are full of hyperparameters. To obtain a good model, one must carefully experiment with hyperparameters such as the number of layers, the number of hidden nodes, the type of non-linearity, the learning rate, and the drop-out parameter, just to name a few. I will discuss general hyperparameter optimization algorithms—including those based on evolutionary strategies, Bayesian techniques, and bandit learning–that can automate this laborious process. Further, I will argue that hyperparameter optimization is especially valuable for low-resource settings, where commonly-used hyperparameters are often suboptimal and small data sizes afford larger search spaces. Finally, I will discuss benchmarks and datasets for evaluating hyperparameter optimization algorithms in practice.

Bio: Kevin Duh is a senior research scientist at the Johns Hopkins University Human Language Technology Center of Excellence (JHU HLTCOE). He is also an assistant research professor in the Department of Computer Science and a member of the Center for Language and Speech Processing (CLSP). His research interests lie at the intersection of Natural Language Processing and Machine Learning, in particular on areas relating to machine translation, semantics, and deep learning. Previously, he was assistant professor at the Nara Institute of Science and Technology (2012-2015) and research associate at NTT CS Labs (2009-2012). He received his B.S. in 2003 from Rice University, and PhD in 2009 from the University of Washington, both in Electrical Engineering.

Keynote Talk: TBD

Loïc Barrault
Meta AI

Abstract: TBD

Bio: Loïc Barrault (M) is a Research Scientist at Meta AI. Previously, he was an Associate Professor at LIUM, University of Le Mans. He obtained his PhD at the University of Avignon in 2008 in the field of automatic speech recognition. Then he did 2 years as researcher and 9 years as Associate Professor at LIUM, Le Mans Université followed by 2 years as Senior Lecturer in the NLP group of the University of Sheffield. Loïc Barrault participated in many international projects, namely EuroMatrix+, MateCAT, DARPA BOLT, and national projects, namely ANR Cosmat, "Projet d'Investissement d'Avenir" PACTE and a large industrial project PEA TRAD. He coordinated the EU ChistERA M2CR project and is currently actively involved in the ChistERA ALLIES project and the French ANR ON-TRAC project. His research work focuses on statistical and neural machine translation, by including linguistics aspects (factored neural machine translation), by considering multiple modalities (multimodal neural machine translation) and by designing lifelong learning methods for MT. He is one of the organisers of the Multimodal Machine Translation shared task at WMT.

Table of Contents

Program

Thursday, August 15, 2024

09:00 - 09:10 *Opening Remarks*

09:10 - 10:05 *Invited Talk 1: Kevin Duh (Johns Hopkins University)*

10:05 - 10:30 *Session 1: Booster Presentations*

KpopMT: Translation Dataset with Terminology for Kpop Fandom
JiWoo Kim, Yunsu Kim and JinYeong Bak

HeSum: a Novel Dataset for Abstractive Text Summarization in Hebrew
Itai Mondshine, Tzuf Paz-Argaman, Asaf Achi Mordechai and Reut Tsarfaty

Challenges in Urdu Machine Translation
Abdul Basit, Abdul Hameed Azeemi and Agha Ali Raza

Low-Resource Cross-Lingual Summarization through Few-Shot Learning with Large Language Models
Gyutae Park, Seojin Hwang and Hwanhee Lee

Enhancing Low-Resource NMT with a Multilingual Encoder and Knowledge Distillation: A Case Study
Aniruddha Roy, Pretam Ray, Ayush Maheshwari, Sudeshna Sarkar and Pawan Goyal

Rule-Based, Neural and LLM Back-Translation: Comparative Insights from a Variant of Ladin
Samuel Frontull and Georg Moser

AGE: Amharic, Ge'ez and English Parallel Dataset
Henok Biadglign Ademtew and Mikiyas Girma Birbo

Adopting Ensemble Learning for Cross-lingual Classification of Crisis-related Text On Social Media
Shareefa Ahmed Al Amer, Mark G. Lee and Phillip Smith

Rosetta Balcanica: Deriving a "Gold Standard" Neural Machine Translation (NMT) Parallel Dataset from High-Fidelity Resources for Western Balkan Languages
Edmon Begoli, Maria Mahbub and Sudarshan Srinivasan

	Irish-based Large Language Model with Extreme Low-Resource Settings in Machine Translation Khanh-Tung Tran, Barry O'Sullivan and Hoang D. Nguyen
10:30 - 11:00	*Coffee/Tea Break*
11:00 - 12:30	*Session 2: Scientific Research Papers*
	Tuning LLMs with Contrastive Alignment Instructions for Machine Translation in Unseen, Low-resource Languages Zhuoyuan Mao and Yen Yu
	Linguistically Informed Transformers for Text to American Sign Language Translation Abhishek Bharadwaj Varanasi, Manjira Sinha and Tirthankar Dasgupta
	Leveraging Mandarin as a Pivot Language for Low-Resource Machine Translation between Cantonese and English King Yiu Suen, Rudolf Chow and Albert Y.s. Lam
	Enhancing Turkish Word Segmentation: A Focus on Borrowed Words and Invalid Morpheme Soheila Behrooznia, Ebrahim Ansari and Zdenek Zabokrtsky
	Super donors and super recipients: Studying cross-lingual transfer between high-resource and low-resource languages Vitaly Protasov, Elisei Stakovskii, Ekaterina Voloshina, Tatiana Shavrina and Alexander Panchenko
12:30 - 14:00	*Lunch*
14:00 - 15:00	*Invited Talk 2: Loïc Barrault (Meta AI)*
15:00 - 16:00	*Session 3: Poster Session*
	KpopMT: Translation Dataset with Terminology for Kpop Fandom JiWoo Kim, Yunsu Kim and JinYeong Bak
	HeSum: a Novel Dataset for Abstractive Text Summarization in Hebrew Itai Mondshine, Tzuf Paz-Argaman, Asaf Achi Mordechai and Reut Tsarfaty

Thursday, August 15, 2024 (continued)

Challenges in Urdu Machine Translation
Abdul Basit, Abdul Hameed Azeemi and Agha Ali Raza

Low-Resource Cross-Lingual Summarization through Few-Shot Learning with Large Language Models
Gyutae Park, Seojin Hwang and Hwanhee Lee

Enhancing Low-Resource NMT with a Multilingual Encoder and Knowledge Distillation: A Case Study
Aniruddha Roy, Pretam Ray, Ayush Maheshwari, Sudeshna Sarkar and Pawan Goyal

Rule-Based, Neural and LLM Back-Translation: Comparative Insights from a Variant of Ladin
Samuel Frontull and Georg Moser

AGE: Amharic, Ge'ez and English Parallel Dataset
Henok Biadglign Ademtew and Mikiyas Girma Birbo

Adopting Ensemble Learning for Cross-lingual Classification of Crisis-related Text On Social Media
Shareefa Ahmed Al Amer, Mark G. Lee and Phillip Smith

Rosetta Balcanica: Deriving a "Gold Standard" Neural Machine Translation (NMT) Parallel Dataset from High-Fidelity Resources for Western Balkan Languages
Edmon Begoli, Maria Mahbub and Sudarshan Srinivasan

Irish-based Large Language Model with Extreme Low-Resource Settings in Machine Translation
Khanh-Tung Tran, Barry O'Sullivan and Hoang D. Nguyen

15:30 - 16:00 *Coffee/Tea Break*

16:00 - 17:30 *Session 4: Scientific Research Papers*

Tokenisation in Machine Translation Does Matter: The impact of different tokenisation approaches for Maltese
Kurt Abela, Kurt Micallef, Marc Tanti and Claudia Borg

Machine Translation Through Cultural Texts: Can Verses and Prose Help Low-Resource Indigenous Models?
Antoine Cadotte, Nathalie André and Fatiha Sadat

Thursday, August 15, 2024 (continued)

	Learning-From-Mistakes Prompting for Indigenous Language Translation You Cheng Liao, Chen-Jui Yu, Chi-Yi Lin, He-Feng Yun, Yen-Hsiang Wang, Hsiao-Min Li and Yao-Chung Fan
	Finetuning End-to-End Models for Estonian Conversational Spoken Language Translation Tiia Sildam, Andra Velve and Tanel Alumäe
	Benchmarking Low-Resource Machine Translation Systems Ana Alexandra Morim Da Silva, Nikit Srivastava, Tatiana Moteu Ngoli, Michael Röder, Diego Moussallem and Axel-Cyrille Ngonga Ngomo
17:30 - 17:40	*Closing remarks*

Tuning LLMs with Contrastive Alignment Instructions for Machine Translation in Unseen, Low-resource Languages

Zhuoyuan Mao[*] and **Yen Yu**
Apple
kevinmzy@gmail.com, yen_yu@apple.com

Abstract

This article introduces contrastive alignment instructions (**AlignInstruct**) to address two challenges in machine translation (MT) on large language models (LLMs). One is the expansion of supported languages to previously unseen ones. The second relates to the lack of data in low-resource languages. Model fine-tuning through MT instructions (**MTInstruct**) is a straightforward approach to the first challenge. However, MTInstruct is limited by weak cross-lingual signals inherent in the second challenge. AlignInstruct emphasizes cross-lingual supervision via a cross-lingual discriminator built using statistical word alignments. Our results based on fine-tuning the BLOOMZ models (1b1, 3b, and 7b1) in up to 24 unseen languages showed that: (1) LLMs can effectively translate unseen languages using MTInstruct; (2) AlignInstruct led to consistent improvements in translation quality across 48 translation directions involving English; (3) Discriminator-based instructions outperformed their generative counterparts as cross-lingual instructions; (4) AlignInstruct improved performance in 30 zero-shot directions.

1 Introduction

Large language models (LLMs) (Brown et al., 2020; Chowdhery et al., 2022; Scao et al., 2022; Touvron et al., 2023a; Muennighoff et al., 2023; OpenAI, 2023; Anil et al., 2023; Touvron et al., 2023b) achieved good performance for a wide range of NLP tasks for prevalent languages. However, insufficient coverage for low-resource languages remains to be one significant limitation. Low-resource languages are either not present, or orders of magnitude smaller in size than dominant languages in the pre-training dataset. This limitation is in part due to the prohibitive cost incurred by curating good quality and adequately sized datasets for pre-training. Incrementally adapting existing multilingual LLMs to incorporate an unseen, low-resource language thus becomes a cost-effective priority to address this limitation. Previous study (de la Rosa and Fernández, 2022; Müller and Laurent, 2022; Yong et al., 2023) explored extending language support using either continual pre-training (Neubig and Hu, 2018; Artetxe et al., 2020; Muller et al., 2021; Ebrahimi and Kann, 2021), or parameter efficient fine-tuning (PEFT) methods (Pfeiffer et al., 2020; Hu et al., 2022; Liu et al., 2022) on monolingual tasks. Extending language support for cross-lingual tasks remains underexplored due to the challenge of incrementally inducing cross-lingual understanding and generation abilities in LLMs (Yong et al., 2023).

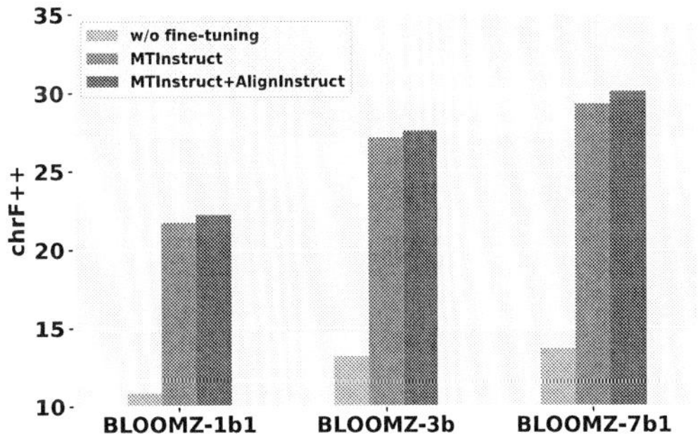

Figure 1: **Average chrF++ scores of BLOOMZ models across 24 unseen languages**, comparing settings of without fine-tuning, fine-tuning with MTInstruct, and fine-tuning that combines MTInstruct and AlignInstruct.

This study focused on machine translation (MT) to highlight the cross-lingual LLM adaptation challenge. The challenge lies in enabling translation for low-resource languages that often lack robust cross-lingual signals. We first explored the efficacy of fine-tuning LLMs with MT instructions (MTInstruct) in unseen, low-resource languages. MTInstruct is a method previously shown to bolster the translation proficiency of LLMs for sup-

[*]Currently at Sony Group Corporation. Work done during Apple internship.

Proceedings of the The Seventh Workshop on Technologies for Machine Translation of Low-Resource Languages (LoResMT 2024), pages 1–25
August 15, 2024 ©2024 Association for Computational Linguistics

ported languages (Li et al., 2023). Subsequently, given that cross-lingual alignments are suboptimal in LLMs as a result of data scarcity of low-resource languages, we proposed contrastive alignment instructions (AlignInstruct) to explicitly provide cross-lingual supervision during MT fine-tuning. AlignInstruct is a cross-lingual discriminator formulated using statistical word alignments. Our approach was inspired by prior studies (Lambert et al., 2012; Ren et al., 2019; Lin et al., 2020; Mao et al., 2022), which indicated the utility of word alignments in enhancing MT. In addition to AlignInstruct, we discussed two word-level cross-lingual instruction alternatives cast as generative tasks for comparison with AlignInstruct.

Our experiments fine-tuned the BLOOMZ models (Muennighoff et al., 2023) of varying sizes (1b1, 3b, and 7b1) for 24 unseen, low-resource languages, and evaluated translation on OPUS-100 (Zhang et al., 2020) and Flores-200 (Costa-jussà et al., 2022). We first showed that MTInstruct effectively induced the translation capabilities of LLMs for these languages. Building on the MTInstruct baseline, the multi-task learning combining AlignInstruct and MTInstruct resulted in stronger translation performance without the need for additional training corpora. The performance improved with larger BLOOMZ models, as illustrated in Fig. 1, indicating that AlignInstruct is particularly beneficial for larger LLMs during MT fine-tuning. When compared with the generative variants of AlignInstruct, our results indicated that discriminative instructions better complemented MTInstruct. Furthermore, merging AlignInstruct with its generative counterparts did not further improve translation quality, underscoring the efficacy and sufficiency of AlignInstruct in leveraging word alignments for MT.

In zero-shot translation evaluation on the OPUS benchmark, AlignInstruct exhibited improvements over the MTInstruct baseline in 30 zero-shot directions between non-English languages, when exclusively fine-tuned with three unseen languages (German, Dutch, and Russian). However, when incorporating supported languages (Arabic, French, and Chinese) the benefits of AlignInstruct were only evident in zero-shot translations where the target language was a supported language. In addition, to interpret the inherent modifications within the BLOOMZ models after applying MTInstruct or AlignInstruct, we conducted a visualization of the layer-wise cross-lingual alignment capabilities of the model representations.

2 Methodology

This section presents MTInstruct as the baseline, and AlignInstruct. The MTInstruct baseline involved fine-tuning LLMs using MT instructions. AlignInstruct dealt with the lack of cross-lingual signals stemming from the limited parallel training data in low-resource languages. The expectation was enhanced cross-lingual supervision cast as a discriminative task without extra training corpora. Following this, we introduced two generative variants of AlignInstruct for comparison.[1]

2.1 Baseline: MTInstruct

Instruction tuning (Wang et al., 2022; Mishra et al., 2022; Chung et al., 2022; Ouyang et al., 2022; Sanh et al., 2022; Wei et al., 2022) has been shown to generalize LLMs' ability to perform various downstream tasks, including MT (Li et al., 2023).

Given a pair of the parallel sentences, $\left((x_i)_1^N, (y_j)_1^M\right)$, where $(x_i)_1^N := x_1x_2\ldots x_N$, $(y_j)_1^M := y_1y_2\ldots y_M$. $x_i, y_j \in \mathcal{V}$ are members of the vocabulary $\mathcal{V}$ containing unique tokens that accommodate languages X and Y. Li et al. (2023) showed that the following MT instructions (MTInstruct) can improve the translation ability in an LLM with a limited number of parallel sentences:

- **Input:** "Translate from Y to X.
  Y: $y_1y_2\ldots y_M$.
  X: "
- **Output**: "$x_1x_2\ldots x_N$."

Note that Li et al. (2023) demonstrated the utility of MTInstruct solely within the context of fine-tuning for languages acquired at pre-training phase. This study called for an assessment of MTInstruct on its efficacy for adapting to previously unsupported languages, denoted as X, accompanied by the parallel data in a supported language Y.

2.2 AlignInstruct

Word alignments have been demonstrated to enhance MT performance (Lambert et al., 2012; Ren et al., 2019; Lin et al., 2020; Mao et al., 2022), both in the fields of statistical machine translation (SMT) (Brown et al., 1993) and neural machine translation (NMT) (Sutskever et al., 2014; Bahdanau et al., 2015). Ren et al. (2019) and Mao

[1]We also discussed monolingual instructions for MT fine-tuning in App. F.

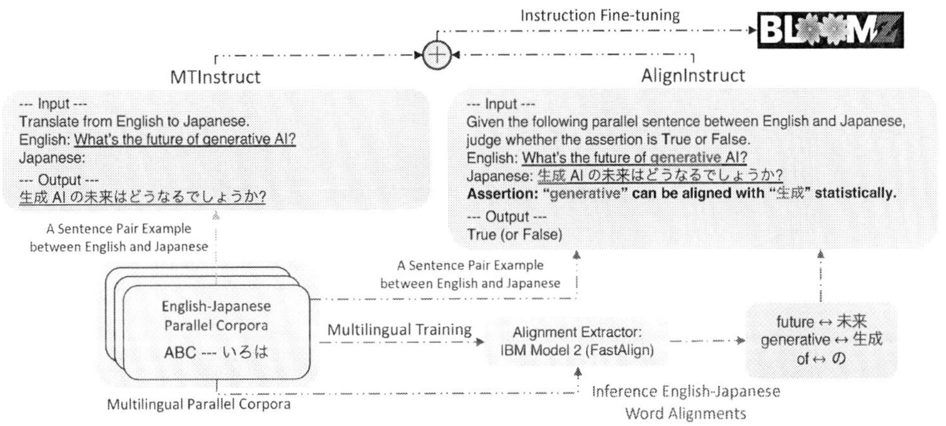

Figure 2: **Proposed instruction tuning methods combining MTInstruct (Sec. 2.1) and AlignInstruct (Sec. 2.2) for LLMs in MT tasks.** $\oplus$ denotes combining multiple instruction patters with a specific fine-tuning curriculum (Sec. 3.2). IBM Model 2 indicates word alignment model of statistical machine translation (Brown et al., 1993).

et al. (2022) reported the utility of SMT-derived contrastive word alignments in guiding encoder-decoder NMT model training. Built upon their findings, we introduced AlignInstruct for bolstering cross-lingual alignments in LLMs. We expected AlignInstruct to enhancing translation performance particularly for languages with no pre-training data and limited fine-tuning data.

As shown in Fig. 2, we employed FastAlign (Dyer et al., 2013) to extract statistical word alignments from parallel corpora. Our approach depended on a trained FastAlign model (IBM Model 2, Brown et al., 1993) to ensure the quality of the extracted word pairs. These high-quality word alignment pairs were regarded as "gold" word pairs for constructing AlignInstruct instructions.[2] Assuming one gold word pair $(x_k x_{k+1}, y_l y_{l+1} y_{l+2})$ was provided for the sentence pair $\left((x_i)_1^N, (y_j)_1^M\right)$, the AlignInstruct instruction reads:

- **Input:** "Given the following parallel sentence between Y and X, judge whether the assertion is True or False.
  Y: $y_1 y_2 \dots y_M$.
  X: $x_1 x_2 \dots x_N$.
  Assertion: "$y_l y_{l+1} y_{l+2}$" can be aligned with "$x_k x_{k+1}$" statistically."
- **Output**: "True" (or "False")

Instructions with the "False" output were constructed by uniformly swapping out part of the word pair to create misalignment. We anticipated that this treatment forced the model to learn to infer the output by recognizing true alignment-enriched instructions. This would require the model to encode word-level cross-lingual representation, a crucial characteristic for MT tasks.

2.3 Generative Counterparts of AlignInstruct

Previous studies (Liang et al., 2022; Yu et al., 2023) have suggested the importance of both discriminative and generative tasks in fine-tuning LLMs. We accordingly considered two generative variants of AlignInstruct. We then compared them with AlignInstruct to determine the most effective training task. As detailed in Sec. 4, our results indicated that these variants underperformed AlignInstruct when applied to unseen, low-resource languages.

2.3.1 HintInstruct

HintInstruct as a generative variant of AlignInstruct was instructions containing word alignment hints. It was inspired by Ghazvininejad et al. (2023), where dictionary hints were shown to improve few-shot in-context leaning. Instead of relying on additional dictionaries, we used the same word alignments described in Sec. 2.2, which were motivated by the common unavailability of high-quality dictionaries for unseen, low-resource languages. Let $\{(x_{k_s} x_{k_s+1} \dots x_{k_s+n_s}, y_{l_s} y_{l_s+1} \dots y_{l_s+m_s})\}_{s=1}^S$ be S word pairs extracted from the sentence pair $\left((x_i)_1^N, (y_j)_1^M\right)$. HintInstruct follows the instruction pattern:

- **Input**: "Use the following alignment hints

[2] Note that these word pairs may not necessarily represent direct translations of each other; instead, they are word pairs identified based on their co-occurrence probability within the similar context. Refer to IBM model 2 in SMT.

and translate from Y to X.
Alignments between X and Y:
– $(x_{k_1}x_{k_1+1}\dots x_{k_1+n_1}, y_{l_1}y_{l_1+1}\dots y_{l_1+m_1})$,
– $(x_{k_2}x_{k_2+1}\dots x_{k_1+n_1}, y_{l_2}y_{l_2+1}\dots y_{l_2+m_2})$,
$\dots$,
– $(x_{k_S}x_{k_S+1}\dots x_{k_S+n_S}, y_{l_S}y_{l_S+1}\dots y_{l_S+m_S})$,
Y: $y_1y_2\dots y_M$.
X: "

- **Output**: "$x_1x_2\dots x_N$."

where S denotes the number of the word alignment pairs used to compose the instructions. Different from AlignInstruct, HintInstruct expects the translation targets to be generated.

2.3.2 ReviseInstruct

ReviseInstruct was inspired by Ren et al. (2019) and Liu et al. (2020) for the notion of generating parallel words or phrases, thereby encouraging a model to encode cross-lingual alignments. A ReviseInstruct instruction contained a partially corrupted translation target, as well as a directive to identify and revise these erroneous tokens. Tokens are intentionally corrupted at the granularity of individual words, aligning with the word-level granularity in AlignInstruct and HintInstruct. ReviseInstruct follows the instruction pattern:[3]

- **Input**: "Given the following translation of X from Y, output the incorrectly translated word and correct it.
Y: $y_1y_2\dots y_M$.
X: $x_1x_2\dots x_kx_{k+1}\dots x_{k+n}\dots x_N$."
- **Output**: "The incorrectly translated word is "$x_kx_{k+1}\dots x_{k+n}$". It should be "$x_jx_{j+1}\dots x_{j+m}$"."

3 Experimental Settings

3.1 Backbone Models and Unseen Languages

Our experiments fine-tuned the BLOOMZ models (Muennighoff et al., 2023) for MT in unseen, low-resource languages. BLOOMZ is an instruction fine-tuned multilingual LLM from BLOOM (Scao et al., 2022) that supports translation across 46 languages. Two lines of experiments evaluated the effectiveness of the MTInstruct baseline and AlignInstruct:

BLOOMZ+24 Tuning BLOOMZ-7b1, BLOOMZ-3b, and BLOOMZ-1b1[4] for 24 unseen, low-resource languages. These experiments aimed to: (1) assess the effectiveness of AlignInstruct in multilingual, low-resource scenarios; (2) offer comparison across various model sizes. We used the OPUS-100 (Zhang et al., 2020)[5] datasets as training data. OPUS-100 is an English-centric parallel corpora, with around 4.5M parallel sentences in total for 24 selected languages, averaging 187k sentence pairs for each language and English. Refer to App. A for training data statistics. We used OPUS-100 and Flores-200 (Costa-jussà et al., 2022)[6] for evaluating translation between English and 24 unseen languages (48 directions in total) on in-domain and out-of-domain test sets, respectively. The identical prompt as introduced in Sec. 2.1 was employed for inference. Inferences using alternative MT prompts are discussed in App. G.

BLOOMZ+3 Tuning BLOOMZ-7b1 with three unseen languages, German, Dutch, and Russian, or a combination of these three unseen languages and another three seen (Arabic, French, and Chinese). We denote the respective setting as **de-nl-ru** and **ar-de-fr-nl-ru-zh**. These experiments assessed the efficacy of AlignInstruct in zero-shot translation scenarios, where translation directions were not presented during fine-tuning, as well as the translation performance when incorporating supported languages as either source or target languages. To simulate the low-resource fine-tuning scenario, we randomly sampled 200k parallel sentences for each language. For evaluation, we used the OPUS-100 supervised and zero-shot test sets, comprising 12 supervised directions involving English and 30 zero-shot directions without English among six languages.

Notably, BLOOMZ's pre-training data includes the English portion of the Flores-200 dataset, potentially leading to data leakage during evaluation (Muennighoff et al., 2023; Zhu et al., 2023a). To mitigate this, our evaluation also compared translation quality before and after fine-tuning, thereby distinguishing the genuine improvements in translation capability attributable to the fine-tuning process (refer to the results in Sec. 4).

3.2 Training Details and Curricula

The PEFT method, LoRA (Hu et al., 2022), was chosen to satisfy the parameter efficiency requirement for low-resource languages, as full-parameter fine-tuning would likely under-specify the mod-

[3]We illustrated examples of HintInstruct and ReviseInstruct in App. E for reference.

[4]https://huggingface.co/bigscience/bloomz

[5]https://opus.nlpl.eu/opus-100.php

[6]https://github.com/facebookresearch/flores/blob/main/flores200/README.md

BLOOMZ model	Objective	OPUS en→xx			OPUS xx→en			Flores en→xx			Flores xx→en		
		BLEU	chrF++	COMET	BLEU	chrF++	COMET	BLEU	chrF++	COMET	BLEU	chrF++	COMET
BLOOMZ-7b1	w/o fine-tuning	3.61	8.82	47.81	6.70	18.49	51.68	2.00	9.35	36.54	9.95	24.47	52.05
	Individual objectives												
	MTInstruct	11.54	25.33	64.54	18.59	33.25	69.84	3.30	17.10	40.58	11.37	27.14	56.33
	AlignInstruct	4.73	9.23	49.85	5.32	12.90	53.26	1.97	8.90	42.35	3.47	11.93	39.58
	Multiple objectives with different curricula												
	MT+Align	**12.28**	**26.17**	**65.54**	**18.72**	**34.02**	**70.69**	3.26	**17.20**	**41.07**	**11.60**	**27.38**	**56.98**
	Align→MT	**11.73**	**25.48**	64.54	17.54	32.62	69.76	**3.35**	**17.21**	**40.85**	11.32	**27.21**	**56.50**
	MT+Align→MT	**12.10**	**26.16**	**65.43**	18.23	**33.54**	**70.60**	3.28	**17.26**	**41.13**	**11.48**	**27.34**	**56.78**
BLOOMZ-3b	w/o fine-tuning	4.63	9.93	48.53	5.90	16.38	48.05	2.00	9.09	39.52	5.86	18.56	47.03
	Individual objectives												
	MTInstruct	10.40	23.08	62.28	16.10	31.15	68.36	2.85	16.23	39.21	8.92	24.57	53.33
	AlignInstruct	1.70	4.05	43.89	0.87	3.20	41.93	0.16	3.09	31.10	0.10	1.80	29.46
	Multiple objectives with different curricula												
	MT+Align	**10.61**	**23.64**	**62.84**	**16.73**	**31.51**	**68.52**	**2.95**	**16.62**	**39.83**	**9.50**	**25.16**	**54.35**
	Align→MT	10.22	22.53	61.99	15.90	30.31	67.79	**3.02**	**16.43**	**39.46**	**9.07**	**24.70**	**53.71**
	MT+Align→MT	**10.60**	**23.35**	**62.69**	**16.58**	**31.64**	**68.98**	**2.93**	**16.57**	**39.78**	**9.41**	**25.08**	**54.13**
BLOOMZ-1b1	w/o fine-tuning	3.76	7.57	46.98	4.78	14.11	49.34	1.24	6.93	38.13	3.49	14.56	43.26
	Individual objectives												
	MTInstruct	7.42	17.85	57.53	11.99	25.59	63.93	2.11	14.40	36.35	5.33	20.65	48.83
	AlignInstruct	2.51	5.29	45.17	3.13	8.92	48.48	0.35	3.79	31.70	1.35	6.43	33.63
	Multiple objectives with different curricula												
	MT+Align	**7.80**	**18.48**	**57.77**	**12.57**	**25.92**	**64.03**	**2.16**	**14.54**	**37.05**	**5.46**	**20.90**	**49.31**
	Align→MT	**7.49**	**18.09**	**57.67**	11.80	24.70	63.29	2.08	14.28	**36.61**	5.24	20.53	48.76
	MT+Align→MT	**7.98**	**18.61**	**57.94**	**12.43**	**25.78**	63.93	**2.16**	**14.46**	**37.02**	**5.37**	**20.67**	**49.01**

Table 1: **Results of BLOOMZ+24 fine-tuned with MTInstruct and AlignInstruct on different curricula** as described in 3.2. Scores that surpass the MTInstruct baseline are marked in **bold**.

els.See App. B for implementation details. How AlignInstruct and MTInstruct are integrated into training remained undetermined. To that end, we investigated three training curricula:

Multi-task Fine-tuning combined multiple tasks in a single training session (Caruana, 1997). This was realized by joining MTInstruct and AlignInstruct training data, denoted as **MT+Align**.[7]

Pre-fine-tuning & Fine-tuning arranges fine-tuning in a two-stage curriculum (Bengio et al., 2009), first with AlignInstruct, then with MTInstruct.[8] This configuration, denoted as **Align→MT**, validates whether AlignInstruct should precede MTInstruct.

Mixed Fine-tuning (Chu et al., 2017) arranged the above curricula to start with MT+Align, followed by MTInstruct, denoted as **MT+Align→MT**.

4 Evaluation and Analysis

This section reports BLEU (Papineni et al., 2002; Post, 2018), chrF++ (Popović, 2015), and COMET (Rei et al., 2020)[9] scores for respective experimental configurations. We further characterized of the degree to which intermediate embeddings were language-agnostic after fine-tuning.

4.1 BLOOMZ+24 Results

Tab. 1 shows the scores for the unmodified BLOOMZ models, as well as BLOOMZ+24 under MTInstruct, AlignInstruct, and the three distinct curricula. Non-trivial improvements in all metrics were evident for BLOOMZ+24 under MTInstruct. This suggests that MTInstruct can induce translation capabilities in unseen languages. Applying AlignInstruct and MTInstruct via the curricula further showed better scores than the baselines, suggesting the role of AlignInstruct as complementing MTInstruct. Align→MT was an exception, performing similarly to MTInstruct. This may indicate the effect of AlignInstruct depends on its cadence relative to MTInstruct in a curriculum.

Superior OPUS and Flores scores under the xx→en direction were evident, compared to the reverse direction, en→xx. This suggests that our treatments induced understanding capabilities more than generative ones. This may be attributed to the fact that BLOOMZ had significant exposure to English, and that we used English-centric corpora. Finally, we noted the inferior performance of Flores than OPUS. This speaks to the challenge of instilling out-of-domain translation abilities in unseen languages. Our future work will focus on enhancing the domain generalization capabilities

[7] Note that AlignInstruct and MTInstruct were derived from the same parallel corpora.

[8] An effective curriculum often starts with a simple and general task, followed by a task-specific task.

[9] COMET scores do not currently support Limburgish (li), Occitan (oc), Tajik (tg), Turkmen (tk), and Tatar (tt) among the 24 languages in the BLOOMZ+24 setting. Thus, we report the average COMET scores for the remaining 19 languages.

Objective	en-af	af-en	en-am	am-en	en-be	be-en	en-cy	cy-en	en-ga	ga-en	en-gd	gd-en
MTInstruct	25.0	38.5	3.0	3.4	8.9	14.0	20.2	33.2	15.6	29.2	13.1	66.0
MT+Align	25.0	*36.9*	**3.4**	**4.9**	*8.3*	13.9	**20.6**	**33.8**	**17.6**	**32.6**	**15.6**	*48.1*
Objective	en-gl	gl-en	en-ha	ha-en	en-ka	ka-en	en-kk	kk-en	en-km	km-en	en-ky	ky-en
MTInstruct	16.9	24.7	12.3	10.0	4.6	10.0	12.6	14.6	19.7	13.9	16.0	21.1
MT+Align	17.1	24.4	**14.6**	**11.4**	4.9	**10.5**	12.3	**15.6**	**20.4**	**14.4**	15.8	**23.3**
Objective	en-li	li-en	en-my	my-en	en-nb	nb-en	en-nn	nn-en	en-oc	oc-en	en-si	si-en
MTInstruct	13.5	21.3	6.2	5.2	12.7	22.2	18.3	27.1	10.0	13.4	5.2	11.5
MT+Align	13.2	**22.3**	**7.6**	**6.3**	**13.5**	**24.2**	**19.0**	**28.5**	*9.1*	13.5	5.1	**13.9**
Objective	en-tg	tg-en	en-tk	tk-en	en-tt	tt-en	en-ug	ug-en	en-uz	uz-en	en-yi	yi-en
MTInstruct	5.5	8.0	24.4	30.4	1.9	3.6	1.2	4.2	3.1	5.7	7.1	14.9
MT+Align	**6.6**	**8.8**	**27.2**	**31.2**	2.1	**5.0**	1.1	**5.5**	**3.5**	**7.4**	**11.1**	*12.8*

Table 2: Language-wise BLEU results on BLOOMZ-7b1 for BLOOMZ+24 fine-tuned using MTInstruct or MT+Align. Scores significantly (Koehn, 2004) outperforming the MTInstruct baseline are emphasized in **bold** while those decreased significantly (Koehn, 2004) are marked in *italics*.

BLOOMZ model	Objective	OPUS en→xx			OPUS xx→en			Flores en→xx			Flores xx→en		
		BLEU	chrF++	COMET	BLEU	chrF++	COMET	BLEU	chrF++	COMET	BLEU	chrF++	COMET
BLOOMZ-7b1	MTInstruct	11.54	25.33	64.54	18.59	33.25	69.84	3.30	17.10	40.58	11.37	27.14	56.33
	MT+Align	**12.28**	**26.17**	**65.54**	**18.72**	**34.02**	**70.69**	3.26	**17.20**	**41.07**	**11.60**	**27.38**	**56.98**
	MT+Hint	**12.12**	**25.92**	**64.60**	18.25	33.18	**70.31**	**3.34**	**17.13**	**41.10**	**11.45**	**27.37**	**56.86**
	MT+Revise	**11.96**	**25.73**	**64.73**	**18.69**	**33.74**	**70.32**	**3.34**	17.10	**41.07**	**11.44**	**27.37**	**56.73**
BLOOMZ-3b	MTInstruct	10.40	23.08	62.28	16.10	31.15	68.36	2.85	16.23	39.21	8.92	24.57	53.33
	MT+Align	**10.61**	**23.64**	**62.84**	**16.73**	**31.51**	**68.52**	**2.95**	**16.62**	**39.83**	**9.50**	**25.16**	**54.35**
	MT+Hint	**10.49**	**23.34**	**62.65**	**16.29**	**31.43**	**68.83**	**3.11**	**16.95**	**39.91**	**9.52**	**25.25**	**54.28**
	MT+Revise	**10.52**	23.03	62.04	**16.22**	30.98	68.28	**2.99**	**16.83**	**39.52**	**9.47**	**25.21**	**53.91**
BLOOMZ-1b1	MTInstruct	7.42	17.85	57.53	11.99	25.59	63.93	2.11	14.40	36.35	5.33	20.65	48.83
	MT+Align	**7.80**	**18.48**	**57.77**	**12.57**	**25.92**	**64.03**	**2.16**	**14.54**	**37.05**	**5.46**	**20.90**	**49.31**
	MT+Hint	**7.71**	**18.15**	**57.76**	11.52	24.88	63.63	**2.21**	**14.61**	**37.24**	**5.47**	**20.78**	**48.97**
	MT+Revise	7.31	**17.99**	57.45	**12.00**	25.33	63.81	2.07	14.32	**36.68**	**5.41**	**20.91**	**49.09**

Table 3: **Results of BLOOMZ+24 fine-tuned combining MTInstruct with AlignInstruct (or its generative variants).** Scores that surpass the MTInstruct baseline are marked in **bold**.

of LLM fine-tuning in MT tasks.

Moreover, we reported the language-wise scores in Tab. 2. Specifically, in the "en-xx" direction, 11 languages showed statistically significant (Koehn, 2004) improvements, and only 2 decreased significantly. In the "xx-en" direction, the improvements were more pronounced, with 18 languages improving significantly (most by over 1 BLEU point) and 3 decreasing significantly. The average improvement for "en-xx" was 0.74, which was substantial, especially given the limited volume of parallel data available for each language. The smaller average increase in "xx-en" can be attributed to a large decrease in one language (gd), likely due to limited training data (which can be potentially addressed with oversampling). The significantly enhanced performance in most individual languages underscores the effectiveness of our proposed methods.

4.2 Assessing AlignInstruct Variants

From Tab. 3, we observed the objectives with AlignInstruct consistently outperformed those with HintInstruct or ReviseInstruct across metrics and model sizes. Namely, easy, discriminative instructions, rather than hard, generative ones, may be preferred for experiments under similar data constraints. The low-resource constraint likely made MTInstruct more sensitive to the difficulty of its accompanying tasks.

Further, combining more than two instruction tuning tasks simultaneously did not guarantee consistent improvements, see Tab. 4. Notably, MT+Align either outperformed or matched the performance of other objective configurations. While merging multiple instruction tuning tasks occasionally resulted in superior BLEU and chrF++ scores for OPUS xx→en, it fell short in COMET scores compared to MT+Align. This indicated that while such configurations might enhance word-level translation quality, as reflected by BLEU and chrF++ scores, due to increased exposure to cross-lingual word alignments, MT+Align better captured the context of the source sentence as reflected by COMET scores. Overall, these instruction tuning tasks did not demonstrate significant synergistic effects for fine-tuning for unseen languages.

Objective	OPUS en→xx			OPUS xx→en			Flores en→xx			Flores xx→en		
	BLEU	chrF++	COMET	BLEU	chrF++	COMET	BLEU	chrF++	COMET	BLEU	chrF++	COMET
MTInstruct	11.54	25.33	64.54	18.59	33.25	69.84	3.30	17.10	40.58	11.37	27.14	56.33
MT+Align	**12.28**	**26.17**	**65.54**	**18.72**	**34.02**	**70.69**	3.26	**17.20**	**41.07**	**11.60**	**27.38**	**56.98**
MT+Align+Revise	**12.08**	**25.73**	**64.55**	**19.23**	**34.32**	**70.60**	**3.33**	**17.25**	**41.17**	**11.60**	**27.61**	**57.22**
MT+Align+Hint	**12.02**	**25.51**	**64.58**	**19.40**	**34.44**	**70.65**	3.25	16.87	**41.13**	**11.58**	**27.48**	**56.93**
MT+Hint+Revise	**12.10**	**25.69**	**64.68**	**19.58**	**34.49**	**70.55**	**3.34**	**17.24**	**41.13**	**11.70**	**27.62**	**57.19**
MT+Align+Hint+Revise	**12.00**	**25.39**	**64.55**	**19.68**	**34.48**	**70.64**	**3.40**	**17.17**	**41.21**	**11.67**	**27.54**	**57.16**

Table 4: **Results of BLOOMZ+24 combining MTInstruct with multiple objectives among AlignInstruct, HintInstruct, and ReviseInstruct on BLOOMZ-7b1.** Scores that surpass MTInstruct are marked in **bold**.

Fine-tuned Languages	Objective	Zero-shot Directions				Supervised Directions			
		Directions	BLEU	chrF++	COMET	Directions	BLEU	chrF++	COMET
-	w/o fine-tuning	overall	6.89	19.14	57.95	en→xx	13.38	26.65	64.28
						xx→en	21.70	42.05	72.72
		seen→seen	16.95	30.78	74.58	en→seen	20.13	32.87	76.99
		seen→unseen	2.30	13.31	49.98	en→unseen	6.63	20.43	51.56
		unseen→seen	7.78	20.07	62.74	seen→en	26.30	48.70	78.22
		unseen→unseen	2.37	14.83	46.06	unseen→en	17.10	35.40	67.23
de-nl-ru	MTInstruct	overall	8.38	22.75	59.93	en→xx	17.05	32.02	69.26
						xx→en	25.13	45.02	76.29
		seen→seen	14.52	27.25	70.48	en→seen	17.60	29.87	73.81
		seen→unseen	6.14	22.82	54.75	en→unseen	16.50	34.17	64.70
		unseen→seen	7.56	19.22	61.99	seen→en	25.73	47.07	77.52
		unseen→unseen	6.85	23.45	54.07	unseen→en	24.53	42.97	75.06
	MT+Align	overall	**8.86**	**23.30**	**60.70**	en→xx	16.63	31.73	68.79
						xx→en	**25.62**	**45.37**	**76.45**
		seen→seen	**14.77**	**27.80**	**71.07**	en→seen	15.80	28.47	72.35
		seen→unseen	**6.31**	**23.08**	**54.81**	en→unseen	**17.47**	**35.00**	**65.24**
		unseen→seen	**8.61**	**20.24**	**63.81**	seen→en	**25.90**	**47.13**	77.47
		unseen→unseen	**7.15**	**23.70**	**54.51**	unseen→en	**25.33**	**43.60**	**75.43**
ar-de-fr-nl-ru-zh	MTInstruct	overall	11.79	26.36	63.22	en→xx	21.18	35.52	70.86
						xx→en	28.35	48.00	77.30
		seen→seen	22.68	35.32	76.39	en→seen	26.20	37.77	78.22
		seen→unseen	7.10	24.50	55.18	en→unseen	16.17	33.27	63.50
		unseen→seen	12.56	24.74	68.83	seen→en	31.97	52.93	79.72
		unseen→unseen	6.78	22.62	53.69	unseen→en	24.73	43.07	74.88
	MT+Align	overall	**12.13**	**26.65**	**63.23**	en→xx	**21.33**	**35.65**	**70.99**
						xx→en	**28.60**	**48.27**	**77.49**
		seen→seen	**23.67**	**36.53**	**76.89**	en→seen	**26.30**	37.63	**78.25**
		seen→unseen	**7.27**	24.32	54.96	en→unseen	**16.37**	**33.67**	**63.73**
		unseen→seen	**12.92**	**25.29**	**69.10**	seen→en	**32.03**	**53.07**	**79.93**
		unseen→unseen	6.68	22.30	53.19	unseen→en	**25.17**	**43.47**	**75.05**

Table 5: **Results of BLOOMZ+3 without fine-tuning or fine-tuned with MTInstruct, or MT+Align.** Scores that surpass the MTInstruct baseline are marked in **bold**. "Seen" and "unseen" refer to whether the language was included in the pre-training of the BLOOMZ model. xx includes seen and unseen languages.

4.3 BLOOMZ+3 Zero-shot Evaluation

Tab. 5 reports the results of the two settings, de-nl-ru and ar-de-fr-nl-ru-zh. Results of MT+Align+Hint+Revise and pivot-based translation are reported in App. C and H. In the de-nl-ru setting, where BLOOMZ was fine-tuned with the three unseen languages, we noticed MT+Align consistently outperformed the MTInstruct baseline across all evaluated zero-shot directions. Notably, MT+Align enhanced the translation quality for unseen→seen and seen→unseen directions compared to w/o fine-tuning and MTInstruct, given that the model was solely fine-tuned on de, nl, and ru data. This suggested AlignInstruct not only benefits the languages supplied in the data but also has a positive impact on other languages through cross-lingual alignment supervision. In terms of supervised directions involving English, we noticed performance improvements associated with unseen languages, and regression in seen ones. The regression may be attributed to forgetting for the absence of seen languages in fine-tuning data. Indeed, continuous exposure to English maintained the translation quality for seen→en. As LoRA is modular, the regression can be mitigated by detaching the LoRA parameters for seen languages.

The ar-de-fr-nl-ru-zh setting yielded a consistently higher translation quality across all directions when compared with the de-nl-ru setting. This improvement was expected, as all the six languages were included. Translation quality improved for when generating seen languages under

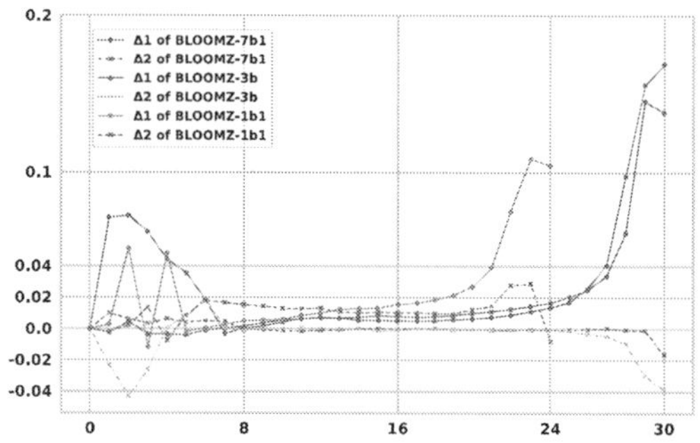

Figure 3: **Differences in cosine similarity of layer-wise embeddings for BLOOMZ+24.** $\Delta 1$ represents the changes from the unmodified BLOOMZ to the one on MTInstruct, and $\Delta 2$ from MTInstruct to MT+Align.

the zero-shot scenario. However, the same observation cannot be made for unseen languages. This phenomenon underscored the effectiveness of AlignInstruct in enhancing translation quality for BLOOMZ's supported languages, but suggested limitations for unseen languages when mixed with supported languages in zero-shot scenarios. In the supervised directions, we found all translation directions surpassed the performance of the MTInstruct baseline. This highlighted the overall effectiveness of AlignInstruct in enhancing translation quality across a range of supervised directions.

4.4 How did MTInstruct and AlignInstruct Impact BLOOMZ's Representations?

This section analyzed the layer-wise cosine similarities between the embeddings of parallel sentences to understand the changes in internal representations after fine-tuning. The parallel sentences were prepared from the English-centric validation datasets. We then mean-pool the outputs at each layer as sentence embeddings and compute the cosine similarities, as illustrated in Fig. 3. Results for BLOOMZ+3 are discussed in App. D.

We observed that, after MTInstruct fine-tuning, the cosine similarities rose in nearly all layers ($\Delta 1$, Fig. 3). This may be interpreted as enhanced cross-lingual alignment, and as indicating the acquisition of translation capabilities. Upon further combination with AlignInstruct ($\Delta 2$, Fig. 3), the degree of cross-lingual alignment rose in the early layers (layers 4 - 7) then diminished in the final layers (layers 29 & 30). This pattern aligned with the characteristics of encoder-decoder multilingual NMT models, where language-agnostic encoder representations with language-specific decoder representations improve multilingual NMT performance (Liu et al., 2021; Wu et al., 2021; Mao et al., 2023). This highlights the beneficial impact of AlignInstruct.

5 Related Work

Prompting LLMs for MT LLMs have shown good performance for multilingual MT through few-shot in-context learning (ICL) (Jiao et al., 2023). Agrawal et al. (2023) and Zhang et al. (2023a) explored strategies to compose better examples for ICL for XGLM-7.5B (Lin et al., 2022) and GLM-130B (Zeng et al., 2023). Ghazvininejad et al. (2023), Peng et al. (2023), and Moslem et al. (2023) claimed that dictionary-based hints and domain-specific style information can improve prompting OPT (Zhang et al., 2022), GPT-3.5 (Brown et al., 2020), and BLOOM (Scao et al., 2022) for MT. He et al. (2023) used LLMs to mine useful knowledge for prompting GPT-3.5 for MT.

Fine-tuning LLMs for MT ICL-based methods do not support languages unseen during pre-training. Current approaches address this issue via fine-tuning. Zhang et al. (2023b) explored adding new languages to LLaMA (Touvron et al., 2023a) with interactive translation task for unseen high-resource languages. However, similar task datasets are usually not available for most unseen, low-resource languages. Li et al. (2023) and Xu et al. (2023a) showed multilingual fine-tuning with translation instructions can improve the translation ability in supported languages. Our study extended their finding to apply in the context of unseen, low-resource languages. In parallel research, Yang et al. (2023) undertook MT instruction fine-tuning in a massively multilingual context for unseen languages. However, their emphasis was on fine-tuning curriculum based on resource availability of languages, whereas we exclusively centered on low-resource languages and instruction tuning tasks.

6 Conclusion

In this study, we introduced AlignInstruct for enhancing the fine-tuning of LLMs for MT in unseen, low-resource languages while limiting the use of additional training corpora. Our multilingual and zero-shot findings demonstrated the strength of AlignInstruct over the MTInstruct baseline and other instruction variants. Our future work pertains to exploring using large monolingual corpora of unseen languages for MT and refining the model capability to generalize across diverse MT prompts.

Limitations

Multilingual LLMs In this study, our investigations were confined to the fine-tuning of BLOOMZ models with sizes of 1.1B, 3B, and 7.1B. We did not experiment with the 175B BLOOMZ model due to computational resource constraints. However, examining this model could provide valuable insights into the efficacy of our proposed techniques. Additionally, it would be instructive to experiment with other recent open-source multilingual LLMs, such as mGPT (Shliazhko et al., 2022) and LLaMa2 (Touvron et al., 2023b).

PEFT Methods and Adapters As discussed in the BLOOM+1 paper (Yong et al., 2023), alternative PEFT techniques, such as $(IA)^3$ (Liu et al., 2022), have the potential to enhance the adaptation performance of LLM pre-training for previously unseen languages. These approaches are worth exploring for MT fine-tuning in such languages, in addition to the LoRA methods employed in this study. Furthermore, our exploration was limited to fine-tuning multiple languages using shared additional parameters. Investigating efficient adaptation through the use of the mixture of experts (MoE) approach for MT tasks (Fan et al., 2021; Costa-jussà et al., 2022; Mohammadshahi et al., 2022; Koishekenov et al., 2023; Xu et al., 2023b) presents another intriguing avenue for LLM fine-tuning.

Instruction Fine-tuning Data Another limitation of our study is that we exclusively explored MT instruction fine-tuning using fixed templates to create MT and alignment instructions. Investigating varied templates (either manually (Yang et al., 2023) or automatically constructed (Zhou et al., 2023)) might enhance the fine-tuned MT model's ability to generalize across different MT task descriptions. Additionally, leveraging large monolingual corpora in unseen languages could potentially enhance the effectiveness of monolingual instructions for MT downstream tasks, offering further insights beyond the resource-constrained scenarios examined in this work. Furthermore, the creation and utilization of instruction tuning datasets, akin to xP3 (Muennighoff et al., 2023), for unseen, low-resource languages could potentially amplify LLMs' proficiency in following instructions in such languages. Zhu et al. (2023b) has investigated multilingual instruction tuning datasets. However, the scalability of such high-quality datasets to thousands of low-resource languages still remains to be addressed.

Comparison with the State-of-the-art Multilingual NMT Models In this study, we refrained from contrasting translations in low-resource languages with best-performing multilingual NMT models like NLLB-200 (Costa-jussà et al., 2022), as our primary objective centered on enhancing the MTInstruct baseline through improved cross-lingual alignment within LLMs, rather than delving into the best combination of techniques for MT fine-tuning in LLMs. In future exploration, our methods can potentially be integrated with the MT fine-tuning paradigm proposed by the concurrent work of Xu et al. (2023a), paving the way for elevating the state-of-the-art translation quality using LLMs.

References

Sweta Agrawal, Chunting Zhou, Mike Lewis, Luke Zettlemoyer, and Marjan Ghazvininejad. 2023. In-context examples selection for machine translation. In *Findings of the Association for Computational Linguistics: ACL 2023*, pages 8857–8873, Toronto, Canada. Association for Computational Linguistics.

Rohan Anil, Andrew M. Dai, Orhan Firat, Melvin Johnson, Dmitry Lepikhin, Alexandre Passos, Siamak Shakeri, Emanuel Taropa, Paige Bailey, Zhifeng Chen, Eric Chu, Jonathan H. Clark, Laurent El Shafey, Yanping Huang, Kathy Meier-Hellstern, Gaurav Mishra, Erica Moreira, Mark Omernick, Kevin Robinson, Sebastian Ruder, Yi Tay, Kefan Xiao, Yuanzhong Xu, Yujing Zhang, Gustavo Hernández Ábrego, Junwhan Ahn, Jacob Austin, Paul Barham, Jan A. Botha, James Bradbury, Siddhartha Brahma, Kevin Brooks, Michele Catasta, Yong Cheng, Colin Cherry, Christopher A. Choquette-Choo, Aakanksha Chowdhery, Clément Crepy, Shachi Dave, Mostafa Dehghani, Sunipa Dev, Jacob Devlin, Mark Díaz, Nan Du, Ethan Dyer, Vladimir Feinberg, Fangxiaoyu Feng, Vlad Fienber, Markus Freitag, Xavier Garcia, Sebastian Gehrmann, Lucas Gonzalez, and et al. 2023. Palm 2 technical report. *CoRR*, abs/2305.10403.

Mikel Artetxe, Sebastian Ruder, and Dani Yogatama. 2020. On the cross-lingual transferability of monolingual representations. In *Proceedings of the 58th Annual Meeting of the Association for Computational Linguistics*, pages 4623–4637, Online. Association for Computational Linguistics.

Dzmitry Bahdanau, Kyunghyun Cho, and Yoshua Bengio. 2015. Neural machine translation by jointly learning to align and translate. In *3rd International Conference on Learning Representations, ICLR 2015, San Diego, CA, USA, May 7-9, 2015, Conference Track Proceedings*.

Yoshua Bengio, Jérôme Louradour, Ronan Collobert, and Jason Weston. 2009. Curriculum learning. In

Proceedings of the 26th Annual International Conference on Machine Learning, ICML 2009, Montreal, Quebec, Canada, June 14-18, 2009, volume 382 of *ACM International Conference Proceeding Series*, pages 41–48. ACM.

Peter F. Brown, Stephen A. Della Pietra, Vincent J. Della Pietra, and Robert L. Mercer. 1993. The mathematics of statistical machine translation: Parameter estimation. *Computational Linguistics*, 19(2):263–311.

Tom B. Brown, Benjamin Mann, Nick Ryder, Melanie Subbiah, Jared Kaplan, Prafulla Dhariwal, Arvind Neelakantan, Pranav Shyam, Girish Sastry, Amanda Askell, Sandhini Agarwal, Ariel Herbert-Voss, Gretchen Krueger, Tom Henighan, Rewon Child, Aditya Ramesh, Daniel M. Ziegler, Jeffrey Wu, Clemens Winter, Christopher Hesse, Mark Chen, Eric Sigler, Mateusz Litwin, Scott Gray, Benjamin Chess, Jack Clark, Christopher Berner, Sam McCandlish, Alec Radford, Ilya Sutskever, and Dario Amodei. 2020. Language models are few-shot learners. In *Advances in Neural Information Processing Systems 33: Annual Conference on Neural Information Processing Systems 2020, NeurIPS 2020, December 6-12, 2020, virtual*.

Rich Caruana. 1997. Multitask learning. *Machine Learning*, 28(1):41–75.

Aakanksha Chowdhery, Sharan Narang, Jacob Devlin, Maarten Bosma, Gaurav Mishra, Adam Roberts, Paul Barham, Hyung Won Chung, Charles Sutton, Sebastian Gehrmann, Parker Schuh, Kensen Shi, Sasha Tsvyashchenko, Joshua Maynez, Abhishek Rao, Parker Barnes, Yi Tay, Noam Shazeer, Vinodkumar Prabhakaran, Emily Reif, Nan Du, Ben Hutchinson, Reiner Pope, James Bradbury, Jacob Austin, Michael Isard, Guy Gur-Ari, Pengcheng Yin, Toju Duke, Anselm Levskaya, Sanjay Ghemawat, Sunipa Dev, Henryk Michalewski, Xavier Garcia, Vedant Misra, Kevin Robinson, Liam Fedus, Denny Zhou, Daphne Ippolito, David Luan, Hyeontaek Lim, Barret Zoph, Alexander Spiridonov, Ryan Sepassi, David Dohan, Shivani Agrawal, Mark Omernick, Andrew M. Dai, Thanumalayan Sankaranarayana Pillai, Marie Pellat, Aitor Lewkowycz, Erica Moreira, Rewon Child, Oleksandr Polozov, Katherine Lee, Zongwei Zhou, Xuezhi Wang, Brennan Saeta, Mark Diaz, Orhan Firat, Michele Catasta, Jason Wei, Kathy Meier-Hellstern, Douglas Eck, Jeff Dean, Slav Petrov, and Noah Fiedel. 2022. Palm: Scaling language modeling with pathways. *CoRR*, abs/2204.02311.

Chenhui Chu, Raj Dabre, and Sadao Kurohashi. 2017. An empirical comparison of domain adaptation methods for neural machine translation. In *Proceedings of the 55th Annual Meeting of the Association for Computational Linguistics (Volume 2: Short Papers)*, pages 385–391, Vancouver, Canada. Association for Computational Linguistics.

Hyung Won Chung, Le Hou, Shayne Longpre, Barret Zoph, Yi Tay, William Fedus, Eric Li, Xuezhi Wang, Mostafa Dehghani, Siddhartha Brahma, Albert Webson, Shixiang Shane Gu, Zhuyun Dai, Mirac Suzgun, Xinyun Chen, Aakanksha Chowdhery, Sharan Narang, Gaurav Mishra, Adams Yu, Vincent Y. Zhao, Yanping Huang, Andrew M. Dai, Hongkun Yu, Slav Petrov, Ed H. Chi, Jeff Dean, Jacob Devlin, Adam Roberts, Denny Zhou, Quoc V. Le, and Jason Wei. 2022. Scaling instruction-finetuned language models. *CoRR*, abs/2210.11416.

Marta R. Costa-jussà, James Cross, Onur Çelebi, Maha Elbayad, Kenneth Heafield, Kevin Heffernan, Elahe Kalbassi, Janice Lam, Daniel Licht, Jean Maillard, Anna Sun, Skyler Wang, Guillaume Wenzek, Al Youngblood, Bapi Akula, Loïc Barrault, Gabriel Mejia Gonzalez, Prangthip Hansanti, John Hoffman, Semarley Jarrett, Kaushik Ram Sadagopan, Dirk Rowe, Shannon Spruit, Chau Tran, Pierre Andrews, Necip Fazil Ayan, Shruti Bhosale, Sergey Edunov, Angela Fan, Cynthia Gao, Vedanuj Goswami, Francisco Guzmán, Philipp Koehn, Alexandre Mourachko, Christophe Ropers, Safiyyah Saleem, Holger Schwenk, and Jeff Wang. 2022. No language left behind: Scaling human-centered machine translation. *CoRR*, abs/2207.04672.

Javier de la Rosa and Andrés Fernández. 2022. Zero-shot reading comprehension and reasoning for spanish with BERTIN GPT-J-6B. In *Proceedings of the Iberian Languages Evaluation Forum (IberLEF 2022) co-located with the Conference of the Spanish Society for Natural Language Processing (SEPLN 2022), A Coruña, Spain, September 20, 2022*, volume 3202 of *CEUR Workshop Proceedings*. CEUR-WS.org.

Chris Dyer, Victor Chahuneau, and Noah A. Smith. 2013. A simple, fast, and effective reparameterization of IBM model 2. In *Proceedings of the 2013 Conference of the North American Chapter of the Association for Computational Linguistics: Human Language Technologies*, pages 644–648, Atlanta, Georgia. Association for Computational Linguistics.

Abteen Ebrahimi and Katharina Kann. 2021. How to adapt your pretrained multilingual model to 1600 languages. In *Proceedings of the 59th Annual Meeting of the Association for Computational Linguistics and the 11th International Joint Conference on Natural Language Processing (Volume 1: Long Papers)*, pages 4555–4567, Online. Association for Computational Linguistics.

Angela Fan, Shruti Bhosale, Holger Schwenk, Zhiyi Ma, Ahmed El-Kishky, Siddharth Goyal, Mandeep Baines, Onur Celebi, Guillaume Wenzek, Vishrav Chaudhary, Naman Goyal, Tom Birch, Vitaliy Liptchinsky, Sergey Edunov, Michael Auli, and Armand Joulin. 2021. Beyond english-centric multilingual machine translation. *J. Mach. Learn. Res.*, 22:107:1–107:48.

Marjan Ghazvininejad, Hila Gonen, and Luke Zettlemoyer. 2023. Dictionary-based phrase-level prompting of large language models for machine translation. *CoRR*, abs/2302.07856.

Zhiwei He, Tian Liang, Wenxiang Jiao, Zhuosheng Zhang, Yujiu Yang, Rui Wang, Zhaopeng Tu, Shuming Shi, and Xing Wang. 2023. Exploring human-like translation strategy with large language models. *CoRR*, abs/2305.04118.

Edward J. Hu, Yelong Shen, Phillip Wallis, Zeyuan Allen-Zhu, Yuanzhi Li, Shean Wang, Lu Wang, and Weizhu Chen. 2022. Lora: Low-rank adaptation of large language models. In *The Tenth International Conference on Learning Representations, ICLR 2022, Virtual Event, April 25-29, 2022*. OpenReview.net.

Wenxiang Jiao, Wenxuan Wang, Jen-tse Huang, Xing Wang, and Zhaopeng Tu. 2023. Is chatgpt A good translator? A preliminary study. *CoRR*, abs/2301.08745.

Philipp Koehn. 2004. Statistical significance tests for machine translation evaluation. In *Proceedings of the 2004 Conference on Empirical Methods in Natural Language Processing*, pages 388–395, Barcelona, Spain. Association for Computational Linguistics.

Yeskendir Koishekenov, Alexandre Berard, and Vassilina Nikoulina. 2023. Memory-efficient NLLB-200: Language-specific expert pruning of a massively multilingual machine translation model. In *Proceedings of the 61st Annual Meeting of the Association for Computational Linguistics (Volume 1: Long Papers)*, pages 3567–3585, Toronto, Canada. Association for Computational Linguistics.

Patrik Lambert, Simon Petitrenaud, Yanjun Ma, and Andy Way. 2012. What types of word alignment improve statistical machine translation? *Mach. Transl.*, 26(4):289–323.

Jiahuan Li, Hao Zhou, Shujian Huang, Shanbo Chen, and Jiajun Chen. 2023. Eliciting the translation ability of large language models via multilingual finetuning with translation instructions. *CoRR*, abs/2305.15083.

Xiaozhuan Liang, Ningyu Zhang, Siyuan Cheng, Zhenru Zhang, Chuanqi Tan, and Huajun Chen. 2022. Contrastive demonstration tuning for pre-trained language models. In *Findings of the Association for Computational Linguistics: EMNLP 2022*, pages 799–811, Abu Dhabi, United Arab Emirates. Association for Computational Linguistics.

Xi Victoria Lin, Todor Mihaylov, Mikel Artetxe, Tianlu Wang, Shuohui Chen, Daniel Simig, Myle Ott, Naman Goyal, Shruti Bhosale, Jingfei Du, Ramakanth Pasunuru, Sam Shleifer, Punit Singh Koura, Vishrav Chaudhary, Brian O'Horo, Jeff Wang, Luke Zettlemoyer, Zornitsa Kozareva, Mona Diab, Veselin Stoyanov, and Xian Li. 2022. Few-shot learning with multilingual generative language models. In *Proceedings of the 2022 Conference on Empirical Methods in Natural Language Processing*, pages 9019–9052, Abu Dhabi, United Arab Emirates. Association for Computational Linguistics.

Zehui Lin, Xiao Pan, Mingxuan Wang, Xipeng Qiu, Jiangtao Feng, Hao Zhou, and Lei Li. 2020. Pre-training multilingual neural machine translation by leveraging alignment information. In *Proceedings of the 2020 Conference on Empirical Methods in Natural Language Processing (EMNLP)*, pages 2649–2663, Online. Association for Computational Linguistics.

Danni Liu, Jan Niehues, James Cross, Francisco Guzmán, and Xian Li. 2021. Improving zero-shot translation by disentangling positional information. In *Proceedings of the 59th Annual Meeting of the Association for Computational Linguistics and the 11th International Joint Conference on Natural Language Processing (Volume 1: Long Papers)*, pages 1259–1273, Online. Association for Computational Linguistics.

Haokun Liu, Derek Tam, Mohammed Muqeeth, Jay Mohta, Tenghao Huang, Mohit Bansal, and Colin Raffel. 2022. Few-shot parameter-efficient fine-tuning is better and cheaper than in-context learning. In *NeurIPS*.

Yinhan Liu, Jiatao Gu, Naman Goyal, Xian Li, Sergey Edunov, Marjan Ghazvininejad, Mike Lewis, and Luke Zettlemoyer. 2020. Multilingual denoising pre-training for neural machine translation. *Transactions of the Association for Computational Linguistics*, 8:726–742.

Zhuoyuan Mao, Chenhui Chu, Raj Dabre, Haiyue Song, Zhen Wan, and Sadao Kurohashi. 2022. When do contrastive word alignments improve many-to-many neural machine translation? In *Findings of the Association for Computational Linguistics: NAACL 2022*, pages 1766–1775, Seattle, United States. Association for Computational Linguistics.

Zhuoyuan Mao, Raj Dabre, Qianying Liu, Haiyue Song, Chenhui Chu, and Sadao Kurohashi. 2023. Exploring the impact of layer normalization for zero-shot neural machine translation. In *Proceedings of the 61st Annual Meeting of the Association for Computational Linguistics (Volume 2: Short Papers)*, pages 1300–1316, Toronto, Canada. Association for Computational Linguistics.

Paulius Micikevicius, Sharan Narang, Jonah Alben, Gregory F. Diamos, Erich Elsen, David García, Boris Ginsburg, Michael Houston, Oleksii Kuchaiev, Ganesh Venkatesh, and Hao Wu. 2018. Mixed precision training. In *6th International Conference on Learning Representations, ICLR 2018, Vancouver, BC, Canada, April 30 - May 3, 2018, Conference Track Proceedings*. OpenReview.net.

Swaroop Mishra, Daniel Khashabi, Chitta Baral, and Hannaneh Hajishirzi. 2022. Cross-task generalization via natural language crowdsourcing instructions. In *Proceedings of the 60th Annual Meeting of the Association for Computational Linguistics (Volume 1: Long Papers)*, pages 3470–3487, Dublin, Ireland. Association for Computational Linguistics.

Alireza Mohammadshahi, Vassilina Nikoulina, Alexandre Berard, Caroline Brun, James Henderson, and Laurent Besacier. 2022. SMaLL-100: Introducing shallow multilingual machine translation model for low-resource languages. In *Proceedings of the 2022 Conference on Empirical Methods in Natural Language Processing*, pages 8348–8359, Abu Dhabi, United Arab Emirates. Association for Computational Linguistics.

Yasmin Moslem, Rejwanul Haque, John D. Kelleher, and Andy Way. 2023. Adaptive machine translation with large language models. In *Proceedings of the 24th Annual Conference of the European Association for Machine Translation*, pages 227–237, Tampere, Finland. European Association for Machine Translation.

Niklas Muennighoff, Thomas Wang, Lintang Sutawika, Adam Roberts, Stella Biderman, Teven Le Scao, M Saiful Bari, Sheng Shen, Zheng Xin Yong, Hailey Schoelkopf, Xiangru Tang, Dragomir Radev, Alham Fikri Aji, Khalid Almubarak, Samuel Albanie, Zaid Alyafeai, Albert Webson, Edward Raff, and Colin Raffel. 2023. Crosslingual generalization through multitask finetuning. In *Proceedings of the 61st Annual Meeting of the Association for Computational Linguistics (Volume 1: Long Papers)*, pages 15991–16111, Toronto, Canada. Association for Computational Linguistics.

Benjamin Muller, Antonios Anastasopoulos, Benoît Sagot, and Djamé Seddah. 2021. When being unseen from mBERT is just the beginning: Handling new languages with multilingual language models. In *Proceedings of the 2021 Conference of the North American Chapter of the Association for Computational Linguistics: Human Language Technologies*, pages 448–462, Online. Association for Computational Linguistics.

Martin Müller and Florian Laurent. 2022. Cedille: A large autoregressive french language model. *CoRR*, abs/2202.03371.

Graham Neubig and Junjie Hu. 2018. Rapid adaptation of neural machine translation to new languages. In *Proceedings of the 2018 Conference on Empirical Methods in Natural Language Processing*, pages 875–880, Brussels, Belgium. Association for Computational Linguistics.

OpenAI. 2023. GPT-4 technical report. *CoRR*, abs/2303.08774.

Long Ouyang, Jeffrey Wu, Xu Jiang, Diogo Almeida, Carroll L. Wainwright, Pamela Mishkin, Chong Zhang, Sandhini Agarwal, Katarina Slama, Alex Ray, John Schulman, Jacob Hilton, Fraser Kelton, Luke Miller, Maddie Simens, Amanda Askell, Peter Welinder, Paul F. Christiano, Jan Leike, and Ryan Lowe. 2022. Training language models to follow instructions with human feedback. In *NeurIPS*.

Kishore Papineni, Salim Roukos, Todd Ward, and Wei-Jing Zhu. 2002. Bleu: a method for automatic evaluation of machine translation. In *Proceedings of the 40th Annual Meeting of the Association for Computational Linguistics*, pages 311–318, Philadelphia, Pennsylvania, USA. Association for Computational Linguistics.

Keqin Peng, Liang Ding, Qihuang Zhong, Li Shen, Xuebo Liu, Min Zhang, Yuanxin Ouyang, and Dacheng Tao. 2023. Towards making the most of chatgpt for machine translation. *CoRR*, abs/2303.13780.

Jonas Pfeiffer, Ivan Vulić, Iryna Gurevych, and Sebastian Ruder. 2020. MAD-X: An Adapter-Based Framework for Multi-Task Cross-Lingual Transfer. In *Proceedings of the 2020 Conference on Empirical Methods in Natural Language Processing (EMNLP)*, pages 7654–7673, Online. Association for Computational Linguistics.

Maja Popović. 2015. chrF: character n-gram F-score for automatic MT evaluation. In *Proceedings of the Tenth Workshop on Statistical Machine Translation*, pages 392–395, Lisbon, Portugal. Association for Computational Linguistics.

Matt Post. 2018. A call for clarity in reporting BLEU scores. In *Proceedings of the Third Conference on Machine Translation: Research Papers*, pages 186–191, Brussels, Belgium. Association for Computational Linguistics.

Alec Radford, Karthik Narasimhan, Tim Salimans, and Ilya Sutskever. 2018. Improving language understanding by generative pre-training.

Jeff Rasley, Samyam Rajbhandari, Olatunji Ruwase, and Yuxiong He. 2020. Deepspeed: System optimizations enable training deep learning models with over 100 billion parameters. In *KDD '20: The 26th ACM SIGKDD Conference on Knowledge Discovery and Data Mining, Virtual Event, CA, USA, August 23-27, 2020*, pages 3505–3506. ACM.

Ricardo Rei, Craig Stewart, Ana C Farinha, and Alon Lavie. 2020. COMET: A neural framework for MT evaluation. In *Proceedings of the 2020 Conference on Empirical Methods in Natural Language Processing (EMNLP)*, pages 2685–2702, Online. Association for Computational Linguistics.

Shuo Ren, Yu Wu, Shujie Liu, Ming Zhou, and Shuai Ma. 2019. Explicit cross-lingual pre-training for unsupervised machine translation. In *Proceedings of the 2019 Conference on Empirical Methods in Natural Language Processing and the 9th International Joint Conference on Natural Language Processing (EMNLP-IJCNLP)*, pages 770–779, Hong Kong, China. Association for Computational Linguistics.

Victor Sanh, Albert Webson, Colin Raffel, Stephen H. Bach, Lintang Sutawika, Zaid Alyafeai, Antoine Chaffin, Arnaud Stiegler, Arun Raja, Manan Dey,

M Saiful Bari, Canwen Xu, Urmish Thakker, Shanya Sharma Sharma, Eliza Szczechla, Taewoon Kim, Gunjan Chhablani, Nihal V. Nayak, Debajyoti Datta, Jonathan Chang, Mike Tian-Jian Jiang, Han Wang, Matteo Manica, Sheng Shen, Zheng Xin Yong, Harshit Pandey, Rachel Bawden, Thomas Wang, Trishala Neeraj, Jos Rozen, Abheesht Sharma, Andrea Santilli, Thibault Févry, Jason Alan Fries, Ryan Teehan, Teven Le Scao, Stella Biderman, Leo Gao, Thomas Wolf, and Alexander M. Rush. 2022. Multitask prompted training enables zero-shot task generalization. In *The Tenth International Conference on Learning Representations, ICLR 2022, Virtual Event, April 25-29, 2022*. OpenReview.net.

Teven Le Scao, Angela Fan, Christopher Akiki, Ellie Pavlick, Suzana Ilic, Daniel Hesslow, Roman Castagné, Alexandra Sasha Luccioni, François Yvon, Matthias Gallé, Jonathan Tow, Alexander M. Rush, Stella Biderman, Albert Webson, Pawan Sasanka Ammanamanchi, Thomas Wang, Benoît Sagot, Niklas Muennighoff, Albert Villanova del Moral, Olatunji Ruwase, Rachel Bawden, Stas Bekman, Angelina McMillan-Major, Iz Beltagy, Huu Nguyen, Lucile Saulnier, Samson Tan, Pedro Ortiz Suarez, Victor Sanh, Hugo Laurençon, Yacine Jernite, Julien Launay, Margaret Mitchell, Colin Raffel, Aaron Gokaslan, Adi Simhi, Aitor Soroa, Alham Fikri Aji, Amit Alfassy, Anna Rogers, Ariel Kreisberg Nitzav, Canwen Xu, Chenghao Mou, Chris Emezue, Christopher Klamm, Colin Leong, Daniel van Strien, David Ifeoluwa Adelani, and et al. 2022. BLOOM: A 176b-parameter open-access multilingual language model. *CoRR*, abs/2211.05100.

Oleh Shliazhko, Alena Fenogenova, Maria Tikhonova, Vladislav Mikhailov, Anastasia Kozlova, and Tatiana Shavrina. 2022. mgpt: Few-shot learners go multilingual. *CoRR*, abs/2204.07580.

Kaitao Song, Xu Tan, Tao Qin, Jianfeng Lu, and Tie-Yan Liu. 2019. MASS: masked sequence to sequence pre-training for language generation. In *Proceedings of the 36th International Conference on Machine Learning, ICML 2019, 9-15 June 2019, Long Beach, California, USA*, volume 97 of *Proceedings of Machine Learning Research*, pages 5926–5936. PMLR.

Ilya Sutskever, Oriol Vinyals, and Quoc V. Le. 2014. Sequence to sequence learning with neural networks. In *Advances in Neural Information Processing Systems 27: Annual Conference on Neural Information Processing Systems 2014, December 8-13 2014, Montreal, Quebec, Canada*, pages 3104–3112.

Hugo Touvron, Thibaut Lavril, Gautier Izacard, Xavier Martinet, Marie-Anne Lachaux, Timothée Lacroix, Baptiste Rozière, Naman Goyal, Eric Hambro, Faisal Azhar, Aurélien Rodriguez, Armand Joulin, Edouard Grave, and Guillaume Lample. 2023a. Llama: Open and efficient foundation language models. *CoRR*, abs/2302.13971.

Hugo Touvron, Louis Martin, Kevin Stone, Peter Albert, Amjad Almahairi, Yasmine Babaei, Nikolay Bashlykov, Soumya Batra, Prajjwal Bhargava, Shruti Bhosale, Dan Bikel, Lukas Blecher, Cristian Canton-Ferrer, Moya Chen, Guillem Cucurull, David Esiobu, Jude Fernandes, Jeremy Fu, Wenyin Fu, Brian Fuller, Cynthia Gao, Vedanuj Goswami, Naman Goyal, Anthony Hartshorn, Saghar Hosseini, Rui Hou, Hakan Inan, Marcin Kardas, Viktor Kerkez, Madian Khabsa, Isabel Kloumann, Artem Korenev, Punit Singh Koura, Marie-Anne Lachaux, Thibaut Lavril, Jenya Lee, Diana Liskovich, Yinghai Lu, Yuning Mao, Xavier Martinet, Todor Mihaylov, Pushkar Mishra, Igor Molybog, Yixin Nie, Andrew Poulton, Jeremy Reizenstein, Rashi Rungta, Kalyan Saladi, Alan Schelten, Ruan Silva, Eric Michael Smith, Ranjan Subramanian, Xiaoqing Ellen Tan, Binh Tang, Ross Taylor, Adina Williams, Jian Xiang Kuan, Puxin Xu, Zheng Yan, Iliyan Zarov, Yuchen Zhang, Angela Fan, Melanie Kambadur, Sharan Narang, Aurélien Rodriguez, Robert Stojnic, Sergey Edunov, and Thomas Scialom. 2023b. Llama 2: Open foundation and fine-tuned chat models. *CoRR*, abs/2307.09288.

Yiren Wang, ChengXiang Zhai, and Hany Hassan. 2020. Multi-task learning for multilingual neural machine translation. In *Proceedings of the 2020 Conference on Empirical Methods in Natural Language Processing (EMNLP)*, pages 1022–1034, Online. Association for Computational Linguistics.

Yizhong Wang, Swaroop Mishra, Pegah Alipoormolabashi, Yeganeh Kordi, Amirreza Mirzaei, Atharva Naik, Arjun Ashok, Arut Selvan Dhanasekaran, Anjana Arunkumar, David Stap, Eshaan Pathak, Giannis Karamanolakis, Haizhi Lai, Ishan Purohit, Ishani Mondal, Jacob Anderson, Kirby Kuznia, Krima Doshi, Kuntal Kumar Pal, Maitreya Patel, Mehrad Moradshahi, Mihir Parmar, Mirali Purohit, Neeraj Varshney, Phani Rohitha Kaza, Pulkit Verma, Ravsehaj Singh Puri, Rushang Karia, Savan Doshi, Shailaja Keyur Sampat, Siddhartha Mishra, Sujan Reddy A, Sumanta Patro, Tanay Dixit, and Xudong Shen. 2022. Super-NaturalInstructions: Generalization via declarative instructions on 1600+ NLP tasks. In *Proceedings of the 2022 Conference on Empirical Methods in Natural Language Processing*, pages 5085–5109, Abu Dhabi, United Arab Emirates. Association for Computational Linguistics.

Jason Wei, Maarten Bosma, Vincent Y. Zhao, Kelvin Guu, Adams Wei Yu, Brian Lester, Nan Du, Andrew M. Dai, and Quoc V. Le. 2022. Finetuned language models are zero-shot learners. In *The Tenth International Conference on Learning Representations, ICLR 2022, Virtual Event, April 25-29, 2022*. OpenReview.net.

Liwei Wu, Shanbo Cheng, Mingxuan Wang, and Lei Li. 2021. Language tags matter for zero-shot neural machine translation. In *Findings of the Association for Computational Linguistics: ACL-IJCNLP 2021*, pages 3001–3007, Online. Association for Computational Linguistics.

Haoran Xu, Young Jin Kim, Amr Sharaf, and Hany Hassan Awadalla. 2023a. A paradigm shift in machine translation: Boosting translation performance of large language models. *CoRR*, abs/2309.11674.

Haoran Xu, Weiting Tan, Shuyue Stella Li, Yunmo Chen, Benjamin Van Durme, Philipp Koehn, and Kenton Murray. 2023b. Condensing multilingual knowledge with lightweight language-specific modules. *CoRR*, abs/2305.13993.

Wen Yang, Chong Li, Jiajun Zhang, and Chengqing Zong. 2023. Bigtrans: Augmenting large language models with multilingual translation capability over 100 languages. *CoRR*, abs/2305.18098.

Zheng Xin Yong, Hailey Schoelkopf, Niklas Muennighoff, Alham Fikri Aji, David Ifeoluwa Adelani, Khalid Almubarak, M Saiful Bari, Lintang Sutawika, Jungo Kasai, Ahmed Baruwa, Genta Winata, Stella Biderman, Edward Raff, Dragomir Radev, and Vassilina Nikoulina. 2023. BLOOM+1: Adding language support to BLOOM for zero-shot prompting. In *Proceedings of the 61st Annual Meeting of the Association for Computational Linguistics (Volume 1: Long Papers)*, pages 11682–11703, Toronto, Canada. Association for Computational Linguistics.

Zhang Ze Yu, Lau Jia Jaw, Wong Qin Jiang, and Zhang Hui. 2023. Fine-tuning language models with generative adversarial feedback. *CoRR*, abs/2305.06176.

Aohan Zeng, Xiao Liu, Zhengxiao Du, Zihan Wang, Hanyu Lai, Ming Ding, Zhuoyi Yang, Yifan Xu, Wendi Zheng, Xiao Xia, Weng Lam Tam, Zixuan Ma, Yufei Xue, Jidong Zhai, Wenguang Chen, Zhiyuan Liu, Peng Zhang, Yuxiao Dong, and Jie Tang. 2023. GLM-130B: an open bilingual pre-trained model. In *The Eleventh International Conference on Learning Representations, ICLR 2023, Kigali, Rwanda, May 1-5, 2023*. OpenReview.net.

Biao Zhang, Barry Haddow, and Alexandra Birch. 2023a. Prompting large language model for machine translation: A case study. In *International Conference on Machine Learning, ICML 2023, 23-29 July 2023, Honolulu, Hawaii, USA*, volume 202 of *Proceedings of Machine Learning Research*, pages 41092–41110. PMLR.

Biao Zhang, Philip Williams, Ivan Titov, and Rico Sennrich. 2020. Improving massively multilingual neural machine translation and zero-shot translation. In *Proceedings of the 58th Annual Meeting of the Association for Computational Linguistics*, pages 1628–1639, Online. Association for Computational Linguistics.

Shaolei Zhang, Qingkai Fang, Zhuocheng Zhang, Zhengrui Ma, Yan Zhou, Langlin Huang, Mengyu Bu, Shangtong Gui, Yunji Chen, Xilin Chen, and Yang Feng. 2023b. Bayling: Bridging cross-lingual alignment and instruction following through interactive translation for large language models. *CoRR*, abs/2306.10968.

Susan Zhang, Stephen Roller, Naman Goyal, Mikel Artetxe, Moya Chen, Shuohui Chen, Christopher Dewan, Mona T. Diab, Xian Li, Xi Victoria Lin, Todor Mihaylov, Myle Ott, Sam Shleifer, Kurt Shuster, Daniel Simig, Punit Singh Koura, Anjali Sridhar, Tianlu Wang, and Luke Zettlemoyer. 2022. OPT: open pre-trained transformer language models. *CoRR*, abs/2205.01068.

Yongchao Zhou, Andrei Ioan Muresanu, Ziwen Han, Keiran Paster, Silviu Pitis, Harris Chan, and Jimmy Ba. 2023. Large language models are human-level prompt engineers. In *The Eleventh International Conference on Learning Representations, ICLR 2023, Kigali, Rwanda, May 1-5, 2023*. OpenReview.net.

Wenhao Zhu, Hongyi Liu, Qingxiu Dong, Jingjing Xu, Lingpeng Kong, Jiajun Chen, Lei Li, and Shujian Huang. 2023a. Multilingual machine translation with large language models: Empirical results and analysis. *CoRR*, abs/2304.04675.

Wenhao Zhu, Yunzhe Lv, Qingxiu Dong, Fei Yuan, Jingjing Xu, Shujian Huang, Lingpeng Kong, Jiajun Chen, and Lei Li. 2023b. Extrapolating large language models to non-english by aligning languages. *CoRR*, abs/2308.04948.

A Training Data Statistics

Training data statistics of BLOOMZ+24 are shown in Tab. 6. Several selected languages involved previously unseen scripts by BLOOMZ, but such fine-tuning is practical as BLOOMZ is a byte-level model with the potential to adapt to any language. Note that our proposed methods can be applied to any byte-level generative LLMs.

B Implementation Details

We employed 128 V100 GPUs for the BLOOMZ+24 and 32 V100 GPUs for the BLOOMZ+3 experiments. The batch sizes were configured at 4 sentences for BLOOMZ-7b1 and 8 sentences for both BLOOMZ-3b and BLOOMZ-1b1, per GPU device. We configured LoRA with a rank of 8, an alpha of 32, and a dropout of 0.1. Consequently, the BLOOMZ-7b1, BLOOMZ-3b, and BLOOMZ-1b1 models had 3.9M, 2.5M, and 1.2M trainable parameters, respectively, constituting approximately 0.05 - 0.10% of the parameters in the original models. We conducted training for 5 epochs, ensuring a stable convergence is achieved. To facilitate this stability, we introduced a warm-up ratio of 0.03 into our training process. Maximum input and output length were set as 384. S for HintInstruct was set as 5 at most. Additionally, we used mixed precision training (Micikevicius et al., 2018) to expedite computation using DeepSpeed (Rasley

Language	ISO 639-1	Language Family	Subgrouping	Script	Seen Script	#sent.
Afrikaans	af	Indo-European	Germanic	Latin	✓	275,512
Amharic	am	Afro-Asiatic	Semitic	Ge'ez	✗	89,027
Belarusian	be	Indo-European	Balto-Slavic	Cyrillic	✗	67,312
Welsh	cy	Indo-European	Celtic	Latin	✓	289,521
Irish	ga	Indo-European	Celtic	Latin	✓	289,524
Scottish Gaelic	gd	Indo-European	Celtic	Latin	✓	16,316
Galician	gl	Indo-European	Italic	Latin	✓	515,344
Hausa	ha	Afro-Asiatic	Chadic	Latin	✓	97,983
Georgian	ka	Kartvelian	Georgian-Zan	Georgian	✗	377,306
Kazakh	kk	Turkic	Common Turkic	Cyrillic	✗	79,927
Khmer	km	Austroasiatic	Khmeric	Khmer	✗	111,483
Kyrgyz	ky	Turkic	Common Turkic	Cyrillic	✗	27,215
Limburgish	li	Indo-European	Germanic	Latin	✓	25,535
Burmese	my	Sino-Tibetan	Burmo-Qiangic	Myanmar	✗	24,594
Norwegian Bokmål	nb	Indo-European	Germanic	Latin	✓	142,906
Norwegian Nynorsk	nn	Indo-European	Germanic	Latin	✓	486,055
Occitan	oc	Indo-European	Italic	Latin	✓	35,791
Sinhala	si	Indo-European	Indo-Aryan	Sinhala	✗	979,109
Tajik	tg	Indo-European	Iranian	Cyrillic	✗	193,882
Turkmen	tk	Turkic	Common Turkic	Latin	✓	13,110
Tatar	tt	Turkic	Common Turkic	Cyrillic	✗	100,843
Uyghur	ug	Turkic	Common Turkic	Arabic	✓	72,170
Northern Uzbek	uz	Turkic	Common Turkic	Latin	✓	173,157
Eastern Yiddish	yi	Indo-European	Germanic	Hebrew	✗	15,010
Total						4,498,632

Table 6: **Statistics of training data for BLOOMZ+24**: 24 unseen, low-resource languages for BLOOMZ. ✓and ✗indicate whether script is seen or unseen.

et al., 2020). We tuned the optimal learning rate for each individual experiment according to validation loss. We conducted all experiments once due to computational resource constraints and reported the average scores across all languages.

C Results of MT+Align+Hint+Revise for BLOOMZ+3

We present the results in Tab. 7. Co-referencing the results in Tab. 5, compared with MT+Align, we observed a clear advantage for the MT+Align+Hint+Revise setting in supervised directions involving English (en→seen and seen→en) in the ar-fr-de-nl-ru-zh setting. This result suggested that AlignInstruct's variants played a crucial role in preserving the BLOOMZ's capabilities for supported languages. However, in all other scenarios, AlignInstruct alone proved sufficient to enhance the performance beyond the MTInstruct baseline, but hard to achieve further improvements with additional instructions.

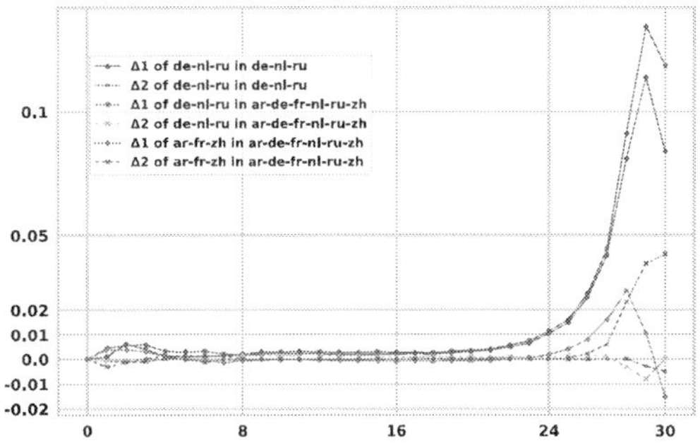

Figure 4: **Differences in cosine similarity of layer-wise embeddings for BLOOMZ+3.** $\Delta 1$ represents the changes from the unmodified BLOOMZ to the one on MTInstruct, and $\Delta 2$ from MTInstruct to MT+Align.

D Representation Change of BLOOMZ+3

The representation change observed in de-nl-ru was consistent with the findings presented in Sec. 4.4, which highlighted an initial increase in cross-lingual alignment in the early layers, followed by a decrease in the final layers. When mixing fine-tuning data with supported languages, the changes

Languages	Zero-shot Directions				Supervised Directions			
	Directions	BLEU	chrF++	COMET	Directions	BLEU	chrF++	COMET
de-nl-ru	overall	**8.94**	**23.53**	**60.67**	en→xx	16.70	31.83	68.98
					xx→en	**25.18**	45.00	**76.45**
	seen→seen	14.00	**27.58**	**70.59**	en→seen	15.97	28.53	**72.69**
	seen→unseen	**6.49**	**23.01**	**54.92**	en→unseen	**17.43**	**35.13**	**65.27**
	unseen→seen	**9.50**	**21.90**	**64.69**	seen→en	25.33	46.70	77.51
	unseen→unseen	6.73	22.70	53.34	unseen→en	**25.03**	**43.30**	**75.39**
ar-de-fr-nl-ru-zh	overall	**12.07**	**26.67**	63.13	en→xx	**21.62**	**36.12**	**70.94**
					xx→en	**28.92**	**48.60**	**77.50**
	seen→seen	**23.52**	**36.13**	**76.62**	en→seen	**26.87**	**38.40**	**78.40**
	seen→unseen	**7.16**	24.48	55.02	en→unseen	**16.37**	**33.83**	63.49
	unseen→seen	**12.91**	**25.23**	**68.91**	seen→en	**32.57**	**53.70**	**80.06**
	unseen→unseen	6.73	**22.65**	53.12	unseen→en	**25.27**	**43.50**	**74.93**

Table 7: **Results of BLOOMZ+3 with MT+Align+Hint+Revise.** Co-referencing Tab. 5, scores that surpass the MTInstruct baseline are marked in **bold**.

exhibited more intricate patterns. As illustrated by ar-fr-zh in ar-de-fr-nl-ru-zh in Fig. 4, sentence alignment declined after MTInstruct fine-tuning but elevated after further combining with AlignInstruct. We leave the interpretation of this nuanced behavior in future work.

E Examples of HintInstruct and ReviseInstruct

We illustrated examples of HintInstruct and ReviseInstruct in Fig. 5.

F Assessing Monolingual Instructions

New language capabilities may be induced through continual pre-training on monolingual next-word prediction tasks (Yong et al., 2023). The coherence of the generated sentences is crucial in MT (Wang et al., 2020; Liu et al., 2020), especially when the target languages are unseen and low-resource. We examined the significance of this approach in fostering the translation quality. We reused the same parallel corpora to avoid introducing additional monolingual datasets.

Given a monolingual sentence, $(x_i)_1^N$, with length N in an unseen language X. The LLM is incrementally trained on the following task:

- **Input**: "Given the context, complete the following sentence: $x_1 x_2 \dots x_{l<N}$,"
- **Output**: "$x_{l+1} x_{l+2} \dots x_N$."

We conducted experiments with two MonoInstruct settings: **MonoInstruct-full**, an objective to generate the entire sentence, and **MonoInstruct-half** for generating the latter half of the sentence given the first half, inspired by GPT (Radford et al., 2018) and MASS (Song et al., 2019), respectively. We reported the MonoInstruct results in Tab. 8. Firstly, we observed that fine-tuning MTInstruct in conjunction with either MonoInstruct-full or MonoInstruct-half harms the MT performance, which could be attributed to the inherent difficulty of monolingual instruction tasks and the limited amount of monolingual data. We found that the

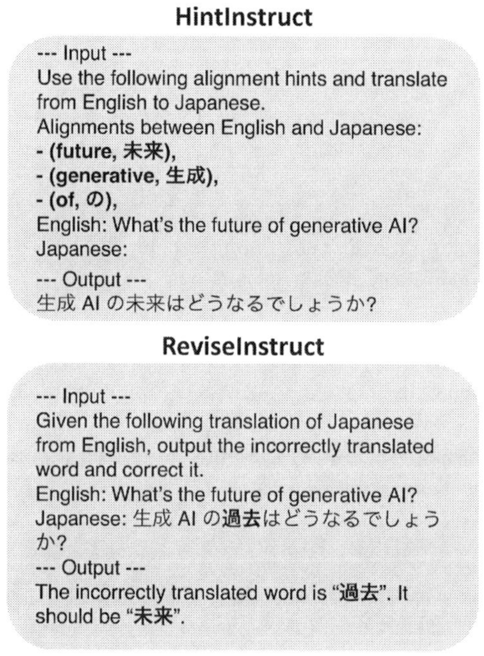

Figure 5: Examples of HintInstruct and ReviseInstruct.

Objective	OPUS en→xx			OPUS xx→en			Flores en→xx			Flores xx→en		
	BLEU	chrF++	COMET	BLEU	chrF++	COMET	BLEU	chrF++	COMET	BLEU	chrF++	COMET
MTInstruct	11.54	25.33	64.54	18.59	33.25	69.84	3.30	17.10	40.58	11.37	27.14	56.33
MT+Mono-full	9.89	22.42	62.52	15.43	29.04	66.64	3.00	16.68	40.49	10.26	25.15	54.17
MT+Mono-half	10.23	22.45	62.22	15.51	29.65	67.29	3.18	16.91	40.57	10.66	26.15	54.80
MT+Mono-full+Align	10.15	22.35	62.22	15.72	29.86	67.70	3.07	16.59	**40.78**	10.61	25.58	55.17
MT+Mono-half+Align	10.09	22.61	62.98	16.00	30.34	67.96	3.10	16.75	**40.70**	10.79	26.27	55.40
MT+Mono-full+Align+Hint+Revise	10.33	23.04	63.19	17.16	31.61	68.26	3.23	16.70	**40.90**	10.98	26.18	55.50
MT+Mono-half+Align+Hint+Revise	10.62	23.10	62.92	17.32	31.80	68.56	3.20	16.93	**41.00**	11.09	26.77	55.99

Table 8: **Results of BLOOMZ+24 fine-tuned incorporating monolingual instructions on BLOOMZ-7b1.** Scores that surpass the MTInstruct baseline are marked in **bold**.

simpler MT+Mono-half yielded better results than MT+Mono-full as richer contexts were provided. However, MonoInstruct still did not improve the MTInstruct baseline. Secondly, further combining MonoInstrcut with AlignInstruct variants yielded improvements compared with MT+Mono-full (or half), but underperformed the MTInstruct baseline. This suggested that improving MT performance with monolingual instructions is challenging without access to additional monolingual data.

G Inference using Different MT Prompts

We investigated the performance of fine-tuned models when using various MT prompts during inference, aiming to understand models' generalization capabilities with different test prompts. We examined five MT prompts for the fine-tuned models of BLOOMZ-7b1, following Zhang et al. (2023a), which are presented in Tab. 9. The results, showcased in Tab. 10, revealed that in comparison to the default prompt used during fine-tuning, the translation performance tended to decline when using other MT prompts. We observed that MT+Align consistently surpasses MTInstruct for xx→en translations, though the results were mixed for en→xx directions. Certain prompts, such as PROMPT-3 and PROMPT-4, exhibited a minor performance drop, while others significantly impacted translation quality. These findings underscored the need for enhancing the models' ability to generalize across diverse MT prompts, potentially by incorporating a range of MT prompt templates during the fine-tuning process, as stated in the Limitations section.

H Zero-shot Translation using English as Pivot

Pivot translation serves as a robust technique for zero-shot translation, especially given that we used English-centric data during fine-tuning. In Tab. 11, we present results that utilize English as an intermediary pivot for translations between non-English language pairs. Our findings indicated that employing the English pivot typically yielded an enhancement of approximately 1.1 - 1.2 BLEU points compared to direct translations in zero-shot directions when fine-tuning BLOOMZ. When contrasting the MTInstruct baseline with our proposed MT+Align, we observed that combining AlignInstruct consistently boosted performance in pivot translation scenarios.

Prompt	Definition
PROMPT-default	Translate from Y to X. Y: $y_1 y_2 \cdots y_M$. X:
PROMPT-1	Y: $y_1 y_2 \cdots y_M$. X:
PROMPT-2	$y_1 y_2 \cdots y_M$. X:
PROMPT-3	Translate to X. Y: $y_1 y_2 \cdots y_M$. X:
PROMPT-4	Translate from Y to X. $y_1 y_2 \cdots y_M$. X:
PROMPT-5	Translate to X. $y_1 y_2 \cdots y_M$. X:

Table 9: **MT prompt variants investigated for fine-tuned models.** These MT prompts are following the design in Zhang et al. (2023a).

I Per Language Result Details of BLOOMZ+24 and BLOOMZ+3

We present per language detailed results of original BLOOMZ-7b1 and fine-tuned BLOOMZ-7b1 models in Tab. 12, 13, 14, 15, 16, 17, 18, 19, respectively for the BLOOMZ+24 and BLOOMZ+3 settings.

Prompt	Objective	en→xx BLEU	en→xx chrF++	en→xx COMET	xx→en BLEU	xx→en chrF++	xx→en COMET
PROMPT-default	MTInstruct	11.54	25.33	64.54	18.59	33.25	69.84
	MT+Align	**12.28**	**26.17**	**65.54**	**18.72**	**34.02**	**70.69**
PROMPT-1	MTInstruct	5.29	11.31	50.20	7.87	20.08	57.46
	MT+Align	**5.30**	**11.38**	**50.95**	**8.93**	**20.77**	**58.38**
PROMPT-2	MTInstruct	2.20	6.68	45.56	7.15	19.08	57.22
	MT+Align	1.91	5.35	43.84	**7.61**	18.80	56.76
PROMPT-3	MTInstruct	10.59	22.69	62.65	15.85	29.93	67.59
	MT+Align	9.20	20.80	60.96	**16.17**	**30.58**	**68.70**
PROMPT-4	MTInstruct	8.67	20.73	61.50	15.20	28.95	66.61
	MT+Align	**8.91**	20.53	**61.64**	**16.25**	**30.67**	**67.94**
PROMPT-5	MTInstruct	6.61	14.55	55.99	10.88	22.41	61.40
	MT+Align	6.02	12.28	52.42	**11.83**	**23.85**	**62.09**

Table 10: **Results of using different MT prompts for BLOOMZ-7b1 fine-tuned models during inference.** Refer to Tab. 9 for details about definitions of different MT prompts. We report the average results for the BLOOMZ+24 setting. Results better than the MTInstruct baseline are marked in **bold**.

MTInstruct	BLEU	chrF++	COMET	**MT+Align**	BLEU	chrF++	COMET
overall	11.79	26.36	63.22	overall	**12.13**	**26.65**	**63.23**
seen→seen	22.68	35.32	76.39	seen→seen	**23.67**	**36.53**	**76.89**
seen→unseen	7.10	24.50	55.18	seen→unseen	**7.27**	24.32	54.96
unseen→seen	12.56	24.74	68.83	unseen→seen	**12.92**	**25.29**	**69.10**
unseen→unseen	6.78	22.62	53.69	unseen→unseen	6.68	22.30	53.19
MTInstruct with English pivot	BLEU	chrF++	COMET	**MT+Align with English pivot**	BLEU	chrF++	COMET
overall	12.99	28.01	65.38	overall	**13.25**	**28.30**	**65.57**
seen→seen	23.10	35.30	76.30	seen→seen	**23.48**	**35.57**	**76.43**
seen→unseen	9.00	27.67	59.54	seen→unseen	**9.28**	**28.03**	**59.73**
unseen→seen	13.18	24.98	68.77	unseen→seen	**13.36**	**25.22**	**68.94**
unseen→unseen	8.57	25.77	58.17	unseen→unseen	**8.83**	**26.07**	**58.42**

Table 11: **Results of BLOOMZ+3 using English as a pivot language for zero-shot translation evaluation.** Results of MT+Align surpassing corresponding those of MTInstruct are marked in **bold**.

Language	OPUS en→xx			OPUS xx→en			Flores en→xx			Flores xx→en		
	BLEU	chrF++	COMET	BLEU	chrF++	COMET	BLEU	chrF++	COMET	BLEU	chrF++	COMET
af	3.8	13.2	56.38	7.6	22.0	59.14	2.6	14.9	33.60	20.1	38.0	65.61
am	0.1	0.3	33.17	0.5	8.3	43.57	0.3	0.6	30.65	1.9	12.6	46.24
be	4.2	5.1	47.26	7.3	17.5	48.57	0.4	3.3	31.58	4.2	22.3	49.27
cy	2.7	10.5	53.21	6.2	16.0	53.25	1.2	11.2	34.17	6.0	20.3	53.45
ga	1.2	10.6	42.85	4.0	16.4	46.05	1.2	11.6	33.94	5.5	19.6	46.97
gd	9.3	16.0	51.40	47.6	55.9	59.30	1.2	11.2	36.28	4.2	18.8	43.73
gl	4.5	25.6	64.93	17.2	36.7	66.07	13.4	38.5	74.77	51.0	67.8	85.77
ha	0.1	5.4	38.42	0.3	11.2	42.58	1.5	10.2	35.77	6.9	18.9	47.37
ka	0.3	1.9	31.97	0.6	9.2	44.48	0.4	1.4	28.81	2.4	17.0	47.57
kk	4.3	4.9	50.51	5.1	14.2	51.51	0.5	1.6	33.66	5.1	19.8	51.40
km	2.8	4.5	51.68	3.9	11.1	50.40	0.8	2.9	39.56	5.6	16.2	50.42
ky	10.0	10.6	54.23	10.3	24.0	55.99	0.6	1.6	30.19	3.8	17.9	48.05
li	6.6	16.2	-	5.9	24.8	-	2.0	14.9	-	9.8	29.8	-
my	1.8	2.4	45.44	3.0	5.0	48.33	0.4	0.8	29.58	1.0	3.7	44.15
nb	5.8	18.2	57.01	13.9	33.0	56.37	3.9	19.3	46.74	19.8	40.3	63.56
nn	6.3	18.6	62.33	8.9	25.3	56.28	3.7	19.7	41.75	16.9	37.5	62.37
oc	6.0	13.6	-	5.1	18.6	-	9.6	33.6	-	53.0	68.5	-
si	0.6	2.0	41.84	1.6	9.4	48.58	0.5	1.4	28.08	1.6	9.1	42.67
tg	0.4	1.4	-	1.1	11.8	-	0.4	1.5	-	3.3	18.0	-
tk	7.9	10.6	-	5.3	13.0	-	0.7	8.7	-	4.2	20.1	-
tt	0.0	1.0	-	0.2	13.3	-	0.3	1.4	-	4.2	20.2	-
ug	0.0	0.4	32.44	0.3	11.2	45.69	0.3	0.9	31.34	3.0	16.5	48.99
uz	0.7	2.1	35.94	1.0	12.8	41.86	1.5	11.5	40.65	3.1	18.7	49.43
yi	7.3	16.5	57.47	4.0	23.0	63.91	0.7	1.7	33.22	2.1	15.6	41.87
avg.	3.61	8.82	47.81	6.70	18.49	51.68	2.00	9.35	36.54	9.95	24.47	52.05

Table 12: Detailed results of BLOOMZ-7b1 without fine-tuning.

Language	OPUS en→xx			OPUS xx→en			Flores en→xx			Flores xx→en		
	BLEU	chrF++	COMET	BLEU	chrF++	COMET	BLEU	chrF++	COMET	BLEU	chrF++	COMET
af	25.0	41.4	71.05	38.5	52.3	78.94	10.1	31.0	45.42	33.9	51.1	72.66
am	3.0	12.8	59.55	3.4	19.8	59.71	0.2	5.2	42.97	1.4	16.0	49.47
be	8.9	14.9	55.16	14.0	24.9	62.37	0.7	12.3	30.90	3.7	21.0	49.99
cy	20.2	38.0	71.55	33.2	49.3	77.72	5.0	20.3	38.38	13.1	30.2	57.47
ga	15.6	37.1	63.87	29.2	49.1	75.94	3.7	21.2	39.17	12.5	30.3	57.53
gd	13.1	24.7	62.14	66.0	69.6	77.70	2.2	19.6	40.75	7.1	22.3	50.05
gl	16.9	37.6	70.62	24.7	43.6	75.62	21.9	45.2	77.26	46.6	64.5	86.86
ha	12.3	32.7	71.75	10.0	29.8	64.51	1.9	17.1	49.24	6.8	22.1	48.81
ka	4.6	18.1	67.39	10.0	24.3	60.50	0.3	6.8	27.46	1.5	14.9	46.10
kk	12.6	19.5	66.07	14.6	28.2	71.80	0.8	13.0	35.76	3.9	19.7	52.24
km	19.7	25.2	63.24	13.9	32.1	75.02	0.5	12.3	35.60	6.2	22.4	56.45
ky	16.0	20.5	66.27	21.1	33.8	73.06	0.9	12.7	36.10	3.0	17.5	50.40
li	13.5	32.8	-	21.3	35.7	-	3.3	19.9	-	14.6	31.4	-
my	6.2	14.3	58.04	5.2	15.6	63.65	0.2	12.9	40.37	1.3	12.7	48.38
nb	12.7	30.4	63.27	22.2	42.1	76.74	7.9	28.4	44.15	25.6	44.3	72.56
nn	18.3	38.0	77.18	27.1	47.7	81.80	7.3	25.7	45.35	24.3	42.9	70.06
oc	10.0	20.0	-	13.4	27.1	-	8.0	27.5	-	46.9	63.5	-
si	5.2	21.4	68.16	11.5	26.4	70.79	0.9	12.9	41.73	3.7	19.2	57.41
tg	5.5	22.0	-	8.0	25.9	-	1.1	15.8	-	3.1	19.6	-
tk	24.4	26.7	-	30.4	37.8	-	0.7	10.8	-	3.9	18.8	-
tt	1.9	17.6	-	3.6	19.6	-	0.4	13.7	-	1.6	14.3	-
ug	1.2	19.7	49.76	4.2	21.2	61.34	0.4	12.9	35.88	1.7	16.7	50.29
uz	3.1	18.2	62.12	5.7	22.0	61.12	0.5	3.6	34.67	3.9	18.8	50.32
yi	7.1	24.3	59.13	14.9	20.2	58.66	0.3	9.5	29.77	2.5	17.2	43.27
avg.	11.54	25.33	64.54	18.6	33.25	68.84	3.30	17.10	40.58	11.37	27.14	56.33

Table 13: Detailed results of BLOOMZ-7b1 fine-tuned with MTInstruct for BLOOMZ+24.

Language	OPUS en→xx			OPUS xx→en			Flores en→xx			Flores xx→en		
	BLEU	chrF++	COMET	BLEU	chrF++	COMET	BLEU	chrF++	COMET	BLEU	chrF++	COMET
af	25.0	41.9	70.72	36.9	52.2	78.68	10.6	31.9	45.84	33.5	51.1	72.84
am	3.4	13.2	60.62	4.9	22.8	62.43	0.3	5.4	44.20	1.4	16.4	51.05
be	8.3	14.5	55.23	13.9	25.1	62.72	0.8	12.5	30.93	3.6	20.6	49.14
cy	20.6	39.0	71.73	33.8	49.4	77.55	4.7	20.3	38.70	14.6	31.5	58.34
ga	17.6	39.3	65.76	32.6	52.7	77.49	3.4	21.4	39.99	13.6	31.6	58.73
gd	15.6	27.2	62.09	48.1	55.4	75.90	2.3	20.3	40.81	7.4	22.0	49.99
gl	17.1	37.2	70.85	24.4	43.3	75.90	21.7	44.9	77.09	45.6	63.5	86.60
ha	14.6	35.0	73.34	11.4	31.3	65.69	1.9	17.3	50.88	7.4	22.5	49.57
ka	4.9	18.9	67.54	10.5	25.3	61.27	0.3	6.9	27.61	2.1	16.0	47.04
kk	12.3	19.3	65.73	15.6	28.0	71.01	0.9	13.0	35.86	4.1	19.8	52.43
km	20.4	26.5	63.38	14.4	35.2	75.62	0.6	12.5	35.44	7.1	22.9	57.81
ky	15.8	19.6	64.74	23.3	35.8	74.70	0.9	13.3	36.71	2.9	17.4	50.06
li	13.2	29.4	-	22.3	38.2	-	3.1	19.7	-	12.5	28.7	-
my	7.6	15.4	58.84	6.3	18.0	66.45	0.3	13.3	40.97	1.2	14.4	50.79
nb	13.5	31.4	64.08	24.2	44.2	77.58	7.9	28.7	44.12	25.5	44.9	72.72
nn	19.0	38.0	77.61	28.5	47.7	81.68	7.0	26.7	46.14	25.8	44.1	70.55
oc	9.1	19.3	-	13.5	27.5	-	7.5	25.9	-	47.3	63.8	-
si	5.1	22.1	69.60	13.9	29.1	72.51	1.1	13.1	43.01	5.6	22.7	61.89
tg	6.6	23.7	-	8.8	27.2	-	0.9	15.6	-	3.4	19.9	-
tk	27.2	26.2	-	31.2	38.7	-	0.7	11.4	-	3.8	18.2	-
tt	2.1	18.6	-	5.0	21.5	-	0.4	13.3	-	1.5	13.7	-
ug	1.1	20.7	51.12	5.5	23.4	63.42	0.4	13.8	37.51	2.1	16.3	50.45
uz	3.5	18.6	62.09	7.4	23.3	62.01	0.2	1.9	34.50	3.7	18.2	50.09
yi	11.1	33.1	70.13	12.8	21.2	60.47	0.4	9.8	30.08	2.6	17.0	42.57
avg.	12.28	26.17	65.54	18.72	34.02	70.69	3.26	17.20	41.07	11.60	27.38	56.98

Table 14: Detailed results of BLOOMZ-7b1 fine-tuned with MT+Align for BLOOMZ+24.

Zero-shot	BLEU	chrF++	COMET	Supervised	BLEU	chrF++	COMET
ar-de	1.4	14.8	56.19	en-ar	11.1	32.4	75.66
ar-fr	21.9	46.1	74.19	en-de	12.2	29.2	59.16
ar-nl	0.6	11.2	56.59	en-fr	26.8	49.2	77.42
ar-ru	3.1	6.2	48.41	en-nl	2.0	16.0	46.52
ar-zh	18.4	14.4	73.65	en-ru	5.7	16.1	49.00
de-ar	2.0	17.8	64.91	en-zh	22.5	17.0	77.90
de-fr	12.0	33.4	63.45	avg.	13.38	26.65	64.28
de-nl	3.7	17.9	47.30				
de-ru	1.3	11.8	45.53				
de-zh	8.9	7.6	61.52				
fr-ar	11.2	33.4	74.20		BLEU	chrF++	COMET
fr-de	4.6	23.4	48.83	ar-en	26.7	48.4	78.12
fr-nl	2.8	17.2	52.14	de-en	21.1	38.5	71.99
fr-ru	3.1	10.4	45.12	fr-en	27.7	49.8	79.46
fr-zh	20.9	17.0	76.20	nl-en	12.3	31.1	61.29
nl-ar	1.3	13.2	59.46	ru-en	17.9	36.6	68.40
nl-de	5.9	22.8	46.49	zh-en	24.5	47.9	77.08
nl-fr	9.6	29.6	58.30	avg.	21.70	42.05	72.72
nl-ru	0.8	9.0	42.83				
nl-zh	3.3	3.7	53.96				
ru-ar	6.5	25.3	68.38				
ru-de	2.0	17.0	48.06				
ru-fr	15.7	38.7	67.54				
ru-nl	0.5	10.5	46.14				
ru-zh	10.7	11.3	67.18				
zh-ar	8.6	29.7	73.47				
zh-de	1.6	17.6	49.90				
zh-fr	20.7	44.1	75.79				
zh-nl	0.6	10.4	48.53				
zh-ru	2.9	8.6	44.13				
avg.	6.89	19.14	57.95				
seen→seen	16.95	30.78	74.58	en→seen	20.13	32.87	76.99
seen→unseen	2.30	13.31	49.98	en→unseen	6.63	20.43	51.56
unseen→seen	7.78	20.07	62.74	seen→en	26.30	48.70	78.22
unseen→unseen	2.37	14.83	46.06	unseen→en	17.10	35.40	67.23

Table 15: Detailed results of BLOOMZ-7b1 without fine-tuning.

Zero-shot	BLEU	chrF++	COMET	Supervised	BLEU	chrF++	COMET
ar-de	4.7	20.9	56.43	en-ar	9.1	27.2	71.47
ar-fr	20.8	42.5	71.47	en-de	19.8	36.1	66.53
ar-nl	7.2	22.9	58.29	en-fr	23.0	44.5	74.98
ar-ru	5.0	21.0	54.73	en-nl	15.5	36.1	64.76
ar-zh	14.0	12.4	67.94	en-ru	14.2	30.3	62.82
de-ar	2.4	16.2	64.53	en-zh	20.7	17.9	74.97
de-fr	11.9	31.2	64.44	avg.	17.05	32.02	69.26
de-nl	9.4	28.1	54.22				
de-ru	5.1	19.6	55.41				
de-zh	4.2	5.8	55.26				
fr-ar	10.1	29.1	70.72		BLEU	chrF++	COMET
fr-de	8.6	27.7	53.77	ar-en	26.5	46.9	76.92
fr-nl	10.3	30.1	57.55	de-en	27.0	44.0	76.97
fr-ru	7.9	26.0	56.82	fr-en	27.5	49.0	78.80
fr-zh	18.1	18.5	72.24	nl-en	21.8	41.3	73.99
nl-ar	2.0	15.1	63.73	ru-en	24.8	43.6	74.23
nl-de	9.7	28.1	52.58	zh-en	23.2	45.3	76.83
nl-fr	13.2	32.3	65.17	avg.	25.13	45.02	76.29
nl-ru	5.1	18.6	55.13				
nl-zh	3.0	5.4	54.34				
ru-ar	5.9	15.0	60.36				
ru-de	5.6	23.8	52.66				
ru-fr	17.9	38.4	68.66				
ru-nl	6.2	22.5	54.41				
ru-zh	7.5	13.6	61.40				
zh-ar	6.7	22.1	67.48				
zh-de	3.3	19.6	51.75				
zh-fr	17.4	38.9	73.00				
zh-nl	4.8	19.3	54.41				
zh-ru	3.5	17.9	49.02				
avg.	8.38	22.75	59.93				
seen→seen	14.52	27.25	70.48	en→seen	17.60	29.87	73.81
seen→unseen	6.14	22.82	54.75	en→unseen	16.50	34.17	64.70
unseen→seen	7.56	19.22	61.99	seen→en	25.73	47.07	77.52
unseen→unseen	6.85	23.45	54.07	unseen→en	24.53	42.97	75.06

Table 16: Detailed results of BLOOMZ-7b1 fine-tuned with MTInstruct for BLOOMZ+3 de-nl-ru.

Zero-shot	BLEU	chrF++	COMET	Supervised	BLEU	chrF++	COMET
ar-de	5.1	20.8	55.25	en-ar	8.4	26.0	70.45
ar-fr	20.3	42.5	71.78	en-de	21.1	36.7	67.15
ar-nl	6.4	21.6	57.48	en-fr	22.9	44.4	74.67
ar-ru	5.2	21.5	55.51	en-nl	16.1	36.8	65.26
ar-zh	16.0	14.1	69.55	en-ru	15.2	31.5	63.30
de-ar	2.4	16.3	64.01	en-zh	16.1	15.0	71.93
de-fr	13.5	34.3	66.25	avg.	16.63	31.73	68.79
de-nl	9.7	28.0	55.00				
de-ru	5.3	19.6	55.61				
de-zh	7.2	7.3	60.64				
fr-ar	10.0	28.2	69.86		BLEU	chrF++	COMET
fr-de	9.2	27.8	54.03	ar-cn	27.1	47.0	76.54
fr-nl	10.8	31.0	58.50	de-en	27.8	44.4	77.57
fr-ru	8.6	26.7	57.07	fr-en	27.1	48.7	78.82
fr-zh	15.9	15.8	70.78	nl-en	22.6	42.2	74.25
nl-ar	2.2	15.4	63.47	ru-en	25.6	44.2	74.46
nl-de	10.2	28.5	53.65	zh-en	23.5	45.7	77.04
nl-fr	14.4	34.4	66.55	avg.	25.62	45.37	76.45
nl-ru	5.3	19.3	55.53				
nl-zh	5.5	6.2	58.77				
ru-ar	6.5	16.0	62.69				
ru-de	6.1	24.3	52.89				
ru-fr	18.2	39.0	69.95				
ru-nl	6.3	22.5	54.36				
ru-zh	7.6	13.3	61.94				
zh-ar	8.7	26.5	70.88				
zh-de	3.0	19.5	50.82				
zh-fr	17.7	39.7	73.56				
zh-nl	4.4	19.3	54.20				
zh-ru	4.1	19.5	50.47				
avg.	8.86	23.30	60.70				
seen→seen	14.77	27.80	71.07	en→seen	15.80	28.47	72.35
seen→unseen	6.31	23.08	54.81	en→unseen	17.47	35.00	65.24
unseen→seen	8.61	20.24	63.81	seen→en	25.90	47.13	77.47
unseen→unseen	7.15	23.70	54.51	unseen→en	25.33	43.60	75.43

Table 17: Detailed results of BLOOMZ-7b1 fine-tuned with MT+Align for BLOOMZ+3 de-nl-ru.

Zero-shot	BLEU	chrF++	COMET	Supervised	BLEU	chrF++	COMET
ar-de	6.9	24.7	58.10	en-ar	14.6	35.6	76.70
ar-fr	26.2	48.2	74.96	en-de	20.4	36.0	65.96
ar-nl	8.8	24.7	59.53	en-fr	27.9	50.0	77.65
ar-ru	6.5	22.7	55.33	en-nl	14.8	34.8	63.11
ar-zh	28.6	22.3	77.64	en-ru	13.3	29.0	61.43
de-ar	3.3	19.8	68.27	en-zh	36.1	27.7	80.31
de-fr	15.2	35.8	67.05	avg.	21.18	35.52	70.86
de-nl	8.2	26.0	53.35				
de-ru	4.4	17.9	54.79				
de-zh	12.0	9.9	65.20				
fr-ar	14.2	35.2	74.84		BLEU	chrF++	COMET
fr-de	8.9	28.4	53.81	ar-en	33.7	53.5	79.81
fr-nl	10.1	29.9	56.92	de-en	27.1	43.9	77.04
fr-ru	8.1	26.0	55.96	fr-en	29.6	51.0	79.60
fr-zh	30.2	25.6	79.43	nl-en	22.0	41.4	73.54
nl-ar	3.1	18.2	67.72	ru-en	25.1	43.9	74.05
nl-de	10.4	27.7	52.67	zh-en	32.6	54.3	79.75
nl-fr	16.9	37.3	68.46	avg.	28.35	48.00	77.30
nl-ru	4.8	17.8	54.71				
nl-zh	8.1	7.0	63.96				
ru-ar	11.9	31.5	72.45				
ru-de	6.1	23.7	52.74				
ru-fr	21.2	42.5	71.71				
ru-nl	6.8	22.6	53.91				
ru-zh	21.3	20.7	74.63				
zh-ar	13.1	34.1	74.92				
zh-de	4.1	22.3	52.13				
zh-fr	23.8	46.5	76.54				
zh-nl	4.8	19.9	54.26				
zh-ru	5.7	21.9	50.60				
avg.	11.79	26.36	63.22				
seen→seen	22.68	35.32	76.39	en→seen	26.20	37.77	78.22
seen→unseen	7.10	24.50	55.18	en→unseen	16.17	33.27	63.50
unseen→seen	12.56	24.74	68.83	seen→en	31.97	52.93	79.72
unseen→unseen	6.78	22.62	53.69	unseen→en	24.73	43.07	74.88

Table 18: Detailed results of BLOOMZ-7b1 fine-tuned with MTInstruct for BLOOMZ+3 ar-de-fr-nl-ru-zh.

Zero-shot	BLEU	chrF++	COMET	Supervised	BLEU	chrF++	COMET
ar-de	6.7	24.2	57.45	en-ar	15.1	35.8	76.76
ar-fr	27.5	49.2	75.21	en-de	20.6	35.9	65.88
ar-nl	8.7	24.8	59.14	en-fr	27.5	49.4	77.46
ar-ru	6.7	21.6	55.04	en-nl	15.0	35.6	63.70
ar-zh	30.1	24.4	78.54	en-ru	13.5	29.5	61.62
de-ar	3.5	19.7	68.39	en-zh	36.3	27.7	80.52
de-fr	15.4	35.8	67.81	avg.	21.33	35.65	70.99
de-nl	9.6	27.3	53.74				
de-ru	4.7	17.9	54.23				
de-zh	12.0	9.9	65.40				
fr-ar	14.9	36.3	74.98		BLEU	chrF++	COMET
fr-de	9.2	28.3	52.96	ar-en	33.9	53.7	79.74
fr-nl	11.3	31.1	57.62	de-en	27.1	43.6	77.13
fr-ru	8.8	26.2	56.31	fr-en	29.7	51.0	80.03
fr-zh	31.1	26.9	79.93	nl-en	22.6	42.3	73.94
nl-ar	3.3	18.5	68.02	ru-en	25.8	44.5	74.07
nl-de	9.4	26.5	52.33	zh-en	32.5	54.5	80.01
nl-fr	17.2	37.3	68.38	avg.	28.60	48.27	77.49
nl-ru	4.4	17.1	53.63				
nl-zh	8.3	7.0	64.08				
ru-ar	12.4	32.1	72.40				
ru-de	5.7	22.9	51.90				
ru-fr	21.5	42.7	72.08				
ru-nl	6.3	22.1	53.32				
ru-zh	22.7	24.6	75.36				
zh-ar	13.9	35.4	75.68				
zh-de	3.6	21.3	51.32				
zh-fr	24.5	47.0	76.98				
zh-nl	4.9	20.3	54.30				
zh-ru	5.5	21.1	50.49				
avg.	12.13	26.65	63.23				
seen→seen	23.67	36.53	76.89	en→seen	26.30	37.63	78.25
seen→unseen	7.27	24.32	54.96	en→unseen	16.37	33.67	63.73
unseen→seen	12.92	25.29	69.10	seen→en	32.03	53.07	79.93
unseen→unseen	6.68	22.30	53.19	unseen→en	25.17	43.47	75.05

Table 19: Detailed results of BLOOMZ-7b1 fine-tuned with MT+Align for BLOOMZ+3 ar-de-fr-nl-ru-zh.

HeSum: a Novel Dataset for Abstractive Text Summarization in Hebrew

Tzuf Paz-Argaman*[,a], Itai Mondshine*[,a], Asaf Achi Mordechai[a], and Reut Tsarfaty[a]

[a]Bar-Ilan University, Israel,
{tzuf.paz-argaman, mondshi1, asaf.achimordechai, reut.tsarfaty}@biu.ac.il

Abstract

While large language models (LLMs) excel in various natural language tasks in English, their performance in lower-resourced languages like Hebrew, especially for generative tasks such as abstractive summarization, remains unclear. The high morphological richness in Hebrew adds further challenges due to the ambiguity in sentence comprehension and the complexities in meaning construction. In this paper, we address this resource and evaluation gap by introducing HeSum, a novel benchmark specifically designed for abstractive text summarization in Modern Hebrew. HeSum consists of 10,000 article-summary pairs sourced from Hebrew news websites written by professionals. Linguistic analysis confirms HeSum's high abstractness and unique morphological challenges. We show that HeSum presents distinct difficulties for contemporary state-of-the-art LLMs, establishing it as a valuable testbed for generative language technology in Hebrew, and MRLs generative challenges in general.[1]

1 Introduction

Recent advances with large language models (LLMs, Brown et al., 2020; Chowdhery et al., 2023) demonstrate impressive capabilities, encompassing diverse tasks such as natural language (NL) understanding and reasoning, including *classification* tasks such as commonsense reasoning (Bisk et al., 2020) and sentiment analysis (Liang et al., 2022), as well as *generative* tasks like summarization and dialogue systems (Cohen et al., 2022). However, these impressive achievements are primarily demonstrated for the English language. Our understanding of how these models perform on low-resource languages is limited, as current evaluations are primarily focused on languages with abundant data (Ahuja et al., 2023; Lai et al., 2023).

This concern is particularly relevant for *morphologically rich languages* (MRLs) such as Hebrew, which is known for their word complexity and ambiguity, leading to processing difficulty (Tsarfaty et al., 2019, 2020). Despite advances in natural language processing for Hebrew, which so far covered tasks as reading comprehension (Keren and Levy, 2021; Cohen et al., 2023), named entity recognition (Bareket and Tsarfaty, 2021), sentiment analysis (Chriqui and Yahav, 2022), and text-based geolocation (Paz-Argaman et al., 2023); a crucial gap persists in the ability to evaluate novel, human-like generated text, as in *abstractive text generation*.

Abstractive text-generation requires both natural language understanding and reasoning over the input, and the ability to generate grammatically, and in particular *morpho-syntactically*, correct text, as well as *semantically* and *morpho-semantically* coherent, fluent text that conveys consistent meanings. Notably, text-generation models are also prone to 'hallucinations' — generating factually incorrect content. These challenges are further amplified in Hebrew due to its morphological richness which leads to a complex realization of sentence structure and meaning.

In order to enable empirically quantified assessment of these aspects of text generation in MRLs, we present a novel benchmark dataset for **He**brew abstractive text **Sum**marization (**HeSum**). HeSum consists of 10,000 articles paired with their corresponding summaries, all of which have been sourced from three different Hebrew news websites, all written by professional journalists. This curated collection offers several key advantages: (i) *High Abstractness* – extensive linguistic analysis validates HeSum's summaries as demonstrably more abstractive even when compared to English benchmarks. (ii) *Unique Hebrew Challenges* – meticulous linguistic analysis pinpoints the inherent complexities specific to Hebrew summarization, offering valuable insights into the nuanced

*Equal contribution.

[1]The dataset, code, and fine-tuned models are publicly available at `https://github.com/OnlpLab/HeSum`

Proceedings of the The Seventh Workshop on Technologies for Machine Translation of Low-Resource Languages (LoResMT 2024), pages 26–36
August 15, 2024

Set	Size	Vocabulary size (over Articles)		Avg. Document Length		Avg. Word Ambiguity	Avg. Morph Anaphors	Avg. Construct-State	BertScore Semantic Similarity
		Lemmas	Tokens	Article	Summary	Article	Article	Summary	Article-Summary
Train	8,000	47,903	269,168	1,427.4	33.2	58	98.8	2.4	76
Validation	1,000	23,134	104,383	1,410.0	33.8	90	87.9	2.5	76
Test	1,000	22,543	102,387	1,507.6	34.7	89	95.7	2.6	74

Table 1: Linguistic Analysis of the HeSum dataset.

characteristics that differentiate it from its English counterpart. And (iii) *Thorough LLM Evaluation* – we conducted a comprehensive empirical analysis using state-of-the-art LLMs, demonstrating that HeSum presents unique challenges even for these contemporary models. By combining high abstractness, nuanced morphological complexities, and a rigorous LLM evaluation, HeSum establishes itself as a valuable resource for advancing the frontiers of abstractive text summarization in MRL settings.

2 The Challenge

Linguistic Challenges in Hebrew Morphologically rich languages (MRLs) pose distinct challenges for generative tasks, above and beyond morphologically impoverished ones such as English.

In MRLs, each input token can be composed of multiple lexical and functional elements, each contributing to the overall structure and semantic meanings of the generated text. For instance, the Hebrew word 'וכשמביתנו' is composed of seven morphemes: 'ו' ('and'), 'כש' ('when'), 'מ' ('from'), 'ה' ('the'), 'בית' ('house'), 'של' ('of'), and 'אנחנו' ('us'). This has ramifications for both the understanding of MRL texts, a process that necessitates morphological segmentation, and for generating MRL texts, requiring morphological fusion. At comprehension, Hebrew poses an additional challenge due to its inherent ambiguity, with many tokens admitting multiple valid segmentations, e.g., 'הקפה' could be interpreted as 'ה'+'קפה' ('the'+'coffee'); as 'הקפה' ('orbit'); or as 'הקף' + 'של' + 'היא' ('perimeter'+'of'+'her'). During generation, the emergence of unseen morphological compositions, where unfamiliar morphemes combine in familiar ways, poses an additional challenge (Hofmann et al., 2021; Gueta et al., 2023). These challenges, coupled with inherent linguistic features like morphological inflections, construct-state nouns (*smixut*), and flexible word order, create a multifaceted challenge for LLMs in processing and generating Hebrew texts.

The HeSum Task We aim to unlock the comprehension-and-generation challenge in MRL settings by first tackling the abstractive text summarization task (Moratanch and Chitrakala, 2016), here focusing on Modern Hebrew.

Given an input document in Hebrew, specifically a news article, our goal is to generate a short, clear, Hebrew summary of the key information in the article. In contrast to *extractive* summarization, here novel morphosyntactic structures need to be generated to communicate the summary.

3 Dataset, Statistics and Analysis

3.1 Data Collection

The HeSum dataset consists of article-and-summary pairs. The articles were collected from three Hebrew news websites: "Shakuf",[2] "HaMakom",[3] and "The Seventh Eye".[4] These websites focus on independent journalism, providing articles on topics such as government accountability, corporate influence, and environmental issues. Each article on these websites is accompanied by an extended subheading written by a professional editor, that serves as a summary of the content. To ensure data quality, articles that were not in Hebrew, or ones that had particularly short summaries (i.e., the extended subheading was less than 10 tokens) were excluded from the dataset.

3.2 Linguistic Analysis

We examined the linguistic, morpho-syntactic and semantic, properties of the HeSum dataset. For the extraction of syntactic and semantic features, we used DictaBert (Shmidman et al., 2023). Additionally, AlephBert (Seker et al., 2022), a Hebrew monolingual BERT-based encoder model (Devlin et al., 2018), was employed to compute semantic similarity between articles and their corresponding summaries, leveraging the BertScore method (Zhang* et al., 2020). Notably, semantic similarity was performed only on article-summary pairs within the model's 512-token limit.

[2]https://shakuf.co.il
[3]https://www.ha-makom.co.il
[4]https://www.the7eye.org.il

Dataset	novel n-grams				CMP	RED (n=1)	RED (n=2)
	n = 1	n = 2	n = 3	n = 4			
CNN/Daily Mail	13.20	52.77	72.20	81.40	90.90	13.73	1.10
XSum	35.76	83.45	95.50	98.49	90.40	5.83	0.16
HeSum	42.00	73.20	82.00	85.36	95.48	4.83	0.10

Table 2: HeSum's Intrinsic Evaluation compared to English Benchmarks (CNN/Daily Mail and XSum).

Table 1 highlights the Hebrew language's multi-faceted complexities as reflected in this task. The notable disparity in the vocabulary size between token and lemma counts underscores extensive morphological richness, necessitating models adept at handling linguistic diversity. The abundance of morphological anaphoric expressions and numerous Hebrew construct-state constructions necessitate advanced models attuned to entity relations that are expressed via Hebrew's unique morphological traits. Lattice analysis reveals a high degree of word ambiguity (numerous lattice paths), highlighting natural language understanding challenges and the consequent difficulty of accurate tokenization for downstream processing tasks. The substantial document length, necessitate the use of models adept at long-form text processing. Finally, the relatively high semantic similarity score indicates effective information distillation in the summaries.

3.3 Summarization Intrinsic Analysis

To assess the challenges of the HeSum summaries we used three established metrics: (i) *Abstractness*: the percentage of summary novel n-grams, unseen in the article (Narayan et al., 2018). (ii) *Compression Ratio (CMP)*: the word count in summary S divided by the word count in article A: $CMP_w(S, A) = 1 - \frac{|S|}{|A|}$. Higher compression ratios indicate greater word-level reduction and, subsequently, potentially a more challenging summarization task (Bommasani and Cardie, 2020). (iii) *Redundancy (RED)*: measures repetitive n-grams within a summary (S) using the form: $RED(S) = \frac{\sum_{i=1}^{m}(f_i - 1)}{\sum_{i=1}^{m} f_i}$ where m is the number of unique n-grams in the summary and $f_i \geq 1$ is the frequency count of a specific n-gram (Hasan et al., 2021).

Table 2 presents a quantitative analysis of HeSum's summarization characteristics, underscoring its challenges. HeSum demonstrates a high degree of abstractness, with approximately half of its unique vocabulary and over 73% of bigrams unseen in the original articles. Furthermore, HeSum presents a significant compression challenge, as summaries average less than 5% of the input article length. Additionally, the analysis reveals minimal redundancy within the summaries, with less than 5% repeated n-grams. These findings underscore HeSum's efficacy in conveying the central ideas of the articles' information in a novel, distillate, and non-redundant manner. Comparative analysis with established abstractive summarization benchmarks, CNN/Daily Mail (Nallapati et al., 2016) and XSum (Narayan et al., 2018), confirms HeSum's high abstractness, compression ratio, and low redundancy, even when compared to these datasets.

4 Experiments

4.1 Experimental setup

Models To demonstrate the complexity of this task, we conducted an evaluation of two LLMs in a zero-shot setting: the GPT-4 model with 32K context window (version 0613), and GPT-3.5-turbo with 16K context (version 0613). To find the most effective prompt format, we tested on the HeSum validation set various prompting strategies, including translating parts of the prompt to English. Ultimately, we adopted the English-translated approach (Brown et al., 2020), where both the instruction and input were translated. The output summaries are strictly in Hebrew. Additionally, to address the limitations of available generative models for Hebrew, we fine-tuned the multilingual mLongT5 model (Uthus et al., 2023) on the HeSum training set with two versions, base (2.37 GB) and large (4.56 GB). mLongT5 is a sequence-to-sequence model based on mT5 (Xue et al., 2020) specifically designed for handling long sequences. Appendix B includes the GPT models' prompting strategies experiments, and the mLongT5 training details.

Automatic Evaluation Metrics To evaluate the generated summaries with respect to the original texts, we used two standardly-used automatic metrics: ROUGE and BertScore.

Model	ROUGE			BertScore	Human Evaluation	
	ROUGE-1	ROUGE-2	ROUGE-L		Coherence	Completeness
GPT-4	13.59	3.70	10.39	77.3	4.48	4.14
GPT-3.5	13.69	3.84	10.55	77.0	4.38	3.98
mLongT5 (fine-tuned)	17.47	7.56	14.68	57.6	3.46	2.10

Table 3: Models' performance on the HeSum test-set.

Phenomenon	GPT-4	GPT-3.5	mLongT5	Example error in Hebrew	Example error translated into English	Explanation
Repetition	0	0	1	האם הוא יכול להיות אלים? אם הוא יכול להיות אלים?...	Can he be violent? If he can be violent?	Duplication with subtle alterations.
Copy from Article	0	0	4	האם עיתונאי יכול להציע ביקורת פומבית על...	Can a journalist make public criticism of...	The model-generated summary replicates a section of the original article.
Non-alphabetic omission	1	0	14	צחצחים	Chachachim	Missing diacritic – it should be 'צ'חצ'חים' instead of 'צחצחים'.
Incorrect disambiguation	1	1	2	...נאומו של הדוד טופז	Uncle Topaz's speech...	'דודו' is incorrectly interpreted as 'דוד' + 'של' ('Uncle' + 'of'), instead of as a man's name – 'דודו', which is why the model added a definite 'ה' to 'דוד'.
Hallucination	3	3	2	...עירב את נח...	...involved Noah...	Noah is not a person mentioned in the article.
Culture transfer	1	1	0	...למנהינת הקמפיין הנבחרת, ננסי ברנדס...	...to the campaign leader-elect, Nancy Brands...	The article refers to Nancy as a 'he', but the summary uses feminine inflection (leader), probably due to Nancy being a common female name in English.
Incorect gender	6	11	1	...חושפות בחקירתם...	...reveal in their investigation...	Gender inflection mismatch: 'reveal' (fem.) clashes with 'their' (masc.).
Incorrect definite (e.g., construct state)	3	2	3	...המשרד המשפטים פירסם...	The Ministry of the Justice published...	Definite articles on both words in 'The Ministry of the Justice' violate Hebrew construct state rules.

Table 4: Error analysis comparing generated summaries from GPT-4, GPT-3.5, and mLongT5 based on 30 inputs.

ROUGE (Lin, 2004) is a widely-used metric in summarization that measures n-gram overlap between generated summaries and human-written references. We calculated ROUGE-1 (unigrams), ROUGE-2 (bigrams), and ROUGE-L scores (longest common subsequence) to capture different levels of granularity. However, n-gram metrics such as ROUGE can struggle with capturing semantic similarity if paraphrases are used. To address this, we also employed BertScore (Zhang* et al., 2020) with AlephBert (Seker et al., 2022) as its backbone. BertScore leverages the pre-trained language model to provide a more semantically meaningful evaluation of the summary.

Human Evaluation To validate the quality of model-generated summaries for the HeSum task, seven independent expert annotators evaluated a total of 186 summaries (62 per model) based on the same set of 62 reference articles. Annotators evaluated each summary using a 1-5 Likert scale (Likert, 1932) based on two key criteria: *coherence*, which assessed the summaries' grammaticality and readability, and *completeness*, which measured the degree to which they capture the main ideas of the articles. To measure the consistency of the annotators' scores, we calculated Krippendorff's α (Krippendorff, 2018) for an interval scale, and received an α score of 0.78 which indicates a good inter-annotator agreement rate.

4.2 Results

Quantitative Analysis Table 3 summarizes the quantitative evaluation results. While mLongT5 consistently achieved higher ROUGE scores, a metric focused on surface-level similarity, GPT-based models exhibited superior performance in BertScore, a semantic similarity metric, and in human evaluation scores that assess coherence and completeness. The consistently higher ROUGE scores of mLongT5 might be partially attributed to limitations in the ROUGE metric itself. ROUGE scores favor summaries that closely mimic the source text, even if they lack originality or fluency. Additionally, n-gram-based metrics like ROUGE may discount grammatically correct sentences that convey the required meaning even with morphological or lexical word variations, or changes in word order, compared to the source text.

Furthermore, when comparing ROUGE to human evaluation we found a negative correlation of human evaluation with ROUGE scores. We computed Pearson correlation coefficients (PCC) and found the coefficients to be around -0.16 with highly statistically significant p-values (less than 2.39×10^{-5}), indicating that higher ROUGE scores do not in actuality correspond to human evaluations of good summaries. Similarly, using Kendall's τ correlations resulted in negative values. Further research is needed for developing automatic summarization metrics that correlate with human scores.

Qualitative Analysis Following the identification of key error categories, we conducted a comparative analysis by randomly selecting 30 summaries generated by each of the three models for the same set of 30 articles. For each model, we then quantified the occurrences of each identified phenomenon within the sampled summaries. The results in Table 4 reveal disparities between the errors of GPT-based models and those of the finetuned mLongT5 on various linguistic phenomena.

The finetuned mLongT5 exhibits pronounced disruptions like repetition (3.33%) and exact copy of sections from the articles (13.33%), which weren't observed in the GPT-based results. However, the GPT-based models demonstrate errors in morphological phenomena specific to Hebrew, such as incorrect gender and wrong definiteness marking on *smixut*, indicating that the morphological richness of the language remains a challenge for these LLMs. Additionally, known phenomena of GPT-based models such as "hallucinations" (Cui et al., 2023; Guerreiro et al., 2023) are also observed in our analysis, as is familiar from other languages.

5 Conclusion

This research seeks to fill a critical gap in the field of LLMs assessment for generative creative tasks in MRLs, by presenting HeSum, a new dataset for Hebrew abstractive summarization, that includes 10K article-summary pairs sourced from professional journalists on Hebrew news websites. HeSum offers three key advantages: high level of abstractness in summarization, distinct challenges specific to the Hebrew language, and a thorough empirical assessment of LLMs using this dataset. By integrating these aspects, HeSum establishes itself as a valuable resource for researchers striving to push the boundaries of generative tasks, and specifically abstractive text summarization in Hebrew.

Limitations

Evaluation Metrics based on n-gram matching, such as BLEU (Papineni et al., 2002), ROUGE (Lin, 2004), and Meteor (Denkowski and Lavie, 2014), are commonly used for evaluating summarization quality in English. However, these metrics can be problematic when applied to Hebrew text. Hebrew allows for more flexible word order compared to English. Additionally, its morphological richness entails that the same concept can be expressed in multiple ways due to variations in prefixes, suffixes, and root conjugations. Furthermore, Hebrew has variations in spelling words due to missing vowels (*Ktiv haser* vs. *Ktiv male*). These factors can lead to n-gram-based metrics overlooking grammatically correct sentences in the generated summary that convey the full meaning even though they show slight differences. Our findings in Section 4.2, which demonstrate a negative correlation between ROUGE scores and human evaluation scores, highlight the limitations of ROUGE evaluation in the context of Hebrew summarization.

Subset of LLMs Although we aspired to evaluate HeSum on a broad range of large language models (LLMs), our current analysis is limited to only two generative models. This might overlook newer models offering potentially superior performance. Additionally, resource constraints prevented us from investigating the behavior of these models in few-shot settings. Having acknowledged that, the timeliness of this resource is uncompromized, as it can be used with contemporary and future models alike, to track advances on this challenge.

Open Access vs. Domain Focus HeSum predominantly comprises articles from news websites, which may bias models' success in this task towards news-style writing, and may not fully capture the linguistic diversity across different genres and domains. The reason for selecting these domains specifically stems from our ability to obtain a permissive license for the resource, allowing open and free access by the community. However, the websites we have chosen – "Shakuf", "HaMakom", and "The Seventh Eye" – deviate from typical news platforms, offering a diverse range of topics that go beyond the typical content found on many popular news websites in Hebrew. This variety ensures that our dataset reflects a broader spectrum of real-world topics.

Dataset Scale vs. Quality In the realm of abstractive summarization, datasets like CNN/Daily Mail (Nallapati et al., 2016) and XSum (Narayan et al., 2018) are commonly employed. These datasets utilize news articles from websites, treating the article content as the document and a corresponding field (often not explicitly intended as a summary) as the summary. However, this approach has faced criticism due to uncertainty about whether the chosen field truly represents a summary (Tejaswin et al., 2021). An alternative approach involves human summarization, but this tends to result in smaller datasets (e.g., PriMock57, Papadopoulos Korfiatis et al., 2022). To advance Hebrew NLP (and the study of generation in MRLs in general) beyond traditional classification tasks, there is a need for extensive generative datasets. Given the current lack of viable alternatives within the NLP community, we have adopted a similar approach to XSUM, albeit with longer summaries. Additionally, collecting human-generated summaries in low-resource languages presents challenges, including the scarcity of crowdsourcing platforms that support Hebrew. To ensure quality, we meticulously reviewed 100 articles, their subheadings, and brief introductory sentences. Ultimately, we chose subheadings as our summary source because they provided more informative content, capturing additional details from the articles. Furthermore, we filtered out articles with subheadings containing very few tokens (10 or fewer) to ensure our summaries adequately represent the article content.

Ethics

Following the generous permission of "Shakuf", "HaMakom", and "The Seventh Eye" — organizations committed to independent journalism, media scrutiny, and transparency in Israel — we were granted the valuable opportunity not only to access and analyze their published articles but also to publish the data for broader research use. This unique collaboration fosters open access and empowers other researchers to build upon the data extracted from their articles and our findings within Hebrew abstraction summarization, expanding knowledge in this important field. Also, we are guaranteed not to have offensive language or hate speech in our data. It should be borne in mind, however, that the opinions or biases reflected in these data may differ from other sources of information (news websites, social media, non-Hebrew news reports, and the like). So, the deployment of technology trained on this resource should be done with care.

Acknowledgements

We wholeheartedly thank Naomi Niddam (Editor-in-Chief, "Shakuf"), Nir Ben-Zvi (CEO, "Shakuf" and "The Seventh Eye"), Shuki Tausig (Editor-in-Chief, "The Seventh Eye"), and Ohad Stone (Creative and digital projects, "Shakuf") for granting us access to and permission to analyze and share their articles for broader research purposes. We also thank Yoav Goldberg, Ido Dagan, Amir David Nissan Cohen, and the participants of the NLP seminar at Bar-Ilan University for their valuable feedback. This research has been funded by a grant from the European Research Council, ERC-StG grant number 677352, a grant by the Israeli Ministry of Science and Technology (MOST), and a KAMIN grant from the Israeli Innovation Authority, for which we are grateful.

References

Kabir Ahuja, Rishav Hada, Millicent Ochieng, Prachi Jain, Harshita Diddee, Samuel Maina, Tanuja Ganu, Sameer Segal, Maxamed Axmed, Kalika Bali, et al. 2023. Mega: Multilingual evaluation of generative ai. *arXiv preprint arXiv:2303.12528*.

Google Translate API. 2023. Google translate api v2 documentation.

Dan Bareket and Reut Tsarfaty. 2021. Neural modeling for named entities and morphology (nemo^2). *Transactions of the Association for Computational Linguistics*, 9:909–928.

Yonatan Bisk, Rowan Zellers, Jianfeng Gao, Yejin Choi, et al. 2020. Piqa: Reasoning about physical commonsense in natural language. In *Proceedings of the AAAI conference on artificial intelligence*, volume 34, pages 7432–7439.

Rishi Bommasani and Claire Cardie. 2020. Intrinsic evaluation of summarization datasets. In *Proceedings of the 2020 Conference on Empirical Methods in Natural Language Processing (EMNLP)*, pages 8075–8096.

Tom Brown, Benjamin Mann, Nick Ryder, Melanie Subbiah, Jared D Kaplan, Prafulla Dhariwal, Arvind Neelakantan, Pranav Shyam, Girish Sastry, Amanda Askell, et al. 2020. Language models are few-shot learners. *Advances in neural information processing systems*, 33:1877–1901.

Aakanksha Chowdhery, Sharan Narang, Jacob Devlin, Maarten Bosma, Gaurav Mishra, Adam Roberts, Paul Barham, Hyung Won Chung, Charles Sutton, Sebastian Gehrmann, Parker Schuh, Kensen Shi, Sasha Tsvyashchenko, Joshua Maynez, Abhishek Rao, Parker Barnes, Yi Tay, Noam Shazeer, Vinodkumar Prabhakaran, Emily Reif, Nan Du, Ben Hutchinson, Reiner Pope, James Bradbury, Jacob Austin, Michael Isard, Guy Gur-Ari, Pengcheng Yin, Toju Duke, Anselm Levskaya, Sanjay Ghemawat, Sunipa Dev, Henryk Michalewski, Xavier Garcia, Vedant Misra, Kevin Robinson, Liam Fedus, Denny Zhou, Daphne Ippolito, David Luan, Hyeontaek Lim, Barret Zoph, Alexander Spiridonov, Ryan Sepassi, David Dohan, Shivani Agrawal, Mark Omernick, Andrew M. Dai, Thanumalayan Sankaranarayana Pillai, Marie Pellat, Aitor Lewkowycz, Erica Moreira,

Rewon Child, Oleksandr Polozov, Katherine Lee, Zongwei Zhou, Xuezhi Wang, Brennan Saeta, Mark Diaz, Orhan Firat, Michele Catasta, Jason Wei, Kathy Meier-Hellstern, Douglas Eck, Jeff Dean, Slav Petrov, and Noah Fiedel. 2023. Palm: Scaling language modeling with pathways. *Journal of Machine Learning Research*, 24(240):1–113.

Avihay Chriqui and Inbal Yahav. 2022. Hebert and hebemo: A hebrew bert model and a tool for polarity analysis and emotion recognition. *INFORMS Journal on Data Science*, 1(1):81–95.

Aaron Daniel Cohen, Adam Roberts, Alejandra Molina, Alena Butryna, Alicia Jin, Apoorv Kulshreshtha, Ben Hutchinson, Ben Zevenbergen, Blaise Hilary Aguera-Arcas, Chung ching Chang, Claire Cui, Cosmo Du, Daniel De Freitas Adiwardana, Dehao Chen, Dmitry (Dima) Lepikhin, Ed H. Chi, Erin Hoffman-John, Heng-Tze Cheng, Hongrae Lee, Igor Krivokon, James Qin, Jamie Hall, Joe Fenton, Johnny Soraker, Kathy Meier-Hellstern, Kristen Olson, Lora Mois Aroyo, Maarten Paul Bosma, Marc Joseph Pickett, Marcelo Amorim Menegali, Marian Croak, Mark Díaz, Matthew Lamm, Maxim Krikun, Meredith Ringel Morris, Noam Shazeer, Quoc V. Le, Rachel Bernstein, Ravi Rajakumar, Ray Kurzweil, Romal Thoppilan, Steven Zheng, Taylor Bos, Toju Duke, Tulsee Doshi, Vincent Y. Zhao, Vinodkumar Prabhakaran, Will Rusch, YaGuang Li, Yanping Huang, Yanqi Zhou, Yuanzhong Xu, and Zhifeng Chen. 2022. Lamda: Language models for dialog applications. In *arXiv*.

Amir Cohen, Hilla Merhav-Fine, Yoav Goldberg, and Reut Tsarfaty. 2023. HeQ: a large and diverse Hebrew reading comprehension benchmark. In *Findings of the Association for Computational Linguistics: EMNLP 2023*, pages 13693–13705, Singapore. Association for Computational Linguistics.

Chenhang Cui, Yiyang Zhou, Xinyu Yang, Shirley Wu, Linjun Zhang, James Zou, and Huaxiu Yao. 2023. Holistic analysis of hallucination in gpt-4v (ision): Bias and interference challenges. *arXiv preprint arXiv:2311.03287*.

Michael Denkowski and Alon Lavie. 2014. Meteor universal: Language specific translation evaluation for any target language. In *Proceedings of the ninth workshop on statistical machine translation*, pages 376–380.

Jacob Devlin, Ming-Wei Chang, Kenton Lee, and Kristina Toutanova. 2018. Bert: Pre-training of deep bidirectional transformers for language understanding. *arXiv preprint arXiv:1810.04805*.

Nuno M Guerreiro, Duarte M Alves, Jonas Waldendorf, Barry Haddow, Alexandra Birch, Pierre Colombo, and André FT Martins. 2023. Hallucinations in large multilingual translation models. *Transactions of the Association for Computational Linguistics*, 11:1500–1517.

Eylon Gueta, Omer Goldman, and Reut Tsarfaty. 2023. Explicit morphological knowledge improves pre-training of language models for hebrew. *arXiv preprint arXiv:2311.00658*.

Tahmid Hasan, Abhik Bhattacharjee, Md Saiful Islam, Kazi Samin, Yuan-Fang Li, Yong-Bin Kang, M Sohel Rahman, and Rifat Shahriyar. 2021. Xl-sum: Large-scale multilingual abstractive summarization for 44 languages. *arXiv preprint arXiv:2106.13822*.

Valentin Hofmann, Janet Pierrehumbert, and Hinrich Schütze. 2021. Superbizarre is not superb: Derivational morphology improves BERT's interpretation of complex words. In *Proceedings of the 59th Annual Meeting of the Association for Computational Linguistics and the 11th International Joint Conference on Natural Language Processing (Volume 1: Long Papers)*, pages 3594–3608, Online. Association for Computational Linguistics.

Omri Keren and Omer Levy. 2021. ParaShoot: A Hebrew question answering dataset. In *Proceedings of the 3rd Workshop on Machine Reading for Question Answering*, pages 106–112, Punta Cana, Dominican Republic. Association for Computational Linguistics.

Klaus Krippendorff. 2018. *Content analysis: An introduction to its methodology*. Sage publications.

Viet Dac Lai, Nghia Trung Ngo, Amir Pouran Ben Veyseh, Hieu Man, Franck Dernoncourt, Trung Bui, and Thien Huu Nguyen. 2023. Chatgpt beyond english: Towards a comprehensive evaluation of large language models in multilingual learning. In *Findings of the Association for Computational Linguistics: EMNLP 2023*, Singapore. Association for Computational Linguistics.

Percy Liang, Rishi Bommasani, Tony Lee, Dimitris Tsipras, Dilara Soylu, Michihiro Yasunaga, Yian Zhang, Deepak Narayanan, Yuhuai Wu, Ananya Kumar, et al. 2022. Holistic evaluation of language models. *arXiv preprint arXiv:2211.09110*.

Rensis Likert. 1932. A technique for the measurement of attitudes. *Archives of psychology*.

Chin-Yew Lin. 2004. Rouge: A package for automatic evaluation of summaries. In *Text summarization branches out*, pages 74–81.

Aviya Maimon and Reut Tsarfaty. 2023. Cohesentia: A novel benchmark of incremental versus holistic assessment of coherence in generated texts. *arXiv preprint arXiv:2310.16329*.

N Moratanch and S Chitrakala. 2016. A survey on abstractive text summarization. In *2016 International Conference on Circuit, power and computing technologies (ICCPCT)*, pages 1–7. IEEE.

Ramesh Nallapati, Bowen Zhou, Cicero dos Santos, Çağlar Gulçehre, and Bing Xiang. 2016. Abstractive text summarization using sequence-to-sequence RNNs and beyond. In *Proceedings of the 20th*

SIGNLL Conference on Computational Natural Language Learning, pages 280–290, Berlin, Germany. Association for Computational Linguistics.

Shashi Narayan, Shay B. Cohen, and Mirella Lapata. 2018. Don't give me the details, just the summary! topic-aware convolutional neural networks for extreme summarization. In *Proceedings of the 2018 Conference on Empirical Methods in Natural Language Processing*, pages 1797–1807, Brussels, Belgium. Association for Computational Linguistics.

Alex Papadopoulos Korfiatis, Francesco Moramarco, Radmila Sarac, and Aleksandar Savkov. 2022. PriMock57: A dataset of primary care mock consultations. In *Proceedings of the 60th Annual Meeting of the Association for Computational Linguistics (Volume 2: Short Papers)*, pages 588–598, Dublin, Ireland. Association for Computational Linguistics.

Kishore Papineni, Salim Roukos, Todd Ward, and Wei-Jing Zhu. 2002. Bleu: a method for automatic evaluation of machine translation. In *Proceedings of the 40th annual meeting of the Association for Computational Linguistics*, pages 311–318.

Tzuf Paz-Argaman, Tal Bauman, Itai Mondshine, Itzhak Omer, Sagi Dalyot, and Reut Tsarfaty. 2023. HeGeL: A novel dataset for geo-location from Hebrew text. In *Findings of the Association for Computational Linguistics: ACL 2023*, pages 7311–7321, Toronto, Canada. Association for Computational Linguistics.

Tanya Reinhart. 1980. Conditions for text coherence. *Poetics today*, 1(4):161–180.

Amit Seker, Elron Bandel, Dan Bareket, Idan Brusilovsky, Refael Greenfeld, and Reut Tsarfaty. 2022. AlephBERT: Language model pre-training and evaluation from sub-word to sentence level. In *Proceedings of the 60th Annual Meeting of the Association for Computational Linguistics (Volume 1: Long Papers)*, pages 46–56, Dublin, Ireland. Association for Computational Linguistics.

Freda Shi, Mirac Suzgun, Markus Freitag, Xuezhi Wang, Suraj Srivats, Soroush Vosoughi, Hyung Won Chung, Yi Tay, Sebastian Ruder, Denny Zhou, et al. 2022. Language models are multilingual chain-of-thought reasoners. *arXiv preprint arXiv:2210.03057*.

Shaltiel Shmidman, Avi Shmidman, and Moshe Koppel. 2023. Dictabert: A state-of-the-art bert suite for modern hebrew. *arXiv preprint arXiv:2308.16687*.

Priyam Tejaswin, Dhruv Naik, and Pengfei Liu. 2021. How well do you know your summarization datasets? In *Findings of the Association for Computational Linguistics: ACL-IJCNLP 2021*, pages 3436–3449, Online. Association for Computational Linguistics.

Reut Tsarfaty, Dan Bareket, Stav Klein, and Amit Seker. 2020. From SPMRL to NMRL: What did we learn (and unlearn) in a decade of parsing morphologically-rich languages (MRLs)? In *Proceedings of the 58th Annual Meeting of the Association for Computational Linguistics*, pages 7396–7408, Online. Association for Computational Linguistics.

Reut Tsarfaty, Shoval Sadde, Stav Klein, and Amit Seker. 2019. What's wrong with Hebrew NLP? and how to make it right. In *Proceedings of the 2019 Conference on Empirical Methods in Natural Language Processing and the 9th International Joint Conference on Natural Language Processing (EMNLP-IJCNLP): System Demonstrations*, pages 259–264, Hong Kong, China. Association for Computational Linguistics.

David Uthus, Santiago Ontañón, Joshua Ainslie, and Mandy Guo. 2023. mlongt5: A multilingual and efficient text-to-text transformer for longer sequences. *arXiv preprint arXiv:2305.11129*.

Linting Xue, Noah Constant, Adam Roberts, Mihir Kale, Rami Al-Rfou, Aditya Siddhant, Aditya Barua, and Colin Raffel. 2020. mt5: A massively multilingual pre-trained text-to-text transformer. *arXiv preprint arXiv:2010.11934*.

Tianyi Zhang*, Varsha Kishore*, Felix Wu*, Kilian Q. Weinberger, and Yoav Artzi. 2020. Bertscore: Evaluating text generation with bert. In *International Conference on Learning Representations*.

A The HeSum Dataset

Collection Protocol Since the websites we collected (Shakuf, HaMakom, and The Seventh Eye) lack archives or RSS feeds, we developed a crawler to systematically navigate through pages, beginning from the homepage and exploring various article links. Leveraging their shared HTML structure, we could efficiently scrape the sites. We excluded pages without textual content, such as multimedia pages or those not in Hebrew. Additionally, articles with summaries of less than 10 tokens were filtered out, as they often lack sufficient detail to be a summary. In addition, all the articles were cleaned from Unicode characters or unrelated content.

Dataset	novel n-grams				CMP	RED (n=1)	RED (n=2)
	n = 1	n = 2	n = 3	n = 4			
CNN/Daily Mail	13.20	52.77	72.20	81.40	90.90	13.73	1.10
XSum	35.76	83.45	95.50	98.49	90.90	5.83	0.16
HeSum	42.00	73.20	82.00	85.36	95.48	4.83	0.10
HeSum (morpheme-based)	17.41	48.02	67.51	76,86	95.57	25.90	2.72

Table 5: HeSum's Intrinsic Evaluation compared to English Benchmarks (CNN/Daily Mail and XSum).

Coherence

1. Very Incoherent: The summary is extremely confusing and lacks any clear connection between sentences.
2. Incoherent: The summary is somewhat understandable.
3. Somewhat Coherent
4. Coherent
5. Very Coherent

Completeness

1. Very Incomplete: The summary lacks essential information and does not convey the main points effectively.
2. Incomplete: The summary provides some information but misses key details.
3. Somewhat Complete
4. Complete
5. Very Complete

Figure 1: Evaluation Criteria

Human Evaluation Details We collected annotations from seven volunteered participants aged 25 and above, all with at least one academic degree. The participants were instructed to rate two parameters – *coherence* and *completeness*, based on known criteria, as depicted in Figure 1. While completeness measures the extent to which the summary captures all the essential information from the source text, coherence is a more complex metric. According to Reinhart (1980), coherence encompasses three core aspects: (i) cohesion, (ii) consistency, and (iii) relevance. While metrics like BertScore can also assess completeness, automatic evaluation of coherence remains a challenge (Maimon and Tsarfaty, 2023). Therefore, the measurement of coherence is evaluated in this work solely by humans.

Model	Rouge1	Rouge2	RougeL	Epochs	Loss
mLongT5-Base	18.62	8.68	15.92	18	2.15
mLongT5-Large	20.22	9.66	18.12	12	1.92

Table 6: mLongT5 performance on validation set and training details.

Data Analysis Table 5 provides a quantitative analysis of HeSum's summarization characteristics, highlighting its challenges. The analysis utilizes two tokenization approaches: word-based (above the dashed line) and morpheme-based (below the dashed line). This distinction allows for a deeper examination of the dataset's abstractness and the influence of morphological features. As the table demonstrates, the number of unique vocabulary items (novel n-grams) decreases when using morpheme tokenization. However, HeSum still exhibits a higher uni-gram count compared to CNN/Daily Mail. This suggests that the task itself inherently involves a high degree of abstractness, and the morphological nature of the data presents an additional challenge.

B Models

Fine-tunning mLongT5 The HeSum corpus exhibits characteristics of long-form text, with an average document length of 2,747 tokens and a 90th percentile reaching 5,276 tokens. This extensive content poses challenges for the vanilla mT5 model, whose capacity for processing such lengths may be limited. Consequently, we have fine-tuned the mLongT5 model (Uthus et al., 2023), which is suitable for handling long inputs. The paper presents results obtained with the base version of mLongT5, which is 2.37 GB. We are also releasing

Dataset	novel n-grams				CMP	RED (n=1)	RED (n=2)
	n = 1	n = 2	n = 3	n = 4			
HeSum	42.00	73.20	82.00	85.36	95.48	4.83	0.10
GPT-4	47.24	80.35	91.37	95.92	91.89	8.14	0.68
GPT-3.5	45.69	80.18	91.73	96.35	93.46	7.53	0.83
mLongT5-large	8.26	30.10	43.50	50.21	95.39	11.89	5.98
mLongT5-base	7.21	28.77	42.06	49.46	92.25	15.74	10.25

Table 7: Intrinsic Evaluation of Summarization. A Comparative Analysis of GPT-4, GPT-3.5, mT5 Models and the Hesum Dataset.

Model	prefix	input	output	ROUGE-1	ROUGE-2	ROUGE-L
GPT-3.5	E	E	E	16.10	4.06	11.43
GPT-3.5	H	H	H	16.34	4.26	11.69
GPT-3.5	E	E	H	12.80	2.30	11.00
mLongT5	—	H	H	17.47	7.56	14.68
GPT-3.5	E	H	H	17.08	4.95	12.46
GPT-3.5	H	H	E	14.35	3.13	9.89
GPT-3.5	E	H	E	14.31	3.11	10.40
GPT-3.5	H	E	H	15.90	4.23	10.80

Table 8: Testing different configurations of language prompting to find the best configuration to evaluate GPT-3.5. 'H' denotes Hebrew and 'E' denotes English. 'prefix' is the instruction to the model, 'input' is the article itself, and the output is the desired summarization language.

a larger model (4.56 GB).[5] The training regimen employed an 8-GPU A100 cluster for 36 hours for the large model, while the base model leveraged a single A100 GPU with 40 GB of memory. Early stopping, utilizing ROUGE-1 as the metric, was implemented to optimize the training process. Further details regarding model performance and implementation specifics are provided in Table 6.

Prompting GPT-based models Here, we leverage the translate-English approach, suggested by (Shi et al., 2022) and (Ahuja et al., 2023), which translates instances from target languages into English before prompting. We decompose the prompt task into three parts: (i) the input article (ii) the instruction (prefix), and (iii) the output. All three parts could be done in either Hebrew or English for the HeSum task. In our experiment, Google Translate API (2023, API, 2023) handled the translation of prompts (input and/or prefix) from Hebrew to English and the translated outputs back to Hebrew for analysis. Testing GPT-3.5 on different configurations of language prompting in the HeSum validation set, we found that the best prompt-language configuration is English-English-English (Table 8). We then applied this prompting strategy to both GPT-3.5 and GPT-4 on the test set. The prompt we used depicted in Figure 2.

[5]https://huggingface.co/biunlp/mT5LongHeSum-large

You are a genius summarizer. Your task is to summarize the main points of the following text. Please follow these instructions step by step:

1. The summary should be concise, consisting of up to 3 sentences.
2. If there are several main topics, create a separate sentence for each topic.
3. The output should be in English.

Figure 2: The prompt we used for the GPT-based models

C Implementation Details

For the intrinsic evaluation of the dataset, we created a Jupyter notebook which computes the different metrics. For computing the n-grams, we used the NLTK package,[6] and for loading and processing the data, we used NumPy[7] and Pandas.[8] For evaluation of the different models, we used the most common ROUGE package for non-English papers,[9] and the HuggingFace implementation of Transformers for BertScore.[10]

[6]https://pypi.org/project/nltk/
[7]https://pypi.org/project/numpy/
[8]https://pypi.org/project/pandas/
[9]https://github.com/csebuetnlp/xl-sum/tree/master/multilingual_rouge_scoring
[10]https://pypi.org/project/transformers/

D Additional Models Performance Analysis

Table 7 presents the intrinsic evaluation results for the models, corresponding to the metrics introduced in Section 3.3. Notably, GPT-based models generate text with greater abstractness, as evidenced by their higher count of novel n-grams compared to the fine-tuned mT5. This finding aligns with mT5's tendency towards repetitive generation, which is further supported by its high RED score and by the qualitative analysis presented in Table 4.

KpopMT: Translation Dataset with Terminology for Kpop Fandom

JiWoo Kim
Sungkyunkwan University
Suwon, South Korea
wldn9705@skku.edu

Yunsu Kim
aiXplain Inc.
Los Gatos, USA
yunsu.kim@aixplain.com

JinYeong Bak
Sungkyunkwan University
Suwon, South Korea
jy.bak@skku.edu

Abstract

While machines learn from existing corpora, humans have the unique capability to establish and accept new language systems. This makes human form unique language systems within social groups. Aligning with this, we focus on a gap remaining in addressing translation challenges within social groups, where in-group members utilize unique terminologies. We propose KpopMT dataset, which aims to fill this gap by enabling precise terminology translation, choosing Kpop fandom as an initiative for social groups given its global popularity. Expert translators provide 1k English translations for Korean posts and comments, each annotated with specific terminology within social groups' language systems. We evaluate existing translation systems including GPT models on KpopMT to identify their failure cases. Results show overall low scores, underscoring the challenges of reflecting group-specific terminologies and styles in translation. We make KpopMT publicly available.[1]

Kpop Fandom Group's Language System	
Korean	원래 덕질 할 때 갠팬 수준으로 최애 위주로만 파는 타입이었음
English	Originally, when I stan, I tended to focus on only my bias almost it seems like solo stan.

Table 1: Example of how specialized terminologies (colorboxes) are used in a global social group.

1 Introduction

One of the most profound distinctions between humans and machines lies in their ability to form a new language system. While machines learn from and rely on existing corpora, humans have the unique capability to establish new social conventions, such as agreeing to call an apple "apple". This inventive ability is deeply intertwined with the social nature of language, wherein words gain influence and become integrated into the vernacular of social groups – termed as social dialect – through social interactions and contexts.

In light of this, our research places a particular emphasis on specific phenomena: Social groups often develop their unique linguistic systems, replete with specific terminologies and jargon, as in Table 1 (Wolfram, 2004; Peterson, 2014). The global surge in social media usage has brought individuals from diverse countries and continents together, forming cohesive communities (Sawyer and Chen, 2012). An example is the Kpop fandom across various regions (Choi et al., 2014); these fans seek to connect and establish interpersonal relationships that transcend language barriers (Malik and Haidar, 2021).

However, the unique linguistic systems of social groups are currently not adequately represented in machine translation (MT) systems. Despite proposals from researchers to consider language diversity in MT (Kumar et al., 2021; Lakew et al., 2018), including cross-domain standard languages (Hu et al., 2019; Currey et al., 2017), local dialects (Abe et al., 2018; Hassan et al., 2017), and related languages (Pourdamghani and Knight, 2017), the specialized language systems of social groups remain underexplored in MT research. For example, Google Translator translates the example sentence in Table 1 as *Originally, when I was a fan, I focused on my favorites. It was the type that only sells.*, which differs from the specialized language system of the group.

In order to promote research in this direction, we argue for the necessity of a benchmark dataset that encompasses the language systems of social groups. This dataset is also crucial for demonstrating the capabilities of the current translation systems specifically tailored to handle the nuances of social group languages.

[1] https://github.com/skswldndi/KpopMT

Proceedings of the The Seventh Workshop on Technologies for Machine Translation of Low-Resource Languages (LoResMT 2024), pages 37–43
August 15, 2024

In our study, we reference the field of terminology-based MT (Xie and Way, 2020; Knowles et al., 2023), which focuses on accurately translating specialized terminology in machine-generated output. Notably, the medical domain has seen significant advancements in this area (Alam et al., 2021; Anastasopoulos et al., 2020), highlighted by the release of datasets that aid the NLP community, particularly those interested in terminology translation and constrained neural MT tasks (Zhang et al., 2023; Wang et al., 2022).

We propose a terminology-tagged MT dataset tailored for social groups, named **KpopMT**. Through human survey, we demonstrate participants in a social group show a strong preference for reference translations in KpopMT compared to translations without terminology. We choose the Kpop fandom as the social group for this initiative, given its global popularity and the widespread sharing of content on social media platforms among fans from diverse countries (Ringland et al., 2022).

KpopMT is collected from Korean posts and comments found on fan-related websites, including X (Twitter). Expert translators fluent in the terminologies used within this social group provide English translations, resulting in 1k sentence pairs, each annotated with specific terminologies. We evaluate existing translation systems, including state-of-the-art models such as GPTs, on KpopMT to identify areas of improvement and establish baseline performance for future research.

2 KpopMT

KpopMT consists of three parts: 1) the parallel sentence tagged with terminologies, 2) termbase which contains parallel glossary, and 3) fandom monolingual dataset. In this section, we illustrate how the parallel sentence and termbase are constructed. We address fandom monolingual dataset in Section 3.1.

In Table 2, we show an example of KpopMT. Capturing the most distinctive part of social groups' language system is terminology, we also provide terminology information. The parallel sentence has fandom-related terms included in both the source and target side, which are annotated as tags.

To ensure translation reliability, we get confirmation from five native English Kpop fans who know both Korean fandom terms and English fandom terms.

2.1 Construction

KpopMT is constructed in two phases. First, we construct parallel sentences. Second, we annotate parallel terminology information in the sentences.

Sentence Phase To obtain sentences that include fandom-related terminology, we make a query list derived from crowd-sourced dictionaries.[2] Using the query list, we manually collect Korean monolingual data from the fan community sites[3][4] and Twitter. Then we hire ten human translators who pass the qualification test, by asking for English translations of ten Korean fandom terms and their meanings. We only hire translators who answer correctly for at least eight terms. Then we ask them to translate Korean sentences into English sentences, resulting in 1,000 sentence pairs.

Please note that we ask them to translate with the inclusion of English fandom terms, such as 'stan.' If there are no specific English fandom terms, we ask the translators to include internet slang in the sentence as a variation of standard language. We also forbid the usage of translation services such as Google Translate.

Terminology Phase In this phase, we mark terms included in the parallel sentences first. After extracting all marked terms, we create a parallel glossary by matching Korean terms with their English counterparts. If there are other possible or morphological variations in English terms, we include them on the target of the glossary, separating them with '|'. Subsequently, experts on the terminology used within fandom and internet slang confirm the consistency of parallel glossary.

Since we separate the sentence phase and the terminology phase, KpopMT is not structured according to the terminologies in this glossary. This complicates the creation of a one-to-one dictionary. For instance, '머글' is not a direct equivalent of only 'local'. Therefore, we opt to begin with the Korean side as it aligns with the actual translation direction in which the data was generated, following Alam et al. (2021).

We categorize the glossary terms into three: **Group-Lexicon**, **Group-NE**, and **Slang**. Group-Lexicon refers to the lexicon unique to the fandom, which may not be understood by those outside the fandom. Group-NE represents elements related to

[2] Naver Open-Dict http://naver.me/xeUyZv8N
[3] Theqoo http://theqoo.net
[4] Instiz http://instiz.net

<table>
<tr><td colspan="2">1. Sentence Phase</td></tr>
<tr><td>Source</td><td>트친 이랑 푸드코트에서 밥 먹다가 용수 만났어요 포카 보여주고 팬이라고 싸인도 받았어요 덕계못 인줄 알았는데</td></tr>
<tr><td>Reference</td><td>I met Yongsoo at food court while eating with my moot . We showed him pc and got an autograph saying that we're fans of him. I thought <u>stan</u> can't get luck to see <u>faves</u></td></tr>
<tr><td colspan="2">2. Terminology Phase</td></tr>
<tr><td>Tag 1</td><td><term id="202" type="slang" source=" 트친 " target=" twitter moots|moots|moot "> moot </term></td></tr>
<tr><td>Tag 2</td><td><term id="146" type="group-NE" source=" 용수 " target=" Yongsoo "> Yongsoo </term></td></tr>
<tr><td>Tag 3</td><td><term id="8" type="group-lexicon" source=" 포카 " target=" pocas|poca|pcs|pc "> pc </term></td></tr>
</table>

Table 2: Example of KpopMT.

the fandom's named entities, such as idol group names or nicknames. Slang encompasses internet slang, which is a variation of standard language. We only apply truecasing to Group-Lexicon and not to Group-NE and Slang, as capitalization is crucial for names and we believe there may be different meanings in truecased slang (e.g., 'ig' and 'IG').

In the end, we tag the sentence pairs on both source and target side with possible terminology translations from the glossary. We tag the sentence pairs with terminology translations only if both source terminology and a corresponding target terminology exist in the reference translation, following Alam et al. (2021). So, we do not tag 'stan' and 'faves' terms in Table 2.

2.2 Key Characteristics

The parallel corpus of KpopMT contains 6k Korean tokens and 12k English tokens, excluding the tags. It has a substantial number of tagged sentences, totaling 1,035, among which the tags categorized as Group-Lexicon are the most prevalent, accounting for 858 (82.8%), followed by Group-NE with 92 (8.8%), and Slang with 85 (8.4%). This indicates that KpopMT contains substantial information on a specific social group, which is Kpop fandom.

In addition, to assess its suitability for evaluating terminology-based translation, we compare KpopMT with TICO-19, widely recognized as the most common terminology machine translation dataset (Table 3) (Anastasopoulos et al., 2020; Odermatt et al., 2023). It is important to note that significant portions of TICO-19 lack any terminological content. KpopMT encompasses more extensive meaningful portions of terms compared to TICO-19.

	Number of Terms				
Dataset	0	1	2	>=3	max
Ours	27.5%	**47.7%**	**19.8%**	**5.0%**	5
TICO-19	**40.2%**	22.6%	6.6%	3.9%	9

Table 3: Comparision with TICO-19 regarding number of terminologies in each line.

Moreover, to demonstrate the necessity of KpopMT, we conduct a human survey involving five native English-speaking Kpop fans. None of them are involved in data construction process. They are given with 80 English sentences, each of which has two versions: samples from KpopMT with fandom-specific terms and expressed in standard language. Fans strongly prefer translations with fandom terms (89.75%) when asked which ones make them feel more connected to fandom members. This highlights the importance of considering cultural factors in communication (Gudykunst, 2003), making KpopMT valuable for both translation accuracy and social connectedness.

3 Experiments

We evaluate existing machine translation systems on KpopMT to assess its difficulty.

3.1 Experimental Setting

Data In our experiments, we utilize two types of data: general standard language data and fandom language data. To acquire the general standard language data, we download a Korean-English dataset (800k) from AI Hub, which is a platform releasing AI data by the Korean government.[5] To obtain the fandom language data, we scrape 40k monolingual

[5]https://www.aihub.or.kr

Systems	Fandom Data	General Data	Finetuned from
M2M		✓	
mBART w/o Fandom		✓	mBART
mBART w/ Fandom	✓	✓	mBART
SL-MT		✓	
Domain Adaptation	✓	✓	SL-MT

Table 4: Features of open-source baselines.

data samples for each language from fan-related websites, employing the query list specified in 2.1. Korean monolingual data has 287k tokens with an average sentence length of 29.79, while English monolingual data has 376k tokens with an average length of 49.61. For evaluation purposes, we employ a test split comprising 500 sentences from our parallel KpopMT.

Baselines We implement two kinds of baselines: open-source machine translation models and proprietary machine translation systems. Our baseline choice considers three factors: general standard language data trained with, fandom monolingual data trained with (Table 4), and state-of-the-art systems.

Regarding general standard language data, we set baselines of M2M, mBART w/o Fandom and Standard Language MT (SL-MT). M2M is a multilingual translation model that can translate between any pair from 100 languages (Fan et al., 2021). mBART w/o Fandom is a finetuned translation model from multilingual Bart (mBART) using general data (Liu et al., 2020). mBART is the state-of-the-art model on IWSLT-17 (Cettolo et al., 2017; Park et al., 2021). SL-MT is a Korean-English state-of-the-art translation model on general standard language data (Park et al., 2020).

Regarding fandom monolingual data, we set baselines of mBART w/ Fandom and Domain Adaptation. mBART w/ Fandom is a finetuned translation model from mBART with an injection of both general parallel data and fandom monolingual data. We use the back-translation technique to make pseudo-parallel data for fandom monolingual data (Sennrich et al., 2016). Domain Adaptation is a finetuned translation model from Standard Language MT, with the technique of iterative back-translation of fandom monolingual data (Hu et al., 2019; Dou et al., 2019). The differences from mBART w/ Fandom are the pretrained model and iteration of back-translation. In a preliminary study, we find that mBART w/ Fandom's performance drops with iterative back-translation.

For proprietary machine translation systems, we experiment with OpenAI's GPT models (GPT-3.5 and GPT-4) and Google Translator. For OpenAI's GPT models (OpenAI, 2023; Eloundou et al., 2023), we assign the role of a Kpop fan to the model. This fan is familiar with terminologies used within the Kpop fandom and internet slang, which has shown empirically the best performance. We provide the prompt in Korean.

Evaluation We evaluate systems on both translation accuracy and terminological accuracy. Translation accuracy is evaluated with standard reference-based MT metrics: SacreBLEU (Post, 2018; Papineni et al., 2002), COMET (Rei et al., 2020), chrF++ (Popović, 2017). Terminology accuracy is evaluated with exact-match term accuracy (EMA) and 1-TERm score (Anastasopoulos et al., 2021). EMA is an accuracy score that searches for exact term translation matches (of the terminology required output) over the original hypothesis. The 1-TERm score is a modification of the TER metric, biased to assign higher edit cost weights for words belonging to a term (and then simply reversed so that a higher score is better). When computing terminology targeted evaluation, we consider synonyms which are split by '|' in the tags. We rank systems according to EMA.

3.2 Results

Table 5 shows overall low scores, underscoring the considerable challenges posed by KpopMT in terms of both terminology-focused content and translation quality.

GPTs Overall, the GPT models demonstrate higher scores than other systems. When examining the words they succeed in generating, they excel in producing certain words compared to other models. 'bias,' 'ult,' and 'stan' are frequently generated, contributing to GPTs' higher EMA scores.

However, Group-Lexicon type faces challenges, especially when excluding those basic words. We conduct an analysis to determine which types of terms GPT-4 could generate or not. We calculate each type's EMA score, resulting in Group-Lexicon 16.3%, Group-NE 21.54%, and Slang 20%. As seen in overall low scores in success translation rate for all types, GPT-4 struggles with generating terminologies, particularly those related to Group-Lexicon. Given the importance of 'Group-Lexicon'

	Systems	Terminology-focused EMA	1-TERm	Translation Quality BLEU	COMET	chrF++
Open Source	M2M	2.4	10.5	4.1	51.2	19.9
	mBART w/o Fandom	6.7	**13.7**	**10.4**	**60.5**	**32.3**
	mBART w/ Fandom	6.4	12.3	9.1	56.6	29.0
	SL-MT	3.8	6.5	8.7	56.4	30.3
	Domain Adaptation	**13.9**	13.3	9.7	57.7	31.2
Proprietary	GPT-3.5-turbo-0613	19.3	1.1	8.7	65.8	32.9
	GPT-4-0613	**26.4**	10.3	9.9	**65.8**	35.0
	Google Translator	10.4	**16.3**	**13.9**	65.4	**35.9**

Table 5: Result on test split set using existing machine translation systems.

in Kpop social groups, this deficiency shows a clear need for better translation in specific social contexts.

General Data We ascertain whether a translation model trained on general standard language data could grasp specific language systems within social groups. Although mBART w/o Fandom displays better performance in translation quality evaluations, its EMA score remains low, indicating a lack of specific knowledge pertaining to social groups.

Fandom Data Our findings suggest that incorporating fandom data into the training process does not consistently yield improved results. The possible explanation is fandom monolingual data during the back-translation process is noisy, resulting in pseudo-parallel data that significantly deviated from general data, which seems to have hindered proper comprehension. Following Michel and Neubig (2018) and calculating the perplexity score of fandom monolingual data using a language model trained with general data, we get 1395.4 for Korean and 713.8 for English. This limitation might prevent effective inference of the meaning and context of relevant terminology.

Translation Quality As highlighted by previous research (Pascual et al., 2020), there exists a tension between fluency of the translation and terminology accuracy in our results. Based on this, we intend to explore in future work whether it is possible to enhance the overall translation quality while preserving social groups' distinctive terminology.

4 Conclusions

Our approach acknowledges the dynamic and evolving nature of language, especially in digitally mediated communities, which are often underrepresented in traditional linguistic resources. We propose a benchmark dataset for social groups' language systems, named KpopMT. 1k parallel dataset contains not only Korean-English parallel sentences but also terminology information of Kpop fandom group. We also make termbase and monolingual data publicly available. We evaluate existing translation approaches on KpopMT to identify their failure cases. Our future plan includes expanding KpopMT to encompass other social groups, such as sports and global movie communities.

Limitations

In the study, we view Kpop fandom as a broad spectrum and do not focus on a specific fandom of any one idol group. There are numerous Kpop Idols, such as BTS, Twice, Seventeen, etc. and each terminology of their fans is distinct from one another. For instance, BTS fans use *Borahae* to mean *I love you*, while Seventeen fans use *horanghae* to mean the same thing.

Ethical Considerations

The created dataset will be released under the terms of the Twitter API. Aside from Tweets, which are sourced from publicly accessible websites, we ensure that there is no violation of copyright or invasion of privacy. To prevent user tracking, we remove any information related to users. All of our dataset is made publicly available through a Creative Commons CC BY-SA 4.0 license.

We compensate volunteer translators with more than the minimum wage in Korea. They are fully aware of their tasks, and we provide them with detailed annotation instructions. After compensation, we anonymize and remove their personal information. Additionally, we carefully filter out data containing hate speech about celebrities to ensure that human translators do not face any risks or harm associated with their participation.

Acknowledgments

We would like to thank the anonymous reviewers for their helpful questions and comments. We further would like to express our gratitude to Jonas Belouadi for discussions, proofreading, and comments on our work. This research was partly supported by the Bio & Medical Technology Development Program of the National Research Foundation (NRF) funded by the Korean government (MSIT) (NRF-2021M3A9E4080780, RS-2023-00252083), Institute of Information & communications Technology Planning & Evaluation (IITP) grant funded by the Korea government (MSIT) (No.2019-0-00421, AI Graduate School Support Program (Sungkyunkwan University).

References

Kaori Abe, Yuichiroh Matsubayashi, Naoaki Okazaki, and Kentaro Inui. 2018. Multi-dialect neural machine translation and dialectometry. In *Proceedings of the 32nd Pacific Asia Conference on Language, Information and Computation*, Hong Kong. Association for Computational Linguistics.

Md Mahfuz Ibn Alam, Ivana Kvapilíková, Antonios Anastasopoulos, Laurent Besacier, Georgiana Dinu, Marcello Federico, Matthias Gallé, Kweonwoo Jung, Philipp Koehn, and Vassilina Nikoulina. 2021. Findings of the wmt shared task on machine translation using terminologies. In *Proceedings of the Sixth Conference on Machine Translation*, pages 652–663.

Antonios Anastasopoulos, Laurent Besacier, James Cross, Matthias Gallé, Philipp Koehn, Vassilina Nikoulina, et al. 2021. On the evaluation of machine translation for terminology consistency. *arXiv preprint arXiv:2106.11891*.

Antonios Anastasopoulos, Alessandro Cattelan, Zi-Yi Dou, Marcello Federico, Christian Federmann, Dmitriy Genzel, Franscisco Guzmán, Junjie Hu, Macduff Hughes, Philipp Koehn, et al. 2020. Tico-19: the translation initiative for covid-19. In *Proceedings of the 1st Workshop on NLP for COVID-19 (Part 2) at EMNLP 2020*.

Mauro Cettolo, Marcello Federico, Luisa Bentivogli, Jan Niehues, Sebastian Stüker, Katsuhito Sudoh, Koichiro Yoshino, and Christian Federmann. 2017. Overview of the IWSLT 2017 evaluation campaign. In *Proceedings of the 14th International Conference on Spoken Language Translation*, pages 2–14, Tokyo, Japan. International Workshop on Spoken Language Translation.

Seong Cheol Choi, Xanat Vargas Meza, and Han Woo Park. 2014. South korean culture goes latin america: Social network analysis of kpop tweets in mexico. *International Journal of Contents*, 10(1):36–42.

Anna Currey, Antonio Valerio Miceli-Barone, and Kenneth Heafield. 2017. Copied monolingual data improves low-resource neural machine translation. In *Proceedings of the second conference on machine translation*, pages 148–156.

Zi-Yi Dou, Junjie Hu, Antonios Anastasopoulos, and Graham Neubig. 2019. Unsupervised domain adaptation for neural machine translation with domain-aware feature embeddings. In *Proceedings of the 2019 Conference on Empirical Methods in Natural Language Processing and the 9th International Joint Conference on Natural Language Processing (EMNLP-IJCNLP)*, pages 1417–1422, Hong Kong, China. Association for Computational Linguistics.

Tyna Eloundou, Sam Manning, Pamela Mishkin, and Daniel Rock. 2023. Gpts are gpts: An early look at the labor market impact potential of large language models. *Preprint*, arXiv:2303.10130.

Angela Fan, Shruti Bhosale, Holger Schwenk, Zhiyi Ma, Ahmed El-Kishky, Siddharth Goyal, Mandeep Baines, Onur Celebi, Guillaume Wenzek, Vishrav Chaudhary, et al. 2021. Beyond english-centric multilingual machine translation. *J. Mach. Learn. Res.*, 22(107):1–48.

William B Gudykunst. 2003. *Cross-cultural and intercultural communication*. Sage.

Hany Hassan, Mostafa Elaraby, and Ahmed Y. Tawfik. 2017. Synthetic data for neural machine translation of spoken-dialects. In *Proceedings of the 14th International Conference on Spoken Language Translation*, pages 82–89, Tokyo, Japan. International Workshop on Spoken Language Translation.

Junjie Hu, Mengzhou Xia, Graham Neubig, and Jaime G Carbonell. 2019. Domain adaptation of neural machine translation by lexicon induction. In *Proceedings of the 57th Annual Meeting of the Association for Computational Linguistics*, pages 2989–3001.

Rebecca Knowles, Samuel Larkin, Marc Tessier, and Michel Simard. 2023. Terminology in neural machine translation: A case study of the canadian hansard. In *Proceedings of the 24th Annual Conference of the European Association for Machine Translation*, pages 481–488.

Sachin Kumar, Antonios Anastasopoulos, Shuly Wintner, and Yulia Tsvetkov. 2021. Machine translation into low-resource language varieties. In *Proceedings of the 59th Annual Meeting of the Association for Computational Linguistics and the 11th International Joint Conference on Natural Language Processing (Volume 2: Short Papers)*, pages 110–121, Online. Association for Computational Linguistics.

Surafel Melaku Lakew, Aliia Erofeeva, and Marcello Federico. 2018. Neural machine translation into language varieties. In *Proceedings of the Third Conference on Machine Translation: Research Papers*, pages 156–164, Brussels, Belgium. Association for Computational Linguistics.

Yinhan Liu, Jiatao Gu, Naman Goyal, Xian Li, Sergey Edunov, Marjan Ghazvininejad, Mike Lewis, and Luke Zettlemoyer. 2020. Multilingual denoising pre-training for neural machine translation. *Transactions of the Association for Computational Linguistics*, 8:726–742.

Zunera Malik and Sham Haidar. 2021. English language learning and social media: Schematic learning on kpop stan twitter. *E-Learning and Digital Media*, 18(4):361–382.

Paul Michel and Graham Neubig. 2018. Mtnt: A testbed for machine translation of noisy text. *Preprint*, arXiv:1809.00388.

Frédéric Odermatt, Béni Egressy, and Roger Wattenhofer. 2023. Cascaded beam search: Plug-and-play terminology-forcing for neural machine translation. *arXiv preprint arXiv:2305.14538*.

OpenAI. 2023. Gpt-4 technical report. *Preprint*, arXiv:2303.08774.

Kishore Papineni, Salim Roukos, Todd Ward, and Wei-Jing Zhu. 2002. Bleu: a method for automatic evaluation of machine translation. In *Proceedings of the 40th Annual Meeting of the Association for Computational Linguistics*, pages 311–318, Philadelphia, Pennsylvania, USA. Association for Computational Linguistics.

Chanjun Park, Sugyeong Eo, Hyeonseok Moon, and Heui-Seok Lim. 2021. Should we find another model?: Improving neural machine translation performance with one-piece tokenization method without model modification. In *Proceedings of the 2021 Conference of the North American Chapter of the Association for Computational Linguistics: Human Language Technologies: Industry Papers*, pages 97–104.

Kyubyong Park, Joohong Lee, Seongbo Jang, and Dawoon Jung. 2020. An empirical study of tokenization strategies for various Korean NLP tasks. In *Proceedings of the 1st Conference of the Asia-Pacific Chapter of the Association for Computational Linguistics and the 10th International Joint Conference on Natural Language Processing*, pages 133–142, Suzhou, China. Association for Computational Linguistics.

Damian Pascual, Beni Egressy, Florian Bolli, and Roger Wattenhofer. 2020. Directed beam search: Plug-and-play lexically constrained language generation. *arXiv preprint arXiv:2012.15416*.

Britt Peterson. 2014. The linguistics of lol. what internet vernacular reveals about the evolution of language. *The Atlantic*, 10:2014.

Maja Popović. 2017. chrf++: words helping character n-grams. In *Proceedings of the second conference on machine translation*, pages 612–618.

Matt Post. 2018. A call for clarity in reporting bleu scores. In *Proceedings of the Third Conference on Machine Translation: Research Papers*, pages 186–191.

Nima Pourdamghani and Kevin Knight. 2017. Deciphering related languages. In *Proceedings of the 2017 Conference on Empirical Methods in Natural Language Processing*, pages 2513–2518, Copenhagen, Denmark. Association for Computational Linguistics.

Ricardo Rei, Craig Stewart, Ana C Farinha, and Alon Lavie. 2020. Comet: A neural framework for mt evaluation. In *Proceedings of the 2020 Conference on Empirical Methods in Natural Language Processing (EMNLP)*, pages 2685–2702.

Kathryn E Ringland, Arpita Bhattacharya, Kevin Weatherwax, Tessa Eagle, and Christine T Wolf. 2022. Army's magic shop: Understanding the collaborative construction of playful places in online communities. In *CHI Conference on Human Factors in Computing Systems*, pages 1–19.

Rebecca Sawyer and Guo-Ming Chen. 2012. The impact of social media on intercultural adaptation.

Rico Sennrich, Barry Haddow, and Alexandra Birch. 2016. Improving neural machine translation models with monolingual data. In *Proceedings of the 54th Annual Meeting of the Association for Computational Linguistics (Volume 1: Long Papers)*, pages 86–96, Berlin, Germany. Association for Computational Linguistics.

Shuo Wang, Peng Li, Zhixing Tan, Zhaopeng Tu, Maosong Sun, and Yang Liu. 2022. A template-based method for constrained neural machine translation. In *Proceedings of the 2022 Conference on Empirical Methods in Natural Language Processing*, pages 3665–3679.

Walt Wolfram. 2004. Social varieties of american english. *Language in the USA: Themes for the twenty-first century*, pages 58–75.

Guodong Xie and Andy Way. 2020. Constraining the transformer nmt model with heuristic grid beam search. In *Proceedings of the 14th Conference of the Association for Machine Translation in the Americas (Volume 1: Research Track)*, pages 36–49.

Jinpeng Zhang, Nini Xiao, Ke Wang, Chuanqi Dong, Xiangyu Duan, Yuqi Zhang, and Min Zhang. 2023. Disambiguated lexically constrained neural machine translation. In *Findings of the Association for Computational Linguistics: ACL 2023*, pages 10583–10596, Toronto, Canada. Association for Computational Linguistics.

Challenges in Urdu Machine Translation

Abdul Basit and **Abdul Hameed Azeemi** and **Agha Ali Raza**
Lahore University of Management Sciences
{a_basit, abdul.azeemi, agha.ali.raza}@lums.edu.pk

Abstract

Recent advancements in Neural Machine Translation (NMT) systems have significantly improved model performance on various translation benchmarks. However, these systems still face numerous challenges when translating low-resource languages such as Urdu. In this work, we highlight the specific issues faced by machine translation systems when translating Urdu language. We first conduct a comprehensive evaluation of English to Urdu Machine Translation with four diverse models: `GPT-3.5` (a large language model), `opus-mt-en-ur` (a bilingual translation model), `NLLB` (a model trained for translating 200 languages) and `IndicTrans2` (a specialized model for translating low-resource Indic languages). The results demonstrate that `IndicTrans2` significantly outperforms other models in Urdu Machine Translation. To understand the differences in the performance of these models, we analyze the Urdu word distribution in different training datasets and compare the training methodologies. Finally, we uncover the specific translation issues and provide suggestions for improvements in Urdu machine translation systems.

1 Introduction

Neural Machine Translation (NMT) has shown remarkable performance on benchmark datasets, particularly following the introduction of transformer architectures (Vaswani et al., 2017). Among these advancements, large language models like `GPT-3.5` and 4 have demonstrated promising potential for machine translation, particularly for resource-rich languages including English, French, and German. However, these models face numerous challenges in translating low-resource languages (e.g., Urdu) due to limited training compared to their high-resource counterparts (Hendy et al., 2023).

Urdu is spoken by over 100 million people worldwide (Haider, 2018). It is predominantly spoken in Pakistan, serving as the national language (Metcalf, 2003) and holds significant cultural importance. Urdu is also spoken in various regions of India, particularly in states like Uttar Pradesh, Bihar, and Telangana, with a sizable population of speakers. However, due to the scarcity of available linguistic resources for Urdu, it is considered a low-resource language (Daud et al., 2017).

In this work, we empirically evaluate four language models for Urdu machine translation: `GPT-3.5` – a large language model, `opus-mt-en-ur` — a bilingual model specifically trained for Urdu translation, `NLLB` — a multilingual translation model designed to cover 200 languages, incorporating a mix of both high-resource and largely low-resource languages and `IndicTrans2` — a multilingual translation model designed for low-resource Indian languages. `IndicTrans2` demonstrates the highest `SacreBLEU` and `Chrf` on five diverse machine translation datasets, followed by `NLLB` , `GPT-3.5` and `opus-mt-en-ur`. To identify the challenges in Urdu machine translation, we examine the translation capability of the four different models qualitatively and highlight the key areas where the bilingual, multilingual, and large language models struggle to perform.

2 Background

Machine translation is a crucial aspect of NLP, automating text translation between languages. It has evolved from rule-based to data-driven and neural approaches. Traditional rule-based systems faced challenges with language complexities, while statistical methods improved but still struggled with syntax and semantics (Okpor, 2014). Neural machine translation (NMT) has significantly improved the performance, employing deep learning models like sequence-to-sequence architectures (Sutskever et al., 2014) for more fluent

Proceedings of the The Seventh Workshop on Technologies for Machine Translation of Low-Resource Languages (LoResMT 2024), pages 44–49
August 15, 2024

and context-aware translations.

The transformer architecture has improved the overall quality of machine translation. Therefore, large language models, such as GPT-3.5, have emerged as potent candidates for machine translation tasks. Numerous studies have been conducted to assess the effectiveness of these modals for neural machine translation. Hendy et al. (2023) demonstrate that GPT-3.5 can generate remarkably fluent and competitive translation outputs, particularly in the zero-shot setting, especially for high-resource language translations. Prior research has demonstrated the remarkable performance of Large Language Models (LLMs) in high-resource bilingual translation tasks, such as English-German translation (Vilar et al., 2022; Zhang et al., 2022). Jiao et al. (2023) observed that GPT-4 performs competitively with commercial translation products for high-resource European languages but demonstrates a notable drop in performance for low-resource and distant languages. Stap and Araabi (2023) show that GPT-4 is unsuitable for extremely low-resource languages. However, there is currently a lack of cross-evaluation of different types of language models for Urdu machine translation.

3 Methodology and Experiments

We conduct empirical evaluation for Urdu machine translation on four types of language models: Large Language Model (LLM), bilingual model, and two multilingual models using five diverse datasets. Through this investigation, we aim to gain insights into the translation capabilities of these language models for the Urdu language.

3.1 Models

GPT-3.5. Large Language Models (LLMs), like GPT-3.5, have demonstrated strong and consistent performance across a range of NLP tasks. We investigate the performance of GPT-3.5 in translating the English source language into Urdu. Leveraging the API for the model GPT-3.5-turbo-0125, we use a specific translation prompt: "Please translate the sentence into Urdu." Additionally, we add the contextual information, "You are a machine translation system", to facilitate the translation process.

Bilingual. For the bilingual experiments, we utilize the opus-mt-en-ur model (Tiedemann, 2020), which has been specifically trained for En $\rightarrow$ Ur machine translation. To facilitate this model's deployment, we use the HuggingFace platform[1]. This enables us to conduct our experiments efficiently and standardize the evaluation process.

Multilingual. We use two multilingual translation models, NLLB and IndicTrans2.

NLLB (Costa-jussà et al., 2022) is a multilingual translation model that supports 200 languages, incorporating a combination of high-resource and low-resource languages. Within the inference process, we specify the source language as English and the target language as Urdu, each identified by their respective language codes eng-Latn and urd-Arab.

IndicTrans2 (Gala et al., 2023) is a specialized model designed to cater to 22 Indic languages, including Urdu. During the inference process, we explicitly specify the source language as English and the target language as Urdu, denoted by the language codes eng-Latn and urd-Arab, respectively.

3.2 Datasets

We evaluate the performance of the selected models on five publicly available test data sets. We utilize the tatoteba-test.eng-urd (Tiedemann, 2020) test set, which is a component of the Tatoeba Translation Challenge. This challenge encompasses numerous test sets created for over 500 languages. Our study exclusively focuses on the publicly available Urdu test set. Secondly, we utilize the Flores 101 dataset (Goyal et al., 2022), which provides a valuable resource for evaluating models on low-resource languages, encompassing 101 such languages. For our study, we concentrate on the Urdu subset of Flores 101 to gauge our model's effectiveness in handling low-resource scenarios. Additionally, we evaluate our models using the Mann Ki Baat (Siripragada et al., 2020) test dataset, which exclusively contains Urdu language content extracted from speeches delivered by the Indian Prime Minister in various Indian languages. Our focus centers on the Urdu subset of Mann Ki Baat. Moreover, we incorporate the UMC005 dataset (Jawaid and Zeman, 2011), a parallel corpus comprising English-Urdu alignments sourced from multiple texts, including the Quran, Bible, Penn Treebank, and EMille corpus. Given the publicly available test sets for the Quran and Bible, we merge these subsets to

[1]https://huggingface.co/Helsinki-NLP/opus-mt-en-ur

	tatoteba-test.eng-urd	Flores101	MKB	UMC 005	Ted Talk
opus-mt-en-ur	12.06	7.09	6.62	14.51	11.84
GPT-3.5	21.68	16.67	12.79	11.87	12.29
NLLB	25.04	21.37	18.52	20.68	**19.55**
IndicTrans2	**30.76**	**27.41**	**21.73**	**20.41**	16.50

Table 1: The SacreBLEU scores of four models on five datasets for Urdu machine translation

	tatoteba-test.eng-urd	Flores101	MKB	UMC 005	Ted Talk
opus-mt-en-ur	0.39	0.28	0.28	0.35	0.34
GPT-3.5	0.48	0.44	0.40	0.37	0.40
NLLB	0.50	0.48	0.45	**0.48**	0.43
IndicTrans2	**0.53**	**0.53**	**0.49**	0.45	**0.44**

Table 2: The CHRF++ scores of four models on five datasets for Urdu machine translation

Model	Train Sentence Pairs	Test Sentence Pairs	Languages	Params
opus-mt-en-ur	1M	1663	1	76.42M
GPT-3.5	NA	NA	NA	NA
NLLB-1.3B	18B	1012	200	1.3B
IndicTrans2	**230.5M**	**2036**	**22**	**1B**

Table 3: A comparison of the training & test splits, number of languages, and the number of parameters of different models.

conduct comprehensive evaluations. Lastly, our models undergo assessment using the TED Talk test dataset (Zweigenbaum et al., 2018). Before evaluation, we preprocess the test data by removing pairs containing symbols in their translations, ensuring a standardized and reliable evaluation process.

3.3 Metrics

We use SacreBLEU (Post, 2018) metric to evaluate the translation performance, which has built-in support for scoring detokenized output using standardized tokenization methods, ensuring a fair and unbiased evaluation of models' translation performance. Additionally, we use CHRF++ (Popović, 2017) scores for assessing translation quality, which is particularly useful when dealing with languages featuring complex sentence structures.

3.4 Results

We present SacreBLEU scores in Table 1 to assess the translation efficacy of the designated models. We observe that GPT-3.5 model exhibits notably superior performance compared to the bilingual model but lags behind the multilingual translation models. NLLB emerges as the runner-up, surpassing both GPT-3.5 and bilingual translation proficiency. IndicTrans2 outperforms all other models on four out of five datasets. However, when scrutinizing more challenging evaluations, as exemplified by the TED Talk test set (Zweigenbaum et al., 2018), the performance of IndicTrans2 surpasses that of the bilingual model and the large language model with scores of 16.50, 12.29, and 11.84. Nevertheless, the NLLB model slightly performs better with a score of 19.55. Additionally, we present Chrf++ scores in the table 2, and our observations indicate that IndicTrans2 outperforms all other models.

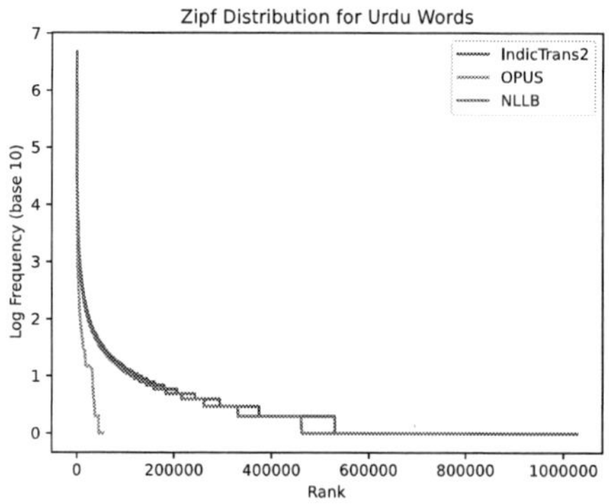

Figure 1: Comparison of Zipf distribution of the training data used in NLLB, IndicTrans2, and OPUS.

To understand why IndicTrans2 performs better than other models, we compare the Zipf distribution of Urdu words present in the training data of NLLB, OPUS and IndicTrans2. Figure 1 shows a significant difference in the Zipf distribution of OPUS compared to other datasets, with significantly fewer types. In contrast, the Zipf distribution of IndicTrans2 and NLLB is more similar, especially for higher-frequency words.

Issue	Source	Actual Translation	Correct Translation	Issue Detail
NER	A **piano** is expensive.	ایک نہایت قیمتی ہے	**پیانو** کافی مہنگا ہے۔	پیانو (piano) is missing in the translated text.
Mistranslation	That will be **funny**.	یہ سُن کر **حیران** رہ جائے گا	وہ بہت **مزاحیہ** ہو گا.	مزاحیہ (funny) is replaced by حیران (surprised) in the translated text.
Word-Repetition	Is this your **first time** in Japan?	کیا یہ جاپان میں **پہلی بار** آپ کی **پہلی بار** ہے؟	کیا تم **پہلی دفعہ** جاپان آئی ہو؟	پہلی بار (first time) is mentioned twice in the translated text.
Literal translation	Cold **weather is perhaps** the only real danger the unprepared will face.	سرد **موسم شاید تیار نہیں** ہونے والوں کے لئے واقعی خطرہ ہوگا	ٹھنڈا **موسم شاید وہ واحد** حقیقی خطرہ ہے جس کا سامنا غیرتیّار فرد کو کرنا پڑے گا	Incorrect phrase in the translated text: موسم شاید تیار نہیں (cold weather is unprepared).
Word-Omission	The protest started around **11:00** local time (UTC+1) on Whitehall opposite the police-guarded entrance to Downing Street, the Prime Minister's official residence	احتجاج کا آغاز مقامی وقت کے مطابق یو ٹی سی وائٹ ہال پر وزیر اعظم کی سرکاری رہائش گاہ ڈاؤننگ اسٹریٹ کے پولیس کے حفاظتی دروازے کے سامنے ہوا	وزیر اعظم کی سرکاری رہائش گاہ کے داخلی راستے کے سامنے پولیس کی حفاظت والے ڈاوننگ اسٹریٹ کے وائٹ ہال پر مقامی وقت کے مطابق تقریبا **11:00** بجے یہ احتجاج شروع ہوا	11:00 missing in the translated text.
Transliteration	These **scarps** were, found all over the moon and appear to be minimally weathered, indicating the geologic events that created them were fairly recent	یہ **سکارپس** پورے چاند پر پائے گئے تھے اور کم سے کم آب و ہوا کے دکھائی دیتے ہیں، جس سے یہ ظاہر ہوتا ہے کہ ان کو پیدا کرنے والے ارضیاتی واقعات کافی حالیہ تھے	چاند کی سطح پر جا بجا پائی جانے والی **کھائیوں** سے معلوم ہوتا ہے کہ وہ کم موسم دیدہ ہیں۔ ان سے ظاہر ہو تا ہے کہ جن جیولوجک حادثات سے ان کی تخلیق ہوئی وہ بہت حالیہ زمانہ کے	سکارپس instead of کھائیوں in the translated text.

Table 4: Different Urdu translation issues present in Neural Machine Translation models.

In the tail of the distribution, we notice a higher frequency for words present in the IndicTrans2 dataset compared to NLLB, which corresponds to a higher BLEU score as well for IndicTrans2 model. This suggests that for training Urdu NMT models, datasets with optimal Urdu word distribution should be prioritized, as observed in the superior performance of IndicTrans2 that shows a Zipf distribution with a better long tail compared to other datasets.

We now outline the training process of IndicTrans2 to understand the reasons behind its superior performance. The training comprises two phases: auxiliary training and downstream training. The auxiliary phase involves back translation to augment large amounts of monolingual corpora (Sennrich et al., 2015a). Subsequent fine-tuning is done on high-quality, human-generated seed data, including BPCC-H-Wiki and the NLLB seed (Costa-jussà et al., 2022). In the second phase, they train on the augmented parallel corpora which combines original data with the back-translated data. Tagged back translation is used (Caswell et al., 2019) for providing additional supervision to the model such that it distinguishes between different data sources during training. This training process combined with high-quality data sources allows IndicTrans2 to perform better than other models on En $\rightarrow$ Ur machine translation.

3.5 Challenges

Our research has unveiled various challenges associated with Urdu machine translation. Some of these challenges are universal across all models, while certain issues are present only in specific models. We enumerate these challenges below.

1. The opus-mt-en-ur model encounters a challenge in the domain of Named Entity Recognition (NER), specifically, its ability to produce accurate translations for certain entities. This issue is observable in the first row of Table 4. This issue was not widely present in the translations done through GPT-3.5 or IndicTrans2 models.

2. When the translation diverges from an accurate representation of the source, it is termed 'Mistranslation' (Freitag et al., 2021). The opus-mt-en-ur model consistently grappled with this issue across all datasets, as demonstrated in the second row of Table 4. In contrast, GPT-3.5 and IndicTrans2 exhibited notably superior proficiency in addressing this challenge.

3. The issue of repetition, which has been noted in almost all text generation models, significantly undermines their overall generation performance (Fu et al., 2021). The

word repetition problem was observed in all three models, namely `opus-mt-en-ur`, `GPT-3.5`, and `IndicTrans2` (third row of Table 4).

4. Machine translation systems have long been noted for their tendency to produce overly literal translations (Dankers et al., 2022). We observe a few instances of literal translations for all selected models in our experiments. An example of literal translation with `GPT-3.5` can be seen in the fourth row of Table 4.

5. NMT systems exhibit a tendency to exclude vital words from the source text, thereby significantly diminishing the overall adequacy of machine translation (Yang et al., 2019). The results indicate that the models still face this challenge for Urdu translation. An example from the text translated by `IndicTrans2` is given in the fifth row of Table 4.

6. Transliteration errors can arise from ambiguous transliterations or inconsistent segmentations between the source and target text (Sennrich et al., 2015b). We observe this issue in different models and an example is given in the last row of Table 4.

4 Limitations and Conclusion

In this work, we investigate the Urdu translation capabilities of four diverse models and uncover the specific challenges. We find that `IndicTrans2` outperforms other models for English to Urdu translation, demonstrating superior performance on `SacreBLEU` and `CHRF++` scores, primarily due to its specialized training process and superior Urdu word distribution in its dataset. We uncover specific Urdu translation issues including named entity recognition, mistranslation, word repetition, literal translations, word omissions, and transliteration errors. Addressing these challenges requires focused efforts on constructing high-quality Urdu training datasets, refining model training methods, and incorporating more robust evaluation metrics. For future work, our evaluation of Urdu machine translation can be extended to additional domain-specific datasets and other low-resource Indic languages to uncover additional issues.

References

Isaac Caswell, Ciprian Chelba, and David Grangier. 2019. Tagged back-translation. *arXiv preprint arXiv:1906.06442*.

Marta R Costa-jussà, James Cross, Onur Çelebi, Maha Elbayad, Kenneth Heafield, Kevin Heffernan, Elahe Kalbassi, Janice Lam, Daniel Licht, Jean Maillard, et al. 2022. No language left behind: Scaling human-centered machine translation. *arXiv preprint arXiv:2207.04672*.

Verna Dankers, Christopher G Lucas, and Ivan Titov. 2022. Can transformer be too compositional? analysing idiom processing in neural machine translation. *arXiv preprint arXiv:2205.15301*.

Ali Daud, Wahab Khan, and Dunren Che. 2017. Urdu language processing: a survey. *Artificial Intelligence Review*, 47:279–311.

Markus Freitag, George Foster, David Grangier, Viresh Ratnakar, Qijun Tan, and Wolfgang Macherey. 2021. Experts, errors, and context: A large-scale study of human evaluation for machine translation. *Transactions of the Association for Computational Linguistics*, 9:1460–1474.

Zihao Fu, Wai Lam, Anthony Man-Cho So, and Bei Shi. 2021. A theoretical analysis of the repetition problem in text generation. In *Proceedings of the AAAI Conference on Artificial Intelligence*, volume 35, pages 12848–12856.

Jay Gala, Pranjal A Chitale, Raghavan AK, Sumanth Doddapaneni, Varun Gumma, Aswanth Kumar, Janki Nawale, Anupama Sujatha, Ratish Puduppully, Vivek Raghavan, et al. 2023. Indictrans2: Towards high-quality and accessible machine translation models for all 22 scheduled indian languages. *arXiv preprint arXiv:2305.16307*.

Naman Goyal, Cynthia Gao, Vishrav Chaudhary, Peng-Jen Chen, Guillaume Wenzek, Da Ju, Sanjana Krishnan, Marc'Aurelio Ranzato, Francisco Guzmán, and Angela Fan. 2022. The flores-101 evaluation benchmark for low-resource and multilingual machine translation. *Transactions of the Association for Computational Linguistics*, 10:522–538.

Samar Haider. 2018. Urdu word embeddings. In *Proceedings of the Eleventh International Conference on Language Resources and Evaluation (LREC 2018)*.

Amr Hendy, Mohamed Abdelrehim, Amr Sharaf, Vikas Raunak, Mohamed Gabr, Hitokazu Matsushita, Young Jin Kim, Mohamed Afify, and Hany Hassan Awadalla. 2023. How good are gpt models at machine translation? a comprehensive evaluation. *arXiv preprint arXiv:2302.09210*.

Bushra Jawaid and Daniel Zeman. 2011. Word-order issues in english-to-urdu statistical machine translation. *Prague Bull. Math. Linguistics*, 95:87–106.

Wenxiang Jiao, Wenxuan Wang, JT Huang, Xing Wang, and ZP Tu. 2023. Is chatgpt a good translator? yes with gpt-4 as the engine. *arXiv preprint arXiv:2301.08745*.

Barbara D Metcalf. 2003. Urdu in india in the 21st century: A historian's perspective. *Social Scientist*, pages 29–37.

Margaret Dumebi Okpor. 2014. Machine translation approaches: issues and challenges. *International Journal of Computer Science Issues (IJCSI)*, 11(5):159.

Maja Popović. 2017. chrf++: words helping character n-grams. In *Proceedings of the second conference on machine translation*, pages 612–618.

Matt Post. 2018. A call for clarity in reporting bleu scores. *arXiv preprint arXiv:1804.08771*.

Rico Sennrich, Barry Haddow, and Alexandra Birch. 2015a. Improving neural machine translation models with monolingual data. *arXiv preprint arXiv:1511.06709*.

Rico Sennrich, Barry Haddow, and Alexandra Birch. 2015b. Neural machine translation of rare words with subword units. *arXiv preprint arXiv:1508.07909*.

Shashank Siripragada, Jerin Philip, Vinay P Namboodiri, and CV Jawahar. 2020. A multilingual parallel corpora collection effort for indian languages. *arXiv preprint arXiv:2007.07691*.

David Stap and Ali Araabi. 2023. Chatgpt is not a good indigenous translator. In *Proceedings of the Workshop on Natural Language Processing for Indigenous Languages of the Americas (AmericasNLP)*, pages 163–167.

Ilya Sutskever, Oriol Vinyals, and Quoc V Le. 2014. Sequence to sequence learning with neural networks. *Advances in neural information processing systems*, 27.

Jörg Tiedemann. 2020. The tatoeba translation challenge realistic data sets for low resource and multilingual mt. *arXiv preprint arXiv:2010.06354*.

Ashish Vaswani, Noam Shazeer, Niki Parmar, Jakob Uszkoreit, Llion Jones, Aidan N Gomez, Łukasz Kaiser, and Illia Polosukhin. 2017. Attention is all you need. *Advances in neural information processing systems*, 30.

David Vilar, Markus Freitag, Colin Cherry, Jiaming Luo, Viresh Ratnakar, and George Foster. 2022. Prompting palm for translation: Assessing strategies and performance. arxiv e-prints, page. *arXiv preprint arXiv:2211.09102*.

Zonghan Yang, Yong Cheng, Yang Liu, and Maosong Sun. 2019. Reducing word omission errors in neural machine translation: A contrastive learning approach.

Susan Zhang, Stephen Roller, Naman Goyal, Mikel Artetxe, Moya Chen, Shuohui Chen, Christopher Dewan, Mona Diab, Xian Li, Xi Victoria Lin, et al. 2022. Opt: Open pre-trained transformer language models. *arXiv preprint arXiv:2205.01068*.

Pierre Zweigenbaum, Serge Sharoff, and Reinhard Rapp. 2018. Overview of the third bucc shared task: Spotting parallel sentences in comparable corpora. In *Proceedings of 11th workshop on building and using comparable corpora*, pages 39–42.

5 Hyperparameters

The hyperparameters used in our experiments are listed below.

Hyperparameters for GPT-3.5	
Batch Size	500
Tokens	1024
Temperature	0
Language Pair	eng-urd

Hyperparameters for `IndicTrans2`	
Batch size	100
Pad token id	1
Scale embedding	True
Model type	IndicTrans
Language pair	eng-urd

Hyperparameters for `NLLB`	
Batch size	100
Pad token id	1
Scale embedding	True
Model type	m2m_100
Language pair	eng-urd

Hyperparameters for `opus-mt-en-ur`	
Batch size	100
pad token id	1
Scale embedding	True
Number of beams	4
Model type	Marian
Language pair	eng-urd

6 Resources

We conduct all our experiments on a privately hosted server on the cloud and use a Tesla K80 GPU to run the inference.

Linguistically Informed Transformers for Text to American Sign Language Translation

Abhishek Bharadwaj Varanasi, Manjira Sinha, Tirthankar Dasgupta, Charudatta Jadhav
TCS Research
[1]{varanasi.abhishek,sinha.manjira,dasgupta.tirthankar,charudatta.jadhav}@tcs.com

Abstract

In this paper we propose a framework for automatic translation of English text to American Sign Language (ASL) which leverages a linguistically informed transformer model to translate English sentences into ASL gloss sequences. These glosses are then associated with respective ASL videos, effectively representing English text in ASL. To facilitate experimentation, we create an English-ASL parallel dataset on banking domain. Our preliminary results demonstrated that the linguistically informed transformer model achieves a 97.83% ROUGE-L score for text-to-gloss translation on the ASLG-PC12 dataset. Furthermore, fine-tuning the transformer model on the banking domain dataset yields an 89.47% ROUGE-L score when fine-tuned on ASLG-PC12 + banking domain dataset. These results demonstrate the effectiveness of the linguistically informed model for both general and domain-specific translations. To facilitate parallel dataset generation in banking-domain, we choose ASL despite having limited benchmarks and data corpus compared to some of the other sign languages.

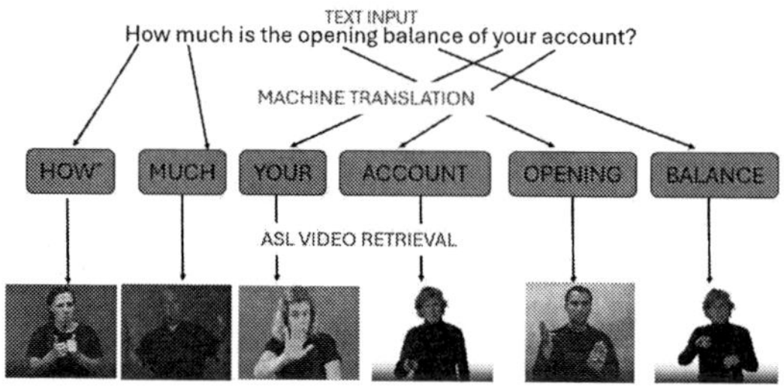

Figure 1: Illustration of text to American Sign Language (ASL) translation using glosses as intermediate step.

1 Introduction

Sign Languages (SL) are the primary means of communications for the deaf community. It is a non-verbal form of communication where deaf individuals use their hands, arms, and facial expressions to share thoughts and ideas. Unlike spoken languages that rely on sound, ASL employs gestures. Recent linguistic studies have confirmed that SLs, like other spoken languages, is a complete natural language with its own syntactical structures and intricate morphological and phonological properties. This complexity includes both sequential and simultaneous affixation of manual and non-manual elements in its structure.

A challenging aspect of sign language translation (SLT) is that Sign Languages (SLs) are multi-channeled and do not have a written form, as noted by (Langer et al., 2014). Consequently, advancements in text-based machine translation (MT) cannot be directly applied to SLs. Historically, researchers have used written representations of SLs to facilitate translation. One common method involves using glosses, which are labels in the spoken language that correspond to sign language components, often including affixes and markers. These glosses act as an intermediary step in developing MT systems that translate between SLs and spoken languages (noted by (Cihan Camgoz et al., 2017; Camgoz et al., 2018); (Chen et al., 2022)), and vice versa ((Stoll et al., 2020); (Saunders et al., 2020)). Other notable works include (Stoll et al., 2020) that proposed an approach using Neural Machine Translation (NMT) and motion graphs to generate sign language videos for a given text. (Moryossef et al., 2023) have proposed a method of converting the text to sign language glosses, extracting the poses for each gloss and translating the poses to a video. In an earlier attempt, (Dasgupta and Basu, 2008) have proposed a method translating text to Indian Sign Language (ISL) using Lexical Functional Grammar while (Sugandhi et al., 2020) talks about generating animated avatar using *HamNoSys* for text to SL translation. For translations from spoken languages to SLs, glosses are used to build the system in two phases: translating text

Proceedings of the The Seventh Workshop on Technologies for Machine Translation of Low-Resource Languages (LoResMT 2024), pages 50–56
August 15, 2024 ©2024 Association for Computational Linguistics

to glosses, and then converting these glosses into video (see Figure 1). These glosses are then input into systems that generate SL content, such as avatar animations or auto-encoder based video generators. Our present research specifically targets the text-to-gloss translation phase, which is crucial for producing accurate sign language animations. However, despite improvements in this area, significant breakthroughs remain elusive, as indicated by Rastgoo et al. (2021).

In this paper we propose a framework for automatic translation of English text to ASL. The key contributions and results of this work are as follows:

1. We leverage a novel method called linguistically informed transformer architecture that takes into account both the word level and different linguistic feature embeddings using a Graph Convolution Network (GCN) for the MT task. The primary focus is to translate English sentences into ASL gloss sequences. These glosses are then associated with respective ASL videos, effectively representing English content in ASL.
2. To facilitate experimentation, we have manually created an English-ASL parallel dataset on banking domain. Banks play a pivotal role in the daily lives of individuals impacting personal finance and economic stability. Hence, facilitating communication for the deaf community in the banking domain is essential. The dataset will be released with this paper.
3. Our preliminary results demonstrated that the linguistically informed transformer model achieves a 97.83% ROUGE-L score for text-to-gloss translation on the ASLG-PC12 dataset. Furthermore, fine-tuning the transformer model on the banking domain dataset yields an 89.47% ROUGE-L score when fine-tuned on ASLG-PC12 + banking domain dataset.

The above results show a significant improvement from the baseline GRU-B model. ASLG-PC12 (Othman and Jemni, 2012), the largest text-to-ASL gloss dataset, offers 87,710 samples but pales in comparison to mainstream language pairs like English to French. Its focus on news and politics limits its applicability across domains, necessitating domain-specific models, increasing data scarcity challenges.

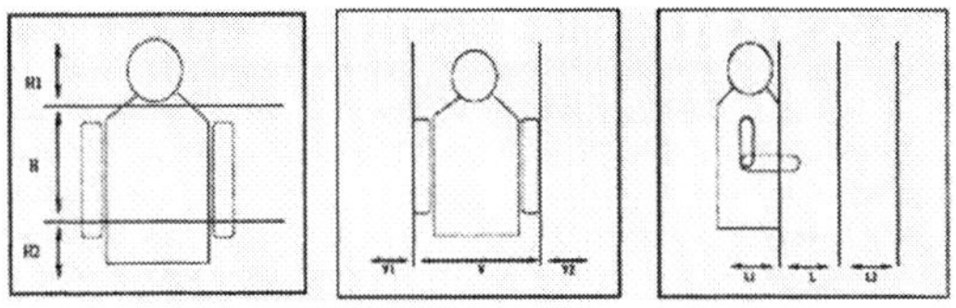

Figure 2: Classification of signing space into horizontal, vertical, and lateral regions.

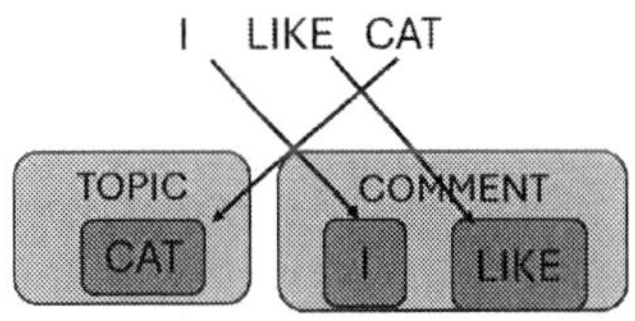

Figure 3: Illustration of Topic-Comment Structure

2 Sign Language (SL) Linguistic Issues

Sign Languages (SL) are visual-spatial natural languages, utilizing manual and non-manual components for linguistic communication (Zeshan, 2003). Manual components include hand shape, orientation, position, and movement, while non-manual components consist of facial expressions, eye gaze, and body posture. Signers utilize a three-dimensional signing space segmented into 27 cubical regions (Sinha, 2003, 2009). Each sign formation adheres to complex constraints akin to spoken languages, with SL morphology primarily derivational. The closed lexical class in SL encompasses classifier hand shapes, discourse markers, and non-manual signs (Zeshan, 2003). Classifier hand shapes offer specific hand configurations representing referent characteristics, as shown in Figure 2.

American Sign Language (ASL) is known to follow a topic-comment structure. This structure positions the main subject or theme (the topic) at the sentence's outset, followed by more specific information (the comment) (Struxness, 2010). By establishing context early in the sentence, ASL users efficiently convey complex ideas (Figure 3). One important aspect of ASL's topic-comment structure is the flexibility in word ordering. While the default order is topic-comment, ASL allows for variations based on emphasis and context. For instance, a speaker might choose to emphasize a particular aspect of the comment by placing it before the topic. This flexibility adds nuance and richness to ASL communication, enabling speakers to convey subtle meanings and emotions effectively (Struxness, 2010). The flexibility in the structure is the reason why a simple rule-based approach is not possible for text to ASL gloss translation.

3 The Linguistically Informed Transformer for Text to ASL Gloss

The existing NMT models excel at capturing intricate data patterns without requiring manual feature engineering, offering end-to-end solutions. However, they often overlook latent linguistic traits crucial for extracting pertinent information. To address this, we propose a transformer-based architecture that integrates word embeddings from the encoder part with diverse linguistic features inherent in text, enhancing automatic text-to-ASL gloss translation.

3.1 Transformer Model

The input to the model is a sentence consisting of a word sequence $x = (x_1, x_2, ..., x_T)$ representations. We then tokenize the sentence x using a wordpiece vocabulary, and then generate the input sequence $\bar{x}$ by concatenating a [CLS] token, the tokenized sentence, and a [SEP] token. Then for each token $\bar{x}_i \in \bar{x}$, we convert it into vector space by summing the token, segment, and position embeddings, thus yielding the input embeddings $h^0 \in R^{(n+2)\times h}$, where h is the hidden size. Next, we use a series of L stacked Transformer blocks to project the input embeddings into a sequence of contextual vectors $h^i \in R^{(n+2)\times h}$. Here, we omit an exhaustive description of the block architecture and refer readers to Vaswani et al. (2017) for more details.

3.2 Syntactic Dependency Graph

Encoding the structural information directly into neural network architecture is not trivial. Marcheggiani and Titov (Marcheggiani and Titov, 2017) proposed a way to incorporate structural information into sequential neural networks through Graph Convolution Networks (GCN) (Webster et al., 2019; Kipf and Welling, 2016). GCNs take graphs as inputs and conduct convolution on each node over their local graph neighborhoods. The syntax structure of a sentence is transferred into a syntactic dependency graph, and GCN is used to encode this graph information. This kind of architecture is already utilized to incorporate syntactic structure with BERT (Devlin et al., 2018) embeddings for several NLP based tasks (Duvenaud et al., 2015).

3.3 Linguistically informed transfomer

We have incorporated the similar method for the present text-gloss translation task in this work. Here, each sentence is parsed into its syntactic dependencies graph and use GCN to consume this structural information. We use pre-trained GLOVE embeddings as our initial hidden states of vertices in GCN. The output hidden states of the GCN is combined with the context embeddings generated by the transformer model's (T5 and BART) encoder and then passed to the decoder unit.

4 Experiments

Dataset: The ASLG-PC12 corpus (Othman and Jemni, 2012): consists of 87,710 bilingual sentences. It contains 1,027,100 English words and 906,477 gloss words, along with 4,662 English word singletons and 6,561 gloss word singletons. The vocabulary for both sign gloss annotation and spoken language comprises 16,788 and 12,344 terms, respectively.

ASL-Bank Dataset: Considering the specificity of the terminology used in banking contexts, we have also built a set of 3597 text- ASL gloss pairs through domain experts. The collected phrases are sourced from banking-related texts and provided to American Sign Language (ASL) experts for manual translation into ASL gloss. Refer Appendix D for data statistics and Appendix E for sample data.

Fine-tuning: We divided the ASLG-PC12 corpus into 52,626 sentences for training, 17,542 sentences for validation, and 17,542 sentences for testing (Amin et al., 2021) and use it to fine-tune a T5-small, T5-base and BART-base model on A100 GPU for 50 epochs (experiment A). For the ASL-Bank dataset, we used 3,166 sentences for training, 395 sentences for validation and 396 sentences for testing. We fine-tuned the three transformer models from experiment A on A100 GPU for 50 epochs. Refer Appendix A and B for more details.

Evaluation: Apart from using the standard MT evaluation parameters like, ROUGE-L (Lin, 2004) and BLUE (Papineni et al., 2002) scores we also advocate using a modified BERTScore (Zhang et al., 2019) as performance metrics. As the BERT models are trained on natural English text, we cannot rely on the sentence embeddings it gives for the ASL gloss sequences for the reasons explained above. Hence, we proposed to get the word embeddings of each gloss present in the ASL gloss sequence and aggregate them to get the sentence embedding of the ASL gloss sequence which can be further used to calculate the cosine similarity score.

5 Results

The results are reported by first comparing the model performance upon fine-tuning on ASLG-PC12 (Othman and Jemni, 2012) dataset between our models of choice T5-small, T5-base (Raffel et al., 2020) and BART-base (Lewis et al., 2019) and a GRU based model from Amin et al. (2021) (Table 1).

Model	GRU-B (Amin et al., 2021)	T5-small*	T5-base*	BART-base*
ROUGE-L	74.37	77.82	**77.83**	77.36
BLEU-1	73.26	77.68	**77.73**	77.21
BLEU-2	69.64	67.16	**67.22**	66.51
BLEU-3	66.68	66.36	**66.43**	65.53
BLEU-4	63.98	64.65	**64.76**	64.66
***Modified* BERTScore**	—	**77.59**	77.58	77.55

Table 1: Comparing scores on ASLG-PC12 test dataset for text to gloss with other work

From table 1, it is clear that the transformer models BART-base, T5-small and T5-base are better performing compared to a GRU model. Further, we check how well these fine-tuned transformer models are performing on our ASL-banking dataset Since ASLG-PC12 dataset has no samples related to banking domain, the scores drop when tested on our banking dataset (Table 2). Hence, we have further fine-tuned the BART-base model, T5-base model and T5-small model on our ASL-banking dataset (Table 3). We also checked if including an equal number of samples from ASLG datatset (i.e., 3597 samples) along with our ASL-banking dataset improves the test scores and we observed that there is a significant improvement in the test scores (Table 4).

Model	T5-small*	T5-base*	BART-base*
ROUGE-L	59.06	**59.13**	57.71
BLEU-1	60.66	**60.98**	59.93
BLEU-2	37.44	**37.74**	36.64
BLEU-3	26.18	**26.42**	25.48
BLEU-4	19.66	**19.85**	19.01
Modified BERTScore	80.45	**80.64**	80.37

Table 2: Test scores when tested on our ASL-banking dataset using the T5-small*, T5-base* and BART-base* models

T5-base model is the best performing transformer model for text-to-ASL translation task on both ASLG-PC12 dataset and our ASL-banking dataset. A few challenges in the text to gloss translation task are: In some cases, word ordering is different within the topic part and the comment part of the predicted texts compared to the gold texts. In case of *wh*-questions, the *wh* word is sometimes placed at the beginning of the sentences and sometimes at the end. In a few sentences, helping verbs and articles are not removed. So, they should be exclusively removed using SpaCy's parts-of-speech tagging. Few words are being replaced by their synonymous words in the gloss translations. It's not a problem while signing the text, but it is reducing the scores of metrics like ROUGE-L and BLEU.

Model	T5-small	T5-base	BART-base
ROUGE-L	68.25	**69.96**	67.92
BLEU-1	71.11	**73.08**	69.80
BLEU-2	64.45	**67.89**	64.19
BLEU-3	53.86	**58.14**	54.14
BLEU-4	46.69	**51.47**	47.27
Modified BERTScore	78.06	**78.16**	78.13

Table 3: Comparing scores on our ASL-Banking test dataset for text to gloss using transformer models after further fine-tuning

Model	T5-small	T5-base	BART-base
ROUGE-L	69.17	**69.47**	65.50
BLEU-1	70.67	**70.83**	66.83
BLEU-2	62.48	**63.05**	57.41
BLEU-3	56.87	**57.74**	50.67
BLEU-4	52.47	**53.58**	45.50
Modified BERTScore	**79.38**	79.37	79.09

Table 4: Comparing scores on our ASL-Banking test dataset using the transformer models fine-tuned on ASLG + ASL-Banking dataset

6 Conclusion

In this paper, we present a linguistically informed transformer architecture towards automatic translation of English text to American Sign Language. The proposed model not only aims at addressing the poor generalization capability of traditional structured prediction models but also exploit the linguistic characteristics present within a text to improve the performance of the translation. We evaluate the performance of the proposed model with respect to a popular baseline model. We observed that the proposed transformer based model along with an additional linguistic information performs much better than existing baseline system.

Limitations

1. This work specifically focuses on text to ASL gloss translation. Hence, the fine-tuned models cannot be used for generating glosses in other sign languages like Indian sign language or British sign language due to differences in structure.
2. As shown in Figure.1, the glosses generated using the proposed framework can be mapped to videos (refer Appendix C) and can be streamed together. But the output has inconsistencies due variation in resolution and people signing from video-to-video. This can be tackled with video generation which is not in the scope of this work.
3. Since the syntactical structure of sign language is very much different from that of natural language, open-source LLMs like LLaMA family can be leveraged by combining external sign language rules. It also helps in tackling the limitation of using a single model for different sign language translations. This can be achieved with techniques like Retrieval Augmented Generation (RAG) but this is not in the scope of this work.

References

Mohamed Amin, Hesahm Hefny, and Mohammed Ammar. 2021. Sign language gloss translation using deep learning models. *International Journal of Advanced Computer Science and Applications*, 12(11).

Necati Cihan Camgoz, Simon Hadfield, Oscar Koller, Hermann Ney, and Richard Bowden. 2018. Neural sign language translation. In *Proceedings of the IEEE conference on computer vision and pattern recognition*, pages 7784–7793.

Yutong Chen, Ronglai Zuo, Fangyun Wei, Yu Wu, Shujie Liu, and Brian Mak. 2022. Two-stream network for sign language recognition and translation. *Advances in Neural Information Processing Systems*, 35:17043–17056.

Necati Cihan Camgoz, Simon Hadfield, Oscar Koller, and Richard Bowden. 2017. Subunets: End-to-end hand shape and continuous sign language recognition. In *Proceedings of the IEEE international conference on computer vision*, pages 3056–3065.

Tirthankar Dasgupta and Anupam Basu. 2008. Prototype machine translation system from text-to-indian sign language. In *Proceedings of the 13th international conference on Intelligent user interfaces*, pages 313–316.

Jacob Devlin, Ming-Wei Chang, Kenton Lee, and Kristina Toutanova. 2018. Bert: Pre-training of deep bidirectional transformers for language understanding. *arXiv preprint arXiv:1810.04805*.

David K Duvenaud, Dougal Maclaurin, Jorge Iparraguirre, Rafael Bombarell, Timothy Hirzel, Alán Aspuru-Guzik, and Ryan P Adams. 2015. Convolutional networks on graphs for learning molecular fingerprints. *Advances in neural information processing systems*, 28.

Thomas N Kipf and Max Welling. 2016. Semi-supervised classification with graph convolutional networks. *arXiv preprint arXiv:1609.02907*.

Gabriele Langer, Susanne König, and Silke Matthes. 2014. Compiling a basic vocabulary for german sign language (dgs)–lexicographic issues with a focus on word senses. In *Proceedings of the XVI EURALEX International Congress: The User in Focus*, pages 767–786.

Mike Lewis, Yinhan Liu, Naman Goyal, Marjan Ghazvininejad, Abdelrahman Mohamed, Omer Levy, Ves Stoyanov, and Luke Zettlemoyer. 2019. Bart: Denoising sequence-to-sequence pre-training for natural language generation, translation, and comprehension. *arXiv preprint arXiv:1910.13461*.

Chin-Yew Lin. 2004. Rouge: A package for automatic evaluation of summaries. In *Text summarization branches out*, pages 74–81.

Diego Marcheggiani and Ivan Titov. 2017. Encoding sentences with graph convolutional networks for semantic role labeling. *arXiv preprint arXiv:1703.04826*.

Amit Moryossef, Mathias Müller, Anne Göhring, Zifan Jiang, Yoav Goldberg, and Sarah Ebling. 2023. An open-source gloss-based baseline for spoken to signed language translation. *arXiv preprint arXiv:2305.17714*.

Achraf Othman and Mohamed Jemni. 2012. English-asl gloss parallel corpus 2012: Aslg-pc12. In *Signlang@ LREC 2012*, pages 151–154. European Language Resources Association (ELRA).

Kishore Papineni, Salim Roukos, Todd Ward, and Wei-Jing Zhu. 2002. Bleu: a method for automatic evaluation of machine translation. In *Proceedings of the 40th annual meeting of the Association for Computational Linguistics*, pages 311–318.

Colin Raffel, Noam Shazeer, Adam Roberts, Katherine Lee, Sharan Narang, Michael Matena, Yanqi Zhou, Wei Li, and Peter J Liu. 2020. Exploring the limits of transfer learning with a unified text-to-text transformer. *Journal of machine learning research*, 21(140):1–67.

Razieh Rastgoo, Kourosh Kiani, and Sergio Escalera. 2021. Sign language recognition: A deep survey. *Expert Systems with Applications*, 164:113794.

Ben Saunders, Necati Cihan Camgoz, and Richard Bowden. 2020. Adversarial training for multi-channel sign language production. *arXiv preprint arXiv:2008.12405.*

Samar Sinha. 2003. A skeletal grammar of indian sign language. *Unpublished master's diss., Jawaharlal Nehru University, New Delhi, India.*

Samar Sinha. 2009. *A grammar of Indian sign language*. Ph.D. thesis, PhD dissertation, Jawaharlal Nehru University, New Delhi, India.

Stephanie Stoll, Necati Cihan Camgoz, Simon Hadfield, and Richard Bowden. 2020. Text2sign: towards sign language production using neural machine translation and generative adversarial networks. *International Journal of Computer Vision*, 128(4):891–908.

Kevin Struxness. 2010. American sign language grammar rules. Technical report, Technical Report,[on-line: http://daphne. palomar. edu/kstruxness/Spring ....

Sugandhi, Parteek Kumar, and Sanmeet Kaur. 2020. Sign language generation system based on indian sign language grammar. *ACM Transactions on Asian and Low-Resource Language Information Processing (TALLIP)*, 19(4):1–26.

Ashish Vaswani, Noam Shazeer, Niki Parmar, Jakob Uszkoreit, Llion Jones, Aidan N Gomez, Łukasz Kaiser, and Illia Polosukhin. 2017. Attention is all you need. *Advances in neural information processing systems*, 30.

Kellie Webster, Marta R Costa-Jussà, Christian Hardmeier, and Will Radford. 2019. Gendered ambiguous pronoun (gap) shared task at the gender bias in nlp workshop 2019. In *Proceedings of the First Workshop on Gender Bias in Natural Language Processing*, pages 1–7.

Ulrike Zeshan. 2003. Indo-pakistani sign language grammar: a typological outline. *Sign Language Studies*, pages 157–212.

Tianyi Zhang, Varsha Kishore, Felix Wu, Kilian Q Weinberger, and Yoav Artzi. 2019. Bertscore: Evaluating text generation with bert. *arXiv preprint arXiv:1904.09675.*

A Hyperparameters used for fine-tuning on ASLG-PC12 dataset

1. Training epochs: 50
2. Learning rate: 1e-5
3. Weight Decay: 1e-6
4. Warm-up Epochs: 10
5. Batch size: 10
6. Gradient accumulation steps: 4
7. Optimizer: Adam

B Hyperparameters used for fine-tuning on our ASL-Banking dataset

1. Training epochs: 50
2. Learning rate: 1e-5
3. Weight Decay: 1e-5
4. Warm-up Epochs: 10
5. Batch size: 2
6. Gradient accumulation steps: 4
7. Attention Dropout: 0.1
8. Optimizer: Adam

The linguistic embeddings which are GCN's output hidden states are combined with the last hidden state of the encoder part as described in section 3.3 during both the fine-tuning processes.

C Video Retriever

The generated ASL gloss sequence is tokenized into individual glosses using SpaCy tokenizer and each gloss is mapped to its corresponding ASL video which is stored in a folder/database. If there is no video match for a particular gloss, we check if it is a common noun or an adjective. If yes, then we try to find a video for its synonym. We use NLTK word-net to find the synonyms. The synonyms are sorted in lexicological order. We iterate through this list and check if there exists a video each of synonym. As soon as we find a synonym which has a video, we break the loop and use this video for signing the original word. If it is neither a common noun nor an adjective or there is no video even for any of its synonyms, we will simply sign it letter-by-letter (as shown in Figure 4).

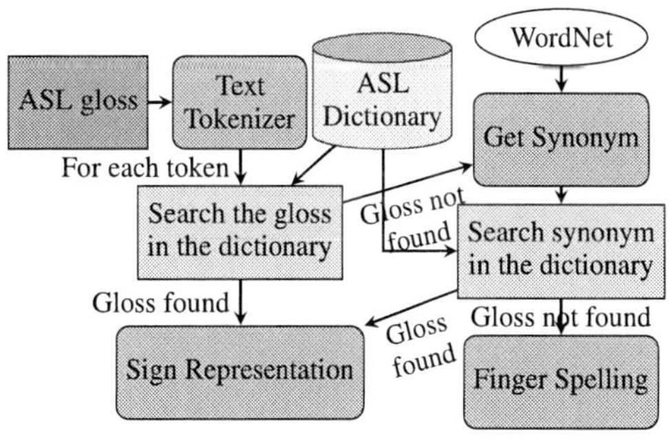

Figure 4: Video Retrieval Process flow

D Data Statistics

Conversational Type	Vocabulary Size	Type	Count
Banker point-of-view	772	Declarative	446
		Interrogative	168
Customer point-of-view	1595	Declarative	502
		Interrogative	2488
		Total:	3597

E Sample Data

English Text	ASL Gloss Sequence
A basic savings account it is. I'll need you to fill out this form with your personal details.	SAVINGS ACCOUNT BASIC, IT IX. FORM THIS FILL-OUT NEED YOU, YOUR PERSONAL DETAILS IX-loc.
A basic savings account it is. I'll need you to fill out this form with your personal details.	SAVINGS ACCOUNT BASIC, IT IX. FORM THIS FILL-OUT NEED YOU, YOUR PERSONAL DETAILS IX-loc.
Can I deposit a check via mobile banking?	DEPOSIT CHECK MOBILE BANKING CAN I?
How can I assist you in updating your contact information for your account?	HOW CAN I ASSIST YOU IN UPDATING YOUR CONTACT INFORMATION FOR YOUR ACCOUNT ?
Your credit check came back clear, so we can proceed with finalizing your account.	CREDIT CHECK YOUR FINISH, CLEAR. ACCOUNT YOUR FINALIZE CAN PROCEED WE.

Low-Resource Cross-Lingual Summarization through Few-Shot Learning with Large Language Models

Gyutae Park, Seojin Hwang, Hwanhee Lee[†]
Department of Artificial Intelligence, Chung-Ang University, Seoul, Korea
{pkt0401, swiftie1230, hwanheelee}@cau.ac.kr

Abstract

Cross-lingual summarization (XLS) aims to generate a summary in a target language different from the source language document. While large language models (LLMs) have shown promising zero-shot XLS performance, their few-shot capabilities on this task remain unexplored, especially for low-resource languages with limited parallel data. In this paper, we investigate the few-shot XLS performance of various models, including Mistral-7B-Instruct-v0.2, GPT-3.5, and GPT-4. Our experiments demonstrate that few-shot learning significantly improves the XLS performance of LLMs, particularly GPT-3.5 and GPT-4, in low-resource settings. However, the open-source model Mistral-7B-Instruct-v0.2 struggles to adapt effectively to the XLS task with limited examples. Our findings highlight the potential of few-shot learning for improving XLS performance and the need for further research in designing LLM architectures and pre-training objectives tailored for this task. We provide a future work direction to explore more effective few-shot learning strategies and to investigate the transfer learning capabilities of LLMs for cross-lingual summarization.

1 Introduction

Cross-Lingual Summarization (XLS) is a task that involves generating a summary in a target language different from the source document's language. It is a complex natural language processing task that requires performing both summarization and machine translation simultaneously. This task is much more challenging than single-language summarization, as it involves overcoming the differences between languages while effectively extracting and compressing key information. Generally, there are two types of pipelines for XLS systems (Leuski et al., 2003; Orăsan and Chiorean, 2008): *summarize-then-translate* and *translate-then-summarize*. The former summarizes the source text first and then translates it, while the latter translates the source text first and then summarizes it.

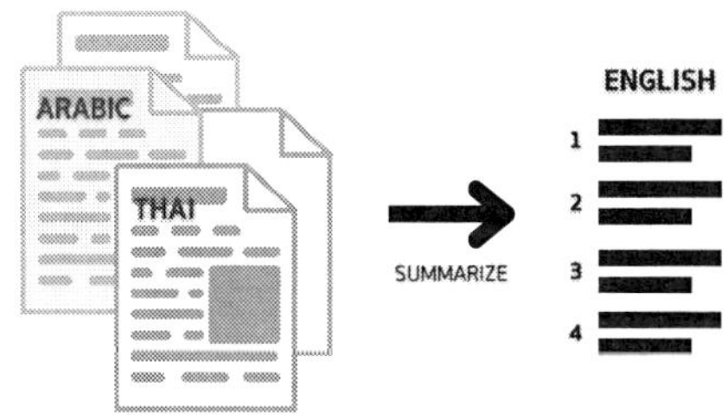

Figure 1: An example of cross-lingual summarization.

However, these pipelines have the disadvantage that errors occurring at each stage can propagate and accumulate, potentially degrading the final performance. To resolve the issues of these pipelines, there has been a lot of research on the end-to-end approach (Zhu et al., 2019; Bai et al., 2021), known as the direct method, which generates the target language summary directly from the source document in a single step. The direct method can mitigate the error propagation problem compared to traditional pipelines and enable more efficient learning.

In parallel with the development of end-to-end approaches, Large Language Models (LLMs) such as GPT-3.5 and GPT-4 (OpenAI, 2023) have demonstrated strong performance in various natural language processing tasks. It is known that these models can significantly improve performance through few-shot learning with only a small number of examples. (Brown et al., 2020) However, directly applying these models to the XLS task is still challenging. Particularly for low-resource languages, where it is difficult to build large-scale

[†]Corresponding author.

Proceedings of the The Seventh Workshop on Technologies for Machine Translation of Low-Resource Languages (LoResMT 2024), pages 57–63
August 15, 2024 ©2024 Association for Computational Linguistics

parallel corpora, the lack of data makes it difficult to fully utilize the performance of pre-trained language models, acting as a major obstacle in XLS research. (Ladhak et al., 2020) Hence, this study aims to explore the XLS performance of various LLMs using a few-shot learning approach through in-context learning, focusing on the direct method.

Our findings demonstrate that few-shot learning enables LLMs, particularly GPT-3.5 and GPT-4, to achieve competitive performance in cross-lingual summarization tasks for low-resource language settings. The results also highlight open-source models' challenges in adapting to the XLS task with limited parallel data. These findings emphasize the potential of few-shot learning in enhancing cross-lingual summarization capabilities and the need for further research in developing effective few-shot strategies and architectures for low-resource languages.

2 Related Work

Cross-lingual summarization (XLS) has undergone significant evolution, shifting from early pipeline approaches like *summarize-then-translate* (Orăsan and Chiorean, 2008; Wan et al., 2010) and *translate-then-summarize* (Leuski et al., 2003; Boudin et al., 2011) to more sophisticated methods utilizing multilingual pre-trained models. These pipelines were initially dominant due to their simplicity but were plagued by error propagation and the limitations inherent to sequential processing tasks. (Parnell et al., 2024) The advent of multilingual pre-trained models such as mBART (Lewis et al., 2020) and mT5 (Xue et al., 2021) marked a transformative shift towards end-to-end approaches, directly generating summaries in the target language and substantially mitigating error propagation issues.

In recent years, the emergence of large language models (LLMs) has revolutionized the field of natural language processing, including XLS. Especially, widely used LLMs like GPT-3.5 and GPT-4 have demonstrated remarkable zero-shot learning capabilities across various tasks. (Brown et al., 2020; Qin et al., 2023; Bubeck et al., 2023) However, the exploration of LLMs in the context of XLS is still in its early stages, with limited research on their zero-shot learning capabilities and even fewer studies focusing on their few-shot learning potential.(Wang et al., 2023) Recent studies have shown promising results in using LLMs for various NLP tasks.(Bang et al., 2023; Yang et al., 2023; Patil and Gudivada, 2024)

However, the specific exploration of these models in XLS scenarios, particularly in the few-shot setting, remains largely unexplored. While some studies have investigated the zero-shot XLS performance of LLMs (Wang et al., 2023), there is a notable lack of research on the few-shot learning capabilities of models such as GPT-3.5, GPT-4, and multilingual LLMs in the XLS domain. Moreover, the disparity in performance between proprietary models like GPT-4 and open-source alternatives in zero-shot settings underscores the necessity for further investigation into the few-shot capabilities of LLMs. This is particularly critical to ensure that advancements in XLS are equitable and accessible across various linguistic and resource settings.

In this paper, we aim to bridge this gap by exploring the few-shot learning capabilities of LLMs in the context of XLS. We focus on the direct method, leveraging the nuanced capabilities of LLMs like GPT-3.5, GPT-4, and open-source models such as Mistral-7B-Instruct-v0.2. The Mistral-7B-Instruct-v0.2 is a 7.3B parameter model that outperforms Llama-2 13B (Touvron et al., 2023b) across all benchmarks and even surpasses Llama-1 34B (Touvron et al., 2023a) on many tasks and particularly noted for its ability to process up to 32k tokens, significantly enhancing its capability for few-shot learning by providing richer context management. (La Plateforme; Jiang et al., 2024) This open-source model has demonstrated strong performance in various natural language processing tasks and offers robust multilingual support. Our aim is to provide comprehensive insights into the practical applications and limitations of these models in low-resource languages, setting the stage for future advancements in the field.

3 Methods

The main objective of our research is to compare and analyze the performance of pre-trained mT5 and few-shot prompt-based GPT-3.5 and GPT-4. Then, we aim to experimentally confirm the impact of their few-shot learning on low-resource language XLS tasks. Additionally, we conduct comprehensive comparison with one of the open-source multilingual LLMs, such as the Mistral-7B-Instruct-v0.2 (La Plateforme; Jiang et al., 2024), to provide a broader perspective on the performance of different LLMs in the XLS task to provide a broader

Input Prompt

Please summarize the following text in English

Example 1

Text: "แผนที่ของนาซายังชี้อีกว่า ระดับของไนโตรเจนไดออกไซด์ มลพิษที่เกิดจากโรงงานอุตสาหกรรม มีปริมาณลดลงด้วยเช่นกันในปีนี้ สอดคล้องกับจำนวนตัวเลขของโรงงานในจีนที่ถูกสั่งปิดโรงงานยุติการผลิตเพื่อกักกันไม่ให้ไวรัสแพร่ระบาด ตัวเลขผู้ติดเชื้อไวรัสโคโรนาสายพันธุ์ใหม่ในจีนขณะนี้อยู่ที่เกือบ 80,000 ราย นับแต่เกิดการระบาดเมื่อปลายปีที่แล้ว ขณะที่พบผู้ติดเชื้อไวรัสชนิดนี้ในอีกกว่า..."
(Nasa's map also shows that the level of nitrogen dioxide pollution caused by industrial plants has also decreased this year, in line with the number of plants in China that have been ...)

Translated summary: "Satellite images have shown a dramatic decline in pollution levels over China, which is ""at least partly"" due to an economic slowdown prompted by the coronavirus, US space agency Nasa says."

Example 2

Text: "นิตยสารเพลย์บอยลงโฆษณาฉบับเดือนมีนาคม-เมษายนของตนทางทวิตเตอร์ 2017 นิตยสารเพลย์บอยซึ่งยุติการตีพิมพ์รูปเปลือยของสาวเพื่อนเล่น ""เพลย์เมท"" ซึ่งเป็นเอกลักษณ์ประจำตัวที่โด่งดังไปเมื่อเดือนมีนาคมปี 2016 ประกาศเปลี่ยนนโยบายแบบกลับหลังหันอีกครั้ง โดยเพลย์บอยฉบับเดือนมีนาคม-เมษายน 2017 จะลงรูปเปลือยของสาวเพลย์เมทบนหน้าปก โดยมีการโฆษณ..."
(Playboy magazine advertised its March-April issue on Twitter 2017. Playboy magazine, which stopped publishing nude photos of playmate girlfriend" Playmate", a well-known identity in ...)

Translated summary: "Playboy magazine has announced it is bringing back nudity, reversing a decision made last year."

Test Text

Text: "สื่อรัสเซียรายงานว่า ศ.โอเลก โซโคลอฟ วัย 63 ปี อยู่ในสภาพมึนเมาและพลัดตกลงไปในแม่น้ำพร้อมด้วยกระเป๋าเป้ซึ่งภายในมีชิ้นส่วนแขนทั้ง 2 ข้างของ น.ส.อนาสตาเซีย เยชเชนโก วัย 24 ปี ในเวลาต่อมา เจ้าหน้าที่ตำรวจได้เข้าตรวจสอบบ้านพักของ ศ.โซโคลอฟ ในนครเซ็นต์ปีเตอร์สเบิร์ก และพบร่างที่ถูกหั่นแยกชิ้นส่วนของ น.ส.เยชเชนโก เจ้าหน้าที่ตรวจสอบแม่น้ำมอยกา..."
(Russian media reported that Prof.Oleg Sokolov, 63, was intoxicated and fell into the river with a backpack containing parts of Ms.Anastasia Yeshchenko, 24, later a police officer examined ...)

Translated summary:

Figure 2: Two-shot prompt construction for cross-lingual summarization from Thai to English.

perspective on the performance of different LLMs in the XLS task and assess the effectiveness of few-shot learning in mitigating the challenges posed by low-resource settings.

3.1 Direct Cross-Lingual Summarization

We focus on the direct cross-lingual summarization method, which generates target language summaries directly from source language documents in an end-to-end manner. Unlike traditional pipelines that involve separate summarization and translation steps, the direct approach combines these tasks into a single, unified process. This allows for a more seamless transfer of information between languages and reduces the potential for error propagation.

3.2 Models

We compare the performance of fine-tuned mT5, GPT-3.5, GPT-4, and Mistral-7B-Instruct-v0.2 on cross-lingual summarization tasks. For GPT-3.5 and GPT-4, specifically GPT-3.5-turbo-0125 and GPT-4-0125-preview models, and Mistral-7B-Instruct-v0.2, we evaluate their performance in zero-shot, one-shot, and two-shot settings. The Mistral-7B-Instruct-v0.2 is particularly noted for its ability to process up to 32k tokens, significantly enhancing its capability for few-shot learning by providing richer context management. This model has been shown to outperform other models like Llama-2-13B across all benchmarks, with robust multilingual support enhancing its utility for diverse linguistic datasets.

3.3 Few-Shot Prompt Construction

For the few-shot learning approach, we construct prompts that include several examples from the validation set. These examples are carefully selected based on their token count, ensuring that the shortest examples are used as the first and second examples in the prompt. This structured approach facilitates effective few-shot learning, even when computational resources are limited.

The direct prompts for few-shot learning, as depicted in Figure 2, are structured to provide the model with two examples of increasing complexity. Each prompt consists of two example texts and their corresponding summaries in the target language. The test text is then appended to the prompt, and the model is expected to generate a summary in English. By including these meticulously chosen examples in the prompt, we aim to provide the model with sufficient context to perform few-shot cross-lingual summarization effectively. This method allows us to explore the capabilities of large language models in low-resource settings where the availability of parallel data is limited.

4 Experiments

4.1 Datasets

We utilize the CrossSum (Bhattacharjee et al., 2023) dataset, a multilingual corpus of summaries in 45 languages. Following the definitions in (Li et al., 2023), we focus on low-resource language pairs with fewer than 1,000 parallel data points. Additionally, we include experiments with Pashto, a medium-resource language with 1,212 parallel data points, to more broadly assess the effective-

Models		Th-En			Gu-En			Mr-En			Pa-En			Bu-En			Si-En		
		Language Pair																	
		R-1	R-2	R-L	R-1	R-2	R-L	R-1	R-2	R-L	R-1	R-2	R-L	R-1	R-2	R-L	R-1	R-2	R-L
mT5-Base (fine-tuning)		29.16	9.79	22.63	24.28	6.40	19.12	25.87	7.28	20.14	30.86	10.27	24.78	28.44	7.50	22.07	28.94	8.17	22.53
GPT-3.5	Zero-shot	14.69	3.84	10.32	12.69	2.80	9.20	13.83	3.04	9.96	14.98	3.78	10.94	13.2	2.21	10.19	13.08	2.11	9.91
	One	15.18	3.95	10.99	13.0	3.12	9.25	14.91	3.73	10.79	14.62	3.93	10.80	15.80	2.43	11.91	13.39	2.34	10.11
	Two	16.56	4.59	11.6	**15.33**	**3.57**	**10.57**	**16.52**	**4.06**	**11.96**	**15.52**	3.96	**11.06**	16.48	2.83	**12.39**	14.03	2.47	9.81
GPT-4	Zero-shot	12.22	3.39	8.59	10.96	2.71	7.63	10.97	2.84	7.90	12.10	3.58	8.55	14.73	3.77	9.84	13.92	3.86	9.45
	One	14.86	4.12	10.51	13.88	3.50	9.27	14.11	3.52	10.09	13.33	4.04	9.43	16.88	**4.48**	11.41	15.03	**4.35**	10.27
	Two	**17.67**	**5.19**	**12.67**	13.63	3.49	9.27	14.97	3.73	10.38	13.65	**4.15**	9.49	**17.38**	4.32	11.73	**15.10**	4.15	**10.39**
Mistral-7B-instruct-v0.2	Zero-shot	8.91	2.12	6.42	6.15	0.68	4.76	7.63	1.55	5.76	7.65	1.62	5.99	7.59	1.06	5.68	7.23	0.99	5.40
	One	10.28	2.51	7.58	7.27	0.79	5.46	8.08	1.42	6.06	7.41	1.21	5.82	8.35	0.91	6.37	8.43	1.06	6.08
	Two	10.10	2.37	7.30	6.31	0.71	4.81	6.66	0.57	5.35	8.96	1.71	6.77	9.55	1.07	7.44	8.21	0.49	6.58

Table 1: Performance comparison of model performance metrics across various language pairs, including R1, R2, and Rouge-L scores. The language pairs are abbreviated as follows: Th-En (Thai to English), Gu-En (Gujarati to English), Mr-En (Marathi to English), Pa-En (Pashto to English), Bu-En (Burmese to English), Si-En (Sinhala to English).

Models		En-Th			En-Gu			En-Mr			En-Pa			En-Bu			En-Si		
		Language Pair																	
		R-1	R-2	R-L	R-1	R-2	R-L	R-1	R-2	R-L	R-1	R-2	R-L	R-1	R-2	R-L	R-1	R-2	R-L
mT5-Base (fine-tuning)		4.59	0.94	4.40	10.14	1.19	9.37	9.38	1.22	8.94	20.12	4.62	17.55	4.85	0.55	4.72	5.62	0.39	5.13
GPT-3.5	Zero-shot	4.78	1.48	4.53	1.40	0.0	1.40	2.05	0.0	2.05	0.0	0.0	0.0	1.70	0.26	1.70	1.22	0.0	1.22
	One	4.5	0.82	4.45	1.60	0.0	1.60	1.02	0.13	1.02	0.0	0.0	0.0	0.58	0.0	1.55	1.72	**1.72**	1.72
	Two	5.29	1.46	5.20	0.55	0.0	0.55	0.88	0.09	0.88	0.0	0.0	0.0	1.55	0.0	1.55	1.63	1.07	1.63
GPT-4	Zero-shot	6.09	1.42	5.84	1.50	0.0	1.50	1.35	0.0	1.35	0.0	0.0	0.0	2.61	0.90	2.61	3.34	**1.72**	3.34
	One	**9.38**	**2.25**	**9.38**	1.22	0.0	1.22	1.48	0.1	1.48	0.0	0.0	0.0	4.62	0.17	4.62	**4.36**	1.15	**4.36**
	Two	8.64	2.16	8.39	**2.05**	0.0	**2.05**	1.31	0.0	1.31	0.0	0.0	0.0	2.02	0.22	2.02	2.53	1.15	2.53
Mistral-7B-instruct-v0.2	Zero-shot	4.33	1.18	4.33	0.23	0.0	0.23	**2.37**	**0.20**	**2.37**	0.0	0.0	0.0	2.64	1.21	2.64	0.06	0.0	0.06
	One	4.39	1.33	4.30	0.51	0.0	0.51	1.64	0.08	1.64	0.0	0.0	0.0	**7.78**	**1.55**	**7.78**	0.74	0.0	0.74
	Two	3.15	0.38	2.94	0.51	0.0	0.51	0.55	0.0	0.55	0.0	0.0	0.0	2.43	0.01	2.10	0.42	0.0	0.42

Table 2: Performance comparison of model performance metrics across various language pairs, including R1, R2, and Rouge-L scores. The language pairs are abbreviated as follows: En-Th (English to Thai), En-Gu (English to Gujarati), En-Mr (English to Marathi), En-Pa (English to Pashto), En-Bu (English to Burmese), and En-Si (English to Sinhala).

ness of our proposed method in diverse linguistic settings. Figure 3 illustrates the distribution of the dataset across different languages for both many-to-one and one-to-many scenarios. The number of parallel data points for each language pair remains consistent in both settings. This symmetry allows us to represent the dataset distribution in a single figure, simplifying the visual representation of the data.

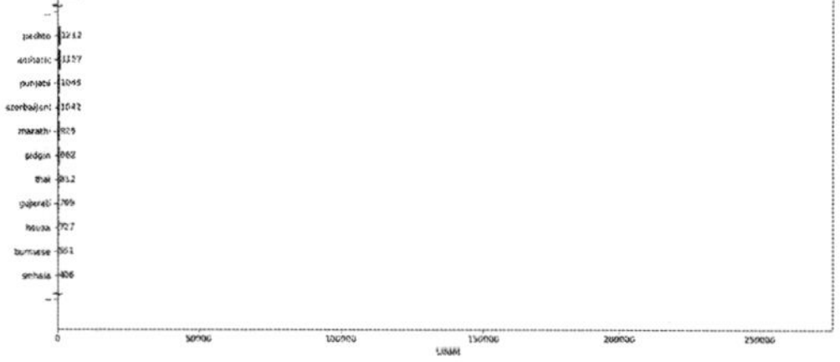

Figure 3: Distribution of English-centric many-to-one and one-to-many datasets in Train data

4.2 Performance Metrics

To evaluate the quality of the generated summaries, we used the ROUGE (Lin, 2004), reporting ROUGE-1/2/L (R-1,2,L). These metrics measure the overlap of unigrams, bigrams, and the longest common subsequences between the generated and reference summaries, respectively.

4.3 Experimental Results

Overall Performance: Fine-tuned mT5 models outperformed most language pairs and experimental settings. Notably, the GPT-3.5 and GPT-4 models demonstrated significant improvements in few-shot scenarios, particularly highlighting their effective adaptation in many-to-one settings, where they summarize from various source languages into English. However, in the one-to-many setting, GPT-3.5, GPT-4, and Mistral-7B-Instruct-v0.2 showed limited performance gains in the one-shot scenario, and their performance either deteriorated or remained unimproved in the two-shot setting.

Moreover, there was no significant performance difference among GPT-3.5, GPT-4, and Mistral-7B-Instruct-v0.2 in the one-to-many setting, indicating the challenges associated with summarizing from English to low-resource languages. The Mistral-7B-Instruct-v0.2 model consistently underperformed compared to the fine-tuned mT5 and the GPT-3.5 and GPT-4 models across most language pairs and few-shot settings, suggesting that it struggles to effectively adapt to the cross-lingual summarization task with limited examples.

Few-Shot Learning Impact: The performance of GPT-3.5 and GPT-4 models competitively improved as the number of shots increased, showcasing their few-shot learning capabilities in cross-lingual summarization. The Mistral-7B-Instruct-v0.2 model exhibited performance gains up to the one-shot setting, with generally increasing ROUGE scores. However, in the two-shot setting, the model's performance showed a decreasing trend, indicating that the benefits of few-shot learning may not consistently extend to higher numbers of shots for this open-source model. This highlights the challenges in applying open-source models to few-shot cross-lingual summarization tasks and suggests that further research is needed to optimize their performance in these settings.

Analysis by Language Pair: The many-to-one approach generally resulted in higher ROUGE scores than the one-to-many approach. This suggests that summarizing in English is relatively more straightforward than summarizing in other languages. However, the performance gap between the two approaches was more pronounced for the Mistral-7B-Instruct-v0.2, indicating its limited ability to generate summaries in non-English target languages compared to the other models. Notably, all models achieved ROUGE scores of 0 for the English to-Pashto language pair across all few-shot settings (see Table 2). This result indicates that few-shot learning did not improve the models' performance for this specific language pair. The English to Pashto results, where all models failed to generate meaningful summaries even with few-shot learning, underscore the limitations of current approaches in handling extremely low-resource language pairs. This finding emphasizes the need for further research in developing more effective few-shot learning strategies and investigating the transfer learning capabilities of LLMs for cross-lingual summarization in such challenging scenarios.

5 Conclusion

This study empirically analyzed the few-shot performance of LLMs in cross-lingual summarization tasks, focusing on low-resource languages using a direct prompting approach. We observed that LLMs demonstrated competitive performance improvements through few-shot learning compared to zero-shot setups particularly in the many-to-one XLS. But, we also demonstrated that there was no significant gain to LLMs in the one-to-many XLS. These findings underscore the need for further research in developing more effective few-shot learning strategies and architectures tailored to low-resource languages.

Limitation

Our study conducts experiments on a limited number of low-resource languages and uses only ROUGE metrics to validate the systems' performance. Future research should explore advanced few-shot learning techniques, such as meta-learning or prompt-tuning, and investigate the impact of pre-training objectives and architectures designed specifically for cross-lingual tasks. This could lead to developing more effective open-source models for low-resource cross-lingual summarization.

Despite these limitations, this research demonstrates the potential of large language models' few-shot learning capabilities in low-resource cross-lingual summarization tasks and provides experimental validation for the proposed research directions. Further work is necessary to extend these findings to additional low-resource languages and advance the few-shot learning capabilities of open-source models like Mistral-7B-Instruct-v0.2.

Acknowledgement

This research was supported by Institute for Information & Communications Technology Planning & Evaluation (IITP) through the Korea government (MSIT) under Grant No. 2021-0-01341 (Artificial Intelligence Graduate School Program (Chung-Ang University)).

References

Yu Bai, Yang Gao, and Heyan Huang. 2021. Cross-lingual abstractive summarization with limited parallel resources. *Preprint*, arXiv:2105.13648.

Yejin Bang, Samuel Cahyawijaya, Nayeon Lee, Wenliang Dai, Dan Su, Bryan Wilie, Holy Lovenia, Ziwei Ji, Tiezheng Yu, Willy Chung, Quyet V. Do, Yan Xu, and Pascale Fung. 2023. A multitask, multilingual, multimodal evaluation of chatgpt on reasoning, hallucination, and interactivity. *Preprint*, arXiv:2302.04023.

Abhik Bhattacharjee, Tahmid Hasan, Wasi Uddin Ahmad, Yuan-Fang Li, Yong-Bin Kang, and Rifat Shahriyar. 2023. Crosssum: Beyond english-centric cross-lingual summarization for 1,500+ language pairs. *Preprint*, arXiv:2112.08804.

Florian Boudin, Stéphane Huet, and Juan-Manuel Torres-Moreno. 2011. A graph-based approach to cross-language multi-document summarization. *Polibits*, 43:113–118.

Tom B. Brown, Benjamin Mann, Nick Ryder, Melanie Subbiah, Jared Kaplan, Prafulla Dhariwal, Arvind Neelakantan, Pranav Shyam, Girish Sastry, Amanda Askell, Sandhini Agarwal, Ariel Herbert-Voss, Gretchen Krueger, Tom Henighan, Rewon Child, Aditya Ramesh, Daniel M. Ziegler, Jeffrey Wu, Clemens Winter, Christopher Hesse, Mark Chen, Eric Sigler, Mateusz Litwin, Scott Gray, Benjamin Chess, Jack Clark, Christopher Berner, Sam McCandlish, Alec Radford, Ilya Sutskever, and Dario Amodei. 2020. Language models are few-shot learners. *Preprint*, arXiv:2005.14165.

Sébastien Bubeck, Varun Chandrasekaran, Ronen Eldan, Johannes Gehrke, Eric Horvitz, Ece Kamar, Peter Lee, Yin Tat Lee, Yuanzhi Li, Scott Lundberg, Harsha Nori, Hamid Palangi, Marco Tulio Ribeiro, and Yi Zhang. 2023. Sparks of artificial general intelligence: Early experiments with gpt-4. *Preprint*, arXiv:2303.12712.

Albert Q. Jiang, Alexandre Sablayrolles, Antoine Roux, Arthur Mensch, Blanche Savary, Chris Bamford, Devendra Singh Chaplot, Diego de las Casas, Emma Bou Hanna, Florian Bressand, Gianna Lengyel, Guillaume Bour, Guillaume Lample, Lélio Renard Lavaud, Lucile Saulnier, Marie-Anne Lachaux, Pierre Stock, Sandeep Subramanian, Sophia Yang, Szymon Antoniak, Teven Le Scao, Théophile Gervet, Thibaut Lavril, Thomas Wang, Timothée Lacroix, and William El Sayed. 2024. Mixtral of experts. *Preprint*, arXiv:2401.04088.

La Plateforme. Mistral AI | frontier AI in your hands. `https://mistral.ai/`. Accessed: 2023-05-10.

Faisal Ladhak, Esin Durmus, Claire Cardie, and Kathleen McKeown. 2020. Wikilingua: A new benchmark dataset for cross-lingual abstractive summarization. *Preprint*, arXiv:2010.03093.

Anton Leuski, Chin-Yew Lin, Liang Zhou, Ulrich Germann, Franz Josef Och, and Eduard Hovy. 2003. Cross-lingual c*st*rd: English access to hindi information. *ACM Transactions on Asian Language Information Processing*, 2(3):245–269.

Mike Lewis, Yinhan Liu, Naman Goyal, Marjan Ghazvininejad, Abdelrahman Mohamed, Omer Levy, Veselin Stoyanov, and Luke Zettlemoyer. 2020. BART: Denoising sequence-to-sequence pre-training for natural language generation, translation, and comprehension. In *Proceedings of the 58th Annual Meeting of the Association for Computational Linguistics*, pages 7871–7880, Online. Association for Computational Linguistics.

Peiyao Li, Zhengkun Zhang, Jun Wang, Liang Li, Adam Jatowt, and Zhenglu Yang. 2023. ACROSS: An alignment-based framework for low-resource many-to-one cross-lingual summarization. In *Findings of the Association for Computational Linguistics: ACL 2023*, pages 2458–2472, Toronto, Canada. Association for Computational Linguistics.

Chin-Yew Lin. 2004. ROUGE: A package for automatic evaluation of summaries. In *Text Summarization Branches Out*, pages 74–81, Barcelona, Spain. Association for Computational Linguistics.

OpenAI. 2023. GPT-4 technical report. ArXiv. Abs/2303.08774.

C Orăsan and OA Chiorean. 2008. Evaluation of a cross-lingual romanian-english multi-document summariser.

Jacob Parnell, Inigo Jauregi Unanue, and Massimo Piccardi. 2024. Sumtra: A differentiable pipeline for few-shot cross-lingual summarization. *Preprint*, arXiv:2403.13240.

Rajvardhan Patil and Venkat Gudivada. 2024. A review of current trends, techniques, and challenges in large language models (llms). *Applied Sciences*, 14(5).

Chengwei Qin, Aston Zhang, Zhuosheng Zhang, Jiaao Chen, Michihiro Yasunaga, and Diyi Yang. 2023. Is ChatGPT a general-purpose natural language processing task solver? In *Proceedings of the 2023 Conference on Empirical Methods in Natural Language Processing*, pages 1339–1384, Singapore. Association for Computational Linguistics.

Hugo Touvron, Thibaut Lavril, Gautier Izacard, Xavier Martinet, Marie-Anne Lachaux, Timothée Lacroix, Baptiste Rozière, Naman Goyal, Eric Hambro, Faisal Azhar, Aurelien Rodriguez, Armand Joulin, Edouard Grave, and Guillaume Lample. 2023a. Llama: Open and efficient foundation language models. *Preprint*, arXiv:2302.13971.

Hugo Touvron, Louis Martin, Kevin Stone, Peter Albert, Amjad Almahairi, Yasmine Babaei, Nikolay Bashlykov, Soumya Batra, Prajjwal Bhargava, Shruti Bhosale, Dan Bikel, Lukas Blecher, Cristian Canton Ferrer, Moya Chen, Guillem Cucurull, David Esiobu, Jude Fernandes, Jeremy Fu, Wenyin Fu, Brian Fuller, Cynthia Gao, Vedanuj Goswami, Naman Goyal, Anthony Hartshorn, Saghar Hosseini, Rui Hou, Hakan Inan, Marcin Kardas, Viktor Kerkez, Madian Khabsa, Isabel Kloumann, Artem Korenev, Punit Singh Koura,

Marie-Anne Lachaux, Thibaut Lavril, Jenya Lee, Diana Liskovich, Yinghai Lu, Yuning Mao, Xavier Martinet, Todor Mihaylov, Pushkar Mishra, Igor Molybog, Yixin Nie, Andrew Poulton, Jeremy Reizenstein, Rashi Rungta, Kalyan Saladi, Alan Schelten, Ruan Silva, Eric Michael Smith, Ranjan Subramanian, Xiaoqing Ellen Tan, Binh Tang, Ross Taylor, Adina Williams, Jian Xiang Kuan, Puxin Xu, Zheng Yan, Iliyan Zarov, Yuchen Zhang, Angela Fan, Melanie Kambadur, Sharan Narang, Aurelien Rodriguez, Robert Stojnic, Sergey Edunov, and Thomas Scialom. 2023b. Llama 2: Open foundation and fine-tuned chat models. *Preprint*, arXiv:2307.09288.

Xiaojun Wan, Huiying Li, and Jianguo Xiao. 2010. Cross-language document summarization based on machine translation quality prediction. In *Proceedings of the 48th Annual Meeting of the Association for Computational Linguistics*, pages 917–926, Uppsala, Sweden. Association for Computational Linguistics.

Jiaan Wang, Yunlong Liang, Fandong Meng, Beiqi Zou, Zhixu Li, Jianfeng Qu, and Jie Zhou. 2023. Zero-shot cross-lingual summarization via large language models. *Preprint*, arXiv:2302.14229.

Linting Xue, Noah Constant, Adam Roberts, Mihir Kale, Rami Al-Rfou, Aditya Siddhant, Aditya Barua, and Colin Raffel. 2021. mT5: A massively multilingual pre-trained text-to-text transformer. In *Proceedings of the 2021 Conference of the North American Chapter of the Association for Computational Linguistics: Human Language Technologies*, pages 483–498, Online. Association for Computational Linguistics.

Jingfeng Yang, Hongye Jin, Ruixiang Tang, Xiaotian Han, Qizhang Feng, Haoming Jiang, Bing Yin, and Xia Hu. 2023. Harnessing the power of llms in practice: A survey on chatgpt and beyond. *Preprint*, arXiv:2304.13712.

Junnan Zhu, Qian Wang, Yining Wang, Yu Zhou, Jiajun Zhang, Shaonan Wang, and Chengqing Zong. 2019. Ncls: Neural cross-lingual summarization. *Preprint*, arXiv:1909.00156.

Enhancing Low-Resource NMT with a Multilingual Encoder and Knowledge Distillation: A Case Study

Aniruddha Roy[1], Pretam Ray[1], Ayush Maheshwari[2], Sudeshna Sarkar[1], Pawan Goyal[1]
[1] Indian Institute of Technology Kharagpur [2] Vizzhy Inc, Bengaluru
{aniruddha.roy, pretam.ray}@iitkgp.ac.in, ayush.maheshwari@vizzhy.com,
{sudeshna, pawang}@cse.iitkgp.ac.in

Abstract

Neural Machine Translation (NMT) remains a formidable challenge, especially when dealing with low-resource languages. Pre-trained sequence-to-sequence (seq2seq) multi-lingual models, such as mBART-50, have demonstrated impressive performance in various low-resource NMT tasks. However, their pre-training has been confined to 50 languages, leaving out support for numerous low-resource languages, particularly those spoken in the Indian subcontinent. Expanding mBART-50's language support requires complex pre-training, risking performance decline due to catastrophic forgetting. Considering these expanding challenges, this paper explores a framework that leverages the benefits of a pre-trained language model along with knowledge distillation in a seq2seq architecture to facilitate translation for low-resource languages, including those not covered by mBART-50. The proposed framework employs a multilingual encoder-based seq2seq model as the foundational architecture and subsequently uses complementary knowledge distillation techniques to mitigate the impact of imbalanced training. Our framework is evaluated on three low-resource Indic languages in four Indic-to-Indic directions, yielding significant BLEU-4 and chrF improvements over baselines[1]. Further, we conduct human evaluation to confirm effectiveness of our approach.

1 Introduction

Neural Machine Translation (NMT) models (Bahdanau et al., 2016; Vaswani et al., 2017; Liu et al., 2020a; Khandelwal et al.) have shown impressive results on benchmark datasets, mainly containing large amounts of parallel data. However, these models face challenges when applied to low-resource languages or languages with rich and diverse morphology. Previous approaches have leveraged pre-trained models trained on extensive corpora (Weng et al., 2019; Wang et al., 2022; Liu et al., 2020b, 2021; Haddow et al., 2022; Roy et al., 2023, 2022) to address these limitations.

Pre-trained multilingual seq2seq-based models based on an encoder-decoder framework such as mBART-50 (Liu et al., 2020b) have been successfully used for various low-resource NMT tasks. Despite being pre-trained with 50 languages, it needs more support for numerous low-resource languages. Expanding the capabilities of mBART-50 to encompass new languages entails a cumbersome process involving the collection of substantial amounts of monolingual data and the execution of pre-training with denoising objectives after initializing mBART-50. This process is time-consuming and may decrease performance on the initial 50 languages when incorporating new ones, a phenomenon known as catastrophic forgetting (French, 1999).

In contrast, encoder-based pretrained model XLM-R (Conneau et al., 2020) is designed to accommodate 100 languages, making it suitable for a wide range of low-resource cross-lingual Natural Language Understanding (NLU) tasks. Both cross-lingual and Machine Translation (MT) functionalities share certain similarities. In cross-lingual scenarios, training and evaluation occur across different languages, while MT systems process input in one language and produce output in another. This distinction prompts several experimental research questions, including: 1) How does an XLM-R based NMT model perform on low-resource morphologically rich languages, particularly those not covered by mBART-50? 2) Given that low-resource NMT may be affected by training imbalances leading to performance degradation, can the application of knowledge distillation further enhance the results?

To address the two aforementioned experimen-

[1]Our code is publicly available at https://github.com/raypretam/Two-step-low-res-NMT

Proceedings of the The Seventh Workshop on Technologies for Machine Translation of Low-Resource Languages (LoResMT 2024), pages 64–73
August 15, 2024

tal research questions, we utilize our base model, which follows a seq2seq framework. Here, we initialize the encoder with the multilingual pretrained model XLM-R large, while decoder layers are initialized from scratch, we call this base approach as XLM-MT. Similar frameworks have been explored in previous studies (Zhu et al., 2020; Li et al., 2023), with our approach sharing similarities with (Chen et al., 2022), who employed it for zero-shot cross-lingual NMT tasks and froze the embedding layers. However, our base approach differs in considering only decoder training. Thereafter, we apply complementary knowledge distillation (CKD) (Shao and Feng, 2022) to the base XLM-MT model to address training imbalances. The objective of this complementary knowledge distillation is to train the student model with knowledge which complements the teacher model and avoid knowledge forgetting, and we refer to this as XLM-MT+CKD. We empirically evaluate our model across three Indic languages and observe significant improvement in BLEU and chrF scores. Finally, we use human evaluation to assess the fluency, relatedness, and correctness of our output. Our contributions are as follows:

1. We repurpose the XLM-based seq2seq framework in conjunction with a complementary knowledge distillation approach to effectively design an NMT model for low-resource MT tasks. To the best of our knowledge, we are the first to integrate these two approaches effectively for NMT tasks.

2. We conduct comprehensive experiments on three Indian languages in four directions that are not included in mBART-50 and demonstrate the significance of our approach in enhancing translation results.

3. We also perform a detailed analysis of the results, including human evaluation and error analysis, for our proposed model.

2 Methodology

Given a source language sentence $X = (x_1, x_2, \ldots, x_S)$, and its corresponding target language translation $Y = (y_1, y_2, \ldots, y_T)$, an NMT model is trained to predict the translated sequence Y' using the maximum log-likelihood estimation (MLE) objective. The probability of predicting the target sequence Y' is computed as $p(Y'|X;\theta) = \prod_{t=1}^{T} p(y_t|y_{0:t-1}, x_{1:S}, \theta)$, where θ represents the model parameters.

2.1 Base Model (XLM-MT)

We initialize encoder layers and encoder embeddings with an unsupervised pre-trained multilingual model, XLM-R large (Conneau et al., 2020) which is trained using masked language model objective. Then, we train the decoder from scratch while freezing the encoder parameters. During training, decoder parameters are learned with an MLE objective. The underlying assumption is that the pre-trained encoder parameters have already learnt a multilingual representation of the source language. As a result, only the decoder is trained using MLE objective while leveraging the encoder embeddings learned by the pre-trained model. $\mathcal{L}_{\theta_{dec}} = \sum_{(X,Y)\in D} \log P(Y|X;\theta_{dec})$ where X and Y represents the source target sentence respectively from the dataset D. The parameter θ_{dec} refers to the parameters of the decoder layers and embedding.

Algorithm 1 Complementary Knowledge Distillation

Input: Training data D, the number of teachers n.
Output: Student model S.
Initialize S and teacher models ($T_{1:n}$) with the base model, XLM-MT.
while not converge **do**
    randomly divides the training data D in mutually exclusive $n+1$ subsets $D_1, D_2, \ldots D_{n+1}$
    for $t = 1$ to $n+1$ **do**
        for $i = 1$ to n **do**
            Train T_i on $D_{O(i,t)}$
        end for
        Train S on D_t using Eq 3
    end for
    for $i = 1$ to n **do**
        $T_i \leftarrow S$ (At the end of each epoch, reinitialize teacher models with the student model:)
    end for
end while
return student model S

2.2 Complementary Knowledge Distillation

Imbalances in training data lead to performance degradation in low-resource NMT due to catastrophic knowledge forgetting (LeCun et al., 2002; Shao and Feng, 2022). We leverage complementary knowledge distillation (CKD) technique (Shao and Feng, 2022) to overcome this problem in low-resource MT. In CKD, n teacher models and a student model S are trained in a complementary manner such that S learns from new training samples while teacher models dynamically provide complementary early samples knowledge to the S. In our case, both teacher and student models are initialized with the parameters of our base model, XLM-MT.

We divide the training set D into $n+1$ mutually exclusive subsets for each epoch. The student model S sequentially learns from D_1 to D_{n+1} while the teacher models learn from all data splits except D_t. To determine the training data for the teacher models at timestep t, we utilize an ordering function, as shown in Eq 1 (Shao and Feng, 2022). This ordering function covers all data splits except D_t, ensuring that the teacher models complement the student model.

$$O(i,t) = \left\{ \begin{array}{cc} i+t, & i+t \leq n+1 \\ i+t-n-1, & i+t > n+1 \end{array} \right\} \quad (1)$$

where, $i \in \{1,2,\ldots,n\}$ and $t \in \{1,2,\ldots,n+1\}$

In the process of word-level knowledge distillation, the student model S benefits from an additional supervision signal, aligning its outputs with the probability outputs of the teacher model T.

$$\mathcal{L}_{KD}(\theta) = -\sum_{t=1}^{T}\sum_{k=1}^{|V|}\sum_{i=1}^{n} \frac{q_i(y_t = k|y_{<t}, X)}{n} \times \log p(y_t = k|y_{<t}, X, \theta) \quad (2)$$

where $|V|$ denotes the number of classes, p denotes the prediction of student and q_i is the prediction of teacher model T_i. To balance the distillation loss and the cross-entropy loss, we introduce a hyperparameter α for interpolation. Finally, the overall objective function is

$$\mathcal{L}(\theta) = \alpha \cdot \mathcal{L}_{KD}(\theta) + (1-\alpha) \cdot \mathcal{L}_{NLL}(\theta) \quad (3)$$

We employ a reinitialization technique (Zhang et al., 2018; Zhu et al., 2018) to facilitate two-way knowledge transfer. After each epoch, we reset the parameters of the teacher models using those of the student model. This reinitialization ensures that the student and teachers begin each epoch with identical settings. We present the training procedure for CKD in Algorithm 1. We apply CKD to our base model in the following 2-step process.

Step 1 - Initialization: In this step, we initialize both the student and teacher models with the model obtained after the first step training (*c.f.*, Section 2.1). This initialization ensures that the student model benefits from the knowledge acquired during the initial decoder training.

Step 2 - CKD: In this step, we apply the complementary KD technique (*c.f.*, Section 2.2) which enables the model to benefit from the transfer of complementary knowledge.

3 Experimental Setup

Dataset: For our experiments, we specifically select three Indic languages, namely Kannada, and Punjabi that are not included in mBART-50, to assess the effectiveness of our approach. We use the Samanantar dataset (Ramesh et al., 2022) for training all our NMT models which contains parallel sentences for 11 Indic language pairs. We consider three languages in 4 directions, namely Hindi-Kannada, Kannada-Hindi, Kannada-Punjabi, and Punjabi-Kannada, containing 2.1 million and 1.1 million parallel sentences respectively. We use the FLORES-200 (Team, 2022) containing 997 and 1012 sentences as our validation and test set respectively.

Implementation Details: We implement our approach using the Fairseq Toolkit (Ott et al., 2019). We use Adam optimizer (Kingma and Ba, 2017) with $\beta_1 = 0.9$ and $\beta = 0.98$. Following the work by Chen et al. (2021), we use learning rates $5e-3$ and $1e-3$ for the base model and CKD, respectively. We set maximum updates of 200K for the base model training and 40K for the CKD. We use 12 layers with 16 attention heads in the decoder. We use the 'Large' variant of XLM-R that has 550 million parameters for our experiments. We set the number of teachers to 1 and $\alpha = 0.95$. We set batch size $=$ 32k, and used beam size $=$ 5 throughout our experiments, and following Shao and Feng (2022) we averaged the last five checkpoints. We use BLEU-4 (Papineni et al., 2002) and chrF (Popović, 2015) score to evaluate our approach. All the models have been trained on single A100 GPUs. None of the training methods consumed more than 96 hours.

Baselines We employ various baseline models for comparison with our approach. To ensure a fair assessment, we train all baseline models using identical training data and assess their performance on the Flores dataset.

Transformer (Vaswani et al., 2017): We uti-

Model	hi-kn	kn-hi	kn-pa	pa-kn	hi-kn	kn-hi	kn-pa	pa-kn
		BLEU				**chrF**		
Transformer	3.60	7.61	1.39	1.04	37.40	34.09	24.19	25.75
Sequence-KD (Kim and Rush, 2016)	4.23	7.88	1.71	1.08	37.43	34.23	24.31	25.89
mBERT-KD (Chen et al., 2020)	4.73	8.67	2.01	1.31	37.47	34.67	24.43	26.22
Selective KD (Wang et al., 2021)	5.35	8.08	2.24	1.19	39.23	35.02	24.57	26.78
Transformer+CKD	4.51	8.89	3.23	1.98	38.54	35.13	24.54	27.01
mBERT-MT (Zhu et al., 2020)	4.98	10.23	3.78	4.17	38.98	35.56	25.01	29.68
SixTp (Chen et al., 2022)	7.01	10.80	6.14	5.45	40.98	35.74	27.62	32.47
XLM-MT (base)	6.08	8.75	6.01	2.98	40.38	35.38	27.12	28.11
XLM-MT + CKD (ours)	**9.15**	**11.46**	**7.23**	**6.43**	**41.11**	**35.88**	**29.12**	**33.98**

Table 1: Performance (BLEU-4 and chrF scores) of our model along with seven baseline models on the FLORES-200 dataset on 3 languages in 4 directions between Indic languages: Hindi ('hi'), Kannada ('kn'), Punjabi ('pa'). We provide additional human evaluation results in Table 4.

lize a standard transformer-based encoder-decoder model, employing six layers for both the encoder and decoder.

Word-level Knowledge Distillation (Kim and Rush, 2016) is a conventional method applied to enhance NMT results by distilling knowledge at the word level.

Sequence-level Knowledge Distillation (Kim and Rush, 2016) is a conventional knowledge distillation technique applied to enhance NMT results by distilling knowledge at the sequence level.

BERT-KD (Chen et al., 2020) is a knowledge extracted from a fine-tuned BERT model is transferred to NMT models.

Selective KD (Wang et al., 2021) refers to the process of distilling and transferring specific, relevant knowledge from a teacher model to a student model. Instead of transferring all the knowledge indiscriminately, this approach involves selecting and distilling the most valuable and informative aspects of the teacher model's knowledge.

mBERT-MT(Zhu et al., 2020), integrates BERT into the NMT process. Initially, BERT is employed to extract representations for an input sequence. Subsequently, these representations are fused with each layer of the NMT model's encoder and decoder using attention mechanisms.

sixTp (Chen et al., 2022) is a sequence-to-sequence (seq-to-seq) model. In its initialization, the encoders are initialized with the XLM-R large model, while the decoder is initialized randomly. The model undergoes a two-stage fine-tuning process. In the initial stage, the encoder layers are frozen, and fine-tuning is performed on the decoders. Subsequently, in the second stage, the model is trained in an end-to-end fashion.

4 Results

Table 1 presents the BLEU-4 and chrF results for Hindi to Kannada, Kannada to Punjabi in both directions. It is noteworthy that Hindi, and Punjabi belong to the Indo-Aryan language family, while Kannada belongs to the Dravidian family. We compare our results against seven competitive baselines, namely, vanilla transformer, knowledge distillation techniques, transformer with CKD, two step training techniques using mBERT and SixTp, which is XLM-R based model. We observe that XLM-MT + CKD achieves BLEU scores within the range of (6.43 to 11.46) consistently surpassing the baselines. We observe an average improvements of 1.22-5.15 BLEU scores across all language pairs. We also present chrF scores in Table 1. Notably, XLM-MT+CKD consistently demonstrates its superiority, outperforming all the baselines with averages of 0.82-4.66 chrF score, across all language pairs. Further, we conduct human evaluation to assess the fluency, relatedness and correctness of the generated text. We present human evaluation results of sixTp and our model, XLM-MT+CKD in Table 4.

We also investigate various variants of our model to validate the effectiveness of our architecture and present results in Table 2. Additionally, we conduct comprehensive error analysis in Section 7.

5 Analysis

How would the method perform with the languages that mBART-50 supported? In addition to the language pairs outlined in Section 3, we extend our exploration to include language pairs supported by mBART-50, facilitating effec-

Model	hi-kn	kn-hi	kn-pa	pa-kn
Transformer	3.60	7.61	2.39	1.04
$\text{Enc}^{\text{XLM-R}}_{\text{train}}$ + Dec	4.72	8.32	5.75	2.11
$\text{Enc}^{\text{XLM-R}}_{\text{no-train}}$ + Dec	6.08	8.75	6.01	2.98
SixTp	7.01	10.80	6.14	5.45
XLM-MT + CKD	**9.15**	**11.46**	**7.23**	**6.43**

Table 2: Performances (BLEU-4 scores) of our model along with its variants. The score in **bold** shows the best scores for the corresponding language pair. Enc + Dec refers to the transformer model without XLM initialization. $\text{Enc}^{\text{XLM-R}}_{\text{train}}$ + Dec refers to joint training of XLM-R based encoder and decoder. $\text{Enc}^{\text{XLM-R}}_{\text{no-train}}$+ + Dec refers to only decoder training.

Model	hi-bn	mr-hi	hi-te
mBART-50	**9.25**	**17.06**	9.35
XLM-MT	8.13	15.78	11.56
XLM-MT + CKD	8.67	15.81	**12.01**

Table 3: Performances BLEU-4 of our model along with mBART-50 model on the FLORES-200 dataset for the translation between Indic languages: Hindi ('hi'), Telugu ('te'), and Bengali ('bn').

tive comparisons with the mBART-50 model. We extracted three language pairs from the Samantar dataset—namely, Hindi-Bengali, Telugu-Hindi, and Marathi-Hindi—and compared our approach with mBART-50. We present the results in Table 3. mBART-50 achieves BLEU-4 scores of 9.35 and 17.06 for the language pairs of Hindi-Bengali and Marathi-Hindi respectively, surpassing the performance of XLM-MT+CKD model. For the Hindi-Telugu pair, our model XLM-MT+CKD achieves better performance than mBART-50.

5.1 Analysis of different model variants

The aim of this analysis is to assess the effectiveness of our model with different approaches in addressing the challenges of machine translation, particularly for low-resource and morphologically rich languages. The obtained BLEU scores are presented in Table 2.

Enc + Dec: To assess the importance of pre-training initialization in the encoder, we compare the performance of XLM-MT, which is initialized with XLM-R large, against a randomly initialized model. We observe that the encoder initialized with XLM-R large produces better performance than the randomly initialized encoder.

$\text{Enc}^{\text{XLM-R}}_{\text{train}}$ + Dec, $\text{Enc}^{\text{XLM-R}}_{\text{no-train}}$ + Dec: To analyze the effectiveness of the two-stage training process employed in XLM-MT, we experiment with two different settings: (a) training encoder and decoder jointly (the second stage), denoted as $\text{Enc}^{\text{XLM-R}}_{\text{train}}$ + Dec, and (b) only training the decoder (the first stage), denoted as $\text{Enc}^{\text{XLM-R}}_{\text{no-train}}$ + Dec. From Table 2, we clearly see the effectiveness of two-stage training compared to only one of these stages across all language pairs.

6 Human Evaluation

We follow a procedure similar to previous studies (Chi et al., 2019; Maurya et al., 2021) to assess the quality of translated sentences in three Indic languages in four Indic-to-Indic language pairs. We randomly selected 50 test data-points for each language pair for evaluation. Three key metrics are used to evaluate the translated sentences: fluency, relatedness, and correctness. Fluency refers to the smoothness and coherence of the generated text, evaluating how well the sentences flow and adhere to grammatical rules. Relatedness measures how well the translated sentences are connected to the given ground truth sentences and capture its key information. Correctness assesses the accuracy and appropriateness of the translated sentences in terms of their meaning and semantics. We present the translated sentences (randomly shuffled) from two models XLM-MT and XLM-MT+CKD to three language experts for each language pair. The selected 12 experts are well versed in the corresponding target language including English. The experts attained a minimum of graduate degree in English and have native proficiency in the target language. The experts are informed about the task and were renumerated as per industry standard norms. The experts rated the sentences on a 5-point scale, with 1 indicating very bad and 5 indicating very good, for each of the three metrics. The final numbers are in Table 4. These are calculated by averaging all

Metric	hi-kn	kn-hi	kn-pa	pa-kn
SixTp				
Fluency	3.13	3.71	2.47	1.97
Correctness	3.04	3.68	2.40	**1.87**
Relatedness	3.18	3.75	2.33	1.92
XLM-MT + CKD				
Fluency	**3.23**	**3.75**	**2.53**	**2.01**
Correctness	**3.71**	**3.92**	**2.47**	1.85
Relatedness	**3.43**	**3.78**	**2.51**	**1.97**

Table 4: Human evaluation results of our approach sixTp and XLM-MT+ CKD for three languages in four directions. The three metrics are Fluency, Relatedness, and Correctness, respectively.

the experts' responses for each parameter. The annotation experts received compensation according to industry standards for their work. We briefed them on the objectives and explicit usage of their annotations

7 Case Study

Table 5 presents several example sentences and their translations by our proposed approach. Notably, there are specific issues with reference 1 in the XLM-MT translations. In reference 1, XLM-MT incorrectly translates the sentence using a wrong gender concept, whereas XLM-MT+CKD translates correctly. Regarding the Kannada sentence in reference 2, the XLM-MT and XLM-MT+CKD approaches provide a correct and meaningful translation, albeit with some paraphrasing.

8 Related Work

Neural Machine Translation (NMT) aims to translate a given source sentence into a target sentence. Typically, an NMT model comprises an encoder, a decoder, and an attention mechanism. The encoder transforms the input sequence into hidden representations while the decoder maps these representations to the target sequence. The attention mechanism, pioneered by (Bahdanau et al., 2016), enhances alignment between words in the source and target languages. Different architectures can be employed for the encoder and decoder, including LSTM (Long Short-Term Memory), CNN (Convolutional Neural Network), and Transformer. The Transformer architecture, introduced by (Vaswani et al., 2017), consists of three sublayers. Transformer has demonstrated state-of-the-art performance in NMT tasks (Barrault et al., 2019).

Prior studies (Imamura and Sumita, 2019; Conneau and Lample, 2019; Yang et al., 2022; Weng et al., 2019; Ma et al., 2020; Zhu et al., 2020) have investigated the integration of pre-trained language encoders into NMT models to bolster supervised translation performance. (Zhu et al., 2020) introduce a BERT-fused model that extracts representations from input sentences and integrates them into the encoder and decoder using attention mechanisms. Recent research (Song et al., 2019) focuses on developing and refining encoder-decoder-based multilingual trained language models for NMT. (Liu et al., 2020c) present mBART, a Transformer-based encoder-decoder model explicitly tailored for NMT applications. Wei et al. finetune the multilingual encoder-based model for low-resource NMT, and they focus on improving the MPE for a more universal representation across languages. (Chen et al., 2021, 2022) have examined a two-stage framework utilizing an encoder-based multilingual language model for zero-shot neural machine translation.

Numerous studies in NMT have incorporated the Knowledge Distillation (KD) framework. (Kim and Rush, 2016) introduced word-level KD for NMT and later proposed sequence-level KD to enhance overall performance. Investigating the efficacy of various token types in KD, (Wang et al., 2021) suggested strategies for selective KD. (Wu et al., 2020) successfully transferred internal hidden states from teacher models to students, achieving positive results. Various KD approaches have also been employed in non-auto-regressive Machine Translation tasks to enhance outcomes. (Gu et al., 2018) improved non-autoregressive model performance by distilling information from an autoregressive model. (Zhou et al., 2021) conducted systematic experiments highlighting the importance of knowledge distillation in training non-auto-

1. Source (Kannada):	Udaharanage, obbaru, motaru karugale rastegala abhivrd'dhige mula karana endu helabahudu. **Translation:** For example, one could say that motor cars were the root cause of the development of roads.
Reference (Punjabi):	Udaharana vajon, koi kahi sakada hai ki motara kara sarakan nu zaruri taura'te vikas vala lai jandi hai. **Translation:** For example, one could say that the motor car essentially leads to development of roads.
XLM-MT+CKD:	Udaharana vajon, koi kahi sakada hai ki motara kara sarakan nu zaruri taura'te vikas vala lai jandi hai. **Translation:** For example, one could say that the motor car essentially leads to development of roads.
2. Source (Hindi) :	kuchh any visheshagyon kee tarah, unhen is baat par sandeh hai ki kya madhumeh ko theek kiya ja sakata hai, yah dekhate hue ki in nishkarshon kee un logon ke lie koee praasangikata nahin hai jinhen pahale se hee taip 1 madhumeh hai. **Translation:** Like some other experts, he is skeptical about whether diabetes can be cured, noting that these findings have no relevance to people who already have type 1 diabetes.
Reference (Kannada):	Madhumehavannu gunapadisalu sadhyave emba bagge itare itara kelavu tajñarante avaru kuda sansaya vyaktapadisuttare, ī sansodhanegaḷu īgagale ṭaip 1 madhumeha hondiruva janarige yavude prayojanagaḷannu nīdilla. **Translation:** Like some other experts, he doubts whether diabetes can be cured, because these conclusions are not practical for people who have previously had type 1 diabetes.
XLM-MT+CKD:	Itara kelavu tajñarante, avaru madhumehavannu gunapadisabahude endu sansayapaduttare, ekendare ī tīrmanagaḷu ī hinde ṭaip 1 madhumeha hondiruva vyaktigaḷige prayogikavagiruvudilla. **Translation:** Like some other experts, he doubts whether diabetes can be cured, because these conclusions are not practical for people who have previously had type 1 diabetes.

Table 5: Sample outputs generated from our proposed approach, where the target languages' source language and translations are specified for each reference.

regressive models, showing its ability to reduce dataset complexity and help model variations in output data. In the realm of multilingual NMT, (Baziotis et al., 2020) used language models as instructors for low-resource NMT models. (Chen et al., 2020) extracted knowledge from fine-tuned BERT and transferred it to NMT models. Furthermore, (Feng et al., 2021) and (Zhou et al., 2021) employed KD to introduce forward-looking information into the teacher-forcing training of NMT models.

9 Conclusion

In this paper, we empirically explored the methods for improving low-resource NMT, particularly for Indic languages. We investigated several strategies for initialization of encoder and decoder, along with the knowledge distillation techniques. We conducted experiment on three low-resource Indic languages in four Indic-to-Indic directions belonging to two language families, specifically focusing on those not covered by mBART-50. Further, we perform additional analysis on languages supported by mBART-50 and high-resource language pairs.

Limitations

A limitation of this study is the increased training time required for the XLM-MT+CKD model due to its addition of complementary knowledge distillation. Furthermore, our validation is limited to low-resource machine translation tasks, although seq2seq models have the potential to be utilized for a wide range of generation tasks, including Question Generation and Summarization in both monolingual and cross-lingual contexts.

Acknowledgement

This work was supported in part by the National Language Translation Mission (NLTM): Bhashini project by the Government of India.

References

Dzmitry Bahdanau, Kyunghyun Cho, and Yoshua Bengio. 2016. Neural machine translation by jointly learning to align and translate.

Loïc Barrault, Ondřej Bojar, Marta R. Costa-jussà, Christian Federmann, Mark Fishel, Yvette Graham, Barry Haddow, Matthias Huck, Philipp Koehn, Shervin Malmasi, Christof Monz, Mathias Müller, Santanu Pal, Matt Post, and Marcos Zampieri. 2019. Findings of the 2019 conference on machine translation (WMT19). In *Proceedings of the Fourth Conference on Machine Translation (Volume 2: Shared Task Papers, Day 1)*, pages 1–61, Florence, Italy. Association for Computational Linguistics.

Christos Baziotis, Barry Haddow, and Alexandra Birch. 2020. Language model prior for low-resource neural machine translation. In *Proceedings of the 2020 Conference on Empirical Methods in Natural Language Processing (EMNLP)*, pages 7622–7634, Online. Association for Computational Linguistics.

Guanhua Chen, Shuming Ma, Yun Chen, Li Dong, Dongdong Zhang, Jia Pan, Wenping Wang, and Furu Wei. 2021. Zero-shot cross-lingual transfer of neural machine translation with multilingual pretrained encoders. In *Proceedings of the 2021 Conference on Empirical Methods in Natural Language Processing*, pages 15–26, Online and Punta Cana, Dominican Republic. Association for Computational Linguistics.

Guanhua Chen, Shuming Ma, Yun Chen, Dongdong Zhang, Jia Pan, Wenping Wang, and Furu Wei. 2022. Towards making the most of cross-lingual transfer for zero-shot neural machine translation. In *Proceedings of the 60th Annual Meeting of the Association for Computational Linguistics (Volume 1: Long Papers)*, pages 142–157, Dublin, Ireland. Association for Computational Linguistics.

Yen-Chun Chen, Zhe Gan, Yu Cheng, Jingzhou Liu, and Jingjing Liu. 2020. Distilling knowledge learned in BERT for text generation. In *Proceedings of the 58th Annual Meeting of the Association for Computational Linguistics*, pages 7893–7905, Online. Association for Computational Linguistics.

Zewen Chi, Li Dong, Furu Wei, Wenhui Wang, Xian-Ling Mao, and Heyan Huang. 2019. Cross-lingual natural language generation via pre-training.

Alexis Conneau, Kartikay Khandelwal, Naman Goyal, Vishrav Chaudhary, Guillaume Wenzek, Francisco Guzmán, Edouard Grave, Myle Ott, Luke Zettlemoyer, and Veselin Stoyanov. 2020. Unsupervised cross-lingual representation learning at scale.

Alexis Conneau and Guillaume Lample. 2019. Cross-lingual language model pretraining. *Advances in neural information processing systems*, 32.

Yang Feng, Shuhao Gu, Dengji Guo, Zhengxin Yang, and Chenze Shao. 2021. Guiding teacher forcing with seer forcing for neural machine translation. In *Proceedings of the 59th Annual Meeting of the Association for Computational Linguistics and the 11th International Joint Conference on Natural Language Processing (Volume 1: Long Papers)*, pages 2862–2872, Online. Association for Computational Linguistics.

Robert French. 1999. Catastrophic forgetting in connectionist networks. *Trends in cognitive sciences*, 3:128–135.

J Gu, J Bradbury, C Xiong, VOK Li, and R Socher. 2018. Non-autoregressive neural machine translation. In *International Conference on Learning Representations (ICLR)*.

Barry Haddow, Rachel Bawden, Antonio Valerio Miceli Barone, Jindřich Helcl, and Alexandra Birch. 2022. Survey of low-resource machine translation. *Computational Linguistics*, 48(3):673–732.

Kenji Imamura and Eiichiro Sumita. 2019. Recycling a pre-trained BERT encoder for neural machine translation. In *Proceedings of the 3rd Workshop on Neural Generation and Translation*, pages 23–31, Hong Kong. Association for Computational Linguistics.

Urvashi Khandelwal, Angela Fan, Dan Jurafsky, Luke Zettlemoyer, and Mike Lewis. Nearest neighbor machine translation. In *International Conference on Learning Representations*.

Yoon Kim and Alexander M. Rush. 2016. Sequence-level knowledge distillation.

Diederik P. Kingma and Jimmy Ba. 2017. Adam: A method for stochastic optimization.

Yann LeCun, Léon Bottou, Genevieve B Orr, and Klaus-Robert Müller. 2002. Efficient backprop. In *Neural networks: Tricks of the trade*, pages 9–50. Springer.

Bryan Li, Mohammad Sadegh Rasooli, Ajay Patel, and Chris Callison-Burch. 2023. Multilingual bidirectional unsupervised translation through multilingual finetuning and back-translation. In *Proceedings of the Sixth Workshop on Technologies for Machine Translation of Low-Resource Languages (LoResMT 2023)*, pages 16–31.

Xuebo Liu, Houtim Lai, Derek F. Wong, and Lidia S. Chao. 2020a. Norm-based curriculum learning for neural machine translation. In *Proceedings of the*

58th Annual Meeting of the Association for Computational Linguistics, pages 427–436, Online. Association for Computational Linguistics.

Xuebo Liu, Longyue Wang, Derek F. Wong, Liang Ding, Lidia S. Chao, Shuming Shi, and Zhaopeng Tu. 2021. On the copying behaviors of pre-training for neural machine translation. In *Findings of the Association for Computational Linguistics: ACL-IJCNLP 2021*, pages 4265–4275, Online. Association for Computational Linguistics.

Yinhan Liu, Jiatao Gu, Naman Goyal, Xian Li, Sergey Edunov, Marjan Ghazvininejad, Mike Lewis, and Luke Zettlemoyer. 2020b. Multilingual denoising pre-training for neural machine translation.

Yinhan Liu, Jiatao Gu, Naman Goyal, Xian Li, Sergey Edunov, Marjan Ghazvininejad, Mike Lewis, and Luke Zettlemoyer. 2020c. Multilingual denoising pre-training for neural machine translation.

Shuming Ma, Jian Yang, Haoyang Huang, Zewen Chi, Li Dong, Dongdong Zhang, Hany Hassan Awadalla, Alexandre Muzio, Akiko Eriguchi, Saksham Singhal, Xia Song, Arul Menezes, and Furu Wei. 2020. Xlm-t: Scaling up multilingual machine translation with pretrained cross-lingual transformer encoders.

Kaushal Kumar Maurya, Maunendra Sankar Desarkar, Yoshinobu Kano, and Kumari Deepshikha. 2021. Zmbart: An unsupervised cross-lingual transfer framework for language generation.

Myle Ott, Sergey Edunov, Alexei Baevski, Angela Fan, Sam Gross, Nathan Ng, David Grangier, and Michael Auli. 2019. fairseq: A fast, extensible toolkit for sequence modeling. In *Proceedings of NAACL-HLT 2019: Demonstrations*.

Kishore Papineni, Salim Roukos, Todd Ward, and Wei-Jing Zhu. 2002. Bleu: a method for automatic evaluation of machine translation. In *Proceedings of the 40th Annual Meeting of the Association for Computational Linguistics*, pages 311–318, Philadelphia, Pennsylvania, USA. Association for Computational Linguistics.

Maja Popović. 2015. chrF: character n-gram F-score for automatic MT evaluation. In *Proceedings of the Tenth Workshop on Statistical Machine Translation*, pages 392–395, Lisbon, Portugal. Association for Computational Linguistics.

Gowtham Ramesh, Sumanth Doddapaneni, Aravinth Bheemaraj, Mayank Jobanputra, Raghavan AK, Ajitesh Sharma, Sujit Sahoo, Harshita Diddee, Mahalakshmi J, Divyanshu Kakwani, Navneet Kumar, Aswin Pradeep, Srihari Nagaraj, Kumar Deepak, Vivek Raghavan, Anoop Kunchukuttan, Pratyush Kumar, and Mitesh Shantadevi Khapra. 2022. Samanantar: The largest publicly available parallel corpora collection for 11 Indic languages. *Transactions of the Association for Computational Linguistics*, 10:145–162.

Aniruddha Roy, Isha Sharma, Sudeshna Sarkar, and Pawan Goyal. 2023. Meta-ed: Cross-lingual event detection using meta-learning for indian languages. *ACM Trans. Asian Low-Resour. Lang. Inf. Process.*, 22(2).

Aniruddha Roy, Rupak Kumar Thakur, Isha Sharma, Ashim Gupta, Amrith Krishna, Sudeshna Sarkar, and Pawan Goyal. 2022. Does meta-learning help mBERT for few-shot question generation in a cross-lingual transfer setting for indic languages? In *Proceedings of the 29th International Conference on Computational Linguistics*, pages 4251–4257, Gyeongju, Republic of Korea. International Committee on Computational Linguistics.

Chenze Shao and Yang Feng. 2022. Overcoming catastrophic forgetting beyond continual learning: Balanced training for neural machine translation. In *Proceedings of the 60th Annual Meeting of the Association for Computational Linguistics (Volume 1: Long Papers)*, pages 2023–2036.

Kaitao Song, Xu Tan, Tao Qin, Jianfeng Lu, and Tie-Yan Liu. 2019. Mass: Masked sequence to sequence pre-training for language generation.

NLLB Team. 2022. No language left behind: Scaling human-centered machine translation.

Ashish Vaswani, Noam Shazeer, Niki Parmar, Jakob Uszkoreit, Llion Jones, Aidan N. Gomez, Lukasz Kaiser, and Illia Polosukhin. 2017. Attention is all you need.

Fusheng Wang, Jianhao Yan, Fandong Meng, and Jie Zhou. 2021. Selective knowledge distillation for neural machine translation. In *Proceedings of the 59th Annual Meeting of the Association for Computational Linguistics and the 11th International Joint Conference on Natural Language Processing (Volume 1: Long Papers)*, pages 6456–6466.

Wenxuan Wang, Wenxiang Jiao, Yongchang Hao, Xing Wang, Shuming Shi, Zhaopeng Tu, and Michael Lyu. 2022. Understanding and improving sequence-to-sequence pretraining for neural machine translation. In *Proceedings of the 60th Annual Meeting of the Association for Computational Linguistics (Volume 1: Long Papers)*, pages 2591–2600, Dublin, Ireland. Association for Computational Linguistics.

Rongxiang Weng, Heng Yu, Shujian Huang, Shanbo Cheng, and Weihua Luo. 2019. Acquiring knowledge from pre-trained model to neural machine translation.

Yimeng Wu, Peyman Passban, Mehdi Rezagholizade, and Qun Liu. 2020. Why skip if you can combine: A simple knowledge distillation technique for intermediate layers.

Jiacheng Yang, Mingxuan Wang, Hao Zhou, Chengqi Zhao, Yong Yu, Weinan Zhang, and Lei Li. 2022. Towards making the most of bert in neural machine translation.

Ying Zhang, Tao Xiang, Timothy M. Hospedales, and Huchuan Lu. 2018. Deep mutual learning. In *2018 IEEE/CVF Conference on Computer Vision and Pattern Recognition*, pages 4320–4328.

Chunting Zhou, Graham Neubig, and Jiatao Gu. 2021. Understanding knowledge distillation in non-autoregressive machine translation.

Jinhua Zhu, Yingce Xia, Lijun Wu, Di He, Tao Qin, Wengang Zhou, Houqiang Li, and Tie-Yan Liu. 2020. Incorporating bert into neural machine translation.

Xiatian Zhu, Shaogang Gong, et al. 2018. Knowledge distillation by on-the-fly native ensemble. *Advances in neural information processing systems*, 31.

Leveraging Mandarin as a Pivot Language for Low-Resource Machine Translation between Cantonese and English

King Yiu Suen
Fano Labs
cyrus.suen@fano.ai

Rudolf Chow
Fano Labs
rudolf@fano.ai

Albert Y.S. Lam
Fano Labs
albert@fano.ai

Abstract

Cantonese, the second most prevalent Chinese dialect after Mandarin, has been relatively overlooked in machine translation (MT) due to a scarcity of bilingual resources. In this paper, we propose to leverage Mandarin, a high-resource language, as a pivot language for translating between Cantonese and English. Our method utilizes transfer learning from pre-trained Bidirectional and Auto-Regressive Transformer (BART) models to initialize auxiliary source-pivot and pivot-target MT models. The parameters of the trained auxiliary models are then used to initialize the source-target model. Based on our experiments, our proposed method outperforms several baseline initialization strategies, naive pivot translation, and two commercial translation systems in both translation directions.

1 Introduction

Cantonese is estimated to have 86.6 million native speakers (Eberhard et al., 2024), primarily spoken in Hong Kong, Macau, Guangdong, Guangxi, and various overseas Chinese communities (Wong et al., 2017). Originating from the same language family as Mandarin, Cantonese shares numerous vocabulary and grammatical similarities with its high-resource counterpart. However, despite these resemblances, the linguistic disparities between Cantonese and Mandarin are substantial enough to render them mutually unintelligible (Snow, 2004; Matthews and Yip, 2013). Consequently, the feasibility of leveraging Mandarin resources to process Cantonese text is widely questioned (Sio and Da Costa, 2019).

Despite the popularity of Cantonese, there has been limited effort for developing a quality translation system for Cantonese. As of the time of writing, Google Translate has yet to support Cantonese. In contrast to Mandarin, parallel corpora for Cantonese are extremely scarce, presenting significant challenges in training neural machine translation (NMT) models for Cantonese.

Researchers have proposed various strategies to address low-resource NMT. A technique that has been shown to be effective is to involve a pivot language. In pivot-based translation, the source sentence is first translated into a pivot language, which is then translated to the target language (De Gispert and Marino, 2006; Wu and Wang, 2007). Despite the simplicity, this method has a few disadvantages. Namely, it requires two translation models for decoding, equivalently doubling the number of parameters as well as the latency; errors from the source-pivot translation may also propagate into the final prediction. As such, studies have been investigating how to directly train a source-target model with the help of the pivot language, such as using the encoder from the source-pivot model and the decoder from the pivot-target model to initialize the source-target model (Kim et al., 2019; Zhang et al., 2022).

The choice of the pivot language is vital to the translation quality (Paul et al., 2009, 2013). Prior research typically selected the pivot language based on the relatedness between source and pivot languages, and the availability of bilingual language resources (Paul et al., 2009, 2013). For Cantonese-English translation, Mandarin is an obvious choice, as it is closely related to Cantonese and there is an abundance of Mandarin-English parallel corpora. However, to the best of our knowledge, no prior studies have examined using Mandarin as a pivot language for translating between Cantonese and English.

In this paper, we aim to bridge the research gap by providing empirical evidence that the usage of Mandarin can improve the translation performance between Cantonese and English. In particular, we use pre-trained Cantonese, Mandarin, and English Bidirectional and Auto-Regressive Transformer (BART; Lewis et al., 2020) models to initial-

Proceedings of the The Seventh Workshop on Technologies for Machine Translation of Low-Resource Languages (LoResMT 2024), pages 74–84
August 15, 2024 ©2024 Association for Computational Linguistics

ize source-pivot and pivot-target translation models. The trained source-pivot and pivot-target translation models are then used to initialize the desired source-target translation model.

2 Background

In this section, we highlight some of the linguistic differences between Cantonese and Mandarin.

2.1 Vocabulary

While there is a considerable lexical overlap between Cantonese and Mandarin, it is estimated that approximately one-third of the vocabularies used in regular Cantonese speeches are absent in Mandarin (Snow, 2004). For example, "umbrella" is "遮" (*ze1*) in Cantonese but "雨傘" (*yǔ sǎn*) in Mandarin (Sio and Da Costa, 2019). In the cases where Cantonese and Mandarin share the same lexical items, it is almost always written with the same character (Snow, 2004). However, even the same Cantonese and Mandarin characters can be used differently (Snow, 2004). For example, "話" (*waa6*) in Cantonese is often used as a verb, meaning "to say". In Mandarin, the same character functions as a noun, meaning "speech". Moreover, there are characters that are unique to Cantonese, such as "冇" (*mou5*; to not have) and "咁" (*gam3*; so). Finally, a number of Cantonese words do not have a standardized written form (Matthews and Yip, 2013). For example, "to give" can be written as "比", "俾", "畀" or "被" in Cantonese (Bauer, 2018), which are all pronounced as "*bei2*".

2.2 Grammar

The differences in grammar between Cantonese and Mandarin are often very subtle. For example, in Cantonese, the noun representing the agent of the action must be present in indirect passive construction (Matthews and Yip, 2013), so "I was scolded" in Cantonese would be "我俾人鬧" (*ngo5 bei2 jan4 naau6*; I + by + person + scolded). In contrast, the agent can be omitted in Mandarin, so the sentence can either be "我被罵" (*wǒ bèi mà*; I + by + scolded) or "我被人罵" (*wǒ bèi rén mà*; I + by + person + scolded). Readers can refer to Snow (2004, p. 47) for more examples of grammatical differences.

2.3 Pronunciation

The pronunciation of the same character often varies between Cantonese and Mandarin. In numerous instances, the characters in Cantonese sound completely different from their Mandarin equivalents. For example, "學習" (to study) is pronounced as "*hok6 zaap6*" in Cantonese but "*xué xí*" in Mandarin, which are substantially different phonetically (Snow, 2004). Although these pronunciation differences are a primary reason why the two languages are not mutually intelligible when spoken, they typically do not impact the written form of the languages, making this issue irrelevant for translation.

2.4 Writing System

There are two written forms of Chinese: traditional and simplified Simplified Chinese, as it name suggests, is a simplified version of traditional Chinese. Simplified characters requires fewer strokes than their traditional counterparts. Cantonese and Mandarin do not inherently dictate which character set is used. Both spoken forms of Chinese can be written in traditional and simplified Chinese characters, although regional preferences exist. Traditional characters are predominantly used in Hong Kong, Macau and Taiwan, while Mainland China, Malaysia and Singapore favor simplified characters.

In our experiments, all simplified characters are converted to traditional characters using OpenCC[1] for smoother transfer learning.

3 Related Work

3.1 Machine Translation for Cantonese

In this section, we review the existing literature on Cantonese MT.

For Cantonese-Mandarin MT, Mak and Lee (2021) examined the feasibility of mining semantically similar sentences from articles on the same subject in Mandarin Wikipedia and Cantonese Wikipedia. Liu (2022) conducted a comparative analysis on the translation performance of Long Short-Term Memory (LSTM) and Transformer model architectures, alongside word-based and byte-pair encoding tokenization methods. Kwok et al. (2023) fine-tuned a pre-trained Mandarin BART using a parallel corpus of 130k sentence pairs from various online resources.

The earliest attempt on Cantonese-English MT was done by Wu and Liu (1999). They developed a statistical MT system that employed a combination of example-based and rule-based methods grounded on a bilingual knowledge base. A more

[1]`https://github.com/yichen0831/opencc-python`

recent effort by Hong et al. (2024) employed back-translation to synthesize a parallel corpus containing 200k sentence pairs. No prior research has studied the use of Mandarin as a pivot language for translating Cantonese to another language.

3.2 Pivot-based Machine Translation

In this section, we review existing approaches to leverage a pivot language in low-resource MT.

The naive approach is to independently train two auxiliary MT models, one for source-pivot and one for pivot-target, decoding twice via the pivot language (De Gispert and Marino, 2006; Wu and Wang, 2007). To reduce prediction errors, one can translate the top-n pivot-language sentences into target language, and then select the highest scoring sentence among the n target-language sentences (Utiyama and Isahara, 2007; R. Costa-jussà et al., 2011). A drawback of this strategy is that the translation speed is n times slower than the naive approach.

Another possibility is to use the pivot language to generate synthetic parallel data. This can be achieved by translating pivot-language sentences in pivot-target parallel corpora into source language (Bertoldi et al., 2008), translating pivot-language sentences in source-pivot parallel corpora into target language (De Gispert and Marino, 2006), or translating pivot monolingual data into source and target languages (Currey and Heafield, 2019).

Finally, one can combine pivoting with transfer learning (Kim et al., 2019). The high-resource source-pivot and pivot-target auxiliary models are first trained independently. Subsequently, a source-target model is initialized with the encoder from the source-pivot model, and the decoder from the pivot-target model. The source-target model is then fine-tuned with source-target data.

4 Proposed Method

Our proposed method is largely based on the transfer learning approach by Kim et al. (2019). A limitation of their approach is the requirement for a large amount of source-pivot and pivot-target parallel data to train the auxiliary models. However, given the scarcity of Cantonese parallel data, it is challenging to train a robust source-pivot model entirely from scratch. To address this issue, we also transfer parameters from pre-trained BART models to the source-pivot and pivot-target models, leveraging the data efficiency of pre-trained language models. We will illustrate our method in terms of Cantonese to English translation, but as our experiments will demonstrate, the method is equally effective in the reverse direction. The core steps of our method are as follows (Figure 1):

1. Pre-train the Cantonese (Yue), Mandarin (Zh) and English (En) BART models with monolingual corpora.

2. (a) Initialize the Yue-Zh model with the encoder from Yue BART and the decoder from Zh BART. Similarly, initialize the Mandarin-English model with the encoder from Zh BART and the decoder from En BART.
   (b) Continue training the Yue-Zh model with Yue-Zh parallel corpora, and the Zh-En model with Zh-En parallel corpora.

3. (a) Initialize the Yue-En model with the encoder from the trained Yue-Zh model and the decoder from the trained Zh-En model.
   (b) Continue training the Yue-En model with Yue-En parallel corpora.

Instead of training our own BART models from scratch, we use the base version of Zh BART model released by Shao et al. (2021) and the base version of En BART model released by Lewis et al. (2020). Both models have the same Transformer architecture (6 encoder and 6 decoder layers, with 12 attention heads and a hidden size of 768). Since there is no publicly available Yue BART model, we continue the pre-training of Zh BART with additional Yue monolingual data, leveraging the shared Chinese character system between Yue and Zh. The vocabularies of Zh BART already contain Cantonese characters, but the original pre-training materials are predominately in Mandarin. Considering the linguistic differences described in Section 2, we believe that this additional pre-training is warranted. Following Lewis et al. (2020), we pre-train Yue BART with the text infilling task: for each sentence, a random number of text spans are sampled, with span lengths drawn from a Poisson distribution ($\lambda = 3$). Each span is replaced with a single `[MASK]` token. The model is trained to reconstruct the original text without knowing how many tokens are missing for each span.

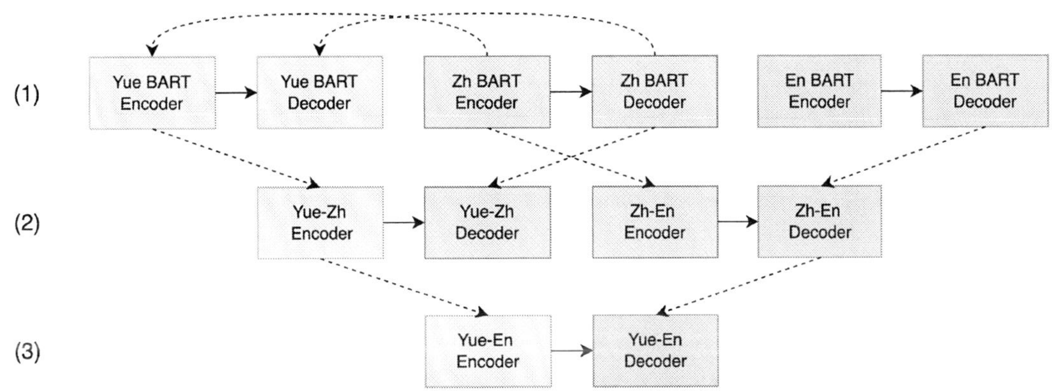

Figure 1: Our proposed pivot-based transfer learning method. Step 1 is the pre-training of BART models. Step 2 is the training of source-pivot and pivot-target models. Step 3 is the training of the source-target model. Solid lines represent translation directions. Dashed lines represent parameter initialization.

Corpus Type	Language	Size
Monolingual	Yue	10.0M
Parallel	Zh-En	17.1M
Parallel	Yue-Zh	31.0K
Parallel	Yue-En	61.7K

Table 1: Number of sentences in monolingual and parallel datasets.

5 Data

In this section, we describe the data used for pre-training and fine-tuning. Table 1 provides a summary of the sizes of the datasets.

5.1 Monolingual Datasets

Our continued pre-training data for Yue BART are composed of web-scraped data from online forums in Hong Kong. To cover a variety of domains, we scraped data from three forums: LIHKG[2], Baby Kingdom[3], and HKEPC[4]. LIHKG, often referred to as the "Reddit of Hong Kong" (Au, 2022), is a multi-category forum with topics including current affairs, gossips, sports, finance and entertainment. Baby Kingdom mainly targets local parents looking for parenting advice. HKEPC contains discussions on the latest technology and reviews on computer products. The text is split into sentences based on punctuation marks. Sentences that contains URL or have fewer than five Chinese characters are removed. This amounts to 10M sentences after pre-processing.

[2] https://lihkg.com
[3] https://baby-kingdom.com
[4] https://hkepc.com

5.2 Parallel Datasets

5.2.1 Mandarin-English

For Mandarin-English data, we use publicly available corpora: News Commentary v18.1 from WMT24 competition[5], UN Parallel Corpus v1.0 (Ziemski et al., 2016) and, WikiMatrix (Schwenk et al., 2019). For WikiMatrix, we filter sentence pairs with alignment quality below the score of 1.04, the same threshold used in Schwenk et al. (2019).

5.2.2 Cantonese-Mandarin

The sources of our Cantonese-Mandarin parallel data include story books[6], language learning websites[7,8], TED talks[9], a previous linguistic study (Wong et al., 2017)[10,11] and a dictionary[12].

5.2.3 Cantonese-English

The sources of our Cantonese-English parallel data include a language learning website[13] and two dictionaries[14,15].

[5] https://www.statmt.org/wmt24/translation-task.html
[6] https://global-asp.github.io/storybooks-hongkong
[7] https://tatoeba.org/
[8] https://www.ilc.cuhk.edu.hk/workshop/Chinese/Cantonese/OnlineTutorial/intro.aspx
[9] https://opus.nlpl.eu/TED2020/zh&zh-tw/v1/TED2020
[10] https://github.com/UniversalDependencies/UD_Cantonese-HK
[11] https://github.com/UniversalDependencies/UD_Chinese-HK
[12] https://kaifangcidian.com/han/yue/
[13] https://opus.nlpl.eu/Tatoeba/yue&en/v2023-04-12/Tatoeba
[14] https://wenlin.com/
[15] https://words.hk/

6 Experiment

In this section, we outline the baselines chosen for comparison. These baselines are selected to address the following research questions:

1. Can continued pre-training on Cantonese monolingual data improve translation performance?
2. Does transfer learning from source-pivot and pivot-target auxiliary models yield better translation performance than transfer learning from BART models?
3. Can direct training of a source-target model mitigate the issue of error propagation associated with naive pivot translation?

Our baselines include different initialization strategies for the Yue-En model. In particular, we choose to initialize the Yue-En encoder using the encoder from one of the followings: Zh BART, Yue BART or Yue-Zh model, and the Yue-En decoder using the decoder from one of the followings: En BART or Zh-En model. These encoder and decoder initialization strategies are fully crossed, resulting in six conditions. Additionally, we include a baseline where all parameters in the Yue-En model are initialized randomly from $N(0, 0.02)$, following the configuration used by Lewis et al. (2020). Moreover, we include pivot translation as a baseline, where source sentences are decoded twice: first through the Yue-Zh model, and then through the Zh-En model. The encoders and decoders are Yue-Zh and Zh-En models are initialized from pre-trained BART models, and are trained on Yue-Zh and Zh-En parallel data respectively. Finally, we compared our proposed method to two existing translation platforms that support translation between Cantonese and English: Azure AI Translator[16] and Baidu Fanyi[17].

To examine whether the same approach would work for translation from English into Cantonese, we also repeat the experiments for English to Cantonese, using Mandarin as a pivot. The translation directions in the auxiliary models are adjusted accordingly.

For all training and inference, we use one NVIDIA GeForce RTX 3090 GPU with a batch of 64. We use the AdamW optimizer (Loshchilov and Hutter, 2019) with a constant learning rate of 3e-5. To speed up training, the models are trained in half (16-bit) precision. We use a maximum of 500K training steps for pre-training Yue BART, and 10 training epochs for fine-tuning source-pivot, pivot-target and source-target models. We randomly select 5% of the parallel corpora as validation sets. The final models are selected based on validation loss. For the source-target model, we additionally select 10% of the parallel corpora to use as the test set. For decoding, we use beam-search with a beam size of 4. The translation performance is measured by the BLEU score (Papineni et al., 2002).

Encoder	Decoder	BLEU
Random	Random	6.03
Zh BART	En BART	15.10
Zh BART	Zh-En	16.94
Yue BART	En BART	17.25
Yue BART	Zh-En	19.33
Yue-Zh	En BART	17.12
Yue-Zh	Zh-En	**19.64**
Pivot Translation		10.12
Azure AI Translator		17.50
Baidu Fanyi		17.21

Table 2: Experiment results for Yue-En translation.

7 Results

In this section, we present the BLEU score of our experiments. Examples of translation results are analyzed in Appendix A. For each example, our model's translation is compared to that from Azure AI Translator and Baidu Fanyi.

7.1 Cantonese to English

Table 2 presents the results of our experiment for Yue-En translation. Random initialization yielded the poorest translation performance, with a BLEU score of just 6.03. This outcome is expected, given that the model is trained on a low-resource parallel corpus. Pivot translation resulted in the second lowest BLEU score of 10.12, likely due to translation error propagation from the Yue-Zh phase to the Zh-En phase.

Initializing the Yue-En model with BART models significantly enhanced translation performance. Specifically, the Zh BART encoder + En BART decoder combination achieved a BLEU score of 15.10. Replacing the Zh BART encoder with the

[16] https://azure.microsoft.com/en-us/products/ai-services/ai-translator

[17] https://fanyi.baidu.com/

Encoder	Decoder	BLEU
Random	Random	13.43
En BART	Zh BART	24.56
En-Zh	Zh BART	27.22
En BART	Yue BART	24.68
En-Zh	Yue BART	27.82
En BART	Zh-Yue	25.01
En-Zh	Zh-Yue	**28.22**
Pivot Translation		15.63
Azure AI Translator		15.70
Baidu Fanyi		17.91

Table 3: Experiment results for En-Yue translation.

Yue BART encoder further improved the BLEU score to 17.25, likely because the Yue BART encoder can more accurately encode Cantonese sentences compared to the Zh BART encoder. This result supports our hypothesis that reusing Mandarin resources without additional pre-training is suboptimal for Cantonese processing.

A similar pattern can be observed when comparing Zh BART encoder + Zh-En decoder (16.94) and Yue BART encoder + Zh-En decoder (19.33). Using an encoder that can interpret Cantonese greatly improve the translation performance. The replacement of En BART decoder with Zh-En decoder also results in higher BLEU scores. This is because the Zh-En decoder, unlike En BART decoder, is trained to interpret the outputs from a Chinese encoder, allowing a smoother transfer learning.

The BLEU score for the Yue-Zh encoder + En BART decoder (17.12) is higher than that of the two baselines that use Zh BART encoder. However, it is lower than other methods except random initialization and pivot translation.

The highest BLEU score of 19.64 was obtained when both auxiliary models were used for initialization (Yue-Zh encoder + Zh-En decoder). The score is very close to that of Yue BART encoder + Zh-En decoder (19.33), likely because the encoders from Yue BART and Yue-Zh share a similar latent space, but the Yue BART encoder is not as finely tuned as the Yue-Zh encoder to generate latent representations interpretable by the Zh-En decoder.

7.2 English to Cantonese

Table 3 presents the results of our experiment for En-Yue translation. Random initialization and pivot translation resulted in the lowest BLEU scores, at 13.43 and 15.63, respectively. Surprisingly, the two commercial translation systems, Azure AI Translator and Baidu Fanyi, performed only marginally better, achieving BLEU scores of 15.70 and 17.91 respectively. All other baselines exhibited significantly higher BLEU scores.

Moreover, models with En-Zh encoder have higher BLEU scores than their counterparts with En BART. Among the models utilizing the En-Zh encoder, the one employing the Zh-Yue decoder achieved the highest BLEU score of 28.22. This once again shows that pivot-based transfer learning can a provide improvement in performance.

8 Conclusion

In this paper, we experiment pivot-based transfer learning as a way to improve the quality of low-resource Cantonese-English translation. Our approach involves transferring the parameters of pre-trained Yue, Zh, and En BART models to auxiliary source-pivot and pivot-target NMT models. These auxiliary models are then fine-tuned with parallel data. Finally, the parameters of the source-pivot encoder and pivot-target decoder are transferred to the desired source-target model. Our results demonstrate significant improvements over randomly initialized models, demonstrating the benefit of transfer learning. Moreover, transferring from models that are trained for related tasks (MT in auxiliary models versus text infilling in BARTs) and languages (Cantonese versus Mandarin) can further enhance the translation performance. Additionally, by training a single source-target model, we reduce the problem of error propagation in naive pivot translation. Finally, our model also outperforms two existing commercial translation systems, Baidu Fanyi and Azure AI Translator. Examples of translation results reveal that our model is better than both understanding and generating Cantonese idioms.

Future work can explore the potential of using Mandarin to generate synthetic Yue-En parallel data by, for example, translating Mandarin sentences in Zh-En parallel data into Cantonese.

Limitations

A limitation of our method is that in order to allow a smooth transfer learning, there should be sufficient monolingual data for the low-resource language to train the initial BART model. Besides, the pivot language should be similar to the low-resource language, so that the auxiliary translation model between the low-resource language and the pivot language can be trained even with limited data. Finally, the pivot language must be a high-resource language that has a large amount of parallel data with the target language. This is necessary to train the auxiliary translation model between the pivot language and the target language. Our method may not generalize well to other low-resource languages if they do not meet these conditions.

References

Yung Au. 2022. Protest, pandemic, & platformisation in hong kong: Towards cities of alternatives. *Digital Geography and Society*, 3:100043.

Robert S Bauer. 2018. Cantonese as written language in hong kong. *Global Chinese*, 4(1):103–142.

Nicola Bertoldi, Madalina Barbaiani, Marcello Federico, and Roldano Cattoni. 2008. Phrase-based statistical machine translation with pivot languages. In *Proceedings of the 5th International Workshop on Spoken Language Translation: Papers*, pages 143–149, Waikiki, Hawaii.

Anna Currey and Kenneth Heafield. 2019. Zero-resource neural machine translation with monolingual pivot data. In *Proceedings of the 3rd Workshop on Neural Generation and Translation*, pages 99–107, Hong Kong. Association for Computational Linguistics.

Adrià De Gispert and Jose B Marino. 2006. Catalan-english statistical machine translation without parallel corpus: bridging through spanish. In *Proceedings of 5th International Conference on Language Resources and Evaluation (LREC)*, pages 65–68.

David M. Eberhard, Gary F. Simons, and Charles D. Fennig. 2024. *Ethnologue: Languages of the World*, 27 edition. SIL International, Dallas, Texas.

Kung Yin Hong, Lifeng Han, Riza Batista-Navarro, and Goran Nenadic. 2024. Cantonmt: Cantonese to english nmt platform with fine-tuned models using synthetic back-translation data. *arXiv preprint arXiv:2403.11346*.

Yunsu Kim, Petre Petrov, Pavel Petrushkov, Shahram Khadivi, and Hermann Ney. 2019. Pivot-based transfer learning for neural machine translation between non-English languages. In *Proceedings of the 2019 Conference on Empirical Methods in Natural Language Processing and the 9th International Joint Conference on Natural Language Processing (EMNLP-IJCNLP)*, pages 866–876, Hong Kong, China. Association for Computational Linguistics.

Raptor Yick-Kan Kwok, Siu-Kei Au Yeung, Zongxi Li, and Kevin Hung. 2023. Cantonese to written chinese translation via huggingface translation pipeline. In *Proceedings of the 2023 7th International Conference on Natural Language Processing and Information Retrieval*, pages 77–84.

Mike Lewis, Yinhan Liu, Naman Goyal, Marjan Ghazvininejad, Abdelrahman Mohamed, Omer Levy, Veselin Stoyanov, and Luke Zettlemoyer. 2020. BART: Denoising sequence-to-sequence pre-training for natural language generation, translation, and comprehension. In *Proceedings of the 58th Annual Meeting of the Association for Computational Linguistics*, pages 7871–7880, Online. Association for Computational Linguistics.

Evelyn Kai-Yan Liu. 2022. Low-resource neural machine translation: A case study of cantonese. In *Proceedings of the Ninth Workshop on NLP for Similar Languages, Varieties and Dialects*, pages 28–40.

Ilya Loshchilov and Frank Hutter. 2019. Decoupled weight decay regularization. In *International Conference on Learning Representations*.

Hei Yi Mak and Tan Lee. 2021. Low-resource nmt: A case study on the written and spoken languages in hong kong. In *Proceedings of the 2021 5th International Conference on Natural Language Processing and Information Retrieval*, pages 81–87.

Stephen Matthews and Virginia Yip. 2013. *Cantonese: A comprehensive grammar*. Routledge.

Kishore Papineni, Salim Roukos, Todd Ward, and Wei-Jing Zhu. 2002. Bleu: a method for automatic evaluation of machine translation. In *Proceedings of the 40th Annual Meeting of the Association for Computational Linguistics*, pages 311–318, Philadelphia, Pennsylvania, USA. Association for Computational Linguistics.

Michael Paul, Andrew Finch, and Eiichrio Sumita. 2013. How to choose the best pivot language for automatic translation of low-resource languages. *ACM Transactions on Asian Language Information Processing (TALIP)*, 12(4):1–17.

Michael Paul, Hirofumi Yamamoto, Eiichiro Sumita, and Satoshi Nakamura. 2009. On the importance of pivot language selection for statistical machine translation. In *Proceedings of Human Language Technologies: The 2009 Annual Conference of the North American Chapter of the Association for Computational Linguistics, Companion Volume: Short Papers*, pages 221–224, Boulder, Colorado. Association for Computational Linguistics.

Marta R. Costa-jussà, Carlos Henríquez, and Rafael E. Banchs. 2011. Enhancing scarce-resource language translation through pivot combinations. In *Proceedings of 5th International Joint Conference on Natural Language Processing*, pages 1361–1365, Chiang Mai, Thailand. Asian Federation of Natural Language Processing.

Holger Schwenk, Vishrav Chaudhary, Shuo Sun, Hongyu Gong, and Francisco Guzmán. 2019. Wikimatrix: Mining 135m parallel sentences in 1620 language pairs from wikipedia. *arXiv preprint arXiv:1907.05791*.

Yunfan Shao, Zhichao Geng, Yitao Liu, Junqi Dai, Fei Yang, Li Zhe, Hujun Bao, and Xipeng Qiu. 2021. Cpt: A pre-trained unbalanced transformer for both chinese language understanding and generation. *arXiv preprint arXiv:2109.05729*.

Joanna Ut-Seong Sio and Luis Morgado Da Costa. 2019. Building the cantonese wordnet. In *Proceedings of the 10th Global WordNet Conference*, pages 206–215.

Don Snow. 2004. *Cantonese as written language: The growth of a written Chinese vernacular*, volume 1. Hong Kong University Press.

Masao Utiyama and Hitoshi Isahara. 2007. A comparison of pivot methods for phrase-based statistical machine translation. In *Human Language Technologies 2007: The Conference of the North American Chapter of the Association for Computational Linguistics; Proceedings of the Main Conference*, pages 484–491, Rochester, New York. Association for Computational Linguistics.

Tak-sum Wong, Kim Gerdes, Herman Leung, and John Lee. 2017. Quantitative comparative syntax on the Cantonese-Mandarin parallel dependency treebank. In *Proceedings of the Fourth International Conference on Dependency Linguistics (Depling 2017)*, pages 266–275, Pisa, Italy. Linköping University Electronic Press.

Hua Wu and Haifeng Wang. 2007. Pivot language approach for phrase-based statistical machine translation. In *Proceedings of the 45th Annual Meeting of the Association of Computational Linguistics*, pages 856–863, Prague, Czech Republic. Association for Computational Linguistics.

Yan Wu and James Liu. 1999. A Cantonese-English machine translation system PolyU-MT-99. In *Proceedings of Machine Translation Summit VII*, pages 481–486, Singapore, Singapore.

Meng Zhang, Liangyou Li, and Qun Liu. 2022. Triangular transfer: Freezing the pivot for triangular machine translation. In *Proceedings of the 60th Annual Meeting of the Association for Computational Linguistics (Volume 2: Short Papers)*, pages 644–650, Dublin, Ireland. Association for Computational Linguistics.

Michał Ziemski, Marcin Junczys-Dowmunt, and Bruno Pouliquen. 2016. The United Nations parallel corpus v1.0. In *Proceedings of the Tenth International Conference on Language Resources and Evaluation (LREC'16)*, pages 3530–3534, Portorož, Slovenia. European Language Resources Association (ELRA).

A Appendix

A.1 Cantonese to English Examples

Table 4 shows a few examples of Yue-En translation. These examples demonstrate that our model is better at understanding Cantonese idioms than existing commercial translation systems, but may potentially contain gender bias.

Example 1 The literal translation of "大佬" (*daai6 lou2*) is the eldest or elder brother, but it can also be used for addressing a person when one is annoyed. In this context, the latter translation is more appropriate. Only our model made the correct translation.

Example 2 The literal translation of "入廠" (*jap6 cong2*) is to enter a factory, but in Cantonese, it is often used to imply "to be hospitalized (for a surgery)". Once again, only our model was able to make the appropriate lexical transformation.

Example 3 "嫌三嫌四" (*jim4 saam1 jim4 sei3*) is an idiomatic expression, which means "to express discontent about something". Azure and Baidu completely failed to translate it.

Example 4 This example shows a common source of errors in the test set: mis-translation of third-person pronouns. In Cantonese, the third-person singular pronoun "佢" (*keoi5*) is gender-neutral, so it may refer to people of any gender. However, our model seems to have a masculine default. This is possibly because masculine pronouns are over-represented in the training corpus.

A.2 English to Cantonese Examples

Table 5 shows a few examples of En-Yue translation. These examples demonstrate that our model is better at generating Cantonese phrases as well.

Example 1 "Shopping mall" is "商場" ("soeng1 coeng4") in Cantonese and "購物中心" ("kau3 mat6 zung1 sam1") in Mandarin. Our model used the Cantonese phrase in its translation, while Azure and Baidu used the Mandarin counterpart, indicating that our model has a stronger understanding of Cantonese. Moreover, our model arguably produced a better translation than the reference sentence, as the counter word "個" (*go3*) in the reference sentence is unnecessary in this context.

Example 2 In this example, our model correctly used the Cantonese particle "丫" (*aa1*) to soften the force of requests, where Azure and Baidu failed to do so. It also correctly translated "please" into "唔該" (*m4 goi1*) to make the request more polite. Even though the word ordering is different from the reference, the translation is perfectly acceptable. In contrast, Azure AI Translator rendered "please" as "請" (*ceng2*), which, while not incorrect, is generally reserved for more formal contexts in Cantonese. However, our model missed the possessive pronoun, "你" (*nei5*; your), in its translation.

Example 3 The translation by our model was exactly the same as the reference sentence. Both Azure and Baidu missed the demonstrative determiner, "個" (*go3*). Azure used a Mandarin vocabulary, "寬" (*kuān*), to represent the word "wide", while the correct Cantonese translation is "闊" (*fut3*). Baidu even mis-translated "basketball court" into a nonsensical word.

Example 1	
Source	大佬！咁貴喎，梗係冇人買啦！ *daai6 lou2 gam3 gwai3 waa1 gang2 hai6 mou5 jan4 maai5 laa1*
Reference	Hey ! It costs too much! People surely won't buy it!
Our approach	Hey , it's so expensive! Of course nobody buys it!
Azure AI Translator	Big brother , it's so expensive, of course no one buys it!
Baidu Fanyi	Eldest brother ! It's so expensive, of course no one bought it!
Example 2	
Source	佢岩岩出院，又試要入廠。 *keoi5 ngaam4 ngaam4 ceot1 jyun2 jau6 si3 jiu3 jap6 cong2*
Reference	He had just left the hospital but then went back in again.
Our approach	He had just left the hospital, and went back to the hospital again.
Azure AI Translator	He had just been discharged from the hospital, and he tried to enter the factory again.
Baidu Fanyi	He has just been discharged and is going to the factory again.
Example 3	
Source	咪再嫌三嫌四啦，廉價酒店係咁架啦。 *mi1 zoi3 jim4 saam1 jim4 sei3 laa1 lim4 gaa3 zau2 dim3 hai6 gam3 gaa3 laa1*
Reference	Please stop bitching . This is what cheap hotels are like.
Our approach	Stop complaining about cheap hotels like that.
Azure AI Translator	Don't be suspicious , that's the case with budget hotels.
Baidu Fanyi	Don't be too picky about three or four anymore, cheap hotels are like this.
Example 4	
Source	佢本來做老師，最近轉行去炒股票。 *keoi5 bun2 loi4 zou6 lou5 si1 zeoi3 gan6 zyun2 hang4 heoi3 caau2 gu2 piu3*
Reference	She was a teacher originally, but she quitted and is now playing with the stock market.
Our approach	He used to be a teacher, but recently he switched to invest in stocks.
Azure AI Translator	He used to be a teacher, but recently he turned to stock speculation.
Baidu Fanyi	He was originally a teacher, but recently he switched to trading stocks.

Table 4: Yue-En translation results of sentences selected from the test set. The light gray color is used to highlight the translations of a specific phrase in the source sentence.

Example 1	
Source	There are many shopping malls in Wong Tai Sin.
Reference	黃大仙有好多個商場。 *wong4 daai6 sin1 jau5 hou2 do1 go3 soeng1 coeng4*
Our approach	黃大仙有好多商場。 *wong4 daai6 sin1 jau5 hou2 do1 soeng1 coeng4* There are many shopping malls in Wong Tai Sin.
Azure AI Translator	黃大仙有許多購物中心。 *wong4 daai6 sin1 jau5 heoi2 do1 kau3 mat6 zung1 sam1* There are many shopping malls in Wong Tai Sin.
Baidu Fanyi	黃大仙有好多購物中心。 *wong4 daai6 sin1 jau5 hou2 do1 kau3 mat6 zung1 sam1* There are many shopping malls in Wong Tai Sin.
Example 2	
Source	Lend me your book, please.
Reference	唔該借你本書俾我丫。 *m4 goi1 ze3 nei5 bun2 syu1 bei2 ngo5 aa1*
Our approach	借本書俾我丫唔該。 *ze3 bun2 syu1 bei2 ngo5 aa1 m4 goi1* Lend me a book please.
Azure AI Translator	請將你既書借畀我。 *cing2 zoeng3 nei5 gei3 syu1 ze3 bei2 ngo5* Please lend me your book.
Baidu Fanyi	唔該將你書畀我。 *m4 goi1 zoeng3 nei5 di1 syu1 bei2 ngo5* Please give your book to me.
Example 3	
Source	The basketball court is ten or so meters wide.
Reference	個籃球場有十幾米闊。 *go3 laam4 kau4 coeng4 jau5 sap6 gei2 mai5 fut3*
Our approach	個籃球場有十幾米闊。 *go3 laam4 kau4 coeng4 jau5 sap6 gei2 mai5 fut3* The basketball court is ten or so meters wide.
Azure AI Translator	籃球場大約有十米寬。 *laam4 kau4 coeng4 daai6 joek3 jau5 sap6 mai5 fun1* Basketball court is about ten meters wide.
Baidu Fanyi	扣場約莫有十米闊。 *kau3 coeng4 joek3 mok6 jau5 sap6 mai5 fut3* Buckle court is about ten meters wide.

Table 5: En-Yue translation results of sentences selected from the test set.

Enhancing Turkish Word Segmentation: A Focus on Borrowed Words and Invalid Morpheme

Soheila Behrooznia
Dept. of CS and IT
IASBS
Zanjan, Iran
s.behrooznia@iasbs.ac.ir

Ebrahim Ansari
Dept. of CS and IT
IASBS
Zanjan, Iran
ansari@iasbs.ac.ir

Zdeněk Žabokrtský
ÚFAL
Charles University
Prague, Czechia
zabokrtsky@ufal.mff.cuni.cz

Abstract

This study addresses a challenge in morphological segmentation: accurately segmenting words in languages with rich morphology. Current probabilistic methods, such as Morfessor, often produce results that lack consistency with human-segmented words. Our study adds some steps to the Morfessor segmentation process to consider invalid morphemes and borrowed words from other languages to improve morphological segmentation significantly. Comparing our idea to the results obtained from Morfessor demonstrates its efficiency, leading to more accurate morphology segmentation. This is particularly evident in the case of Turkish, highlighting the potential for further advancements in morpheme segmentation for morphologically rich languages.

1 Introduction

Morphological analysis refers to the examination of word structure. It involves breaking down words into smaller units called morphemes and studying the different morphological rules that can apply to these units (Manning, 1998; Goldsmith, 2010). These rules include inflectional morphology rules, which generate different forms of a word without altering its core meaning, and derivational morphology rules, which create new words based on existing ones by modifying their meanings (Stump, 2001). While both types of rules are important, recent studies have emphasized inflectional morphological analysis more.

Several methods for performing morphological segmentation include supervised, semi-supervised, and unsupervised approaches. Supervised techniques involve using labeled data, such as a collection of previously segmented words, to train a model to recognize similar patterns in new data. However, obtaining large enough datasets to cover all living languages can be prohibitively resource-intensive, requiring significant manual labor and expertise. As a result, many researchers instead opt for unsupervised techniques, which rely solely on raw text data gathered from diverse sources like news articles, movie subtitles, or online content (Virpioja et al., 2011).

Another common technique for morphological segmentation is rule-based approaches, which utilize manually crafted rules to identify morpheme boundaries within words (Narasimhan, 2014). Although effective when implemented correctly, creating and maintaining these rules can be costly and time-consuming, especially for less commonly spoken languages. Consequently, only some practical applications employ this method.

When applying morphological segmentation, it is crucial to consider how morphemes are positioned within language units, as this can vary widely across different languages. For instance, specific languages may place prefixes before roots, while others might use suffixes after roots. Moreover, the complexity of morphological segmentation can pose additional challenges, particularly when creating annotated data, which tends to be expensive and time-consuming. To address this issue, our proposed solution involves developing a comprehensive model capable of handling multiple languages simultaneously. Specifically, we will focus on improving morphological segmentation performance for agglutinative languages such as Finnish and Turkish (Durrant, 2013), which exhibit high levels of morphological complexity.

To accomplish this goal, our project will leverage freely available word lists and perform extensive preprocessing steps to ensure consistency and accuracy. Preprocessing will entail converting each dataset into individual lines containing single words, ensuring uniformity in letter casing and font styles, and eliminating extraneous elements such as punctuation marks, numerals, and duplicated entries. Once completed, we will apply two distinct algorithms to segment the processed data. Our pri-

Proceedings of the The Seventh Workshop on Technologies for Machine Translation of Low-Resource Languages (LoResMT 2024), pages 85–93
August 15, 2024 ©2024 Association for Computational Linguistics

mary algorithm will be Morfessor, a probabilistic model explicitly designed for morphological segmentation tasks. We anticipate that evaluating and refining the resulting segmentations through targeted modifications will yield significant improvements in overall performance.

2 Review of Literature

The supervised approach of morphological segmentation uses word information such as part-of-speech (POS) tags, morphological rules, morpheme dictionaries, etc. The unsupervised approach exploits morphemes from a raw corpus (Arabsorkhi and Shamsfard, 2006). This approach has been studied in different languages. There are some mathematical frameworks for modeling methodologies:

- Maximum Likelihood (ML)
- Probabilistic Maximum a Posteriori (MAP)
- Finite state automata (FSA)

MAP modeling is based on the Minimum Description Length (MDL) principle, which considers accuracy and model complexity. An FSA can specify the various word forms (Creutz and Lagus, 2007).

The first Turkish morphology analyzer is Oflazer's model. It is implemented using a PC-KIMMO environment (Oflazer, 1994), which is a computational approach for two-level analyzers (Antworth and McConnell, 1998) and addressing:

- Various forms of words as stated by inflections and derivations
- The dictionary's inability to store up all inflected or derived forms of a word

Külekcŷ and Özkan (2001) proposed a model for dealing with word segmentation. Despite being suggested for Turkish, this model can be used for other languages. In contrast to Oflazer's model, the united stream of characters is used in this model. As a result, to detect segmented morphemes, this model should consider the root and achievable boundaries (Külekcŷ and Özkan, 2001).

Zemberek is an open-source framework for Turkic languages using Latin script that includes language structure information and NLP operations. The standard morphological parser identifies the root and potential suffixes (Akın and Akın, 2007).

Another morphological analyzer is TRmorph, a two-level and rule-based analyzer proposed by Cöltekin (2010). It uses the Stuttgart Finite State Transducer (SFST) tools and consists of 3 major components: a finite state machine (FSA), a set of two-level rules, and a lexicon that keeps the class of root and some lexical irregularities (Cöltekin, 2010). This lexicon is hand-made to be an error-free lexicon created during implementation. Based on morpho-phonological considerations, TRmorph considers morpheme alternations. Morphophonological alternation is dependent on phonological alternation. Therefore, Turkish vowels and consonants can be dismissed, reproduced, or revised to the closest harmonic letter. For example:

- ben (I) $\rightarrow$ ben + ((y)) a $\rightarrow$ bana (for me)
- hak (right) $\rightarrow$ hak + ((n)) ı $\rightarrow$ hakkı (his right)

Spoken Turkish follows a two-level rule system for phonetics, while morphotactics is encoded as finite state machines for word categories like verbs and nouns (Oflazer, 1994). Furthermore, Turkish words have two classes in the Morphotactics part: nominal and verbal. All categories except verbs are in nominal class. Nominal morphotactic is simple. Instead, verbal morphotactics is complicated and has many exceptions. So, both morphotactics should be used simultaneously. This analyzer has been updated and uses the Foma FST compiler, a C compiler, and converts the input to the FST, and the lexicon of TRmorp is a raw text file precisely the prior version (Cöltekin, 2010).

In Turkish, adding morphemes to a word's root or stem can change it from a noun to a verb or vice versa. These morphemes can also create adverbial constructs. This language has exceptions, and Persian, Arabic, and other foreign entered words are considered one of them. The morphological analyzer, used by Şahin et al. (2013), is a two-level analyzer with over 49321 entries, arranged under 14 parts of speech. Their model uses flag diacritics. Flag diacritics' main usage goal is adding a small quantity of memory to the finite state machine during the generation and analysis steps at run-time. If we do not have this, state transitions depend only on the current state and input symbols (Şahin et al., 2013). This model is used in ITU Turkish NLP Web Service[1] consists of different elements such as Tokenizer, Normalizer, Morphology analyzer, Morphology disambiguation, et cetera. In ITU, Components are categorized under four

[1] `http://tools.nlp.itu.edu.tr`

groups: preprocessing, morphological processing, multiword expression handling, and syntactic processing (Eryiğit, 2014). In ITU, the morphological layer uses a rule-based analyzer that is proposed by Şahin et al. (2013) as well as HFST-Helsinki FST proposed by Lindén et al. (2009) and a hybrid morphological disambiguator (Eryiğit, 2014).

Besides Turkish-specified morphological analyzers, some unsupervised methods can be used for languages without exception. Morfessor is used in our project in this way.

Creutz and Lagus (2002) proposed the main idea of Morfessor in 2002, and they improved their model and named it Morfessor. Morfessor is an unsupervised generative probabilistic model for predicting morphological segmentation. The first version of it is named Morfessor Baseline (Creutz and Lagus, 2007). Then, the idea expanded and introduced other versions, such as Morfessor 1.0, Morfessor FlatCat, Allomorfessor, and Morfessor 2.0 (Creutz and Lagus, 2002; Creutz, 2003; Creutz and Lagus, 2004, 2005). However, the Baseline version is still popular as a morphological analyzer even though other versions have improved the results. Morfessor is well suited for rich morphology languages such as Finnish, Estonian, and German. It uses a corpus of unannotated text as input and produces a segmentation of words observed in the text as its output. Unlike most morphological models, Morfessor is not restricted to the count of morphemes. Morphological analyzers must be built for each language, but Morfessor is a general model for unsupervised and semi-supervised morphological segmentation (Creutz and Lagus, 2007, 2002; Creutz, 2003; Creutz and Lagus, 2004, 2005).

It has been proved that the weighted function leads to better results. Creutz and Lagus (2005) introduced a semi-supervised model based on the Morfessor Baseline. The semi-supervised approach is an excellent way for humans to prepare annotated data manually since data is expensive and complicated to obtain. An important question, however, is how many annotated words are required. Kohonen et al. have proved that 100 manually segmented words is enough and can improve output quality (Creutz and Lagus, 2005).

The algorithm processes all combinations of training data in one cycle. For each combination, it checks every possible two-part division and picks the one with the lowest cost. The cost can decrease or stay the same at each step, which means the algorithm will eventually stop working when the cost drops below a certain level. There is also a way to use this algorithm to decode messages, which involves finding the best division for a new message without changing the program's settings (Creutz and Lagus, 2005). A newer version, Morfessor 2.0, has additional features that allow it to divide messages even when it does not have all the information it needs (Kohonen et al., 2010).

The impact of the smaller size of the annotated data on the cost function is insignificant compared to the likelihood of the unannotated data. Therefore, additional weighting parameters should be included in the annotated data to avoid the adverse effects of annotations on the cost function (Creutz and Lagus, 2007).

The second feature of Morfessor 2.0 is an online and batch training mode. So, the model needs to know how much the final size of training data is, and it has access to only one word of training data at a time. Morfessor 2.0 can skip analyzed compounds and constructions randomly since the variant compounds can be found in the current text. Morfessor 2.0 produces the n-best segmentation of multiple generated segmentations for every compound via the Viterbi algorithm. This feature lets the algorithm extract the most conceivable segmentation for a compound (Smit et al., 2014).

In other studies, Vania and Lopez (2017), and Haghdoost et al. (2019) investigated the effects of different approaches to breaking down words into smaller units for language modeling purposes (Haghdoost et al., 2019, 2020).

Vania and Lopez (2017) examined ten languages with diverse structural properties and trained word-level language models while adding granular information about the constituent parts of each word throughout the training process. After comparing several segmentation techniques, they concluded that character-based models produced superior outcomes overall. Moreover, rule-based approaches tailored to each language's distinct characteristics significantly outperformed alternative partitioning strategies (Vania and Lopez, 2017).

Meanwhile, Haghdoost et al. explored the utility of Morfessor—both supervised and unsupervised variants—for generating morphological networks in Persian and Turkish. Specifically, they determined that the supervised approach was preferable for their objectives, enabling them to incorporate newly segmented words into their lexicon (Haghdoost et al., 2019). Furthermore, they employed both Morfessor versions to establish a Turkish morphological network, thereby revealing relationships among segmented words through a tree-like framework similar to manual segmentation (Haghdoost et al., 2020).

Additionally, research on 50 distinct languages revealed disparities in the difficulty levels associated with crafting language models due to fluctuations in grammatical architectures (Gerz et al., 2018). Prior work demonstrated that Morfessor mitigates morphological impacts for numerous languages, and morphologically driven partitions enhance cross-lingual language modeling (Creutz and Lagus, 2007; Park et al., 2021).

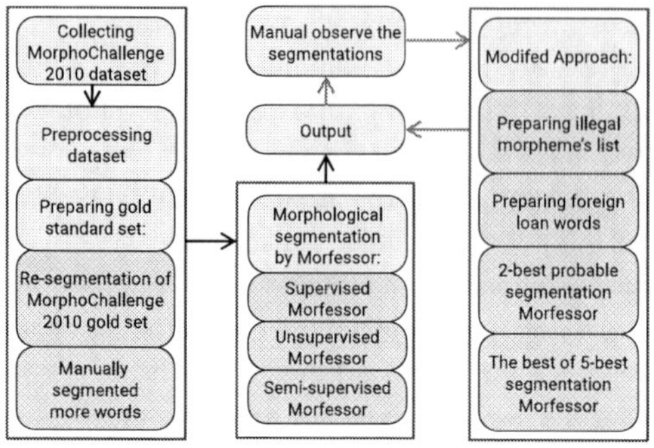

Figure 1: Our approach for Turkish morphological segmentation

3 Our Experiment

Our project aims to accurately segment morphemes using Morfessor, as natural language word lists are time-consuming and labor-intensive to create manually. We address the challenge of creating raw and segmented datasets by using the MorphoChallenge 2010 Turkish dataset[2] as input to Morfessor. Our contributions include gold-segmented words, invalid morphemes (i.e., morphemes not included in the language), and a list of entered foreign words (borrowing words from other languages). Preparing Datasets is not the only part of our work. We use them in different types of Morfessor: supervised, semi-supervised, and unsupervised. Then, we observe the behavior of Morfessor in the segmentation process and according to this, we add some steps to the segmentation process to enhance the performance of Morfessor that will be discussed completely. To put it in a nutshell, our modified process of Morfessor does not let the entered foreign words become separated. It also uses an invalid morpheme dataset to prevent their breaking down from the words. Also, we produce the second and best probable segmentation by Morfessor. All of these experiments are done with the same input dataset- are evaluated and compared with each other. Let's dive into the details in the following subsections.

3.1 Datasets

We use four datasets for our research:

1. word list file: This file contains 617,298 unique Turkish words with their frequency of occurrence. However, as we were interested in finding roots and morphemes, and all types of morphemes are essential, all words were equally treated. Doing so allows us to gain insights into the language's internal workings and better understand how meanings are constructed. Therefore, we removed the frequency of the words and numbers, punctuation marks, and other unnecessary items in the pre-processing phase.

2. Gold standard file: We used the MorphoChallenge 2010 gold standard file consisting of 1000 words, but with some changes. We reviewed this gold standard set and noticed that some words can be more re-segmented according to the language rules to create derived words for improving the accuracy of our evaluation. We also randomly selected 1000 unique words from the word list file, segmented them manually, and merged these new segmentations with the corrected gold standard file. This resulted in a dataset of 2000 segmented words without overlap between these samples, of which 20% was used for testing, and the remainder was used for training or addition to the word list file, following our semi-supervised approach.

3. Borrowed words: This dataset contains foreign words that have entered Turkish throughout history and culture. We manually gathered this dataset from websites and online Turkish texts. The foreign word dataset contains 5553 French, 1,523 Persian, 1,188 English, and 626 Arabic words that entered Turkish.

4. Invalid morphemes: This dataset contains a small number of letter combinations recognized as morphemes by Morfessor but not actual morphemes.

[2] `http://morpho.aalto.fi/events/morphochallenge2010/datasets.shtml`

3.2 Data Processing

We used the word list file as input to Morfessor in three ways: supervised, unsupervised, and semi-supervised. The output of all approaches was the first probable segmentation of data. We also produced the two most probable segmentations for each word to observe the segmentation process in the next probable segmentations.

3.3 Applying Morfessor

Experimentation with Morfessor progressed in three primary manners: supervised, semi-supervised, and unsupervised Morfessor. Each experimental setup featured varying degrees of human intervention.

- **Supervised Morfessor:** We leveraged 1,600 segmented words as a training set and reserved 400 words for testing purposes, sourcing both sets randomly from the pool of gold standard segmented words. This configuration remained consistent throughout all the approaches tested.

- **Semi-supervised Morfessor:** Under this setting, we combined 1,600 segmented words along with 8,400 unsegmented words to formulate the baseline input dataset. Employing a hybrid mix of segmented and unsegmented words enabled the algorithm to learn from a broader array of examples, thereby enhancing its adaptability towards segmentation tasks.

- **Unsupervised Morfessor:** Lastly, we presented the algorithm with a random assortment comprising 10,000 unsegmented words extracted from the word lists. Completely devoid of any prior guidance, the unsupervised version of Morfessor embarked upon discovering meaningful segmentations autonomously. It should be mentioned that the words are the same in the datasets we use in each experiment in order to have fair results.

These divergent strategies allowed us to gauge the efficacy of Morfessor across a spectrum of scenarios, ranging from heavily guided environments to entirely self-reliant conditions. Ultimately, understanding the nuances of Morfessor's performance under various circumstances shall aid us in optimizing its application for real-world problems.

3.4 Invalid Morpheme Handling

We developed a process to handle invalid morphemes in the output of Morfessor. This process aimed to prepare a list of invalid morphemes that cannot be used in Turkish and then to use this list to select the most probable segmentation for each word. The process worked as follows:

- We produced the first two most probable segmentations for each word.

- We selected the second segmentation if there were invalid morphemes in the first segmentation.

- If there were also invalid morphemes in the second segmentation, we selected the most probable candidate that did not contain any invalid morphemes.

- If no valid segmentation existed, we returned the first one.

3.5 Evaluation

During the evaluation process, we consider the segmented portions, the word boundaries, and morphemes. Ensuring precise delineation of morpheme boundaries plays a pivotal role in determining the quality of the segmentation results, alongside taking into consideration the typical morphemes encountered in both the output and gold segmentation files. We used Precision and Recall as the metrics of evaluation to compare our results. For Morpheme segmentation, segmented parts of the word must be evaluated. Additionally to segmented characters, the start and end of a word are crucial to determining a boundary and evaluating the boundary Precision and Recall. The final component of segmentation evaluation is the correct segmentation.

$$Precision = \frac{TruePositive}{TruePositive + FalsePositive}$$

$$Recall = \frac{TruePositive}{TruePositive + FalseNegative}$$

For instance, in the output word "danesh gah" and the gold set "dan esh gah" (daneshgah is a Persian word for university), we have two segmented morphemes in "danesh gah" but the gold segmentation has three segmented morphemes that one of them occurs in the output, i.e. "dan esh gah". Therefore, morpheme precision for this word is $\frac{1}{3}$. We should consider the first and end of the word for boundary precision. So in the gold set for this word, we have two spaces between three segmentations: first and end (i.e., $2+1+1$), and in output, we have one space between segmented morphemes plus the first and end of the word (i.e., $1+1+1$). Therefore, the boundary precision will be $\frac{3}{4}$. Segmentation precision is correct or not, so it will be $\frac{0}{1}$, i.e., 0.

As discussed in 3.3, we used Morfessor to segment our data. This is essential for later evaluation and comparison with Morfessor itself. The Morfessor with semi-supervised learning is effective on the given data, and we will continue to utilize this approach in the subsequent stages of our experiments.

Morfessor- Turkish	BP	MP	SP	BR	MR	SR
Supervised	0.570	0.093	0.037	0.372	0.055	0.037
Unsupervised	0.583	0.130	0.032	0.468	0.097	0.032
Semi-supervised	**0.614**	**0.134**	**0.052**	**0.485**	**0.099**	**0.052**

Table 1: Evaluation of Morfessor on Turkish input (BR: boundary recall, BP: boundary precision, MR: morpheme recall, MR: morpheme precision, SR: segmentation recall, SP: segmentation precision)

4 Results and Observations

Curious about Morfessor's inner workings, we examined Morfessor's output via visual inspection. Starting with a random selection of 200,000 words from the word list, we focused on the semi-supervised Morfessor's behavior. Segmenting 1,600 words from the gold standard file, we allocated 400 words as the evaluation test set. The random words were selected because we only wanted to observe the Morfessor in an unbiased and fair way.

Throughout the segmentation process, Morfessor adeptly identified suffixes and partitioned associated suffix groups into one or multiple components. Nonetheless, it maintained a reasonable count of word fragments. Syllabification played a vital role, enabling efficient segmentation with reduced syllable counts.

Morfessor categorized words lacking suffixes into two classes: monosyllabic and polysyllabic. Monosyllabic words remained undivided, whereas polysyllabic counterparts experienced arbitrary breakage into smaller pieces.

Segmenting words attached with suffixes, Morfessor isolated the base word and either singular or compound suffixes, subject to word length and contextual factors. Diminutive suffixes could face division or remain cohesive according to the prevailing situation. Overall, Morfessor's functional design shed light on its competence in achieving satisfactory segmentation outcomes.

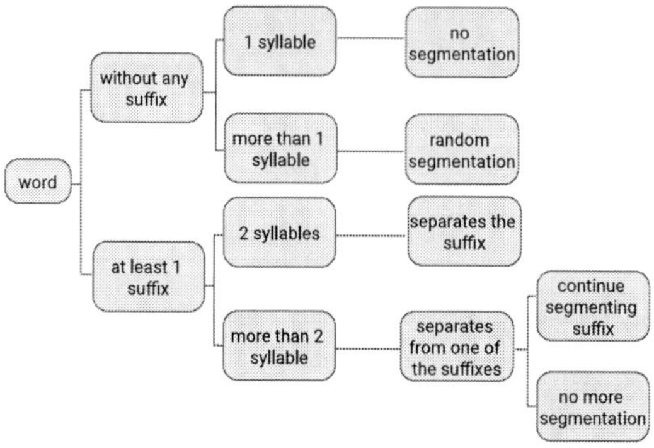

Figure 2: How Morfessor separates the words in general

As a result, the Morfessor has its logic to separate words, sometimes leading to errors. For example, the suffix "ler" indicates the plural form of the word and should be separated from the root word. However, when this suffix combines with another suffix like "ler i", Morfessor incorrectly separates the word into the root word and "leri". Alternatively, "roman", a French word that means novel, is broken down due to its last syllable "an", which is precisely similar to the "an" suffix in Turkish. Morfessor separates words more or halts them if there is more than one legal and invalid suffix in a more than two-syllable word structure. Therefore, foreign word splitting is a challenge that should be solved.

Based on our observations, we can derive additional insights:

1. Morfessor does not segment words into the smallest possible units. We, therefore, choose the second segmentation in the first concept.

2. The second concept is to select the best segmentation from Morfessor's five possible outputs. We select the segmentation that does not contain invalid suffixes.

3. The third concept is to keep foreign-borrowed words intact. We implement these concepts by randomly selecting 9000 words from the Turkish dataset and dividing the gold standard file into 400 words for the test set and 1600 for the training set. Morfessor is also trained on these 1600 words. Therefore, our input dataset contains 10600 words.

As we see in Table 1, the semi-supervised Morfessor has the best result. Therefore, we chose it as the benchmark for our further experience to examine our idea and evaluate it. The results are in Table 2.

Semi-supervised Morfessor	BP	MP	SP	BR	MR	SR
1-best segmentation	0.576	0.114	0.052	0.444	0.082	0.052
2-best segmentation	0.579	0.117	0.055	0.441	0.083	0.055
The invalid morphemes segmentation	0.579	0.118	0.052	0.440	0.084	0.052
Considering borrowed words	**0.627**	**0.158**	**0.140**	**0.531**	**0.128**	**0.140**

Table 2: Results of the most probable best segmentation and considering borrowing words in Turkish (BR: boundary recall, BP: boundary precision, MR: morpheme recall, MR: morpheme precision, SR: segmentation recall, SP: segmentation precision)

Morfessor generates the most likely segmentation as the "1-best". To better understand the impact of other possible segmentations, we choose the "2-best" segmentation. The table shows that precision improves slightly while recall decreases slightly. Another option is to select the best of the "5-best" segmentations while accounting for invalid morphemes. If an invalid morpheme is detected, Morfessor will choose the subsequent segmentation that does not contain that morpheme. If no segmentations are missing, the algorithm will return the first segmentation as the best. Because the results did not improve significantly, we tried another idea. In this case, we used the foreign borrowed words we prepared. We will check to see if Morfessor produced any borrowed words. If so, Morfessor should combine the segments, as these are prohibited morphemes.

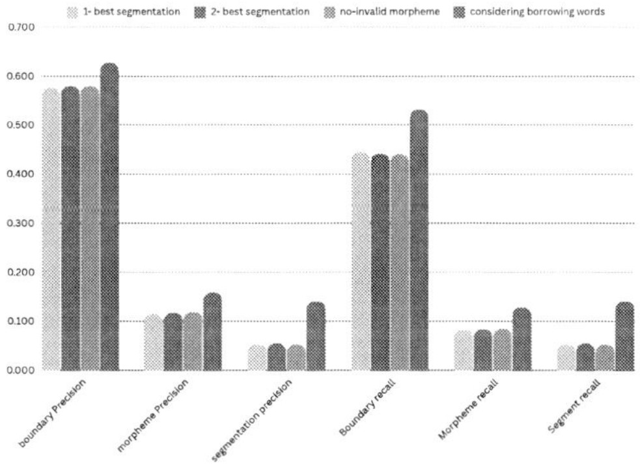

Figure 3: Illustration of the observed ideas

The graph shows that considering borrowed words significantly improved Morfessor's performance. This suggests that having a dataset of borrowed words can improve Morfessor's accuracy and obtain a more detailed segmentation list.

5 Conclusion

In this study, we decided to focus on Morfessor 2.0, a powerful probabilistic tool designed for morphological segmentation specifically tailored for the Turkish language. Our objective was clear: achieve accurate morpheme segmentation in Turkish and discover methods to improve Morfessor's overall performance. We started by utilizing the MorphoChallenge 2010 Turkish dataset, then expanded our sources by gathering extra data comprising borrowed words and even invalid morphemes.

Taking a closer look at different methodologies, our research involved three main approaches—supervised, semi-supervised, and unsupervised learning applied to Morfessor. When measuring Morfessor's effectiveness, we relied on six essential evaluation metrics: boundary recall, boundary precision, morpheme recall, morpheme precision, segmentation recall, and segmentation precision. After thorough analysis, one particular technique stood out among the rest—the semi-supervised approach demonstrated superior accuracy compared to the others.

While exploring how Morfessor functions, we noticed some remarkable abilities; primarily, it excels in recognizing suffixes and breaking them down into smaller sets. Crucially, though, it avoids excessive fragmentation during this breakdown process. Despite those strengths, however, there were still difficulties faced in segmenting foreign terms. Addressing this challenge head-on, we suggested innovative strategies to boost Morfessor's capacity to handle foreign vocabulary better. These creative solutions entailed examining alternative segmentations (second-best), discarding faulty morphemes, and incorporating borrowed phrases from various languages. Upon merging incorrect morphemes and foreign loans throughout the segmentation procedure, we witnessed notable progress in both precision and recall ratios related to Turkish. For interested readers, you can find all relevant experiments and corresponding outputs on our project's GitHub page [3].

Wrapping up our investigation, we believe our work constitutes a major leap forward in crafting a far-reaching segmentation algorithm equipped to skillfully tackle the labyrinthine nuances found in not only Turkish but also other highly inflected languages. As part of our future plans, we intend

[3] https://github.com/Soheila-Behrooznia/TurkishMorphologySegmentation

to spotlight and incorporate even more extensive catalogs of foreign terminology present in Turkish, ultimately leading to enhanced precision concerning segmented word directories.

Acknowledgements

This work has been partially supported by Charles University Research Centre program No. 24/SSH/009.

We would like to thank three anonymous reviewers for their very insightful feedback.

References

Ahmet Afsin Akın and Mehmet Dündar Akın. 2007. Zemberek, an open source nlp framework for turkic languages. *Structure*, 10(2007):1–5.

Evan Antworth and S McConnell. 1998. Pc-kimmo reference manual. *A two-level processor for morphological analysis, version*, 2(0).

Mohsen Arabsorkhi and Mehrnoush Shamsfard. 2006. Unsupervised discovery of persian morphemes. In *Demonstrations*, pages 175–178.

Cagri Cöltekin. 2010. A freely available morphological analyzer for turkish. In *LREC*, volume 2, pages 19–28.

Mathias Creutz. 2003. Unsupervised segmentation of words using prior distributions of morph length and frequency. In *Annual Meeting of the Association for Computational Linguistics*, pages 280–287. ACL.

Mathias Creutz and Krista Lagus. 2002. Unsupervised discovery of morphemes. *arXiv preprint cs/0205057*.

Mathias Creutz and Krista Lagus. 2005. Inducing the morphological lexicon of a natural language from unannotated text. In *Proceedings of the International and Interdisciplinary Conference on Adaptive Knowledge Representation and Reasoning (AKRR'05)*, volume 1, pages 51–59.

Mathias Creutz and Krista Lagus. 2007. Unsupervised models for morpheme segmentation and morphology learning. *ACM Transactions on Speech and Language Processing (TSLP)*, 4(1):1–34.

Mathias Johan Philip Creutz and Krista Hannele Lagus. 2004. Induction of a simple morphology for highly-inflecting languages. In *7th Meeting of the ACL Special Interest Group in Computational Phonology (SIGPHON)*, pages 43–51.

Philip Durrant. 2013. Formulaicity in an agglutinating language: The case of turkish. *Corpus Linguistics and Linguistic Theory*, 9(1):1–38.

Gülşen Eryiğit. 2014. Itu turkish nlp web service. In *Proceedings of the Demonstrations at the 14th Conference of the European Chapter of the Association for Computational Linguistics*, pages 1–4.

Daniela Gerz, Ivan Vulić, Edoardo Ponti, Jason Naradowsky, Roi Reichart, and Anna Korhonen. 2018. Language modeling for morphologically rich languages: Character-aware modeling for word-level prediction. *Transactions of the Association for Computational Linguistics*, 6:451–465.

John A Goldsmith. 2010. Segmentation and morphology. *The handbook of computational linguistics and natural language processing*, pages 364–393.

Hamid Haghdoost, Ebrahim Ansari, Zdenek Žabokrtský, Mahshid Nikravesh, and Mohammad Mahmoudi. 2020. Morphological networks for persian and turkish: What can be induced from morpheme segmentation? *Prague Bull. Math. Linguistics*, 115:105–128.

Hamid Haghdoost, Ebrahim Ansari, Zdeněk Žabokrtský, and Mahshid Nikravesh. 2019. Building a morphological network for persian on top of a morpheme-segmented lexicon. In *Proceedings of the Second International Workshop on Resources and Tools for Derivational Morphology*, pages 91–100.

Oskar Kohonen, Sami Virpioja, and Krista Lagus. 2010. Semi-supervised learning of concatenative morphology. In *Proceedings of the 11th Meeting of the ACL Special Interest Group on Computational Morphology and Phonology*, pages 78–86.

M Oguzhan Külekcỳ and Mehmed Özkan. 2001. Turkish word segmentation using morphological analyzer. In *Seventh European Conference on Speech Communication and Technology*.

Krister Lindén, Miikka Silfverberg, and Tommi Pirinen. 2009. Hfst tools for morphology–an efficient open-source package for construction of morphological analyzers. In *State of the Art in Computational Morphology: Workshop on Systems and Frameworks for Computational Morphology, SFCM 2009, Zurich, Switzerland, September 4, 2009. Proceedings*, pages 28–47. Springer.

Christopher D Manning. 1998. The segmentation problem in morphology learning. In *New Methods in Language Processing and Computational Natural Language Learning*.

Karthik Rajagopal Narasimhan. 2014. *Morphological segmentation: an unsupervised method and application to Keyword Spotting*. Ph.D. thesis, Massachusetts Institute of Technology.

Kemal Oflazer. 1994. Two-level description of turkish morphology. *Literary and linguistic computing*, 9(2):137–148.

Hyunji Hayley Park, Katherine J Zhang, Coleman Haley, Kenneth Steimel, Han Liu, and Lane Schwartz. 2021. Morphology matters: A multilingual language modeling analysis. *Transactions of the Association for Computational Linguistics*, 9:261–276.

Muhammet Şahin, Umut Sulubacak, and Gülşen Eryiğit. 2013. Redefinition of turkish morphology using flag diacritics. In *The 10th Symposium on Natural Language Processing*. Thammasat University.

Peter Smit, Sami Virpioja, Stig-Arne Grönroos, Mikko Kurimo, et al. 2014. Morfessor 2.0: Toolkit for statistical morphological segmentation. In *The 14th Conference of the European Chapter of the Association for Computational Linguistics (EACL), Gothenburg, Sweden, April 26-30, 2014*. Aalto University.

Gregory T Stump. 2001. *Inflectional morphology: A theory of paradigm structure*, volume 93. Cambridge University Press.

Clara Vania and Adam Lopez. 2017. From characters to words to in between: Do we capture morphology? *arXiv preprint arXiv:1704.08352*.

Sami Virpioja, Ville T Turunen, Sebastian Spiegler, Oskar Kohonen, and Mikko Kurimo. 2011. Empirical comparison of evaluation methods for unsupervised learning of morphology. *Traitement Automatique des Langues*, 52(2):45–90.

Super donors and super recipients: Studying cross-lingual transfer between high-resource and low-resource languages

Vitaly Protasov[1] **Elisei Stakovskii**[3] **Ekaterina Voloshina**[3*]
Tatiana Shavrina[3*] **Alexander Panchenko**[1,2]
[1]AIRI [2]Skoltech [3]Independent researcher
{protasov, panchenko}@airi.net {eistakovskii, voloshina.e.yu, rybolos}@gmail.com

Abstract

Despite the increasing popularity of multilingualism within the NLP community, numerous languages continue to be underrepresented due to the lack of available resources. Our work addresses this gap by introducing experiments on cross-lingual transfer between 158 high-resource (HR) and 31 low-resource (LR) languages. We mainly focus on extremely LR languages, some of which are first presented in research works. Across 158 $*$ 31 HR–LR language pairs, we investigate how continued pretraining on different HR languages affects the mT5 model's performance in representing LR languages in the LM setup. Our findings surprisingly reveal that the optimal language pairs with improved performance do not necessarily align with direct linguistic motivations, with subtoken overlap playing a more crucial role. Our investigation indicates that specific languages tend to be almost universally beneficial for pretraining (*super donors*), while others benefit from pretraining with almost any language (*super recipients*). This pattern recurs in various setups and is unrelated to the linguistic similarity of HR-LR pairs. Furthermore, we perform evaluation on two downstream tasks, part-of-speech (POS) tagging and machine translation (MT), showing how HR pretraining affects LR language performance.

1 Introduction

According to the Endangered Languages Project (Belew, 2019), more than 3000 languages are at risk of extinction. In recent years, the NLP community has undoubtedly broadened its efforts and presented very ambitious projects (NLLB Team et al., 2022; Bapna et al., 2022) to incorporate more and more languages into practical use. However, even well-known multilingual transformer models (e.g., mBERT (Devlin et al., 2019), XLM-R (Conneau et al., 2020), and mT5 (Xue et al., 2021)) and cross-lingual benchmarks (XGLUE (Liang et al., 2020), XTREME (Ruder et al., 2021)) cover only about 100 of the most presented languages.

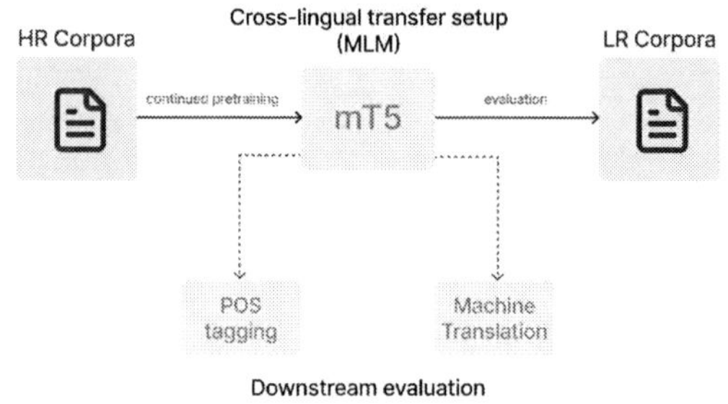

Figure 1: The workflow of cross-lingual transfer between HR and LR languages with further downstream evaluation on POS-tagging and MT tasks.

In this work, we aim to tackle this gap in underrepresentation or even the absence of experiments for LR languages, considering constraints in both labeled and unlabeled text data, as well as linguistic knowledge and experimental base. We present the study of cross-lingual transfer in the case of extremely LR languages, examining how continued pretraining on HR languages impacts model performance on LR languages in the Masked Language Modeling (MLM) setup with additional measurements of its effects on downstream performance (see Figure 1 for more details). We aim to explore whether it is possible to conduct model pretraining on HR languages and observe improvements compared to zero-shot performance when evaluating on unseen LR languages. Additionally, we measure model performance on downstream tasks: POS tagging and MT.

In more detail, we first collect a dataset with raw text data (see Appendix A.3 for the list of lan-

*Research was done while at AIRI.

Proceedings of the The Seventh Workshop on Technologies for Machine Translation of Low-Resource Languages (LoResMT 2024), pages 94–108
August 15, 2024 ©2024 Association for Computational Linguistics

guages and Section 3 for criteria of LR and HR languages). Next, we exclude some languages due to data quality issues. Thereby, we experiment with 158 HR and 31 LR languages, resulting in 4898 HR-LR language pairs for further investigation of cross-lingual transfer. Next we assess the zero-shot performance of the mT5 model on the raw data from LR languages. Afterward, we perform continued pretraining of the model with the MLM objective on data from each HR language and evaluate performance of fine-tuned models on all LR languages. Finally, we analyze the factors, such as data and linguistic features, that lead to successful cross-lingual transfer between HR and LR languages. We also measure the downstream performance of successful HR-LR language pairs in POS tagging and MT tasks for LR languages with available annotated data. We do not use data from LR languages during training and use it for evaluation only. We use the term **donor** to denote the languages that serve as sources for knowledge transfer through continued pretraining. On the other hand, we use the term **recipient** to indicate the languages used to evaluate transfer learning efficiency.

The main **contributions** of this work can be summarized as follows: (i) We collect and present the dataset with 189 languages. (ii) We conduct cross-lingual transfer experiments between 158 HR and 31 LR languages. (iii) We interpret cross-lingual transfer results across data and linguistic features. (iv) We investigate how cross-lingual transfer impacts the performance of downstream tasks, focusing mainly on the POS tagging and MT tasks. The code is available[1].

2 Related Work

The cross-lingual transfer involves leveraging existing resources available for HR languages to improve methods for LR languages. This approach can be particularly beneficial for LR languages that lack extensive linguistic resources and data for NLP applications. Wu and Dredze (2020) state that the mBERT's performance for LR languages is not on par with that for HR languages, and there is an unequal representation of languages within models. Libovický et al. (2019) show that mBERT context embeddings capture similarities between languages, but achieving a proper cross-lingual representation requires the availability of parallel corpora, which is lacking for most LR languages. Malkin et al. (2022) show that the selection of pretraining languages significantly impacts the performance, indicating that there are more effective donors than English. Additionally, Turc et al. (2021) show that Russian and German can serve as better donors for reliable transfer. Fujinuma et al. (2022) experiment with different number of languages during pretraining and find it promising in terms of impact on performance on unseen languages. There are also different suggested strategies for choosing the proper donor language. Kocmi and Bojar (2018) propose using vocabulary overlap to find a better HR donor. Lauscher et al. (2020) demonstrate that typological motivation in language selection positively impacts the transfer learning scores, as well as the size of the source language. Muller et al. (2021) show that the type of language script used plays an essential role, and transliteration helps to improve the quality of transfer learning. Eronen et al. (2023) also show that fine-tuning on linguistically similar languages (defined using WALS (Dryer and Haspelmath, 2013) improves the performance on several downstream tasks. Muller et al. (2022) investigate cross-lingual transfer using diverse data, revealing that morphology and language modeling performance are strong predictors of its success. Dolicki and Spanakis (2021); Lin et al. (2019) establish that no individual WALS feature stands out as the most crucial across various tasks.

Transfer learning has long emerged as a pivotal technique in machine translation, particularly for LR languages. Zoph et al. (2016) introduce an approach that uses HR language data to enhance neural machine translation (NMT) for LR language pairs, achieving notable improvements in their translation quality. Further exploration by Aji et al. (2020) reveal that word embeddings are a critical component of transfer learning, and their proper alignment is essential for optimal results. These findings highlight the critical role of transfer learning in addressing challenges associated with the limited availability of linguistic data in NMT.

The studies mentioned above focus on well-resourced languages with labeled data, which has resulted in neglecting LR languages that already lack available data. This study aims to address this gap by investigating cross-lingual transfer for several understudied LR languages.

[1]Code: https://github.com/Vitaly-Protasov/LR_Transfer

3 HR-LR Multilingual Corpus

We assemble from various existing sources a text corpus. Appendix A.3 lists all used languages.

3.1 Text sources

To assemble a corpus for the need of cross-lingual experiments, we use a wide range of linguistic resources in addition to commonly used corpora. We deliberately do not include projects, such as Oscar (Ortiz Suárez et al., 2019) and Cleaned Colossal Common Crawl (Raffel et al., 2020) because they are already partially represented in the training set of large language models such as XLM-R and mT5. The general corpus includes text materials from the following projects: (i) Wikipedia in every language available (CC BY-SA); (ii) Universal Dependencies project[2] (de Marneffe et al., 2021) (original texts without annotation, the license for every treebank is different, mainly GNU GPL 3.0/LGPLLR/CC BY-based); (iii) The Hamburg Center for Language Corpora (HZSK-PUB)[3] (primary linguistic research textual data, not restricted by copyright or personal data protection); (iv) The Endangered Languages Archive[4] (text content only, no multimedia, non-commercial private research or educational activity); (v) Corpora with annotated languages of CIS countries[5] (Krylova et al., 2015).

3.2 Text processing

We aggregate languages according to their official names and codes presented in a large database, The World Atlas of Language Structures (WALS[6]) (Dryer and Haspelmath, 2013). To ensure high data quality for language processing, we exclude languages with a high presence of HTML tags in the collected data, accounting for 15% of the gathered data. We assume that a large amount of code would significantly affect results, as HTML tags are easier to predict than words in natural languages.

We collect both HR and LR languages. We define a LR language based on a specific range of tokens: 10k tokens as a lower bound and 350k tokens as an upper bound (Yang et al., 2019). Thus, we categorize languages exceeding the upper bound as HR ones. Refer to Appendix A.2 for the list of all languages we collected.

[2]https://universaldependencies.org
[3]https://corpora.uni-hamburg.de/hzsk
[4]https://www.elararchive.org
[5]http://web-corpora.net
[6]https://wals.info/feature

4 Cross-lingual Transfer Methodology

The main goal of our experiments is to figure out whether the training on HR language donors improves the modeling of LR recipient languages, try to interpret it and to observe possible performance of transfer learning in downstream tasks.

4.1 Base model

In our experiments, we utilize the widely used pretrained multilingual language model mT5[7](Xue et al., 2021). It is an encoder-decoder model trained on 101 languages from the mC4 dataset. It was originally pretrained in the transfer learning procedure and has shown itself well in transferring knowledge. We think the encoder-decoder architecture is more flexible and has more possible applications for future works than only encoder or decoder-based models. Due to its multitask finetuning, we decided not to use its another version, mT0 (Muennighoff et al., 2023). Considering our lack of labeled data, exploring its multitask zero-shot performance is unnecessary here.

4.2 MLM pretrainig on donor languages

Following the original article of the mT5, we use the Masked Language Modeling (MLM) objective for the continued pretraining on HR donor languages. More specifically, in the case of mT5 model, this is a denoising task for prediction masked spans (sequential set) of tokens. Similarly to the original paper, we also utilize *early stopping*. We limit the data to perform the training for all languages under the same conditions and minimize the training time: 500k sampled sentences are chosen for continued pretraining on each HR language. We conduct this procedure 5 times to consider the variance of results based on different subsets of training data. We then average the results from the top-performing checkpoints within each training iteration. Textual data sourced from HR languages is employed during both the training and validation steps, while LR language data is utilized during the testing step only to measure the performance on unseen LR languages.

4.3 Evaluation on low-resource languages

We use the perplexity metric (Brown et al., 1992) to evaluate the MLM step. Perplexity has its limitations when evaluating language modeling performance, which may become evident in downstream

[7]https://huggingface.co/google/mt5-base

tasks. Since we deeply explore the results of cross-lingual transfer, we also plan to conduct downstream evaluation afterward to see whether the continued pretraining on HR languages impacts the downstream performance on LR languages. Here, we first measure the zero-shot model's performance in modeling all 31 LR languages. Secondly, we use the best model's checkpoints from each run after continued pretraining on different HR language and evaluate them across all LR languages.

4.4 Analysis of transfer learning results

We are also interested in exploring potential factors that affect cross-lingual transfer results, determining whether they lead to success or failure in various language pairs. Following Lin et al. (2019), we utilize linguistic and data-level features to interpret cross-lingual transfer results.

4.4.1 Data-level analysis

Regarding the data level, we calculate the subtoken overlap between languages. We measure the overlap between unique subtokens in HR-LR pairs:

$$o_{12} = \frac{S_1 \cup S_2}{S_2}, \tag{1}$$

where S_1 is the set of unique subtokens of donor (HR) languages, and S_2 is the set of unique target (LR) languages subtokens. In our experiments, we use the mT5 tokenizer. Here, we consider how the subtoken overlap between HR and LR languages relates to the model's performance in LR languages after continued pretraining in donor languages.

4.4.2 Linguistic-level analysis

We investigate language similarity by leveraging their typological characteristics. According to previous works, we consider WALS features. We deliberately avoid relying on GramBank (Skirgård et al., 2023) and `lang2vec` (Littell et al., 2017). GramBank, despite its extensive data coverage, offers features that are quite specific and narrow in scope, resulting in a heterogeneous and uninformative set for our purposes. On the other hand, `lang2vec` represents each feature from the WALS as one-hot encoding vectors, which increases the number of features. This might affect the outcomes of statistical tests due to the interdependence of many of these features. To interpret the results, we employ the Logistic regression model (Hosmer and Lemeshow, 2000) to obtain coefficients associated with input features. These coefficients serve as indicators of the strength in the relationship between input features and target variables learned during model training. This analysis enables us to assess the importance of various language features in achieving successful transfer learning results.

To mitigate biases in absolute perplexity values, we use binary targets to indicate if perplexity decreases (1) or remains unchanged (0) after continued pretraining. Each data point in our training dataset is represented as a binary vector, where every element signifies whether both languages share the same value for a specific linguistic feature (1) or not (0). Finally, we consider the regression coefficients to identify which typological characteristics should be shared between donor and target languages for successful cross-lingual transfer.

4.5 Downstream evaluation

4.5.1 POS tagging task

We consider the POS tagging task since it is one of the few tasks with annotated data available for the LR languages. Specifically, we utilize datasets from UD treebanks. However, only 6 out of the 31 LR languages have data available: *Bambara, Bhojpuri, Cantonese, Coptic, Guarani, Komi-Zyryan.*

To evaluate the cross-lingual transfer performance of different HR-LR pairs in POS tagging, we train logistic regression on top of mT5 embeddings. Our training and validation data come from a donor HR language's training and validation sets extracted from the UD corpus. Afterward, we assess the model's performance on target LR languages' test sets taken from their UD corpora.

4.5.2 Machine translation task

Additionally, we aim to experiment with another downstream task – Machine Translation (MT). Here, we use data from the NLLB project (NLLB Team et al., 2022; Bapna et al., 2022) as the only open-source dataset with MT data for extremely LR languages that we consider. This dataset contains parallel corpora for numerous language pairs, but in the case of LR languages, we see that only a few of them contain parallel HR-LR corpora, and only for two HR languages, such as English and Afrikaans, there are HR-LR datasets: 8 pairs for English and 7 pairs for Afrikaans.

While evaluating the MT setup, we aim to explore how cross-lingual transfer impacts the model's performance on different HR-LR pairs. To do this, we follow a series of steps. First, we conduct separate experiments for each HR-LR pair

LR language	LR perplexity (zero-shot)	HR language (best)	LR perplexity after training
Akan	33.07	Afrikaans	**30.04**
Atikamekw	61.72	Afrikaans	**49.77**
Bambara	51.67	Lithuanian	**38.39**
Bhojpuri	**31.27**	Hindi	113.48
Cantonese	58.27	Slovene	**53.3**
Chichewa	**13.72**	Afrikaans	43.55
Coptic	**4.72**	Afrikaans	10.21
Dagbani	**47.81**	Slovene	57.71
Greenlandic (South)	**35.55**	Afrikaans	39.68
Guaraní	3.99	French	**3.04**
Kashmiri	**26.27**	Lithuanian	34.90
Komi-Zyrian	110.02	Yazva	**66.56**
Koryak	88.66	Slovene	**53.28**
Kurmanji	**32.44**	Afrikaans	66.22
Madurese	33.61	Afrikaans	**31.81**
Nanai	72.91	Slovene	**38.38**
Quiché	165.78	Slovene	**63.78**
Romani (Lovari)	**25.1**	Afrikaans	40.43
Rundi	**21.92**	Afrikaans	33.50
Samoan	**12.52**	Lithuanian	23.88
Sesotho	**12.77**	Afrikaans	26.21
Shor	167.74	Slovene	**98.91**
Sranan	35.44	Afrikaans	**14.09**
Swati	**40.65**	Afrikaans	53.08
Tabassaran	57.19	Slovene	**50.54**
Tat (Muslim)	**70.32**	Afrikaans	82.90
Tofa	62.38	Slovene	**61.98**
Tsakhur	41.74	Slovene	**25.60**
Tsonga	**40.41**	Afrikaans	48.76
Udi	**55.01**	Afrikaans	72.88
Yukaghir (Kolyma)	104.8	Slovene	**68.45**

Table 1: Comparison of zero-shot results of the mT5 model on LR languages with the results after continued pretraining on HR languages. We highlight the best scores among language pairs.

by training the out-of-the-box model in the MT setup and evaluating its performance afterward. This allows us to measure the performance before the cross-lingual transfer. Then, we select the best-performing model checkpoints for each HR donor after continued pretraining and repeat training and evaluation on MT data using these selected checkpoints. Finally, we compare the model's performance on the MT task before and after cross-lingual transfer across various HR-LR pairs.

To ensure consistency in the obtained results, we intend to use identical test sets across all experiments with specific HR-LR pairs. This enables us to compare and analyze the impact of cross-lingual transfer on the MT results more accurately. Also, following the approach we do in Section 4.5.1, we restrict the training data to match the number of tokens available in the least-resourced language pair to ensure a fair comparison.

5 Results and Analysis

5.1 General cross-lingual transfer results

In Table 1, you can see the comparison of the zero-shot results with the best results after continued pretraining on HR donors. Across 16 out of 31 LR languages, continued pretraining resulted in diminished perplexity scores. In this context, «best» refers to the lowest perplexity score attained among all iterations of continued pretraining. We also examine the most effective HR donors. Figure 4 illustrates relative perplexity scores between zero-shot results and results after continued pretraining across the most effective HR-LR pairs (refer to Appendix A.1 and Appendix A.2 for results for all 4898 HR-LR pairs). After pretraining on *Slovene*, the model demonstrates lower perplexity for 14 LR languages. Similar results are observed for *Afrikaans*, also with 14 LR languages, *Lithuanian* with 12, and *French* with 11.

As well as Turc et al. (2021), we observe that *English* may not be the optimal language for cross-lingual transfer. In our experiments, *Afrikaans* and *Slovene* show the best performance in cross-lingual transfer for extremely low-resource languages. Thus, we consider them as «super-donors» in the scope of our experiments. There are also instances where such languages as *Guaraní* and *Coptic* exhibit universal target characteristics after pretraining on various HR languages.

5.2 Correlation with subtoken overlap

To assess how the overlap of subtokens in data affects the performance of different HR-LR language pairs, we calculate the Pearson correlation coefficient between these data features and the results of cross-lingual transfer for these pairs.

We observe a moderate correlation between subtoken overlap and Δperplexity ($r_{stat} = -0.33$, $p_{value} < 0.01$), where Δperplexity is a difference between results before and after continued pretraining. This indicates that as the degree of subtoken overlap grows, we observe a decrease in perplexity on LR languages (see Figure 2 for the distribution of different pairs in such axes).

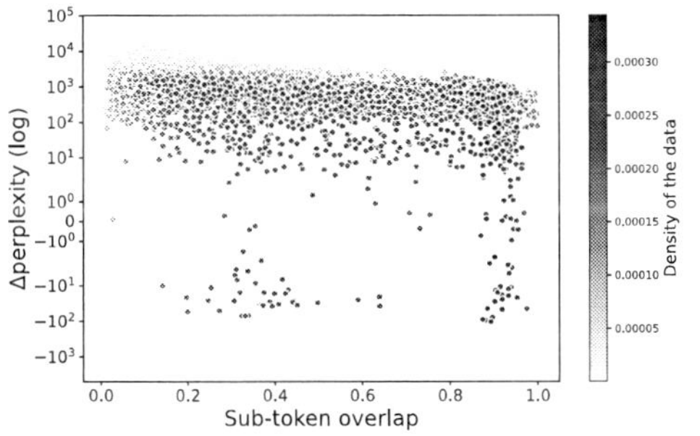

Figure 2: The correlation of subtoken overlap between HR and LR languages and Δperplexity (perplexity values are given in logarithmic scale). Darker colors show a greater density of points, where each point represents a HR-LR pair.

5.3 Interpretation using linguistic features

We also utilize linguistic features to interpret cross-lingual transfer results. To maintain the validity of our findings, we exclude features not annotated in at least half of the considered languages. Thus, we have only 21 out of 194 WALS features for analysis; 12 are specifically related to word order, and the rest to morphology. It is important to note that the absence of annotation in WALS may lead to possible gaps in our analysis. Thus, some crucial factors may be missed. We utilize these features for training the logistic regression model (see Appendix 3 for regression coefficients of 21 linguistic features we relied on).

Surprisingly, the genealogical family feature has a negative coefficient, suggesting that the model performs better when the donor and target languages are unrelated. At the same time, positive coefficients are observed for similar morphological features (e.g., *prefixing* vs. *suffixing*), indicating whether features like *Tense* or *Number* tend to be expressed with prefixes or suffixes. The word order typically does not play an important role, as only the order of *verb* and *object* appears to be significant.

5.4 Downstream evaluation results

5.4.1 POS tagging results

In this downstream evaluation, we investigate whether continued pretraining can help in POS tagging experiments. Here, for each LR language, we compare how well models trained on the best donors from the MLM setup perform against models trained in three randomly chosen languages. We want to determine if training on the best language yields better results for POS tagging than training on random ones. As described in 4.5.1, we train logistic regression using word embeddings to identify part-of-speech. If a word consists of multiple tokens, we use their average embedding. Additionally, we limit the training data to the number of tokens available in the least-resourced donor language for fair comparison. We evaluate performance using both Accuracy and F1-score metrics.

Table 2 shows the results for 6 LR languages with available data. When trained on the best HR donors, such as *Bambara, Bhojpuri, Guarani, Komi-Zyryan*, the model achieves the best performance in at least one metric. However, for *Cantonese* and *Coptic*, the best donors from MLM experiments do not result in the highest performance. In Figure 5, you can see the heatmap of POS tagging results for all considered HR languages in the case of the aforementioned 6 LR languages.

LR	HR	Setup	Accuracy	F1-score
	Arabic	random	0.266 ± 0.000	0.284 ± 0.0
	Armenian	random	0.344 ± 0.000	0.381 ± 0.000
	Dutch	random	0.159 ± 0.0	0.175 ± 0.0
Bambara	Lithuanian	best	$\mathbf{0.378} \pm 0.004$	$\mathbf{0.368} \pm 0.004$
	Arabic	random	0.364 ± 0.0	0.428 ± 0.0
	German	random	0.5 ± 0.0	0.504 ± 0.0
	Persian	random	0.648 ± 0.000	0.627 ± 0.000
Bhojpuri	Hindi	best	$\mathbf{0.705} \pm 0.000$	$\mathbf{0.722} \pm 0.000$
	Italian	random	0.165 ± 0.000	0.175 ± 0.000
	Polish	random	$\mathbf{0.468} \pm 0.000$	$\mathbf{0.447} \pm 0.000$
	Russian	random	0.411 ± 0.000	0.388 ± 0.000
Cantonese	Slovene	best	0.351 ± 0.000	0.373 ± 0.000
	Danish	random	0.052 ± 0.000	0.013 ± 0.000
	German	random	0.073 ± 0.000	0.092 ± 0.000
	Irish	random	$\mathbf{0.208} \pm 0.000$	$\mathbf{0.121} \pm 0.000$
Coptic	Afrikaans	best	0.146 ± 0.000	0.1 ± 0.000
	Faroese	random	0.208 ± 0.000	0.214 ± 0.000
	French	random	0.188 ± 0.000	$\mathbf{0.229} \pm 0.000$
	Irish	random	0.167 ± 0.000	0.167 ± 0.000
Guarani	Slovak	best	$\mathbf{0.25} \pm 0.000$	0.186 ± 0.000
	Chinese	random	0.369 ± 0.000	0.334 ± 0.000
	Estonian	random	0.519 ± 0.000	0.42 ± 0.000
Komi-Zyryan	Urdu	random	0.431 ± 0.000	0.456 ± 0.000
	Slovene	best	$\mathbf{0.581} \pm 0.000$	$\mathbf{0.536} \pm 0.001$

Table 2: The comparison shows evaluation results on POS tagging for 6 LR languages after pretraining on the most effective donors from MLM experiments, compared to 3 randomly selected HR languages. We observe that utilizing the best donors for transfer learning achieves better results in the POS tagging task compared to employing random HR languages.

5.4.2 Machine translation results

In contrast to the POS tagging, our data availability here is significantly limited. As mentioned in Section 4.5.2, we have a substantial amount of annotated data only for Afrikaans and English, total-

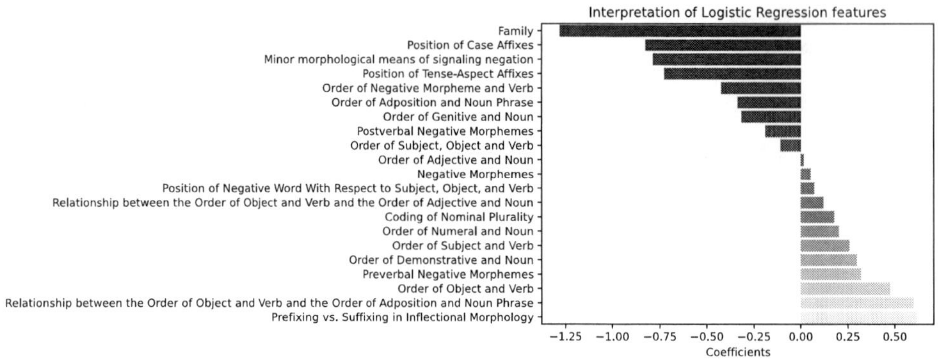

Figure 3: Coefficients of the WALS features obtained from the Logistic Regression model for the interpretation of cross-lingual transfer results.

ing 7 and 8 HR-LR pairs, respectively. Based on the general cross-lingual transfer results (Section 5.1), we observe that *Afrikaans* tends to perform better as a super-donor, while *English* does not show satisfactory results in that regard. Therefore, we decide to proceed with evaluation in Machine Translation setup using data of *Afrikaans* only. As supported by Figure 4, we limit our scope only to the top-performing HR donors.

In Figure 6, you can see the results of the MT setup where we perform fine-tuning on 7 *Afrikaans*-LR pairs. We report the comparisons using the $\Delta chrf$ metric, which indicates the difference in results with and without transfer learning on different HR languages. You can see that cross-lingual transfer significantly boosts MT performance in evaluating *Afrikaans-Sesotho*, *Afrikaans-Swati*, and *Afrikaans-Tsonga*. However, there is no improvement in the evaluation of *Afrikaans-Chichewa*. When looking at absolute values, cross-lingual transfer experiments demonstrated the most significant improvement in performance when applied to *Afrikaans-Akan* and *Afrikaans-Sesotho* pairs, with an increase of more than 0.2 in the *chrf*.

5.5 Super donors and super recipients

Surprisingly, as Figures 4,5,6 (but much more apparent from the heatmaps presented in the Appendix A.2) corresponding to the MLM, POS, and MT tasks respectively, show, a fraction of LR languages tend to be *super recipients*, benefiting unconditionally from all other HR languages. Additionally, some HR languages tend to be *super donors*, benefiting all languages unconditionally, regardless of the donor's or recipient's linguistic characteristics. Furthermore, the sets of such super donors and super recipients do not tend to generalize completely across tasks (MLM, POS, MT).

5.6 Further discussion

Our experiments demonstrate that transferring knowledge from HR languages during continued pretraining can enhance the performance of the mT5 model in the MLM setup across various LR languages. Subsequent downstream evaluation also exhibits such improvement, particularly in the case of the POS tagging and Machine Translation tasks.

The analysis of the MLM experiments reveals that most word order features have no significant impact. HR-LR language pairs from the same families correlate negatively with the results; however, this correlation shifts to positive when they share the same morphological feature as *affix*. Additionally, a higher degree of overlap between subtokens in languages tends to yield better performance in cross-lingual transfer. Meanwhile, other characteristics show no significant correlation with the results from MLM experiments. At the language level, *Afrikaans* and *Slovene* are determined as the best donor languages, and continued pretraining on them tends to better results across most LR languages examined in this study. It aligns with the findings of Turc et al. (2021), who identified a different pair of Germanic and Slavic languages, German and Russian, as the best donors. Most languages that exhibit promising results as donors belong to the Indo-European language family, specifically falling under the classification of Standard Average European (SAE) languages (Haspelmath, 2008). However, languages with the best results are peripheral members of the SAE continuum, i.e., have only some characteristics of SAE languages.

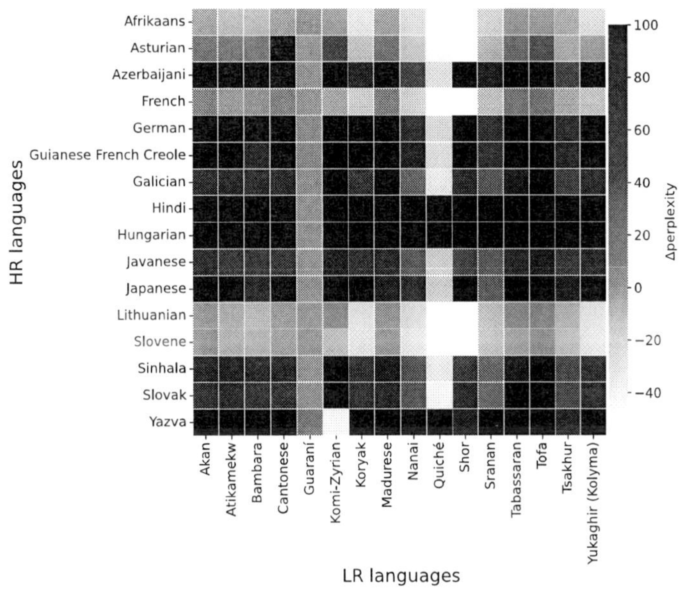

Figure 4: This heatmap illustrates the HR and LR languages where mT5 achieved lower perplexity scores than zero-shot performance. The colors represent the difference (Δperplexity) in perplexity after cross-lingual transfer by the continued pretraining on donors versus the zero-shot setup. Please refer to Appendix A.2 for detailed results of all LR and HR languages considered.

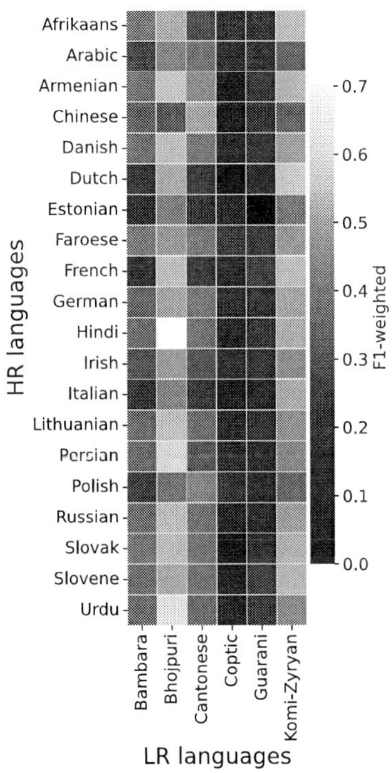

Figure 5: POS tagging results for 6 LR languages with available data in Universal Dependencies after training on HR donors from Table 2.

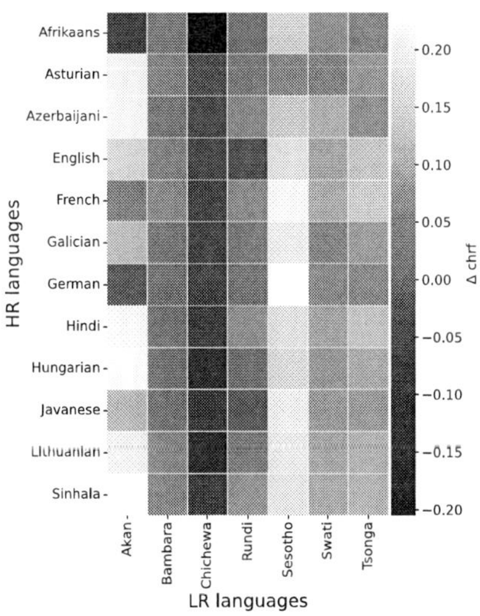

Figure 6: Machine Translation results for 7 *Afrikaans*-LR pairs. Here, we measure the difference between the model's performance with and without continued pretraining on different HR donors and report the results in the $\Delta chrf$ metric. It is important to note that fine-tuning and evaluation for MT were explicitly conducted on these 7 pairs.

In downstream evaluation, the findings from POS tagging demonstrate that employing optimal donor languages during pretraining outperforms pretraining on randomly selected languages in most cases. In Machine Translation, our investigation focuses on a particular pipeline for translation from *Afrikaans* to various LR. Consequently, we can conclude that pretraining on well-performing HR donors from the MLM step contributes to enhanced translation performance, particularly for extremely low-resource languages that we consider.

6 Conclusion

In this work, we present extensive experiments on cross-lingual transfer for HR-LR language pairs, leveraging HR languages for continued pretraining of the mT5. We observe that the performance of cross-lingual transfer significantly correlates with morphological features. Additionally, a higher degree of overlap between subtokens can contribute to better performance. Meanwhile, other characteristics do not significantly correlate with cross-lingual transfer results. We also observe improved downstream evaluation results, showing successful POS tagging and MT tasks performance. Finally, some LR languages tend to be *super recipients*, namely benefiting from all languages, and some HR languages tend to be *super donors* namely benefiting all languages with no apparent linguistic relation between donor and recipient.

References

Alham Fikri Aji, Nikolay Bogoychev, Kenneth Heafield, and Rico Sennrich. 2020. In neural machine translation, what does transfer learning transfer? In *Proceedings of the 58th Annual Meeting of the Association for Computational Linguistics*, pages 7701–7710, Online.

Ankur Bapna, Isaac Caswell, Julia Kreutzer, Orhan Firat, Daan van Esch, Aditya Siddhant, Mengmeng Niu, Pallavi Baljekar, Xavier Garcia, Wolfgang Macherey, Theresa Breiner, Vera Axelrod, Jason Riesa, Yuan Cao, Mia Xu Chen, Klaus Macherey, Maxim Krikun, Pidong Wang, Alexander Gutkin, Apurva Shah, Yanping Huang, Zhifeng Chen, Yonghui Wu, and Macduff Hughes. 2022. Building machine translation systems for the next thousand languages.

Anna Belew. 2019. The endangered languages project (elp): Collaborative infrastructure and knowledge-sharing to support indigenous and endangered languages. In *Proceedings of the Language Technologies for All (LT4All)*.

Peter F. Brown, Vincent J. Della Pietra, Robert L. Mercer, Stephen A. Della Pietra, and Jennifer C. Lai. 1992. An estimate of an upper bound for the entropy of english. *Comput. Linguist.*, 18(1):31–40.

Alexis Conneau, Kartikay Khandelwal, Naman Goyal, Vishrav Chaudhary, Guillaume Wenzek, Francisco Guzmán, Edouard Grave, Myle Ott, Luke Zettlemoyer, and Veselin Stoyanov. 2020. Unsupervised cross-lingual representation learning at scale. In *Proceedings of the 58th Annual Meeting of the Association for Computational Linguistics*, pages 8440–8451, Online. Association for Computational Linguistics.

Marie-Catherine de Marneffe, Christopher D. Manning, Joakim Nivre, and Daniel Zeman. 2021. Universal dependencies. *Comput. Linguistics*, 47(2):255–308.

Jacob Devlin, Ming-Wei Chang, Kenton Lee, and Kristina Toutanova. 2019. BERT: pre-training of deep bidirectional transformers for language understanding. In *Proceedings of the 2019 Conference of the North American Chapter of the Association for Computational Linguistics: Human Language Technologies, NAACL-HLT 2019, Minneapolis, MN, USA, June 2-7, 2019, Volume 1 (Long and Short Papers)*, pages 4171–4186. Association for Computational Linguistics.

Blazej Dolicki and Gerasimos Spanakis. 2021. Analysing the impact of linguistic features on cross-lingual transfer. *CoRR*, abs/2105.05975.

Matthew S. Dryer and Martin Haspelmath, editors. 2013. *WALS Online*. Max Planck Institute for Evolutionary Anthropology, Leipzig.

Juuso Eronen, Michal Ptaszynski, and Fumito Masui. 2023. Zero-shot cross-lingual transfer language selection using linguistic similarity. *Inf. Process. Manag.*, 60(3):103250.

Yoshinari Fujinuma, Jordan L. Boyd-Graber, and Katharina Kann. 2022. Match the script, adapt if multilingual: Analyzing the effect of multilingual pretraining on cross-lingual transferability. In *Proceedings of the 60th Annual Meeting of the Association for Computational Linguistics (Volume 1: Long Papers), ACL 2022, Dublin, Ireland, May 22-27, 2022*, pages 1500–1512. Association for Computational Linguistics.

Martin Haspelmath. 2008. 107. the european linguistic area: Standard average european. In *2. Halbband Language Typology and Language Universals 2. Teilband*, pages 1492–1510. De Gruyter Mouton.

David W. Hosmer and Stanley Lemeshow. 2000. Introduction to the logistic regression model. In *Applied Logistic Regression*.

Tom Kocmi and Ondřej Bojar. 2018. Trivial transfer learning for low-resource neural machine translation. In *Proceedings of the Third Conference on Machine Translation: Research Papers*, pages 244–252, Brussels, Belgium. Association for Computational Linguistics.

Irina Krylova, Boris Orekhov, Ekaterina Stepanova, and Lyudmila Zaydelman. 2015. Languages of russia: Using social networks to collect texts. In *Russian summer school in information retrieval*, pages 179–185. Springer.

Anne Lauscher, Vinit Ravishankar, Ivan Vulić, and Goran Glavaš. 2020. From zero to hero: On the limitations of zero-shot language transfer with multilingual Transformers. In *Proceedings of the 2020 Conference on Empirical Methods in Natural Language Processing (EMNLP)*, pages 4483–4499, Online. Association for Computational Linguistics.

Yaobo Liang, Nan Duan, Yeyun Gong, Ning Wu, Fenfei Guo, Weizhen Qi, Ming Gong, Linjun Shou, Daxin Jiang, Guihong Cao, Xiaodong Fan, Bruce Zhang, Rahul Agrawal, Edward Cui, Sining Wei, Taroon Bharti, Ying Qiao, Jiun-Hung Chen, Winnie Wu, Shuguang Liu, Fan Yang, Rangan Majumder, and Ming Zhou. 2020. XGLUE: A new benchmark dataset for cross-lingual pre-training, understanding and generation. *CoRR*, abs/2004.01401.

Jindrich Libovický, Rudolf Rosa, and Alexander Fraser. 2019. How language-neutral is multilingual bert? *CoRR*, abs/1911.03310.

Yu-Hsiang Lin, Chian-Yu Chen, Jean Lee, Zirui Li, Yuyan Zhang, Mengzhou Xia, Shruti Rijhwani, Junxian He, Zhisong Zhang, Xuezhe Ma, Antonios Anastasopoulos, Patrick Littell, and Graham Neubig. 2019. Choosing transfer languages for cross-lingual learning. In *Proceedings of the 57th Annual Meeting of the Association for Computational Linguistics*, pages 3125–3135, Florence, Italy. Association for Computational Linguistics.

Patrick Littell, David R Mortensen, Ke Lin, Katherine Kairis, Carlisle Turner, and Lori Levin. 2017. Uriel and lang2vec: Representing languages as typological, geographical, and phylogenetic vectors. In *Proceedings of the 15th Conference of the European Chapter of the Association for Computational Linguistics: Volume 2, Short Papers*, pages 8–14.

Dan Malkin, Tomasz Limisiewicz, and Gabriel Stanovsky. 2022. A balanced data approach for evaluating cross-lingual transfer: Mapping the linguistic blood bank. In *Proceedings of the 2022 Conference of the North American Chapter of the Association for Computational Linguistics: Human Language Technologies, NAACL 2022, Seattle, WA, United States, July 10-15, 2022*, pages 4903–4915. Association for Computational Linguistics.

Niklas Muennighoff, Thomas Wang, Lintang Sutawika, Adam Roberts, Stella Biderman, Teven Le Scao, M. Saiful Bari, Sheng Shen, Zheng Xin Yong, Hailey Schoelkopf, Xiangru Tang, Dragomir Radev, Alham Fikri Aji, Khalid Almubarak, Samuel Albanie, Zaid Alyafeai, Albert Webson, Edward Raff, and Colin Raffel. 2023. Crosslingual generalization through multitask finetuning. In *Proceedings of the 61st Annual Meeting of the Association for Computational Linguistics (Volume 1: Long Papers), ACL 2023, Toronto, Canada, July 9-14, 2023*, pages 15991–16111. Association for Computational Linguistics.

Benjamin Muller, Antonios Anastasopoulos, Benoît Sagot, and Djamé Seddah. 2021. When being unseen from mBERT is just the beginning: Handling new languages with multilingual language models. In *Proceedings of the 2021 Conference of the North American Chapter of the Association for Computational Linguistics: Human Language Technologies*, pages 448–462, Online. Association for Computational Linguistics.

Benjamin Muller, Deepanshu Gupta, Jean-Philippe Fauconnier, Siddharth Patwardhan, David Vandyke, and Sachin Agarwal. 2022. Languages you know influence those you learn: Impact of language characteristics on multi-lingual text-to-text transfer. In *Transfer Learning for Natural Language Processing Workshop, 03 December 2022, New Orleans, Louisiana, USA*, volume 203 of *Proceedings of Machine Learning Research*, pages 88–102. PMLR.

NLLB Team, Marta R. Costa-jussà, James Cross, Onur Çelebi, Maha Elbayad, Kenneth Heafield, Kevin Heffernan, Elahe Kalbassi, Janice Lam, Daniel Licht, Jean Maillard, Anna Sun, Skyler Wang, Guillaume Wenzek, Al Youngblood, Bapi Akula, Loic Barrault, Gabriel Mejia Gonzalez, Prangthip Hansanti, John Hoffman, Semarley Jarrett, Kaushik Ram Sadagopan, Dirk Rowe, Shannon Spruit, Chau Tran, Pierre Andrews, Necip Fazil Ayan, Shruti Bhosale, Sergey Edunov, Angela Fan, Cynthia Gao, Vedanuj Goswami, Francisco Guzmán, Philipp Koehn, Alexandre Mourachko, Christophe Ropers, Safiyyah Saleem, Holger Schwenk, and Jeff Wang. 2022. No language left behind: Scaling human-centered machine translation.

Pedro Javier Ortiz Suárez, Benoît Sagot, and Laurent Romary. 2019. Asynchronous pipelines for processing huge corpora on medium to low resource infrastructures. In *Proceedings of the Workshop on Challenges in the Management of Large Corpora (CMLC-7) 2019. Cardiff, 22nd July 2019*, pages 9 – 16, Mannheim. Leibniz-Institut für Deutsche Sprache.

Colin Raffel, Noam Shazeer, Adam Roberts, Katherine Lee, Sharan Narang, Michael Matena, Yanqi Zhou, Wei Li, and Peter J. Liu. 2020. Exploring the limits of transfer learning with a unified text-to-text transformer. *J. Mach. Learn. Res.*, 21:140:1–140:67.

Sebastian Ruder, Noah Constant, Jan A. Botha, Aditya Siddhant, Orhan Firat, Jinlan Fu, Pengfei Liu, Junjie Hu, Dan Garrette, Graham Neubig, and Melvin Johnson. 2021. XTREME-R: towards more challenging and nuanced multilingual evaluation. In *Proceedings of the 2021 Conference on Empirical Methods in Natural Language Processing, EMNLP 2021, Virtual Event / Punta Cana, Dominican Republic, 7-11 November, 2021*, pages 10215–10245. Association for Computational Linguistics.

Hedvig Skirgård, Hannah J Haynie, Damián E Blasi, Harald Hammarström, Jeremy Collins, Jay J Latarche, Jakob Lesage, Tobias Weber, Alena Witzlack-Makarevich, Sam Passmore, et al. 2023. Grambank reveals the importance of genealogical constraints on linguistic diversity and highlights the impact of language loss. *Science Advances*, 9(16):eadg6175.

Iulia Turc, Kenton Lee, Jacob Eisenstein, Ming-Wei Chang, and Kristina Toutanova. 2021. Revisiting the primacy of english in zero-shot cross-lingual transfer. *CoRR*, abs/2106.16171.

Shijie Wu and Mark Dredze. 2020. Are all languages created equal in multilingual bert? In *Proceedings of the 5th Workshop on Representation Learning for NLP, RepL4NLP@ACL 2020, Online, July 9, 2020*, pages 120–130. Association for Computational Linguistics.

Linting Xue, Noah Constant, Adam Roberts, Mihir Kale, Rami Al-Rfou, Aditya Siddhant, Aditya Barua, and Colin Raffel. 2021. mt5: A massively multilingual pre-trained text-to-text transformer. In *Proceedings of the 2021 Conference of the North American Chapter of the Association for Computational Linguistics: Human Language Technologies, NAACL-HLT 2021, Online, June 6-11, 2021*, pages 483–498. Association for Computational Linguistics.

Ze Yang, Wei Wu, Jian Yang, Can Xu, and Zhoujun Li. 2019. Low-resource response generation with template prior. In *Proceedings of the 2019 Conference on Empirical Methods in Natural Language Processing and the 9th International Joint Conference on Natural Language Processing (EMNLP-IJCNLP)*, pages 1886–1897, Hong Kong, China. Association for Computational Linguistics.

Barret Zoph, Deniz Yuret, Jonathan May, and Kevin Knight. 2016. Transfer learning for low-resource neural machine translation. In *Proceedings of the 2016 Conference on Empirical Methods in Natural Language Processing*, pages 1568–1575, Austin, Texas. Association for Computational Linguistics.

A Appendix

A.1 The most efficient high-resource languages

Table 3 lists the most effective HR languages for cross-lingual transfer with the corresponding LR languages with decreased perplexity.

A.2 Cross-lingual transfer results

Figures 7 and 8 depict the heatmaps of various LR-HR language pairs, with corresponding colors indicating perplexity scores measured in the MLM setup. These scores represent the average values across 5 runs of continued pretraining on each HR language. Here, you can see 158 high-resource and 31 low-resource languages.

A.3 Statistics of the collected corpus

As we discussed in Section 3, we gathered the corpus of textual data for 189 languages. In order to divide language by high and low resource, we first calculated some statistics for each language. In Table 4, you can see official names, number of symbols and tokens for each language. We used the tokenizer from the mT5 model for text tokenization.

HR language	LR languages with lowered perplexity
Afrikaans	Akan, Atikamekw, Bambara, Cantonese, Komi-Zyrian Koryak, Madurese, Nanai, Quiché, Shor Sranan, Tofa, Tsakhur, Yukaghir (Kolyma)
Asturian	Koryak, Nanai, Quiché, Shor, Sranan Tsakhur, Yukaghir (Kolyma)
Azerbaijani	Quiché
French	Atikamekw, Bambara, Guaraní, Komi-Zyrian, Koryak Nanai, Quiché, Shor, Sranan, Tsakhur Yukaghir (Kolyma)
German	Quiché
Guianese French Creole	Quiché
Hindi	Guaraní
Hungarian	Guaraní
Japanese	Quiché
Javanese	Quiché
Lithuanian	Atikamekw, Bambara, Cantonese, Guaraní, Koryak Madurese, Nanai, Quiché, Shor, Sranan Tsakhur, Yukaghir (Kolyma)
Sinhala	Quiché
Slovak	Quiché
Slovene	Atikamekw, Bambara, Cantonese, Komi-Zyrian, Koryak Madurese, Nanai, Quiché, Shor, Sranan Tabassaran, Tofa, Tsakhur, Yukaghir (Kolyma)
Yazva	Komi-Zyrian

Table 3: High-resource languages that were used for training the mT5-Base, which achieved a lower perplexity metric than in zero-shot performance on low-resource languages.

Name	N_tokens, kk	N_symbols, kk	Name	N_tokens, kk	N_symbols, kk
Abaza	1.33	2.35	Buriat	172.16	344.66
Acehnese	1.47	3.09	Choctaw	0.001	0.002
Arabic (Egyptian)	157.47	291.76	Cebuano	1365.37	3319.73
Afrikaans	46.5	126.33	Chamorro	0.06	0.13
Akan	0.33	0.62	Chechen	378.15	477.3
Albanian	0.002	0.005	Cherokee	0.17	0.22
Amharic	5.37	6.85	Chukchi	4.08	5.12
Arabic (Moroccan)	1.1	2.07	Chuvash	277.48	442.77
Arabic (Modern Standard)	1.83	1.83	Chichewa	0.28	0.75
Apurinã	0.002	0.0035	Cantonese	0.02	0.02
Archi	0.0012	0.0019	Coptic	0.1	0.13
Arabic (Lebanese)	0.0015	0.0026	Crimean Tatar	1.24	2.6
Armenian (Eastern)	0.12	0.26	Cornish	0.9	1.88
Armenian (Western)	0.09	0.17	Catalan	463.18	1168.29
Armenian (Iranian)	212.94	569.39	Chatino (Yaitepec)	1.21	3.05
Adyghe (Shapsugh)	3.32	5.58	Cheyenne	0.06	0.1
Altai (Southern)	2.46	4.6	Czech	336.81	819.13
Assamese	11.18	18.87	Dagbani	0.28	0.55
Asturian	117.6	304.59	Dogri	0.006	0.009
Atayal	0.71	1.35	Dhivehi	4.35	5.77
Atikamekw	0.33	0.71	Dargwa	11.64	23.4
Avar	5.73	10.82	Danish	0.52	1.46
Awadhi	0.57	1.04	Dutch	598	1675.76
Aymara (Central)	0.92	1.81	Dutch (Zeeuws)	1.43	3.12
Azerbaijani	90.5	230.74	English	7920.93	24002.62
Azari (Iranian)	39.73	74.9	Estonian	97.8	265.66
Balinese	2.04	4.87	Even	0	0.01
Bambara	0.17	0.31	Ewe	0.085	0.153
Beja	0.003	0.003	Faroese	4.17	9.4
Bengali	28.14	56.44	Finnish	243.97	715.36
Bhojpuri	0.01	0.02	Frisian (North)	2.74	5.65
Bikol	3.39	8.63	French	1541.64	4046.63
Belorussian	168.71	467.04	Frisian	0.007	0.016
Breton	21.79	43.06	Frisian (Western)	29.12	69.47
Burmese	26.12	64.79	Fuzhou	1.95	2.86
Bashkir	58.9	122.15	Gaelic (Scots)	4.52	9.25
Bislama	0.13	0.28	Gagauz	0.43	1.02
Basque	12.73	35.51	Georgian	65.7	149.49
Bugis	0.98	2.05	German	6.94	21.3
Bulgarian	147.44	367.2	Guianese French Creole	0.53	1.06

Name	N_tokens, kk	N_symbols, kk	Name	N_tokens, kk	N_symbols, kk	Name	N_tokens, kk	N_symbols, kk
Gilaki	1.33	2.38	Kinyarwanda	0.71	1.65	Samoan	0.31	0.61
Guajajara	0.0016	0.0023	Kurmanji	0.02	0.04	Sango	0.04	0.06
Galician	108.96	282.46	Karakalpak	0.71	1.55	Serbian-Croatian	375.92	828.15
Greek (Modern)	167.59	387.4	Kannada	40.49	94.87	Sindhi	9.28	15
German (Ripuarian)	1.01	2.21	Kongo	0.12	0.26	Seediq	1.14	2.28
Gorontalo	1.3	3.1	Komi-Permyak	1.82	3.19	Sesotho	0.22	0.49
Greenlandic (South)	0.15	0.36	Korean	254.45	318.2	Shan	5.09	7.59
German (Timisoara)	1761.41	5469.18	Kapampangan	1.85	4.41	Shona	1.32	3.11
Guaraní	0.03	0.02	Karachay-Balkar	4.38	9.14	Shor	0.18	0.31
Gujarati	19.35	34.67	Kurdish (Central)	16.77	29.46	Slovene	92.81	239
German (Viennese)	9.44	21.27	Karelian	0.01	0.02	Seminole	0	0
German (Zurich)	0.003	0.006	Koryak	0.25	0.43	Sinhala	18.78	37.48
Hakka	1.67	2.68	Khanty	0.0004	0.0005	Saami (Northern)	1.27	2.62
Hausa	5.58	13.62	Kumyk	1.16	2.45	Solon	1.49	2.93
Hawaiian	0.53	1.02	Komi-Zyrian	0.03	0.05	Somali	3.51	8.41
Haitian Creole	7.72	15.97	Lak	16.46	30.72	Sorbian (Upper)	3.71	7.64
Hebrew (Modern)	308.46	623.18	Lao	1.74	4.17	Spanish	1233.15	3408.23
Hindi	81.33	160.75	Latvian	54.26	135.41	Sranan	0.2	0.43
Hungarian	297.86	779.47	Luganda	1.47	3.38	Sardinian	3.39	7.95
Icelandic	23.58	55.33	Ladin	0.45	0.94	Sorbian (Lower)	0.83	1.69
Igbo	1.16	2.27	Lezgian	10.34	18.87	Santali	6.21	8.12
Ilocano	4.39	10.03	Low German	20.84	51.3	Sotho (Northern)	0.84	1.86
Indonesian	0.28	0.89	Lingala	0.53	1.06	Sundanese	12.54	31.15
Ingush	8.09	14.27	Lithuanian	78.83	199.57	Slovincian	1.2	2.14
Indonesian (Jakarta)	209.58	612.28	Liv	0.004	0.009	Slovak	91.75	224.02
Irish	0.27	0.6	Ladino	1.31	3.25	Swahili	14.32	35.39
Irish (Munster)	15.82	34.2	Luxemburgeois	17.24	41.58	Swedish	0.36	0.99
Italian	1018.44	2776.36	Mari (Hill)	1.71	2.91	Swati	0.14	0.34
Itelmen	0.0005	0.0008	Maithili	2.86	5.27	Swedish (Västerbotten)	882.57	2204.72
Italian (Genoa)	2.57	4.9	Maori	1.2	2.25	Tagalog	21.96	54.45
Italian (Napolitanian)	1.99	3.9	Macedonian	83.34	211.18	Tahitian	0.11	0.19
Italian (Turinese)	12.27	23.48	Madurese	0.2	0.42	Tajik	20.91	43.76
Javanese	17.44	43.98	Meithei	0.47	0.94	Tashlhiyt	0.53	0.89
Jamaican (Creole)	0.42	0.9	Mingrelian	4.43	8.19	Tabassaran	0.06	0.11
Japanese	750.08	1244.1	Marathi	17.82	36.2	Telugu	79.39	178.59
Kabardian	18.8	29.62	Minangkabau	34.7	86.25	Thai	79.96	226.41
Kashmiri	0.13	0.22	Mongol (Khamnigan)	13.48	30.69	Tigrinya	0.13	0.14
Kazakh	72.64	184.75	Malgwa	21.64	48.87	Turkmen	4.05	8.47
Kabyle	1.58	2.83	Maltese	5.37	11.79	Tamil	0.03	0.08
Kabiyé	1.84	2.39	Malay	83.7	241.85	Tibetan (Modern Literary)	34.98	41.26
Galician	108.96	282.46	Mari (Meadow)	189.06	275.65	Tat (Muslim)	0.06	0.11
Greek (Modern)	167.59	387.4	Mordvin (Moksha)	1.45	2.24	Tongan	0.36	0.65
German (Ripuarian)	1.01	2.21	Mandarin	497.71	659.72	Tofa	0.03	0.06
Gorontalo	1.3	3.1	Mansi	2.58	3.99	Tok Pisin	0.16	0.34
Greenlandic (South)	0.15	0.36	Manx	1.57	3.07	Tsakhur	0.09	0.15
German (Timisoara)	1761.41	5469.18	Mordvin (Erzya)	7.81	15.25	Tsonga	0.25	0.58
Guaraní	0.03	0.02	Mon	4.98	7.33	Tamil (Spoken)	65.88	188.99
Gujarati	19.35	34.67	Marshallese	0.002	0.003	Tswana	0.5	1.15
German (Viennese)	9.44	21.27	Mundurukú	0.002	0.002	Tetun	0.42	1.01
German (Zurich)	0.003	0.006	Malayalam	45.49	118.33	Tulu	1.14	2.15
Hakka	1.67	2.68	Mazanderani	2.73	5.08	Tupi	0.006	0.008
Hausa	5.58	13.62	Nanai	0.24	0.41	Turkish	169.37	468.8
Hawaiian	0.53	1.02	Nauruan	0.13	0.26	Tuvan	24.8	51.9
Haitian Creole	7.72	15.97	Navajo	5.67	8.52	Tatar	59.84	127.89
Hebrew (Modern)	308.46	623.18	Ndonga	0.003	0.008	Udi	0.1	0.16
Hindi	81.33	160.75	Nadroga	0.2	0.43	Udmurt	4.76	9.24
Hungarian	297.86	779.47	Nepali	13.5	27.54	Ukrainian	619.13	1523.74
Icelandic	23.58	55.33	Nias	0.36	0.77	Urdu	57.23	110.15
Igbo	1.16	2.27	Norwegian	224.43	608.76	Urubú-Kaapor	0.001	0.001
Ilocano	4.39	10.03	Narom	0.98	1.96	Uyghur	12.66	18.24
Indonesian	0.28	0.89	Neo-Aramaic (Assyrian)	0.0026	0.0021	Uzbek	45.15	104.75
Ingush	8.09	14.27	Nenets (Tundra)	0.47	0.78	Venda	0.11	0.25
Indonesian (Jakarta)	209.58	612.28	Nivkh (South Sakhalin)	0.73	1.14	Veps	2.96	6.83
Irish	0.27	0.6	Newar (Dolakha)	24.93	45.29	Vietnamese	424.35	742.98
Irish (Munster)	15.82	34.2	Oirat	7.97	14.12	Welsh	40.94	82.34
Italian	1018.44	2776.36	Ossetic	2.96	4.91	Wolof	1.3	2.54
Itelmen	0.0005	0.0008	Oriya	16.53	18.51	Warlpiri	0	0
Italian (Genoa)	2.57	4.9	Panjabi	27.68	42.51	Wu	6.67	9.11
Italian (Napolitanian)	1.99	3.9	Papiamentu	11.04	19.5	Waray-Waray	187.45	446.09
Italian (Turinese)	12.27	23.48	Pangasinan	0.63	1.29	Xhosa	0.61	1.56
Javanese	17.44	43.98	Polish	629.24	1616.18	Yi	0.001	0.001
Jamaican (Creole)	0.42	0.9	Portuguese	600.72	1550.9	Yukaghir (Kolyma)	0.026	0.044
Japanese	750.08	1244.1	Provençal	32.42	76.25	Yakut	16.84	33.18
Kabardian	18.8	29.62	Persian	298.12	601.61	Yiddish (Lithuanian)	7.43	14.58
Kashmiri	0.13	0.22	Qafar	0	0.0001	Yoruba	4.69	8.03
Kazakh	72.64	184.75	Quiché	0.02	0.04	Yup'ik (Central)	0.004	0.009
Kabyle	1.58	2.83	Romani (Lovari)	0.2	0.49	Yurt Tatar	2.28	4.04
Kabiyé	1.84	2.39	Rundi	0.14	0.31	Yukaghir (Tundra)	0	0.01
Kirghiz	27.32	65.52	Romanian	195.88	485.41	Yazva	14.23	25.9
Khakas	1.44	2.89	Romansch (Sursilvan)	5.07	12.59	Zazaki	5.46	10.8
Khmer	10.98	28.84	Russian	2372.32	6397.2	Zhuang (Northern)	0.28	0.52
Kikuyu	0.18	0.34	Rutul	0.36	0.67	Zulu	1	2.34

Table 4: All languages presented in the data we collected and used for the experiments.This table includes all collected languages with number of symbols and tokens (tokenized by mT5-Base tokenizer), where "kk" - millions.

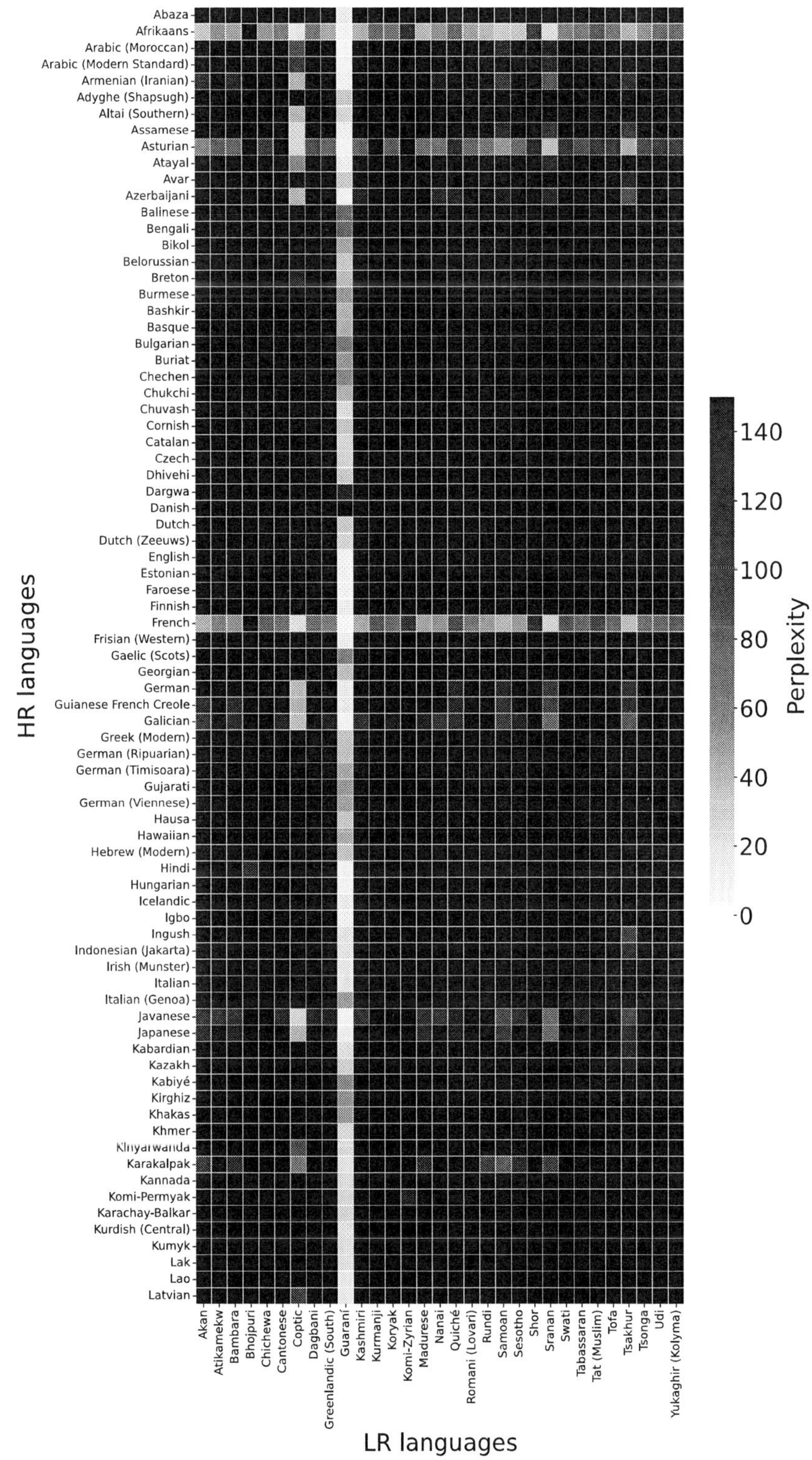

Figure 7: Heatmap for the first 79 high-resource languages with absolute perplexity scores of 31 low-resource languages.

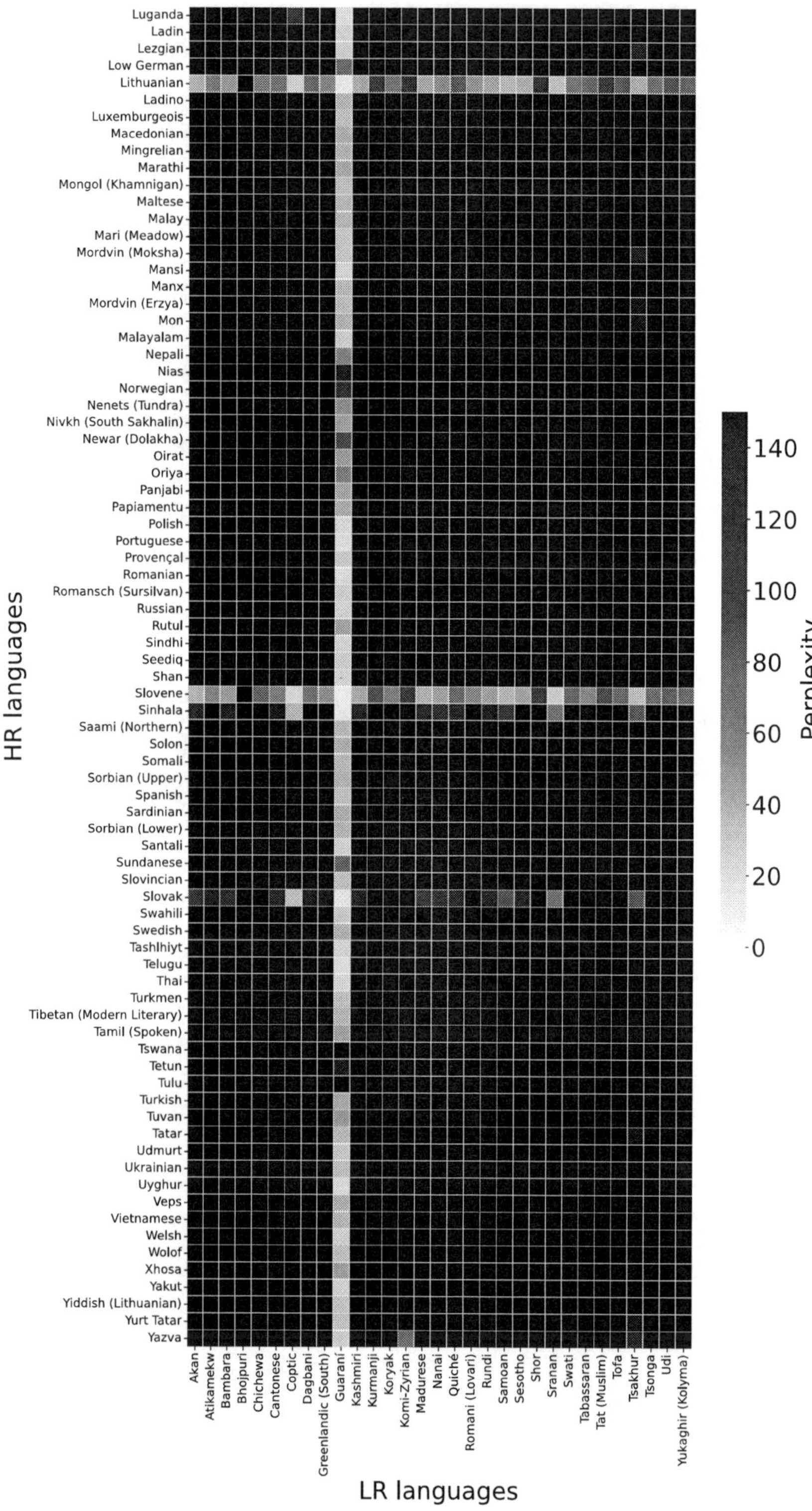

Figure 8: Heatmap for the second 79 high-resource languages with absolute perplexity scores of 31 low-resource languages.

Tokenisation in Machine Translation Does Matter: The impact of different tokenisation approaches for Maltese

Kurt Abela[1] **Kurt Micallef**[1] **Marc Tanti**[2] **Claudia Borg**[1]

[1]Department of Artificial Intelligence, University of Malta
[2]Institute of Linguistics and Language Technology, University of Malta
{kurt.abela, kurt.micallef, marc.tanti, claudia.borg}@um.edu.mt

Abstract

In Machine Translation, various tokenisers are used to segment inputs before training a model. Despite tokenisation being mostly considered a solved problem for languages such as English, it is still unclear as to how effective different tokenisers are for morphologically rich languages. This study aims to explore how different approaches to tokenising Maltese impact machine translation results on the English-Maltese language pair. We observed that the OPUS-100 dataset has tokenisation inconsistencies in Maltese. We empirically found that training models on the original OPUS-100 dataset led to the generation of sentences with these issues. We therefore release an updated version of the OPUS-100 parallel English-Maltese dataset, referred to as OPUS-100-Fix, fixing these inconsistencies in Maltese by using the MLRS tokeniser. We show that after fixing the inconsistencies in the dataset, results on the fixed test set increase by 2.49 BLEU points over models trained on the original OPUS-100. We also experimented with different tokenisers, including BPE and SentencePiece to find the ideal tokeniser and vocabulary size for our setup, which was shown to be BPE with a vocabulary size of 8,000. Finally, we train different models in both directions for the ENG-MLT language pair using OPUS 100 Fix by training models from scratch as well as fine-tuning other pre-trained models, namely mBART-50 and NLLB, where a finetuned NLLB model performed best.

1 Introduction

Tokenisation tends not to be given much attention in Machine Translation (MT), particularly since it is thought of as a solved problem for languages such as English (Erdmann, 2020). However, it can become an issue when generic tokenisers are applied to languages that have particular syntactic rules that are different from those commonly found in English. This is reflected by Domingo et al. (2019) who demonstrate that different tokenisers affect language pairs very differently. Moreover, several modern neural machine translation approaches also employ subword tokenisation in conjuction with word tokenisers as part of the preprocessing step (Wei et al., 2021; Xu et al., 2021; Oravecz et al., 2022). Not much thought tends to be given to the impact that tokenisation could have on the results of the machine translation. It is well known however, that tokenisation affects BLEU results (Post, 2018). In our research, we investigate the impact that different tokenisation approaches can have on the MT evaluation of Maltese, a morphologically rich language with Semitic roots. We experiment with different tokenisers, namely BPE (Sennrich et al., 2016a), SentencePiece (Kudo and Richardson, 2018), Moses Tokeniser (Koehn et al., 2007), OpenNMT Tokeniser (Klein et al., 2017), and a regex tokeniser specifically built for Maltese (Gatt and Čéplö, 2013). We refer to this as the MLRS tokeniser.

It was seen that most regular word-level English tokenisers do not tokenise/detokenise everything correctly. For example, it was seen that if the MT output has characters such as "-", an English detokeniser usually splits this character from other words by adding a space. This is the correct approach for English, but in Maltese most articles contain "-" and should remain joined as one word in the output (such as *il-kelb*, (the dog) should be tokenised as *il- kelb* rather than *il - kelb*.

In order to carry out an empirical evaluation of different tokenisation approaches, we also consider different Machine Translation (MT) approaches, including a baseline system trained from scratch using the base Transformer architecture (Vaswani et al., 2017), a model based on the large Transformer architecture, a fine-tuned mBART-50 model (Tang et al., 2020), NLLB (out-of-the-box) (Costa-jussà et al., 2022) and a fine-tuned version of NLLB, referred to as NLLB-FT.

Proceedings of the The Seventh Workshop on Technologies for Machine Translation of Low-Resource Languages (LoResMT 2024), pages 109–120
August 15, 2024 ©2024 Association for Computational Linguistics

Notably, the pre-trained model mBART-50 does not contain previous knowledge of Maltese whereas NLLB has encountered Maltese during its training.

Another challenge that we face when training NMT systems for low-resource languages is the lack of high-quality publicly available data. For our experiments, we utilize the OPUS-100 dataset (Zhang et al., 2020a). However, upon further analysis, we noticed that the Maltese documents contained several tokenisation errors that added spacing where there should be none. These errors do not occur in a systematic way, which motivated us to look into the impact that such inconsistencies would have on the results. Evaluation metrics such as BLEU, tend to favour a larger number of n-grams. The type of errors present in OPUS-100 were producing more tokens and this could result in an inflated BLEU score.

To this end, we investigate the impact of incorrect tokenisation in OPUS-100 when Maltese is the target language. Our translation efforts focus on the English - Maltese language pair since English is normally used as the source language whenever the target is Maltese, both in a research setting but also in an application scenario.

Our contributions are the following:

(C1) We release an updated version of the Maltese part of OPUS-100, referred to as OPUS-100-Fix,[1] fixing the tokenisation inconsistencies with the Maltese sentences and show how the outputs are improved when trained on OPUS-100-Fix.

(C2) We conduct a thorough evaluation of MT models trained with different word and subword tokenisers, including different vocabulary sizes.

(C3) We further train new models for the English-Maltese language pair on OPUS-100-Fix, including fine-tuning of mBART-50 and NLLB as well training new models from scratch, obtaining better results than a baseline.

2 Literature Review

2.1 Tokenisation

There are different approaches to tokenisation and the type of approach taken might depend on the language or the task at hand. Word-level tokenisers split the text into individual tokens, usually denoted by spaces or other markers. However, in languages such as Mandarin, such approaches are not appropriate since there are no clear boundaries between words. Word-level tokenisers might also not be ideal for morphologically rich languages (Alyafeai et al., 2023), as there is no shared information between words that share the same stem or lemma but have different prefixes or suffixes.

A hybrid approach is known as subword tokenisation where rare/compound words are split into smaller subwords and frequent words are kept as tokens in their entirety. This has become a very common approach in neural systems. By using subword tokenisers such as Byte-Pair Encodings (BPE) (Sennrich et al., 2016b) or SentencePiece (Kudo and Richardson, 2018), the input text can be efficiently tokenised into subwords and passed to the neural MT systems.

In spite of the different conditions that languages present, using a subword tokeniser is generally taken as the defacto approach for many languages (albeit sometimes with another tokenisation approach, such as including a word-level tokeniser (Wei et al., 2021; Xu et al., 2021; Oravecz et al., 2022)), including Maltese.

The following subsections explore popular tokenisation algorithms that will be used for our experiments.

2.1.1 BPE

BPE (Sennrich et al., 2016a) is an unsupervised subword tokeniser. It iteratively merges the most frequent pair of consecutive bytes in the training set to build a vocabulary of subword units, until the predetermined vocabulary size is reached. Throughout our experiments, we will use the original BPE algorithm as mentioned in the original paper.[2]

2.1.2 SentencePiece

Similar to BPE, SentencePiece is also an unsupervised subword tokeniser and the vocabulary size is also pre-determined. Internally, SentencePiece supports two algorithms: Unigram Language Model (Kudo, 2018) and BPE (Sennrich et al., 2016a). Apart from this, it also implements subword regularization which is not done in the original (subword-nmt) implementation of BPE.

The Unigram tokeniser is different to BPE in the sense that it starts from a big vocabulary and iteratively removes tokens until it reaches the specified vocabulary size. It takes into account the whole

[1] https://huggingface.co/datasets/MLRS/OPUS-MT-EN-Fixed

[2] https://github.com/rsennrich/subword-nmt

training set and selects the tokens that maximise the likelihood of the data. It tries to determine the optimal vocabulary of subword units by choosing token boundaries based on the inidividual character frequencies.

Throughout this research, whenever training our own SentencePiece tokeniser, we will experiment with both versions of SentencePiece, one which internally uses BPE and one which internally uses Unigram.

2.1.3 MLRS Tokeniser

The tokeniser from MLRS (Gatt and Čéplö, 2013)[3] is also used. It utilizes regular expressions to tokenise linguistic expressions that are specific to Maltese, such as separating certain prefixes and articles.

2.1.4 Moses Tokeniser

The MosesDecoder (Koehn et al., 2007) package contains a tokeniser[4] that is commonly used and is intended to be language-agnostic, since it simply separates punctuation from words while at the same time keeping URLs and dates intact. Apart from this, it also normalizes characters such as quotes.

2.1.5 OpenNMT Tokeniser

The OpenNMT Tokeniser (Klein et al., 2017) is very similar to the Moses Tokeniser, in the sense that it is language-agnostic, normalizes characters such as quotes and also separates punctuation from words. Contrastively, it does not keep certain words intact such as URLs and dates, and instead splits them as it would any other words.

2.2 Pre-trained Multilingual Models

According to Liu et al. (2020), using mBART-25 as the pre-trained model has been shown to improve translations over a randomly initialized baseline in low/medium resource language. mBART-25 is a transformer model trained on the BART (Lewis et al., 2019) objective. It is trained on 25 different languages. mBART-25 was later extended to include 25 more languages and was called mBART-50 (Tang et al., 2020). However, neither model included Maltese.

A more recent multilingual model is No Language Left Behind (NLLB) (Costa-jussà et al., 2022). NLLB-200 is a large multilingual model trained on 200 languages, one of which is Maltese. The architecture is built on the standard Transformer encoder-decoder architecture (Vaswani et al., 2017). The dataset used to train NLLB was collected from various sources, some of which were in the Maltese language. The fact that NLLB is already pre-trained with Maltese knowledge allows us to experiment both with fine-tuning the model further on our dataset but also to experiment with evaluating the pre-trained NLLB model out-of-the-box.

2.3 Previous MT Approaches for Low-Resource Languages

Most MT systems nowadays contain a number of pre-processing and post-processing techniques. Low quality datasets often have noise in them and pre-processing techniques are vital to ensure that this noise is not passed to the MT systems. Filtering data before training is a common pre-processing approach (Morishita et al., 2022; Oravecz et al., 2022; Tars et al., 2022; Rikters and Miwa, 2023). There are numerous techniques, such as language identification, removing duplicate sentence pairs, sentences where the word or length ratio between the source and target is greater than a specified amount, sentence pairs that have a high cosine similarity or whose source and target sentences are identical etc. Oravecz et al. (2022) go a step further and remove specific segments of noise patterns that were noticed in a particular dataset.

There are also post-processing techniques that can be done, to choose the best output from a number of possible outputs. One such technique is the reranking technique, used by Morishita et al. (2022) and Cruz (2023). The authors use this technique to select the most likely candidate from a set of candidates, using a Source-to-Target Neural Machine Translation (NMT) system, a Target-to-Source NMT system and a Masked Language Model. The overall score is how likely each system is to choose that particular output for the current input. For the Masked Language Model, different pre-trained models were used depending on the target language since naturally the model needs to be trained on the target language to give accurate results.

2.4 Maltese Machine Translation

Limited research exists in the context of Maltese machine translation.

There are works on multilingual MT systems, trained on multilingual corpora which include Mal-

[3] https://mlrs.research.um.edu.mt/index.php?page=demos

[4] https://www.statmt.org/moses/

tese. Zhang et al. (2020b) used OPUS-100 (Zhang et al., 2020c) to train a multilingual system that achieved 47.4 and 62.3 BLEU in the ENG $\rightarrow$ MLT and MLT $\rightarrow$ ENG directions respectively. Ma et al. (2020) presented a MT system based on a pre-trained language model which is further fine-tuned on OPUS-100. They achieved 48.0 and 63.0 BLEU in the ENG $\rightarrow$ MLT and MLT $\rightarrow$ ENG directions respectively. More recently, Yang et al. (2022) created a multilingual model that is first trained on high-resource languages with the aim of transferring knowledge to the low-resource languages. They achieved 49.9 and 65.8 BLEU in the ENG $\rightarrow$ MLT and MLT $\rightarrow$ ENG directions respectively.

Williams et al. (2023) proposed a submission for the 2023 IWSLT speech translation task. Their system is a cascade solution where they utilize a fine-tuned XLS-R model for ASR and a fine-tuned version of mBART-50 as the MT model.

3 Methodology

3.1 Fixing OPUS-100

3.1.1 Original Dataset

The OPUS-100 dataset (Zhang et al., 2020c) dataset contains parallel sentences for over 100 languages. In our case, we are using the English-Maltese portion of this dataset. It contains over a million sentences.

After performing initial experiments, we noticed that this dataset has a number of tokenisation issues on the Maltese side. The inconsistencies identified are the following:

1. Additional spacing between words and their articles (such as *il-kelb (the dog)* sometimes incorrectly being represented as *il- kelb*). A quick estimate shows that 23.2% of the articles are incorrectly tokenised.

2. Additional spacing between specific words that include apostrophes (such as *ta' (of)* being represented as *ta '*)

3. Inconsistent characters to represent an apostrophe, where sometimes the curled apostrophe/smart quote character is used instead of the straight quote.

Curiously, the mistakes do not appear to be consistent throughout the dataset, but a significant amount of the sentences do contain a combination of these errors.

One snippet of a sentence in the OPUS-100 test set is: "*Id- doża ta ' Temodal tista ' [...]*", meaning "*The Temodal dose may [...]*". Here, one can see Inconsistency 1 (with the term *Id- doża*, which should be *Id-doża*) and Inconsistency 2 (with the terms *ta '* and *tista '*, which should be *ta'* and *tista'* respectively).

These tokenisation errors appear in both the training set and the test set. BLEU works with n-grams, therefore if a specific word is split up by a space, they get rewarded for two words being correct rather than one, leading to inflated results. This is evidently the case with issues 1 and 2 above. If a system is taught to split *ta'* into *ta '*, then BLEU will reward it as if it got two words after each other correct rather than treat it as one word as it should be.

3.1.2 OPUS-100-Fix

As detailed in Section 3.1.1, the original Maltese portion of the OPUS-100 dataset has inconsistencies, namely with articles and words containing punctuation, which affect the BLEU score as well as the quality of the translations. Thus, we set out to fix the three issues noted in Section 3.1.1.

Firstly, to fix the issue of the word and its article being separated, we used the detokeniser created for Maltese by MLRS[5] to get a list of all the possible articles. The detokeniser searches for the articles using regular expressions. The articles found followed by a dash and another word were merged together.

Secondly, to fix the issue of common Maltese particles with apostrophes at the end having the apostrophe split from the word (such as *ta '*), once again we use the MLRS detokeniser which internally uses regular expressions to get a list of possible particles. These particles that are immediately followed by a space and an apostrophe have the space removed. Therefore they are merged together as one word.

Lastly, all occurrences of the curled apostrophe character were changed to the standard apostrophe character.

3.2 Evaluating different Tokenisers

A common technique in NMT is to tokenise the input first. There are various tokenisers, some of which are word-level or rule-based and some of which are subword tokenisers. One can also combine different tokenisers (Wei et al., 2021; Xu et al.,

[5] mlrs.research.um.edu.mt

2021), by first tokenising using the word tokenisers and then feeding this to the subword tokenisers.

When it comes to neural approaches that deal with Maltese, we expect that the most appropriate tokenisation technique is a subword tokeniser. This is due to the fact that character-level embeddings in Maltese do not store enough information and word-level tokenisation does not take advantage of stem/lemma similarity, with Maltese being morphologically rich.

In our experiment, we try three different subword tokenisers, namely SentencePiece (which by default adapts the Unigram tokenisation algorithm), the adapted version of BPE used within SentencePiece as well as the original BPE tokeniser. We also use three word-level tokenisers. Two of the word-level tokenisers are popular in the field (namely MosesDecoder (Koehn et al., 2007) and OpenNMT (Klein et al., 2017)) and another one of which is specifically designed for Maltese (the tokeniser from MLRS (Gatt and Čéplö, 2013)). Following (Wu et al., 2016) and (Denkowski and Neubig, 2017), who suggested tokeniser vocabulary sizes should be between 8,000 and 32,000, we use three different vocabulary sizes: 8,000, 16,000 and 32,000.

3.3 Different architectures trained on OPUS-100-Fix

We set out to experiment with different architectures and techniques to set baseline results for models trained on OPUS-100-Fix. Each model has three variations. The first variation is the model as it is, with standard pre-processing and post-processing. The second variation, detailed in Section 3.3.1 includes an additional pre-processing step, where the data is filtered thoroughly before being passed on for training. The third variation, detailed in Section 3.3.2 is a post-processing step to make a better choice from the potential outputs.

3.3.1 Filtering of Data

We follow the most common approaches used in WMT shared tasks (Morishita et al., 2022; Oravecz et al., 2022; Tars et al., 2022) to filter data before feeding it to train the system. A number of operations are performed on the training set, namely by removing sentences:

- Over 150 words in either the source or target text.
- Containing single words with more than 40 characters in either the source or target text.
- Where the ratio between the total character count and the number of words is greater than 12 for both the source and target text.
- Where the ratio of the number of words in the source text to the number of words in the target text exceeds 4.
- Where the ratio of the total character count in the source text to the total character count in the target text exceeds 6.
- Where the source and target texts are identical.
- Where the cosine similarity between bag-of-words vector representations of the source and target text is greater than 0.96.

3.3.2 Noisy Channel Reranking

Following Morishita et al. (2022), we implement a post-processing technique to select the best output from the best 5 possibilities. Instead of selecting the best output using just the Source-to-Target NMT system, we also use a Target-to-Source NMT system, and a Masked Language Model. The overall score is determined by evaluating how probable it is for each model to choose the given output for the given input.

For example, the Target-to-Source system scores how likely it is that the source sentence is the output produced given the target sentence. The Masked Language Model scores how likely it is that the target sentence is produced in that particular order. This is done by masking tokens one by one, which results in pseudo-log-likelihood scores, as described by Salazar et al. (2019). This process is designed to ensemble different results from differ ent models to get a better output. In the case of Maltese, we trained a basic Language Model (LM) trained on the OPUS-100-Fix training set. The hyperparameters are detailed in Section A.1.

4 Evaluation

4.1 Experiment Setup

All models are built using the Fairseq (Ott et al., 2019) library. Fairseq is a library that allows for easy implementation of a machine translation system through CLI commands, meaning minimal code is needed to create a fully working machine translation system. Throughout all experiments, we wanted to keep the hyperparameters the same to ensure a fair assessment. The hyperparameters are detailed in Section A.2.

Given that these experiments focus on tokenisation issues which are present only on the Maltese portion, we present results in the ENG $\rightarrow$ MLT direction, however we also list all results in the MLT $\rightarrow$ ENG direction in the appendix for completeness.

4.1.1 Transformer (base) - Baseline Model

The architecture for the first model is the base transformer architecture by Vaswani et al. (2017) with six encoder and decoder layers with 512 dimensions each. There are eight attention heads for both the encoders and decoders, with 2,048 dimensions for each.

4.1.2 Transformer (large)

The second model trained from scratch is based on the Transformer (large) submission detailed by Vaswani et al. (2017). As described by the authors, the big architecture has six encoder and decoder layers with 1,024 dimensions each. There are 16 attention heads for both encoders and decoders with 4,096 dimensions each.

4.1.3 mBART50 fine-tuned

For this system, a pre-trained mBART-50 model (Tang et al., 2020) was used and fine-tuned on our data. Following Williams et al. (2023), an mBART-50 model was used over mBART-25, since the former was found to perform better.

The architecture of mBART-50 is based on the architecture of mBART-25 (Liu et al., 2020), which itself is a modified version of Vaswani et al. (2017). In their case, they use 12 encoder and decoder layers of 1,024 dimensions on 16 attention heads.

4.1.4 NLLB

Costa-jussà et al. (2022) proposed a model trained on 200 distinct languages, including Maltese, called NLLB as described in Section 2.2. Since this includes Maltese, 2 experiments were conducted: **pre-trained** and **fine-tuned**. For pre-trained, the model was used as-is *out-of-the-box* without further training and evaluated on the test sets. For fine-tuned, the model was further trained on the training sets. In both cases once again Fairseq (Ott et al., 2019) was used to fine-tune and infer the results. This model is also the biggest model that is being experimented with, since it has 24 encoder and decoder layers with 2,048 dimensions on 16 attention heads. The attention heads have 8,192 dimensions each. Due to resource constraints, we only experimented with the 600M parameter version in this study.

4.2 Results

To evaluate the systems, the BLEU and CHRF2 scores are the metrics used. Although BLEU has its pitfalls (Kocmi et al., 2021), it is still used in a lot of previous papers and thus can be used to compare our results to previous literature. Moreover, although there are neural based metrics nowadays such as COMET (Rei et al., 2020) it is not yet clear as to how well they work with the Maltese language and correlate to human scores.

4.2.1 OPUS-100 vs OPUS-100-Fix

Following the issues found in OPUS-100, OPUS-100-Fix was created that fixed these issues to satisfy Contribution C1. We created an experiment to train two Transformer (large) models: one using the original OPUS-100 dataset and another using the fixed OPUS-100-Fix dataset. We then tested these models on both test sets. An additional experiment was done where we detokenised the output of the model trained on the original OPUS-100, to measure the extent to how much the BLEU scores inflate when evaluated on the original test set. For example, if the model outputs *il- kelb*, it will detokenise it to *il-kelb* before evaluating. In all cases, a SentencePiece (Unigram) tokeniser is trained with a vocabulary size of 8,000.

The BLEU results can be seen in Table 1. The model trained on OPUS-100-Fix achieves the best BLEU score when evaluated on the fixed test set, outperforming even the model trained on OPUS-100 with the detokenised output. The CHRF2 scores can be found in the appendix.

The model trained on OPUS-100 achieves the best BLEU score (51.48) when evaluated on the OPUS-100 test, but achieves the lowest (48.38) when evaluated on the OPUS-100-Fix test set. This shows how inflated the results on the original OPUS-100 are, as described in Section 3.1.1. Naturally, this only occurs if the MT output itself contains these errors, hence why the BLEU score drops by a significant amount when we detokenise the output (or train on a clean training set) and evaluate on the OPUS-100 test set.

We note that detokenising post-hoc seems to perform marginally worse than training on OPUS-100-Fix in both testing scenarios. We note that

Training Set	OPUS-100 Test Set	OPUS-100-Fix Test Set
OPUS-100	51.48	48.38
OPUS-100 (Detokenised Output)	46.27	49.54
OPUS-100-Fix	47.00	50.87

Table 1: BLEU scores of Transformer (large) models trained on OPUS-100 and OPUS-100-Fix (ENG → MLT).

the main difference is that the system trained on OPUS-100 tends to not include the articles when possible, such as writing *Kummenti* instead of *Il-Kummenti* (meaning *Comments* instead of *The comments*), potentially due to the conflicting examples in the training set.

One can also notice the increase in the BLEU score that happens once the test set is fixed, where the model trained on OPUS-100-Fix achieves 47.00 BLEU on the OPUS-100 test set but 50.87 BLEU on the OPUS-100-Fix test set. This is obviously not the case with the model trained on OPUS-100, since the output contains the same tokenisation errors found in the training set.

4.2.2 Evaluating different Tokenisers

Following the tokenisation errors found in the OPUS-100 dataset, we set out to satisfy Contribution C2 by experimenting with different tokenisers as a preprocessing step to see whether there are significant differences in the tokeniser used in an MT system in the context of Maltese.

Table 2 shows the Transformer (large) and the NLLB-FT models using the different tokenisers described in Section 3.2. Throughout this experiment, every tokeniser used has 8,000 vocabulary size.

In the case of NLLB-FT, the model is pre-trained on a tokeniser that adapts SentencePiece. Therefore, when evaluating on NLLB-FT, we must use their pre-trained SentencePiece model. This is not the case with the Transformer (large) model, therefore we can perform additional experiments on this model with other tokenisers, including BPE.

Our results show that overall, there does not seem to be significant improvements when pairing a subword tokeniser with another word-level tokeniser. Using the Transformer (Large) model, a BPE tokenizer alone works best in both directions, whereas when using NLLB-FT, the pre-trained SentencePiece model alone performs the best. The best performing model overall was NLLB-FT with 52.25 BLEU and 76.14 CHRF2 scores.

We also set out to determine which vocabulary sizes work best in our experiments. We used a Transformer (Large) model throughout as this allows us to experiment with using and training our own subword tokenisers from scratch. For this experiment we used both versions of SentencePiece as well as BPE with three different vocabulary sizes: 8k, 16k and 32k.

Model	BLEU	CHRF2
Transformer (large)		
SentencePiece-Unigram (SP-U)	50.87	74.96
SP-U + MLRS	50.36	75.29
SP-U + Moses	51.17	75.09
SP-U + OpenNMT	50.91	75.08
SentencePiece BPE (SP-BPE)	50.94	75.04
SP-BPE + MLRS	49.08	74.66
SP-BPE + Moses	51.25	75.18
SP-BPE + OpenNMT	50.94	75.04
Byte Pair Encoding (BPE)	51.29	75.08
BPE + MLRS	49.82	75.04
BPE + Moses	50.24	74.62
BPE + OpenNMT	51.29	75.07
NLLB-FT		
SentencePiece Unigram (SP-U)	**52.25**	**76.14**
SP-U + MLRS	50.32	75.86
SP-U + Moses	50.86	75.21
SP-U + OpenNMT	51.74	75.75

Table 2: Models trained and evaluated on OPUS-100-Fix (ENG → MLT).

The results can be seen in Table 3. In all cases having a smaller vocabulary size achieves the highest BLEU and CHRF2 scores. It is interesting that there is a very sharp drop in performance when using SentencePiece (both the unigram version and BPE version) with higher vocabulary sizes. We experimented with different vocabulary sizes between 8,000 and 16,000 for the unigram version and 16,000 and 32,000 for the BPE version and a drop in performance is observed as the vocabulary size is increased. The overall best performing model is the original BPE with a vocabulary size of 8,000 in both directions.

For completeness, we present the results of the above experiments in the MLT → ENG direction

Vocabulary Size	BLEU	CHRF2
BPE		
8,000	**51.29**	**75.08**
16,000	50.00	74.56
32,000	41.67	68.20
SentencePiece (Unigram)		
8,000	50.87	74.96
16,000	2.73	18.48
32,000	0.05	16.32
SentencePiece (BPE)		
8,000	50.94	75.04
16,000	50.76	74.70
32,000	1.39	15.41

Table 3: Transformer (Large) trained on OPUS-100-Fix (ENG → MLT) with different tokenisers.

Model	BLEU	CHRF2
Transformer (base)	48.64	73.77
Filtering of data	47.38	72.81
Noisy Channel Reranking	47.75	73.01
Transformer (large)	51.29	75.08
Filtering of data	50.93	74.86
Noisy Channel Reranking	51.44	75.28
mBART50 fine-tuned	50.25	74.12
Filtering of data	49.09	73.39
Noisy Channel Reranking	49.40	73.62
NLLB Pre-trained	39.69	71.72
NLLB-FT	52.25	76.14
Filtering of data	**52.65**	**76.29**
Noisy Channel Reranking	52.03	75.85

Table 4: Models trained and evaluated on OPUS-100-Fix (ENG → MLT)

in Section C.

4.2.3 Different architectures trained on OPUS-100-Fix

We also set out to satisfy Contribution C3, by evaluating different models and techniques using this new OPUS-100-Fix dataset as well as using the optimal tokenisers and the optimal vocabulary sizes from the previous section. These models were therefore all trained using BPE with a vocabulary size of 8,000, except for the pre-trained models (mBART50 and NLLB), in which case their respective tokenisers were used.

The results can be seen in Table 4. The NLLB pre-trained model (out-of-the-box) achieves the lowest BLEU and CHRF2 scores, whereas NLLB-FT achieves the highest. In almost all cases, filtering seems to hurt performance except in the NLLB-FT model. This could be due to the general lack of data, which is less of an issue in the case of NLLB-FT since it is pretrained. Reranking is also generally an improvement over filtering but still overall worse than not doing either.

For completeness, the results in the MLT → ENG direction can be seen in Section D.

5 Conclusion

This paper presents an updated version of OPUS-100, OPUS-100-Fix, which fixes numerous inconsistencies in the Maltese data. It is seen that by fixing these inconsistencies, the results improve. Apart from that, we also experiment with numerous tokenisers where we observed that using BPE alone, with a vocabulary size of 8,000, achieves the best results on our data. We finally experiment with different models, both fine-tuned (including NLLB and mBART) and those trained from scratch, and it can be seen that fine-tuning NLLB yields the best performance.

5.1 Limitations

The metrics used to present the results are BLEU and CHRF2, and as seen in Kocmi et al. (2021), may not directly agree with human evaluation.

Apart from this, although OPUS-100 is a commonly used dataset, it is not human reviewed and therefore it could have other types of noise than those fixed in this research such as incorrect translations that could affect performance. For accurate comparisons between models, especially pre-trained models that are potentially trained on higher quality data, it would be better to ensure that the test set is manually reviewed and validated.

5.2 Future Work

For future work it would be beneficial to utilize monolingual data. It is assumed that if we use backtranslation to include the monolingual data, certain techniques such as filtering of data will lead to a higher performance increase.

Apart from this, a LM was trained from scratch using our limited training set for the reranking technique. It would be beneficial to experiment with using a larger Maltese LM trained on more data for this technique, such as BERTu (Micallef et al., 2022).

Acknowledgements

We acknowledge support from the LT-Bridge Project (GA 952194) and DFKI for access to the Virtual Laboratory. We further acknowledge funding by Malta Enterprise.

References

Zaid Alyafeai, Maged S Al-shaibani, Mustafa Ghaleb, and Irfan Ahmad. 2023. Evaluating various tokenizers for arabic text classification. *Neural Processing Letters*, 55(3):2911–2933.

Marta R Costa-jussà, James Cross, Onur Çelebi, Maha Elbayad, Kenneth Heafield, Kevin Heffernan, Elahe Kalbassi, Janice Lam, Daniel Licht, Jean Maillard, et al. 2022. No language left behind: Scaling human-centered machine translation. *arXiv preprint arXiv:2207.04672*.

Marta R. Costa-jussà, James Cross NLLB Team, Onur Çelebi, Maha Elbayad, Kenneth Heafield, Kevin Heffernan, Elahe Kalbassi, Janice Lam, Daniel Licht, Jean Maillard, Anna Sun, Skyler Wang, Guillaume Wenzek, Al Youngblood, Bapi Akula, Loic Barrault, Gabriel Mejia Gonzalez, Prangthip Hansanti, John Hoffman, Semarley Jarrett, Kaushik Ram Sadagopan, Dirk Rowe, Shannon Spruit, Chau Tran, Pierre Andrews, Necip Fazil Ayan, Shruti Bhosale, Sergey Edunov, Angela Fan, Cynthia Gao, Vedanuj Goswami, Francisco Guzmán, Philipp Koehn, Alexandre Mourachko, Christophe Ropers, Safiyyah Saleem, Holger Schwenk, and Jeff Wang. 2022. No language left behind: Scaling human-centered machine translation.

Jan Christian Blaise Cruz. 2023. Samsung r&d institute philippines at wmt 2023. *arXiv preprint arXiv:2310.16322*.

Michael Denkowski and Graham Neubig. 2017. Stronger baselines for trustable results in neural machine translation. *arXiv preprint arXiv:1706.09733*.

Miguel Domingo, Mercedes García-Martínez, Alexandre Helle, Francisco Casacuberta, and Manuel Herranz. 2019. How much does tokenization affect neural machine translation? In *International Conference on Computational Linguistics and Intelligent Text Processing*, pages 545–554. Springer.

Alexander Erdmann. 2020. *Practical Morphological Modeling: Insights from Dialectal Arabic*. The Ohio State University.

Albert Gatt and Slavomír Čéplö. 2013. Digital corpora and other electronic resources for maltese. In *Corpus linguistics*, pages 96–97. UCREL Lancaster.

Guillaume Klein, Yoon Kim, Yuntian Deng, Jean Senellart, and Alexander M Rush. 2017. Opennmt: Open-source toolkit for neural machine translation. *arXiv preprint arXiv:1701.02810*.

Tom Kocmi, Christian Federmann, Roman Grundkiewicz, Marcin Junczys-Dowmunt, Hitokazu Matsushita, and Arul Menezes. 2021. To ship or not to ship: An extensive evaluation of automatic metrics for machine translation. *arXiv preprint arXiv:2107.10821*.

Philipp Koehn, Hieu Hoang, Alexandra Birch, Chris Callison-Burch, Marcello Federico, Nicola Bertoldi, Brooke Cowan, Wade Shen, Christine Moran, Richard Zens, et al. 2007. Moses: Open source toolkit for statistical machine translation. In *Proceedings of the 45th annual meeting of the association for computational linguistics companion volume proceedings of the demo and poster sessions*, pages 177–180. Association for Computational Linguistics.

Taku Kudo. 2018. Subword regularization: Improving neural network translation models with multiple subword candidates. *Preprint*, arXiv:1804.10959.

Taku Kudo and John Richardson. 2018. Sentencepiece: A simple and language independent subword tokenizer and detokenizer for neural text processing. *arXiv preprint arXiv:1808.06226*.

Mike Lewis, Yinhan Liu, Naman Goyal, Marjan Ghazvininejad, Abdelrahman Mohamed, Omer Levy, Ves Stoyanov, and Luke Zettlemoyer. 2019. Bart: Denoising sequence-to-sequence pre-training for natural language generation, translation, and comprehension. *arXiv preprint arXiv:1910.13461*.

Yinhan Liu, Jiatao Gu, Naman Goyal, Xian Li, Sergey Edunov, Marjan Ghazvininejad, Mike Lewis, and Luke Zettlemoyer. 2020. Multilingual denoising pre-training for neural machine translation. *Preprint*, arXiv:2001.08210.

Shuming Ma, Jian Yang, Haoyang Huang, Zewen Chi, Li Dong, Dongdong Zhang, Hany Hassan Awadalla, Alexandre Muzio, Akiko Eriguchi, Saksham Singhal, et al. 2020. Xlm-t: Scaling up multilingual machine translation with pretrained cross-lingual transformer encoders. *arXiv preprint arXiv:2012.15547*.

Kurt Micallef, Albert Gatt, Marc Tanti, Lonneke van der Plas, and Claudia Borg. 2022. Pre-training data quality and quantity for a low-resource language: New corpus and BERT models for Maltese. In *Proceedings of the Third Workshop on Deep Learning for Low-Resource Natural Language Processing*, pages 90–101, Hybrid. Association for Computational Linguistics.

Makoto Morishita, Keito Kudo, Yui Oka, Katsuki Chousa, Shun Kiyono, Sho Takase, and Jun Suzuki. 2022. Nt5 at wmt 2022 general translation task. In *Proceedings of the Seventh Conference on Machine Translation (WMT)*, pages 318–325.

Csaba Oravecz, Katina Bontcheva, David Kolovratník, Bogomil Kovachev, and Christopher Scott. 2022. etranslation's submissions to the wmt22 general machine translation task. In *Proceedings of the Seventh Conference on Machine Translation (WMT)*, pages 346–351.

Myle Ott, Sergey Edunov, Alexei Baevski, Angela Fan, Sam Gross, Nathan Ng, David Grangier, and Michael Auli. 2019. fairseq: A fast, extensible toolkit for sequence modeling. In *Proceedings of NAACL-HLT 2019: Demonstrations*.

Matt Post. 2018. A call for clarity in reporting BLEU scores. In *Proceedings of the Third Conference on Machine Translation: Research Papers*, pages 186–191, Brussels, Belgium. Association for Computational Linguistics.

Ricardo Rei, Craig Stewart, Ana C Farinha, and Alon Lavie. 2020. Comet: A neural framework for mt evaluation. *arXiv preprint arXiv:2009.09025*.

Matīss Rikters and Makoto Miwa. 2023. Aist airc submissions to the wmt23 shared task. In *Proceedings of the Eighth Conference on Machine Translation*, pages 155–161.

Julian Salazar, Davis Liang, Toan Q Nguyen, and Katrin Kirchhoff. 2019. Masked language model scoring. *arXiv preprint arXiv:1910.14659*.

Rico Sennrich, Barry Haddow, and Alexandra Birch. 2016a. Neural machine translation of rare words with subword units. In *Proceedings of the 54th Annual Meeting of the Association for Computational Linguistics (Volume 1: Long Papers)*, pages 1715–1725, Berlin, Germany. Association for Computational Linguistics.

Rico Sennrich, Barry Haddow, and Alexandra Birch. 2016b. Neural machine translation of rare words with subword units. *Preprint*, arXiv:1508.07909.

Yuqing Tang, Chau Tran, Xian Li, Peng-Jen Chen, Naman Goyal, Vishrav Chaudhary, Jiatao Gu, and Angela Fan. 2020. Multilingual translation with extensible multilingual pretraining and finetuning. *arXiv preprint arXiv:2008.00401*.

Maali Tars, Taido Purason, and Andre Tättar. 2022. Teaching unseen low-resource languages to large translation models. In *Proceedings of the Seventh Conference on Machine Translation (WMT)*, pages 375–380.

Ashish Vaswani, Noam Shazeer, Niki Parmar, Jakob Uszkoreit, Llion Jones, Aidan N Gomez, Łukasz Kaiser, and Illia Polosukhin. 2017. Attention is all you need. *Advances in neural information processing systems*, 30.

Daimeng Wei, Zongyao Li, Zhanglin Wu, Zhengzhe Yu, Xiaoyu Chen, Hengchao Shang, Jiaxin Guo, Minghan Wang, Lizhi Lei, Min Zhang, et al. 2021. Hwtsc's participation in the wmt 2021 news translation shared task. In *Proceedings of the Sixth Conference on Machine Translation*, pages 225–231.

Aiden Williams, Kurt Abela, Rishu Kumar, Martin Bär, Hannah Billinghurst, Kurt Micallef, Ahnaf Mozib Samin, Andrea DeMarco, Lonneke van der Plas, and Claudia Borg. 2023. Um-dfki maltese speech translation. In *Proceedings of the 20th International Conference on Spoken Language Translation (IWSLT 2023)*, pages 433–441.

Yonghui Wu, Mike Schuster, Zhifeng Chen, Quoc V Le, Mohammad Norouzi, Wolfgang Macherey, Maxim Krikun, Yuan Cao, Qin Gao, Klaus Macherey, et al. 2016. Google's neural machine translation system: Bridging the gap between human and machine translation. *arXiv preprint arXiv:1609.08144*.

Jitao Xu, Sadaf Abdul Rauf, Minh Quang Pham, and François Yvon. 2021. Lisn@ wmt 2021. In *6th Conference on Statistical Machine Translation*.

Jian Yang, Yuwei Yin, Shuming Ma, Dongdong Zhang, Zhoujun Li, and Furu Wei. 2022. Hlt-mt: High-resource language-specific training for multilingual neural machine translation. *arXiv preprint arXiv:2207.04906*.

Kyra Yee, Yann Dauphin, and Michael Auli. 2019. Simple and effective noisy channel modeling for neural machine translation. In *Conference on Empirical Methods in Natural Language Processing*.

Biao Zhang, Philip Williams, Ivan Titov, and Rico Sennrich. 2020a. Improving massively multilingual neural machine translation and zero-shot translation. *arXiv preprint arXiv:2004.11867*.

Biao Zhang, Philip Williams, Ivan Titov, and Rico Sennrich. 2020b. Improving massively multilingual neural machine translation and zero-shot translation. *arXiv preprint arXiv:2004.11867*.

Biao Zhang, Philip Williams, Ivan Titov, and Rico Sennrich. 2020c. Improving massively multilingual neural machine translation and zero-shot translation.

A Hyperparameters

A.1 Language Model Hyperparameters

For the noisy channel reranking, we used the following hyperparameters. The same hyperparameters as[6] were used to train the model, namely, a dropout of 0.1, Adam optimizer with betas of 0.9 and 0.98, weight decay of 0.01, a learning rate of 0.0005 with an inverse square root scheduler, warmup updates of 4,000, and an initial learning rate of 1e-07. 2,048 max tokens were passed per batch per GPU with an update frequency of 16 per GPU. Two GPUs were used to train the system. In the case of English, we used the pre-trained LM described in Yee et al. (2019).

[6] https://github.com/facebookresearch/fairseq/blob/main/examples/language_model/README.md

A.2 Experiment Setup Hyperparameters

We follow the same hyperparameters as Williams et al. (2023). An Adam optimizer is used with the Adam betas being 0.9 and 0.98. Label smoothed cross entropy is used with a label smoothing of 0.2. The dropout probability is 0.1 and the weight decay is set to 1e-04 . The maximum tokens per batch was set to 2,048. Finally, the learning rate is set to 1e-03, but the initial learning rate is actually smaller, at 1e-07 and increases using a learning rate scheduler to linearly increase the rate after 4,000 steps. Once the learning rate reaches 1e-03, the rate is then decayed by the inverse square root of the update number.

The validation occurs every 10,000 steps, where the BLEU score on the dev set is calculated. The model keeps training with a patience of 10, meaning that if the model does not improve this BLEU score after 10 validation steps, then it stops training.

For standard generation, the beam size is set to 5. After the sentences are inferred, the sentences are detokenised using the respective tokeniser used and scored using Sacrebleu (Post, 2018).

B OPUS-100 vs OPUS-100-Fix

Table 5 shows the CHRF2 scores of the experiments described in Section 4.2.1.

C Evaluating different Tokenisers - MLT $\rightarrow$ ENG

Table 6 shows the MLT $\rightarrow$ ENG results using the different tokenisers.

Table 7 shows the MLT $\rightarrow$ ENG results using the different vocabulary sizes. Similar results to the ENG $\rightarrow$ MLT are achieved.

D Different architectures trained on OPUS-100-Fix - MLT $\rightarrow$ ENG

Table 8 shows the BLEU and CHRF2 scores for different architectures trained and evaluated on OPUS-100-Fix.

Training Set	OPUS-100 Test Set	OPUS-100-Fix Test Set
OPUS-100	75.01	74.85
OPUS-100 (Detokenised Output)	75.00	74.84
OPUS-100-Fix	75.14	**74.96**

Table 5: CHRF2 scores of Transformer (large) models trained on OPUS-100 and OPUS-100-Fix (ENG → MLT).

Model	BLEU	CHRF2
Transformer (large)		
SentencePiece Unigram (SP-U)	61.94	77.12
SP-U + MLRS Tokeniser	61.27	76.91
SP-U + Moses Tokeniser	61.91	77.18
SP-U + OpenNMT Tokeniser	61.94	77.12
SentencePiece BPE (SP-BPE)	62.45	77.45
SP-BPE + MLRS Tokeniser	64.08	78.45
SP-BPE + Moses Tokeniser	62.28	77.46
SP-BPE + OpenNMT Tokeniser	62.45	77.45
Byte Pair Encoding (BPE)	64.47	78.92
BPE + MLRS Tokeniser	63.40	78.25
BPE + Moses Tokeniser	64.44	78.86
BPE + OpenNMT Tokeniser	64.45	78.91
NLLB-FT		
SentencePiece Unigram (SP-U)	**68.04**	**81.17**
SP-U + MLRS Tokeniser	67.70	80.89
SP-U + Moses Tokeniser	63.42	79.76
SP-U + OpenNMT Tokeniser	67.14	80.54

Table 6: Models trained and evaluated on OPUS-100-Fix (MLT → ENG).

Vocabulary Size	BLEU	CHRF2
BPE		
8,000	**64.47**	**78.92**
16,000	64.08	78.69
32,000	60.83	76.47
SentencePiece (Unigram)		
8,000	61.94	77.12
16,000	3.36	18.80
32,000	2.14	16.03
SentencePiece (BPE)		
8,000	62.45	77.45
16,000	60.38	76.21
32,000	3.16	17.16

Table 7: Transformer (Large) trained on OPUS-100-Fix (MLT → ENG) with different tokenisers.

Model	BLEU	CHRF2
Transformer (base)	61.67	77.05
Filtering of data	61.76	76.97
Noisy Channel Reranking	62.08	77.21
Transformer (large)	64.47	78.92
Filtering of data	64.67	78.90
Noisy Channel Reranking	65.07	79.33
mBART50 fine-tuned	64.14	78.28
Filtering of data	57.57	73.13
Noisy Channel Reranking	58.66	74.05
NLLB Pre-trained	60.11	77 .82
NLLB-FT	**68.04**	**81.17**
Filtering of data	66.98	80.46
Noisy Channel Reranking	65.78	79.42

Table 8: Models trained and evaluated on OPUS-100-Fix (MLT → ENG)

Machine Translation Through Cultural Texts: Can Verses and Prose Help Low-Resource Indigenous Models?

Antoine Cadotte
Université du Québec à Montréal
antoine.cadotte@courrier.uqam.ca

Nathalie André
École Kanatamat, Matimekush-Lac John
nathalie.andre@ecolekanatamat.ca

Fatiha Sadat
Université du Québec à Montréal
sadat.fatiha@uqam.ca

Abstract

We propose the first MT models for Innu-Aimun, an Indigenous language in Eastern Canada, in an effort to provide assistance tools for translation and language learning. This project is carried out in collaboration with an Innu community school and involves the participation of other participants, within the framework of a meaningful consideration of Indigenous perspectives. Our contributions in this paper result from the three initial stages of this project. First, we aim to align bilingual Innu-Aimun/French texts with collaboration and participation of Innu-Aimun locutors. Second, we present the training and evaluation results of the MT models (both statistical and neural) based on these aligned corpora. And third, we collaboratively analyze some of the translations resulting from the MT models. We also see these developments for Innu-Aimun as a useful case study for answering a larger question: in a context where few aligned bilingual sentences are available for an Indigenous language, can cultural texts such as literature and poetry be used in the development of MT models?

1 Introduction

Innu-Aimun, formerly known as Montagnais (ISO code moe,[1] Glottolog mont1268)[2], is the language of the Innu, an Indigenous people present in the Quebec and Labrador provinces of Canada. It is a polysynthetic language, member of the Algonquian language family and part of the Cree Innu Naskapi dialect continuum (Drapeau, 2014b).

According to the latest Statistics Canada census (2021), an estimated 11,605 locutors speak Innu-Aimun, when including the related Naskapi language.[3] This figure has seen a negative variation compared to the previous census (2016), [4] and UNESCO considers Innu-Aimun to be endangered/unsafe.[5] This echoes other assessments made by language specialists (Baraby et al., 2017; Drapeau, 2014a, 2011).

A lack of available services in Innu-Aimun has been documented, with insufficient availability of professional translators and interpreters, for Innu-Aimun and for all Indigenous languages in Quebec.[6] In a revitalisation effort, a new professional Innu-Aimun translation and interpretation program is being offered.[7] In this context and with the aim of helping Innu-Aimun translators as well as language learners and users in general, we are taking the first steps to develop a Machine Translation (MT) system for the Innu-Aimun language and French language pair. This project is carried out in collaboration with the Innu-Aimun teaching staff of Innu community school École Kanatamat. The project also involves the participation of students in Innu-Aimun translation and interpretation from the new college program at Cégep de Sept îles.

Innu-Aimun being originally an oral language, the Innu have a rich tradition of oral storytelling but also, since more recently, an ever growing written, literature, including novels and poetry (St-Gelais, 2022). It is for the most part written in French, with some publications in bilingual Innu-Aimun and French editions. Although working with literary and poetic data presents big challenges, such as artistic and figurative translations or particular writing styles, we take these constraints as an opportunity to answer the following questions: Can these types of texts have a positive impact on the results of Machine Translation models for Innu-Aimun and French languages?

Innu-Aimun, as is generally the case with Indigenous language in Canada, is not covered by

[1] ISO 639-3 - moe
[2] Glottolog - mont1268
[3] Statistics Canada: Indigenous languages in Canada, 2021
[4] Indigenous languages across Canada
[5] UNESCO World Atlas of Languages - Montagnais
[6] Final report of the Viens Commission (in French)
[7] Innu-Aimun Interpretation and Translation program at Cégep de Sept-Îles (in French)

Proceedings of the The Seventh Workshop on Technologies for Machine Translation of Low-Resource Languages (LoResMT 2024), pages 121–127
August 15, 2024

currently available MT systems. It is also underrepresented—if not absent—of Large Language Models (LLM) which are increasingly used as translation tools. In the face of recent questioning on the cultural sensitivity and awareness of general NMT models and LLMs, we propose a more culturally-aware approach, based on cultural texts and involving collaboration and participation of Innu-Aimun locutors.

Our paper is structured as follows. We present a brief state-of-the-art related to our topic in Section 2 and our proposed methodology for the present study in Section 3. Section 4 presents results from the first MT models as well as qualitative observations and analyses. Section 5 concludes this paper.

2 Related Works

The existing language technologies for Innu-Aimun today are mainly online language tools, such as a bilingual dictionary, a verb conjugation application and learning games (Junker et al., 2016). Similar tools exist for the neighboring language of Eastern Cree.[8] Other important building blocks, such as morphological models, have been developed for related languages among which Plains Cree is notable (Arppe et al., 2016). A word segmentation tool based on deep learning has also been proposed for Innu-Aimun (Tan Le et al., 2022).

The only Indigenous language for which MT currently exists in Canada is Inuktitut. The development of MT for Inuktitut was made possible by the availability of the Nunavut Hansard Corpus, constructed from the bilingual Inuktitut-English debates of the Legislative Assembly (Joanis et al., 2020). This availability of data also made it possible to improve word segmentation (Le and Sadat, 2020) and the study of gender biases in the bilingual corpus (Hansal et al., 2022; Le et al., 2023).

As several computational linguists have noted (notably Bird (2020)), it is primordial, when working on Indigenous language technology or resource development, to adopt a community-based and collaborative approach, to avoid repeating colonial research patterns. An exemplary participatory approach to Neural Machine Translation (NMT) was demonstrated in the Masakhane Project for African languages (Nekoto et al., 2020). Closer to Indigenous languages in Canada, Bontogon (2016) has taken the necessary but often overlooked step of human evaluation of the Indigenous language learning tool, in this case including by native speakers.

In addition to research approaches, closer attention has also been brought to the cultural awareness in machine translation tools themselves, especially with the recent advent and ubiquity of Large Language Models (LLM). For example, Yao et al. (2024) have underlined the limits of NMT models and LLMs when it comes to translating sentences with cultural content and proposed a data curation pipeline and an evaluation metric to better address this issue. Masoud et al. (2024) have benchmarked the performance of several state-of-the-art LLMs on cultural differences, using three of the largest and most represented cultural groups (American, Chinese, and Arab) and have noticed significant challenges even at this level of representation.

3 Proposed Methodology

3.1 Creation of Innu-Aimun/French alignments with collaboration and participation of Innu-Aimun locutors

Two main reference aligned corpora are used for evaluation as part of this comparative study, based on three bilingual Innu-Aimun and French texts. The first corpus, denonated as **kapesh** is based on literary texts by Innu author An Antane Kapesh.[9] These texts were manually aligned with the participation of Innu-Aimun translation students acting as single annotators.

The second corpus, denonated as **youth**, is based on a collection of poems written by Innu youth,[10] for which a sample representing 25% of the poems from the original text were manually aligned, with verses being treated as short sentences. Part of these the manual alignments for this sample of poems were performed by Innu-Aimun translation students, with every poem aligned by a single annotator. Another part was aligned in collaboration with the Innu-Aimun teaching staff from Kanatamat school. The goal was to allow immediate community benefits from the collaboration, even at the data collection and validation stage. These took the form of the creation of elementary-level exercises based on the poems in *Nin Auass* and their alignments formed in collaboration with the teaching staff.

[8] An example is the bilingual East Cree dictionary

[9] *Eukuan nin matshi-manitu innu-ishkueu* (Kapesh, 2019) and *Tanite nene etutamin nitassi?* (Kapesh, 2020)

[10] The collection is titled *Nin Auass* (Bacon and Morali, 2021)

Based on this sample of manually aligned poems, we evaluated several automated alignment methods, found that, for the type and quantity of text in the **youth** corpus, the best alignment method was Gale and Church (1993). Hence the remaining 75 % was automatically aligned with this method.

Table 1: Studied corpora

Corpus	Domain	Nb sentences
kapesh	Novel/Essay	1280
youth	Youth poems	1907

Table 1 present the aforementioned bilingual corpora with their domain and their total number of sentences (before splitting).

3.2 Evaluating MT performance of aligned texts as one corpus

The main objective of this first MT study involving the Innu-Aimun language is to examine its feasibility with the available published bilingual texts (Innu-Aimun and French), mostly literary and poetic texts. Given the small amount of texts, our approach is to assess how these texts behave as a single unified corpus. Similarly to Joanis et al. (2020), we train/validate and test on the same resulting corpus, as the data is too limited to conduct a generalization study (i.e. testing on an entirely different corpus than the one used in training/validation).

We test two types of MT methods: Statistical Machine Translation (SMT), as proposed by Koehn et al. (2003) and Neural Machine Translation (NMT). While neural methods have achieved state of the art for many high-resourced languages, the statistical approach requires less data and testing it is particularly relevant in low-resource contexts such as ours. The model used for NMT is based on the standard Transformer architecture (Vaswani et al., 2017).

For the distribution between the training, validation and test sets, a portion equivalent to 85% of the corpus is reserved for training, then the rest (15%) is divided in two for validation and testing (7.5% each). This split scheme was chosen because of the low availability of bilingual data for training. Datasets were cleaned and then segmented using language-agnostic BPE (Sennrich et al., 2016) with a vocabulary size of 16K.

Metrics used for NMT and SMT results quantitative evaluations are sacrebleu (Post, 2018) and ChrF++ (Popović, 2015).

In addition to quantative evaluation, the Innu-Aimun teaching staff from Kanatamat also contributed to a series of qualitative observation and analyses, for a small sample of translations generated by the SMT models.

4 Evaluations

4.1 Quantitative evaluations of MT Models

Tables 2 and 3 respectively present the results of the NMT and SMT evaluations for different combinations of individual corpora. The **kapesh** model is trained and evaluated solely on the **kapesh** corpus, the **youth** model is trained and evaluated solely and the **youth** corpus and the **kapesh+youth** model is trained and evaluated on a combination of both corpora.

From our NMT results, we can conclude that at this scale of data (i.e. less than four thousand sentences), NMT performance does not seem to be viable for any usage. The SMT results show that, for the Innu-Aimun/French pair at this data scale, the statistical approach to machine translation generally performs much better than the neural approach. This hypothesis of SMT superiority over NMT is statistically significant with $p < 0.05$ for both corpora and their combinated scores. Statistical significance was tested using Bootstrap Resampling, proposed for MT by Koehn (2004), and suggested by Dror et al. (2018). We used the latters' implementation of the algorithm specified by Berg-Kirkpatrick et al. (2012).

The overall best quantitative results are achieved by the **kapesh**-only SMT model. Its scores are much higher than the **youth**-only scores, but only slightly higher than that of the combined **kapesh+youth** scores.

4.2 Qualitative observations

Since the combined evaluation set include sentences/verses from both corpora, it is hard to discriminate impact of the combination on each of the corpora. The following subsection examines in detail and qualitatively a set of SMT-generated translations, from individual and combined models, to better understand this impact.

Those translations were collaboratively analyzed, involving computational linguistics researchers and Innu-Aimun teaching staff. This also allows to gain a more concrete and qualitative appreciation of the generated translations quality.

Tables 4, 5 and 6 present example translations

Table 2: NMT evaluations of Innu-Aimun/French corpora

Corpus	moe-fr (BLEU)	moe-fr (ChrF++)	fr-moe (BLEU)	fr-moe (ChrF++)
kapesh	**0.28**	**13.4**	**0.62**	**13.2**
youth	0.05	7.0	0.11	5.2
kapesh+youth	0.19	12.3	0.25	13.1

Table 3: SMT evaluations of Innu-Aimun/French corpora

Corpus	moe-fr (BLEU)	moe-fr (ChrF++)	fr-moe (BLEU)	fr-moe (ChrF++)
kapesh	**4.41**	**22.7**	**4.16**	**33.6**
youth	0.652	11.4	0.249	20.9
kapesh+youth	4.22	20.9	3.27	30.7

from the kapesh corpus, while tables 7, 8 and 9 present example from the youth corpus.

In table 4, the two translations seem quite far from the reference one when we compare the words. However, from the perspective of an Innu-Aimun locutor, the general meaning of the translated sentence from the kapesh+youth model can still be understood. In this translation, it is rather the syntax that is not good. The sentence could have been considered a better translation without the last five words (" à ce qu'il dit ").

In table 5, the translation of the kapesh model is more incomplete: it is partially composed of Innu-Aimun words. We can see in the translation of the kapesh+youth model that the French words " chose " and " je vais " (Kapesh, 2020) are also used in the reference translation. However, for the translation of the kapesh+youth model to be a good representation of the concepts in the source sentence, the concept of "other" should be removed and the concept "say" should be added.

In table 6, the translation of the kapesh model is syntactically incorrect in French. The translation of the combined kapesh+youth model, even if it does not represent a complete sentence, could be considered correct except for its plural (the source sentence is singular only).

In table 7, the youth model uses the Innu word " *kie* " rather than the word " et " (Bacon and Morali, 2021): the presence of the kapesh sentences during training allowed the model to perfect its translation, perhaps by taking advantage of the frequency of the word pair kie/et in this other corpus.

In table 8, we see that training on both youth and kapesh corpora allows to generate a more complete sentence than training on youth alone. In collaboration with the Innu-Aimun teaching staff, we can confirm that "moi je suis le loup" is a not only a correct translation, but it is also closer to the literal meaning that the reference translation, which is a more figurative one.

In table 9, although the kapesh+youth model translation gets none of the words of from the reference translation, it is a correct translation of the source sentence. This hints that the very low BLEU and ChrF++ scores of the youth model might not reflect the actual quality of the translations. Additionally, similarly to the previous example, it is actually closer to the literal meaning of the source sentence.

We can emphasize two key points from the above observations. First, we can see that poetry can contribute to an MT corpus: the youth corpus allows the kapesh corpus to get better, more precise translations for its literary sentences. Second, even though they were considered somewhat imprecise, with artistic quality (e.g. rhymes) often being prioritized over translation accuracy, the youth verses can be properly translated by an SMT model. This is true especially when the training also involves sentences from a literary corpus, as the translations can then become more complete and syntatically correct.

We can also conclude that poetry can be involved in—and be useful for—low-resource MT for an Indigenous language, especially if other quality textual sources are scarce. In that matter, quantitative scores might not be suitable for proper evaluation of the generated translations, since the latter can greatly differ from the reference ones even, if they are correct.

Overall, the results show that while interesting

Table 4: Qualitative comparison of kapesh SMT model, with and without youth: example #1

Source sentence (Innu-Aimun)	« Ne auass tapuetueu nenu etikut. » (Kapesh, 2020)
Translation (Reference)	« L'enfant se laisse convaincre. » (Kapesh, 2020)
Translation (kapesh SMT Model)	**l'enfant** est qu'il *tapuetueu* ce que lui dit.
Translation (kapesh+youth SMT Model)	**l'enfant** est d'accord avec ce que lui dit à ce qu'il.

Table 5: Qualitative comparison of kapesh SMT model, with and without youth: example #2

Source sentence (Innu-Aimun)	« Mak kutak tshekuan tshe uitamatan. » (Kapesh, 2020)
Translation (Reference)	« Je vais te dire encore une chose. » (Kapesh, 2020)
Translation (kapesh SMT Model)	la *uitamatan* et les autres.
Translation (kapesh+youth SMT Model)	et les autres **choses** que **je vais**.

Table 6: Qualitative comparison of kapesh SMT model, with and without youth: example #3

Source sentence (Innu-Aimun)	« Mak kutak tshekuan. » (Kapesh, 2020)
Translation (Reference)	« Et il y a autre chose. » (Kapesh, 2020)
Translation (kapesh SMT Model)	**et** les **autres** y.
Translation (kapesh+youth SMT Model)	**et** les **autres choses**.

Table 7: Qualitative comparison of youth SMT model, with and without kapesh: example #1

Source sentence (Innu-Aimun)	« kie nutin » (Bacon and Morali, 2021)
Translation (Reference)	« et le vent » (Bacon and Morali, 2021)
Translation (youth SMT Model)	*kie* **le vent**
Translation (kapesh+youth SMT Model)	**et le vent**

Table 8: Qualitative comparison of youth SMT model, with and without kapesh: example #2

Source sentence (Innu-Aimun)	« NIN MAIKAN » (Bacon and Morali, 2021)
Translation (Reference)	« MOI LE LOUP » (Bacon and Morali, 2021)
Translation (youth SMT Model)	je **loup**
Translation (kapesh+youth SMT Model)	**moi** je suis un **loup**

Table 9: Qualitative comparison of youth SMT model, with and without kapesh: example #3

Source sentence (Innu-Aimun)	« shashish shash »(Bacon and Morali, 2021)
Translation (Reference)	« les jours s'éternisent »(Bacon and Morali, 2021)
Translation (youth SMT Model)	la longtemps
Translation (kapesh+youth SMT Model)	il Y A LONGTEMPS déjà

results can be achieved with a few thousand sentences available, fully ready-to-use MT will require more than the current data for Innu-Aimun.

5 Conclusion

The current study has shown how difficult it can be to obtain good translations when first developing MT for an Indigenous language for which there are very few sentence pairs, and yet how the literary and poetic texts available, even if written in particular styles, can potentially contribute to building a general corpus for MT. We have also shown how at the present scale and types of available text for Innu-Aimun and French, SMT offers much better results than NMT. We carried this project collaboratively, involving both computational linguistics researchers and Innu-Aimun teaching staff, and with the participation of Indigenous and non-Indigenous speakers of Innu-aimun.

Acknowledgments

The authors are grateful to all anonymous reviewers for their suggestions and fruitful recommendations. Also, we are very thankful to all Indigenous and non-Indigenous collaborators and partners. This work has been partially supported by the Northern Scientific Training Program (NSTP).

References

Antti Arppe, Jordan Lachler, Trond Trosterud, Lene Antonsen, and Sjur N. Moshagen. 2016. Basic Language Resource Kits for Endangered Languages: A Case Study of Plains Cree. In *Proceedings of the LREC 2016 Workshop "CCURL 2016 – Towards an Alliance for Digital Language Diversity"*, pages 1–8, Portorož (Slovenia).

J. Bacon and L. Morali, editors. 2021. *Nin Auass. Moi l'enfant: Poèmes de la jeunesse innue*. Mémoire d'encrier.

Anne-Marie Baraby, Marie-Odile Junker, and Yvette Mollen. 2017. A 45-year old language documentation program first aimed at speakers: the case of the Innu.

Taylor Berg-Kirkpatrick, David Burkett, and Dan Klein. 2012. An empirical investigation of statistical significance in NLP. In *Proceedings of the 2012 Joint Conference on Empirical Methods in Natural Language Processing and Computational Natural Language Learning*, pages 995–1005, Jeju Island, Korea. Association for Computational Linguistics.

Steven Bird. 2020. Decolonising Speech and Language Technology. In *Proceedings of the 28th International Conference on Computational Linguistics*, pages 3504–3519, Barcelona, Spain (Online). International Committee on Computational Linguistics.

Megan A. Bontogon. 2016. *Evaluating nêhiyawêtân: A computer assisted language learning (CALL) application for Plains Cree*. Ph.D. thesis, University of Alberta.

L. Drapeau. 2011. *Les langues autochtones du Québec: Un patrimoine en danger*. Presses de l'Université du Québec.

Lynn Drapeau. 2014a. Bilinguisme et érosion lexicale dans une communauté montagnaise. In Pierre Martel and Jacques Maurais, editors, *Langues et sociétés en contact: Mélanges offerts à Jean-Claude Corbeil*, pages 363–376. Max Niemeyer Verlag.

Lynn Drapeau. 2014b. *Grammaire de la langue innue*. PUQ.

Rotem Dror, Gili Baumer, Segev Shlomov, and Roi Reichart. 2018. The hitchhiker's guide to testing statistical significance in natural language processing. In *Proceedings of the 56th Annual Meeting of the Association for Computational Linguistics (Volume 1: Long Papers)*, pages 1383–1392, Melbourne, Australia. Association for Computational Linguistics.

William A. Gale and Kenneth W. Church. 1993. A Program for Aligning Sentences in Bilingual Corpora. *Computational Linguistics*, 19(1):75–102. Place: Cambridge, MA Publisher: MIT Press.

Oussama Hansal, Ngoc Tan Le, and Fatiha Sadat. 2022. Indigenous language revitalization and the dilemma of gender bias. In *Proceedings of the 4th Workshop on Gender Bias in Natural Language Processing (GeBNLP)*, pages 244–254, Seattle, Washington. Association for Computational Linguistics.

Eric Joanis, Rebecca Knowles, Roland Kuhn, Samuel Larkin, Patrick Littell, Chi-kiu Lo, Darlene Stewart, and Jeffrey Micher. 2020. The Nunavut Hansard Inuktitut–English Parallel Corpus 3.0 with Preliminary Machine Translation Results. In *Proceedings of the 12th Language Resources and Evaluation Conference*, pages 2562–2572, Marseille, France. European Language Resources Association.

Marie-Odile Junker, Yvette Mollen, Hélène St-Onge, and Delasie Torkornoo. 2016. Integrated web tools for Innu language maintenance. In *Papers of the 44th Algonquian Conference*, pages 192–210.

A.A Kapesh. 2019. *Je suis une maudite Sauvagesse: Eukuan nin matshi-manitu innushkueu*. Mémoire d'encrier.

A.A. Kapesh. 2020. *Qu'as-tu fait de mon pays? Tanite nene etutamin nitassi?* Mémoire d'encrier.

Philipp Koehn. 2004. Statistical significance tests for machine translation evaluation. In *Proceedings of the 2004 Conference on Empirical Methods in Natural Language Processing*, pages 388–395, Barcelona, Spain. Association for Computational Linguistics.

Philipp Koehn, Franz J. Och, and Daniel Marcu. 2003. Statistical phrase-based translation. In *Proceedings of the 2003 Human Language Technology Conference of the North American Chapter of the Association for Computational Linguistics*, pages 127–133.

Ngoc Tan Le, Oussama Hansal, and Fatiha Sadat. 2023. Challenges and issue of gender bias in under-represented languages: An empirical study on Inuktitut-English NMT. In *Proceedings of the Sixth Workshop on the Use of Computational Methods in the Study of Endangered Languages*, pages 89–97, Remote. Association for Computational Linguistics.

Tan Ngoc Le and Fatiha Sadat. 2020. Low-Resource NMT: an Empirical Study on the Effect of Rich Morphological Word Segmentation on Inuktitut. In *Proceedings of the 14th Conference of the Association for Machine Translation in the Americas (Volume 1: Research Track)*, pages 165–172, Virtual. Association for Machine Translation in the Americas.

Reem I. Masoud, Ziquan Liu, Martin Ferianc, Philip Treleaven, and Miguel Rodrigues. 2024. Cultural alignment in large language models: An explanatory analysis based on Hofstede's cultural dimensions. *Preprint*, arXiv:2309.12342.

Wilhelmina Nekoto, Vukosi Marivate, Tshinondiwa Matsila, Timi Fasubaa, Taiwo Fagbohungbe, Solomon Oluwole Akinola, Shamsuddeen Muhammad, Salomon Kabongo Kabenamualu, Salomey Osei, Freshia Sackey, Rubungo Andre Niyongabo, Ricky Macharm, Perez Ogayo, Orevaoghene Ahia, Musie Meressa Berhe, Mofetoluwa Adeyemi, Masabata Mokgesi-Selinga, Lawrence Okegbemi, Laura Martinus, Kolawole Tajudeen, Kevin Degila, Kelechi Ogueji, Kathleen Siminyu, Julia Kreutzer, Jason Webster, Jamiil Toure Ali, Jade Abbott, Iroro Orife, Ignatius Ezeani, Idris Abdulkadir Dangana, Herman Kamper, Hady Elsahar, Goodness Duru, Ghollah Kioko, Murhabazi Espoir, Elan van Biljon, Daniel Whitenack, Christopher Onyefuluchi, Chris Chinenye Emezue, Bonaventure F. P. Dossou, Blessing Sibanda, Blessing Bassey, Ayodele Olabiyi, Arshath Ramkilowan, Alp Öktem, Adewale Akinfaderin, and Abdallah Bashir. 2020. Participatory research for low-resourced machine translation: A case study in African languages. In *Findings of the Association for Computational Linguistics: EMNLP 2020*, pages 2144–2160, Online. Association for Computational Linguistics.

Maja Popović. 2015. chrF: character n-gram F-score for automatic MT evaluation. In *Proceedings of the Tenth Workshop on Statistical Machine Translation*, pages 392–395, Lisbon, Portugal. Association for Computational Linguistics.

Matt Post. 2018. A call for clarity in reporting BLEU scores. In *Proceedings of the Third Conference on Machine Translation: Research Papers*, pages 186–191, Brussels, Belgium. Association for Computational Linguistics.

Rico Sennrich, Barry Haddow, and Alexandra Birch. 2016. Neural Machine Translation of Rare Words with Subword Units. In *Proceedings of the 54th Annual Meeting of the Association for Computational Linguistics (Volume 1: Long Papers)*, pages 1715–1725, Berlin, Germany. Association for Computational Linguistics.

Myriam St-Gelais. 2022. *Une histoire de la littérature innue*. PUQ, Tshakapesh Institute, Montréal, Canada.

Ngoc Tan Le, Antoine Cadotte, Mathieu Boivin, Fatiha Sadat, and Jimena Terraza. 2022. Deep learning-based morphological segmentation for indigenous languages: A study case on Innu-Aimun. In *Proceedings of the Third Workshop on Deep Learning for Low-Resource Natural Language Processing*, pages 146–151, Hybrid. Association for Computational Linguistics.

Ashish Vaswani, Noam Shazeer, Niki Parmar, Jakob Uszkoreit, Llion Jones, Aidan N Gomez, Ł ukasz Kaiser, and Illia Polosukhin. 2017. Attention is all you need. In *Advances in Neural Information Processing Systems*, volume 30. Curran Associates, Inc.

Binwei Yao, Ming Jiang, Diyi Yang, and Junjie Hu. 2024. Benchmarking llm-based machine translation on cultural awareness. *Preprint*, arXiv:2305.14328.

Rule-Based, Neural and LLM Back-Translation: Comparative Insights from a Variant of Ladin

Samuel Frontull and **Georg Moser**
Department of Computer Science
University of Innsbruck, Innsbruck, Austria
{samuel.frontull, georg.moser}@uibk.ac.at

Abstract

This paper explores the impact of different back-translation approaches on machine translation for Ladin, specifically the Val Badia variant. Given the limited amount of parallel data available for this language (only 18k Ladin–Italian sentence pairs), we investigate the performance of a multilingual neural machine translation model fine-tuned for Ladin–Italian. In addition to the available authentic data, we synthesise further translations by using three different models: a fine-tuned neural model, a rule-based system developed specifically for this language pair, and a large language model. Our experiments show that all approaches achieve comparable translation quality in this low-resource scenario, yet round-trip translations highlight differences in model performance.

1 Introduction

In recent years, a variety of methods have been developed to apply neural machine translation (NMT) also in low-resource scenarios (Shi et al., 2022; Haddow et al., 2022; Ranathunga et al., 2023). The back-translation technique has shown to be particularly effective in such settings (Sennrich et al., 2016; Edunov et al., 2018), offering the potential for substantial improvements in translation quality.

This work investigates the influence of the back-translation model selection for a low-resource language. We do this, by comparing the results obtained by fine-tuning a pre-trained multilingual NMT model using synthesised translations generated by (i) a NMT system fine-tuned on the available parallel data, (ii) a rule-based machine translation (RBMT) system developed for the specific language pair, and (iii) a large language model (LLM) prompted to translate given texts, accompanied by 8 exemplary samples.

The quality of the synthesised data, which in turn is determined by the underlying models used to generate it, matters (Burlot and Yvon, 2018). In our case, the synthesised translations originate from three models based on a different paradigm. Thus, the synthesised data is characterised by the specific strengths and weaknesses of the respective paradigms.

Rule-based systems are robust and computationally lightweight, but may face challenges in dealing with ambiguity. Moreover, they lag behind at the grammatical level. Neural models show a high ability to adapt to provided texts, but perform less well when confronted with out-of-domain data (Shen et al., 2021). In contrast, language model-based approaches (LLMs) are praised for their ability to produce fluent, coherent texts, but they are prone to hallucinations (Rawte et al., 2023). It is therefore an interesting question to investigate how this affects the quality of the NMT models trained on this data. This comparative analysis sheds light on the nuanced contrasts inherent in the different MT methods.

Our results show that in this low-resource scenario the back-translation model does not have a significant impact, and the performance of the models converges to similar results in terms of BLEU/chrF++ points. This assertion is supported by an empirical analysis carried out on the Val Badia variant of Ladin. Our main contributions are:

- we are the first to explore MT for Ladin in general, with a specific focus on the Val Badia variant,
- we compare an RBMT-, an NMT- and an LLM-based back-translation, providing insights into the efficacy of the methods for Ladin,
- we establish baseline results and make the test data, the RBMT system, as well as the best-performing models publicly available

Proceedings of the The Seventh Workshop on Technologies for Machine Translation of Low-Resource Languages (LoResMT 2024), pages 128–138
August 15, 2024 ©2024 Association for Computational Linguistics

In Section 2 we describe our data collection and corpus creation process. In Section 3 we present the three different methods used for the back-translation of monolingual Ladin data into Italian. Section 4 gives an overview of the conducted experiments and Section 5 presents the obtained results. Section 6 discusses related work and similar approaches. In Section 7, we summarize and discuss future work.

The Ladin Language Ladin is an officially recognised minority language, and thus taught in schools, used in the media, and employed in public administration. For this reason, an effective machine translation system could make a significant contribution to facilitating and supporting communication in this language. However, Ladin is still an unexplored language in the field of machine translation. Indeed, nearly no parallel data[1] is publicly available for this language, except for a few hundred samples on OPUS (Tiedemann, 2012). This language, spoken by around 30,000 people in the northern Italian Dolomite regions, exhibits significant diversity across its five main variants (*Val Badia*, *Gherdëina*, *Fascia*, *Fodom*, *Anpezo*), each shaped uniquely by its development in different valleys. This diversity is not only evident in the spoken language but has also resulted in distinct standards for written communication. The first author of the paper originates from the *Val Badia* and is a native speaker of Ladin. Therefore, in this work we concentrate on the standard written language of this valley. In the rest of the paper, we will use *lvb* as language code to refer to this variant of Ladin, and *ita* for Italian.

2 Data

This section gives an overview of the linguistic resources available for the Ladin language and describes the method employed to collect data for the specific Val Badia variant of Ladin.

2.1 Available Resources

Publicly accessible parallel data for Ladin is scarce. The Open Parallel Corpus (Tiedemann, 2012) e.g. lists 1543 Ladin–German, 220 Ladin–Italian, and 81 Ladin–English sentences. However, these texts are mainly specific to the variants of Gherdëina and Fassa and were not disseminated by public institutions. For our experiments, we were provided with the archive of the weekly newspaper *La Usc di Ladins*[2] and a digitised version of the dictionary Ladin Val Badia – Italian (Moling et al., 2016). From these data sources we extracted monolingual texts as well as a small dataset of parallel sentences. We furthermore used the dictionary as the basis for implementing a RBMT system. The collection of other parallel texts is time-consuming and has therefore been left for future work.

2.2 Parallel Data

The Ladin (Val Badia) – Italian dictionary (Moling et al., 2016) contains, alongside the word entries, also sentences that illustrate their usage. For these sentences the corresponding Italian translation is also given. We have collected this data to create our training dataset, which contains a total of 18,139 sentences. These sentences are basic and short because they were created specifically to illustrate the use of words and phrases. The average length is 23.43 and 25.69 characters for Ladin and Italian respectively. This dataset has been publicly released.[3]

2.3 Ladin Monolingual Data

The Ladin newspaper *La Usc di Ladins*, digitally archived since 2012, provides an extensive dataset of monolingual texts. These texts are published in five different variants, each corresponding to one of the five Ladin valleys. We extracted these texts from the PDF documents and segmented them into individual sentences using the NLTK library (Bird et al., 2009), specifically setting Italian as the language to accommodate Ladin. In total, we accumulated 1,937,608 sentences. These sentences had to be categorised by variant, as described below.

Variant Classification In order to train a variant classifier, labeled training data is essential. However, the monolingual data from the newspaper PDFs lacked these labels. Therefore, we collected the texts from the newspaper's website.[4] Here, the article excerpts are categorized according to their origin valleys and the corresponding language variants, allowing us to create a labeled dataset.

We gathered a corpus of 7,766 article excerpts with a total of 42,745 individual sentences for training. These sentences were then split into training (comprising 75% of the sentences) and test data

[1] In a machine readable format.

[2] https://www.lausc.it/

[3] https://www.doi.org/10.57967/hf/1878

[4] https://www.lausc.it

variant	# sentences	# characters
val-badia	746.704	71.619.515
gherdeina	491.575	57.704.414
fascia	407.605	52.504.357
fodom	146.049	16.615.059
anpezo	145.674	16.425.301

Table 1: Variant classification of monolingual data.

(the remaining 25%). Using the 2,500 most frequent 3-gram characters as features, we trained an XGBoost variant-classifier (Chen and Guestrin, 2016). On the test data, our classifier achieved 94.48% accuracy in classifying these 5 labels.

The resulting model was used to predict the variant of each of the 1,937,608 sentences in the monolingual dataset. Table 1 reports the respective number of classifications (and the total number of characters) for each variant. 746,704 sentences were classified as `val-badia` and were considered for further processing.

Data Preparation Because of the spelling reform in 2015, we further processed the sentences classified as `val-badia` to exclude any with words that are no longer valid. To do this, we used the implementation of our RBMT system which is explained in more detail in Section 3.2. We used the system to identify unknown words and tried to adapt them to the new spelling according to certain rules. Sentences where this was not possible were left out. This process ensured that the filtered sentences fully adhered to the new spelling, which also facilitated the rule-based translations. We collected a total of 274,665 sentences ($\approx$ 31% of the extracted sentences) which constitute the monolingual Ladin data we used in our experiments. Among the unused sentences, $\approx 100k$ contain only one unknown word/typo so there would be still potential to acquire additional data if additional time were spent analysing and preparing these texts.

2.4 Italian Monolingual Data

As monolingual data for Italian, we used the `ELRC-CORDIS_News` dataset[5] from OPUS (Tiedemann, 2012), which contains 123,691 Italian sentences.

2.5 Test Data

This section introduces the three test sets on which the models were evaluated. This test data differs considerably from the training data, so that it can be considered out-of-domain data.

Testset 1 This dataset includes the statute of the *Stiftung Südtiroler Sparkasse*, a nonprofit foundation dedicated to supporting and promoting various initiatives and projects, primarily within the province of Bolzano. The document is rich in formal and legal terminology. It contains 424 sentences[6].

Testset 2 This dataset is a festive compendium of the history of the region associated with this language (Kager, 2022). It combines historical narratives with legal and administrative statements. The result is a mixture of stylistic elements and lexical domains. It contains 833 sentences[7].

Testset 3 This dataset delves into the literary realm with the classic story of Pinocchio (Collodi, 2017), a text rich in narrative prose, dialogue and idiomatic expressions, challenging the models with its creative and figurative language. It contains 1563 sentences[8].

3 Back-translation Strategies

The so-called *back-translation*, first introduced in Sennrich et al. (2016), refers to the process of automatic translation of monolingual texts in the target language to the source language. This method of enriching additional training data in the source-to-target translation direction (where the target side remains authentic) has proven to be particularly effective and is particularly valuable in low-resource scenarios. In this section we present the three different back-translation strategies used in our research to translate monolingual Ladin texts into Italian.

3.1 Neural MT

There is evidence that low-resource languages benefit from multilingual models (Aharoni et al., 2019). For this reason, we opted to utilise a pre-trained, multilingual model, specifically the `Helsinki-NLP/opus-mt-ine-ine`[9] model available from the Hugging Face Model Hub, as our

[5]https://elrc-share.eu/

[6]https://huggingface.co/datasets/sfrontull/stiftungsparkasse-lld_valbadia-ita

[7]https://huggingface.co/datasets/sfrontull/autonomia-lld_valbadia-ita

[8]https://huggingface.co/datasets/sfrontull/pinocchio-lld_valbadia-ita

[9]https://huggingface.co/Helsinki-NLP/opus-mt-ine-ine

base model. This model, which is part of OPUS-MT (Tiedemann and Thottingal, 2020), was trained to translate between 135 Indo-European languages, to which Ladin and Italian also belong.

The Marian MT model, configured for `Helsinki-NLP/opus-mt-ine-ine`, features 6 encoder and 6 decoder layers, each with 8 attention heads and a feed-forward dimension of 2048. The model employs a beam search size of 6, a dropout rate of 0.1, and an embedding size of 512. It shares embeddings between the encoder and decoder.

We fine-tuned this model for the two translation directions *lvb* $\rightarrow$ *ita* and *ita* $\rightarrow$ *lvb* on the available authentic training data. We trained a single model for both directions by using the tags »`ita`« for *lvb* $\rightarrow$ *ita* and »`lld_Latn`« [10] for the opposite direction as prefixes of the source text. In the rest of the paper, we refer to this fine-tuned model as `N1`. For fine-tuning, we utilized the AdamW optimizer[11] with the defaults settings.

The fine-tuning greatly improves the model in both translation directions, as the scores reported in Table 4 and 3 show. This demonstrates that the data is reliable and that the model adapts well.

3.2 Rule-based MT

For low-resource languages, RBMT frameworks offer a crucial advantage: leveraging linguistic expertise to overcome the limitations of data-driven methods (Khanna et al., 2021). Considering the similar sentence structure and composition of Ladin and Italian (they are both Romance languages), it can be assumed that a rule-based MT system can also perform well without excessive structural transfer work. The available Ladin Val Badia-Italian dictionary served as the foundation for the rule-based MT system we developed in Apertium (Forcada and Tyers, 2016) for this language pair.

This dictionary provides, in addition to the individual words and word translations, also a list of all inflected forms for each lemma. To effectively utilise this dictionary within our translation system, we mapped the lexicographical data to paradigms within the framework of Apertium (monodix format). Specifically, we created 742 paradigms for a total of 19,034 lemmas. This extensive set includes multiple lexical categories: 597 adverbs, 3,366 adjectives, 11,496 nouns, 162 pronouns, and 2,439 verbs. Additionally, we incorporated proper nouns, short phrases, and wordgrams that were identified during the monolingual text extraction process. The resulting bilingual dictionary contains a total of 30,468 entries. The integration with Apertium was facilitated by connecting to and reusing the pre-existing module for Italian[12]. The Ladin module[13] and the Ladin–Italian[14] module can be found on GitHub. In the rest of the paper, we refer to this RBMT system as `R1`.

According to `aq-covtest`[15] `R1` has a coverage of 96.66% on Testset 1, 95.81% on Testset 2 and 95.90% on Testset 3. However, since we did not develop disambiguation modules, we designed the system to select the first suggestion in cases of morphological and lexical ambiguity, which can sometimes result in incorrect choices that may distort the meaning of the texts. To counteract this, and to further enhance the rule-based translation system, we extracted the 900 most common word n-grams from the texts and added their corresponding translations as entries to the bilingual dictionary.

In addition to the data, we have also included 13 1-level structural transfer rules to avoid common errors. For example, in Ladin, the word *pa* is used to emphasize a question. In Italian, however, there is no corresponding word for this purpose. We have therefore developed a rule to exclude this word from the translation. The other rules include gender correction, dealing with reflexive verbs and prepositions.

3.3 MT with a Large Language Model

LLMs have shown remarkable capability in understanding and generating human-like text across various languages and domains (Brown et al., 2020). However, their performance in MT tasks exhibits significant variability across languages, especially when comparing high-resource languages to low-resource languages (Robinson et al., 2023). We explore the utilisation of a LLM, specifically *GPT-3.5 Turbo* (OpenAI, 2024), to generate translations from Ladin to Italian. The process involved leverag-

[10]We (re)used the tag »`lld_Latn`« because it is listed as a valid target language ID, as few Ladin texts were already included in the training of this model.

[11]`https://huggingface.co/docs/transformers/v4.41.0/en/main_classes/optimizer_schedules#transformers.AdamW`

[12]`https://github.com/apertium/apertium-ita`

[13]`https://github.com/schtailmuel/apertium-lld-ita`

[14]`https://github.com/schtailmuel/apertium-lld`

[15]`https://wikis.swarthmore.edu/ling073/Apertium-quality`

ing the advanced capabilities of the LLM, accessed through the `gpt-3.5-turbo-0125` API endpoint. In the rest of the paper, we refer to this LLM as `L1`.

To enhance throughput and reduce the number of API requests, we generated the translation of 16 Ladin texts in a single request. We provided a set of 8 example translations in JSON format, randomly selected from the available authentic training data and instructed the LLM to generate translations for 16 Ladin texts, which were also provided as a JSON dictionary, with empty Italian translations. Listing 1 (Appendix A) showcases an exemplary prompt.

With this prompting approach, we translated the entire monolingual Ladin corpus into Italian. By providing the exemplary translations as JSON, we were able to reduce the failure rate (invalid/incomplete answers). The extent to which these examples also helped with the translation itself remains open. The entire process spanned approximately 100 hours, with an average processing time of around 22 seconds per request.

4 Experiments

We used the `opus-mt-ine-ine`[16] model as base model for the experiments. In the rest of the paper, we use `BM` to refer to this model. We fine-tuned `BM` with the various data sets using the Transformers library (Wolf et al., 2020), specifically leveraging the `Seq2SeqTrainer` module. We always trained a single model for both directions using the corresponding prefixes.

We configured the training to process batches of 16 samples, and restricted the input and output sequences to a maximum of 128 tokens to ensure manageable computation loads. The models were evaluated each 16,000 steps. As a stopping criterion, we used three consecutive evaluations resulting in an improvement of less than 0.2 chrF points on the validation set. For training, we utilised an NVIDIA TITAN RTX graphics card with 24 GB. In total, we have trained 15 models:

- Model `N1`: `BM` fine-tuned with the available parallel data consisting of 18,139 sentences.
- Models `N2/R2/L2`: `BM` fine-tuned with authentic data and Ladin monolingual data backtranslated (BT) to Italian using `N1/R1/L1` respectively.

[16]`https://huggingface.co/Helsinki-NLP/opus-mt-ine-ine`

	Testset 1	Testset 2	Testset 3
ref	425.7	306.3	697.4
BM	545.8	325.8	595.7
N1	1237.6	437.8	805.3
N2	633.3	414.0	695.1
N3	484.5	331.8	606.8
N4	367.5	323.4	605.4
N5	476.2	320.9	593.4
R1	559.5	421.5	727.8
R2	593.8	405.7	722.2
R3	434.8	309.5	601.0
R4	402.4	305.3	594.3
R5	387.8	306.1	608.1
L1	380.3	294.3	517.8
L2	695.6	406.1	675.3
L3	396.0	345.4	634.4
L4	377.0	318.0	563.7
L5	393.3	316.1	569.6

Table 2: Mean perplexity (*ita*) of selected models.

- Models `N3/R3/L3`: This iteration extends the training base of `N2/R2/L2` by integrating Italian monolingual data that has been translated into Ladin utilising `N2/R2/L2` respectively.
- Models `N4/R4/L4`: `BM` fine-tuned with same training data as `N3/R3/L3` models, but with Ladin and Italian monolingual data backtranslated with `N3/R3/L3` model.
- Models `N5/R5/L5`: This iteration extends the training base of `N4/R4/L4` by adding also the forward-translations (FT) as training data.
- Models `A1/A2`: `A1` was trained on the combined training data used to trained `N4`, `R4` and `L4`. In `A2` we additionally included the forward-translations into the training data.

We refer to the models `N1`, ..., `N5` that were trained with NMT backtranslated data as `N`-models. Analogously, we use the term `R`-models and `L`-models to refer to RBMT and LLM models, respectively.

Models `N4/R4/L4` illustrate the gains achieved through iterative back-translation (Hoang et al., 2018). Additionally, models `N5/R5/L5` demonstrate potential improvements achievable with synthetically generated forward-translation data.

We evaluated these models on the 3 test sets presented in Section 2.5. The results are presented and analysed in the following section.

Ladin (Val Badia) → Italian		Testset 1 BLEU / chrF++	Testset 2 BLEU / chrF++	Testset 3 BLEU / chrF++
NMT opus-mt-ine-ine	BM	8.17/34.81	8.07/34.27	2.29/21.12
BM fine-tuned with authentic data	N1	12.65/41.55	11.49/39.90	11.83/36.40
+ *lvb* monolingual BT with N1	N2	13.01/42.98	12.40/41.26	13.23/36.84
+ *ita* monolingual BT with N2	N3	21.98/50.32	19.37/47.35	15.01/39.15
+ *lvb* and *ita* monolingual BT with N3	N4	22.90/50.67	21.12/48.38	16.17/40.41
+ *lvb* and *ita* monolingual FT with N3	N5	21.49/49.94	20.53/48.16	15.10/39.47
RBMT apertium-lld-ita	R1	11.38/39.72	11.60/41.49	8.48/34.48
BM fine-tuned with authentic data				
+ *lvb* monolingual BT with R1	R2	14.43/42.76	13.27/42.00	13.99/37.37
+ *ita* monolingual BT with R2	R3	22.17/50.33	19.27/48.17	15.89/40.19
+ *lvb* and *ita* monolingual BT with R3	R4	21.36/50.24	20.27/49.08	16.34/**40.76**
+ *lvb* and *ita* monolingual FT with R3	R5	22.50/50.64	20.37/49.04	**16.36**/40.47
LLM gpt-3.5-turbo-0125	L1	**26.77**/**53.20**	21.17/48.52	10.37/32.36
BM fine-tuned with authentic data				
+ *lvb* monolingual BT with L1	L2	12.93/43.20	12.21/41.21	13.22/36.94
+ *ita* monolingual BT with L2	L3	22.69/50.74	20.37/48.40	15.26/38.99
+ *lvb* and *ita* monolingual BT with L3	L4	23.01/51.17	21.38/49.24	15.12/39.37
+ *lvb* and *ita* monolingual FT with L3	L5	23.11/50.84	20.86/48.50	15.19/39.29
ALL BM fine-tuned with authentic data				
+ *lvb* and *ita* monolingual BT with N3, R3, L3	A1	23.58/50.68	21.30/48.78	15.32/39.56
+ *lvb* and *ita* monolingual FT with N3, R3, L3	A2	24.12/51.42	**22.24**/**49.69**	15.98/39.64

Table 3: Evaluation Results for Ladin to Italian Translation

5 Results and Discussion

The results of the various experiments conducted are presented in Table 3 and Table 4, where the SacreBLEU (Post, 2018) and chrF++ (Popović, 2015) scores for different models and test sets are detailed. To facilitate comparison, the best scores for each approach have been underlined, and the overall best scores for each testset are highlighted in bold.

Additionally, as recommended in Edunov et al. (2020), in Table 2 we report the mean perplexity values for the Italian translations generated by the different models to complement BLEU's emphasis on adequacy. Perplexity measures how well a language model can predict the next word in a sequence based on the preceding words. Lower perplexity means that the model is more confident and accurate in its predictions, indicating that it can better reproduce the structure and patterns of the language it generates. Therefore, we present the mean perplexity values obtained from GPT-2 (Radford et al., 2019) , computed using the implementation available from Hugging Face[17].

[17]https://huggingface.co/spaces/evaluate-metric/perplexity

Several findings can be deduced from these results, and will be discussed below. In general, there is evidence that augmenting the training data with monolingual data through back-translation is effective. N1 shows that fine-tuning the model with only authentic training data substantially improves the results in both directions (compared to BM) in terms of BLEU/chrF++ points. This shows on the one hand that the training is effective and on the other hand that the available data is adequate. However, it is also evident that the model generates less fluent text, as indicated by the perplexity scores which increase for this model.

The results reveal a progression in difficulty among the test sets, where Testset 3 emerges as the most challenging one. On this test set, all approaches achieve similar low scores, suggesting the presented approach may face limitations with more complex texts.

In the translation direction *lvb* → *ita*, the best results were achieved by combining the different back-translations, as model A2 results indicate. This emphasises the importance of a broad and diversified dataset. Remarkably, the A2 model is also competitive in the reverse translation direction (*ita*

Italian → Ladin (Val Badia)		Testset 1 BLEU / chrF++	Testset 2 BLEU / chrF++	Testset 3 BLEU / chrF++
NMT `opus-mt-ine-ine`	BM	0.08/5.34	0.55/13.68	0.05/6.86
BM fine-tuned with authentic data	N1	10.22/37.11	10.14/37.48	12.76/35.31
+ *lvb* monolingual BT with N1	N2	19.09/46.92	18.05/45.44	16.50/37.46
+ *ita* monolingual BT with N2	N3	19.54/47.02	19.45/46.21	**16.66**/37.36
+ *lvb* and *ita* monolingual BT with N3	N4	19.61/46.35	19.16/45.63	16.40/37.84
+ *lvb* and *ita* monolingual FT with N3	N5	20.24/46.72	19.39/45.88	15.56/36.97
RBMT `apertium-lld-ita`	R1	4.94/37.50	4.50/36.89	3.19/27.44
BM fine-tuned with authentic data				
+ *lvb* monolingual BT with R1	R2	19.18/46.59	16.96/44.97	15.21/36.76
+ *ita* monolingual BT with R2	R3	19.86/46.83	17.70/45.69	15.04/36.60
+ *lvb* and *ita* monolingual BT with R3	R4	20.93/47.65	19.32/46.58	16.65/**38.16**
+ *lvb* and *ita* monolingual FT with R3	R5	19.97/46.88	18.65/46.19	16.61/38.12
LLM `gpt-3.5-turbo-0125`	L1	5.54/29.03	3.84/28.98	1.16/18.60
BM fine-tuned with authentic data				
+ *lvb* monolingual BT with L1	L2	**22.09**/**48.69**	19.71/46.59	14.16/35.67
+ *ita* monolingual BT with L2	L3	21.59/48.23	**19.96**/**49.96**	14.23/35.81
+ *lvb* and *ita* monolingual BT with L3	L4	20.82/47.86	19.87/46.59	16.55/38.04
+ *lvb* and *ita* monolingual FT with L3	L5	20.93/47.70	19.38/46.37	15.84/37.29
ALL BM fine-tuned with authentic data				
+ *lvb* and *ita* monolingual BT with N3, R3, L3	A1	19.83/47.16	19.94/46.40	16.54/37.91
+ *lvb* and *ita* monolingual FT with N3, R3, L3	A2	20.81/47.50	19.71/46.36	16.36/37.82

Table 4: Evaluation Results for Italian to Ladin Translation

to *lvb*), although it does not achieve the best results.

A comparison of the models N1, R1 and L1 suggests that the LLM generates more fluent texts (low perplexity) but perhaps does not always accurately reproduce the meaning, as attested by the performance on Testset 3 (low perplexity but also low BLEU score). In this assessment, the RBMT system R1 also performs better than the fine-tuned NMT model N1. One of the reasons for the high perplexity values of N1 is that this model tends to hallucinate because it has been fine-tuned with a small data set. However, this does not seem to affect the performance as the models trained on this data do not perform considerably worse.

The performance of the LLM varies significantly, with pronounced differences between the three test sets in both directions of translation. The significant difference observed between Testset 1 and Testset 2 in the translation direction from *lvb* → *ita* cannot be seen in the R- and N-models. It remains unclear to what extent the LLM benefits from the given examples in the prompt. However, by providing an example, the propensity for errors was minimised, resulting in fewer mistakes during execution. Even though LLMs are not (yet) suitable for generating texts in low-resource languages out-of-the-box (see performance of L1 in Table 4), Ladin and low-resource languages in general could benefit from this technology. Our experiments show that models trained on back-translations from L1 performed best on Testset 1 and Testset 2 in the translation direction *ita* → *lvb*.

The inclusion of forward translations in the training data did not consistently improve the models, with the exception of the R-models for *lvb* → *ita*. This suggests that these synthesised texts introduce too much noise. However, model A2 was able to benefit from this data in the translation direction *lvb* → *ita*. Filtering this data could slightly improve the model.

As the models achieve similar scores on the test data, we also examined the quality of round-trip translations to gain additional insights. For this, we used 10k sentences from the monolingual Ladin and Italian data (which were also used for training, hence the high scores), translated them into the other language and then back-translated them. This concept of so-called *round-trip translation* is a suitable evaluation method (Zhuo et al., 2023). We used the R4/N4/L4 models for this purpose, ap-

A/B	*lvb* $\xrightarrow{A}$ *ita* $\xrightarrow{B}$ *lvb*	*ita* $\xrightarrow{A}$ *lvb* $\xrightarrow{B}$ *ita*
	BLEU / chrF++	BLEU / chrF++
N4/N4	70.57 / 82.56	64.19 / 81.26
N4/R4	58.57 / 74.50	47.16 / 72.09
N4/L4	63.90 / 78.09	59.47 / 78.46
R4/N4	70.80 / 82.20	68.38 / 83.00
R4/R4	**80.12** / **88.94**	**68.51** / **84.73**
R4/L4	70.36 / 81.98	67.41 / 82.68
L4/N4	63.72 / 77.53	57.02 / 76.54
L4/R4	57.13 / 73.32	46.95 / 71.52
L4/L4	72.31 / 83.69	65.74 / 82.02

Table 5: Results for Round-Trip Translations

plying one model A for one direction and the same or a different model B for the opposite direction. Table 5 shows the obtained results. It can be clearly seen that the results are worse when a different model is used for the reverse translation. This shows that although the models achieve similar results with the test data, they work differently. The R4 model proves to be the most stable here, as its translations can be back-translated well by all three models. For other combinations, a high variance can be observed.

The translation models N4[18], R4[19], and L4[20] have been released on Hugging Face, making them accessible for further research and application.

6 Related Work

Data augmentation such as back-translation (Sennrich et al., 2016; Hoang et al., 2018) and transfer learning (Zoph et al., 2016) are established strategies to improve MT systems. These concepts are discussed in Haddow et al. (2022); Ranathunga et al. (2023), with a focus on low-resource scenarios. The fact that the synthesised data plays a critical role in the quality of the systems trained on it, as it also introduces a certain degree of noise, was discussed extensively in Edunov et al. (2018); Xu et al. (2022). It was shown that tagging synthetic data can be beneficial in the training process (Caswell et al., 2019). In our work we do not apply advanced techniques to differentiate synthetic from real translations in training. The fact that RBMT systems can still be valuable for low-resource languages and can even help to achieve better results was also demonstrated for Northern Sámi (Aulamo et al., 2021) . In our experiments, we could also observe this in the translation direction *lvb* $\rightarrow$ *ita*. This could be due to the ability of the RBMT system to provide general knowledge that is not available in the relatively limited parallel training datasets (Aulamo et al., 2021). The use of LLMs for MT and different prompting techniques was investigated in Zhang et al. (2023) and their performance in the machine translation of low-resource languages has already been analysed in Moslem et al. (2023). Even if they struggle to generate texts in low-resource languages (Robinson et al., 2023), it has already been claimed that they can contribute to advances in machine translation of such languages. Our work is an example of how LLMs can be used in machine translation of a low-resource language; however, further prompt engineering is needed to make better use of such models.

7 Conclusion

In this work, we conducted a detailed comparison of RBMT, NMT and LLMs for back-translation in a low-resource scenario. We have tested various back-translation approaches and evaluated them for a previously unexplored language in the field of machine translation.

Our current methodology involved the exclusion of numerous Ladin monolingual sentences. However, this filtering would be less important for the translation direction *lvb* $\rightarrow$ *ita*. This previously discarded data could be re-incorporated to improve the performance of the models in this particular translation direction.

The round-trip translation scores indicate that the initial back-translation with the RBMT system leads to more robust models. Improving the ambiguity resolution of this rule-based translation system could lead to even better results.

The simplicity of the prompts used to feed the LLMs provides a further starting point for investigations. In particular, the question arises as to whether the results can be improved by further prompt engineering, e.g., by including the meaning for the distinct words occurring in a text using the available dictionary. Investigating the effects of prompt optimisation could provide new insights into maximising the efficiency of LLMs in machine translation, especially in low-resource scenarios.

We plan to address these research questions in our future work.

[18]https://doi.org/10.57967/HF/2695
[19]https://doi.org/10.57967/HF/2693
[20]https://doi.org/10.57967/HF/2694

Acknowledgements

This research was conducted in collaboration with the Ladin Cultural Institute *Micurà de Rü* and funded by the *Regione Autonoma Trentino-Alto Adige/Südtirol*.

References

Roee Aharoni, Melvin Johnson, and Orhan Firat. 2019. Massively multilingual neural machine translation. In *Proceedings of the 2019 Conference of the North American Chapter of the Association for Computational Linguistics: Human Language Technologies, Volume 1 (Long and Short Papers)*, pages 3874–3884, Minneapolis, Minnesota. Association for Computational Linguistics.

Mikko Aulamo, Sami Virpioja, Yves Scherrer, and Jörg Tiedemann. 2021. Boosting neural machine translation from Finnish to Northern Sámi with rule-based backtranslation. In *Proceedings of the 23rd Nordic Conference on Computational Linguistics (NoDaLiDa)*, pages 351–356, Reykjavik, Iceland (Online). Linköping University Electronic Press, Sweden.

Steven Bird, Ewan Klein, and Edward Loper. 2009. *Natural language processing with Python*. O'Reilly Media, Inc.

Tom B. Brown, Benjamin Mann, Nick Ryder, Melanie Subbiah, Jared Kaplan, Prafulla Dhariwal, Arvind Neelakantan, Pranav Shyam, Girish Sastry, Amanda Askell, Sandhini Agarwal, Ariel Herbert-Voss, Gretchen Krueger, Tom Henighan, Rewon Child, Aditya Ramesh, Daniel M. Ziegler, Jeffrey Wu, Clemens Winter, Christopher Hesse, Mark Chen, Eric Sigler, Mateusz Litwin, Scott Gray, Benjamin Chess, Jack Clark, Christopher Berner, Sam McCandlish, Alec Radford, Ilya Sutskever, and Dario Amodei. 2020. Language models are few-shot learners. *CoRR*, abs/2005.14165.

Franck Burlot and François Yvon. 2018. Using monolingual data in neural machine translation: a systematic study. In *Proceedings of the Third Conference on Machine Translation: Research Papers*, pages 144–155, Brussels, Belgium. Association for Computational Linguistics.

Isaac Caswell, Ciprian Chelba, and David Grangier. 2019. Tagged back-translation. In *Proceedings of the Fourth Conference on Machine Translation (Volume 1: Research Papers)*, pages 53–63, Florence, Italy. Association for Computational Linguistics.

Tianqi Chen and Carlos Guestrin. 2016. Xgboost: A scalable tree boosting system. In *Proceedings of the 22nd ACM SIGKDD International Conference on Knowledge Discovery and Data Mining*, KDD '16, page 785–794, New York, NY, USA. Association for Computing Machinery.

Carlo Collodi. 2017. *Les aventöres de Pinocchio*. Istitut Ladin Micurá de Rü, San Martin de Tor.

Sergey Edunov, Myle Ott, Michael Auli, and David Grangier. 2018. Understanding back-translation at scale. In *Proceedings of the 2018 Conference on Empirical Methods in Natural Language Processing*, pages 489–500, Brussels, Belgium. Association for Computational Linguistics.

Sergey Edunov, Myle Ott, Marc'Aurelio Ranzato, and Michael Auli. 2020. On the evaluation of machine translation systems trained with back-translation. In *Proceedings of the 58th Annual Meeting of the Association for Computational Linguistics*, pages 2836–2846, Online. Association for Computational Linguistics.

Mikel L. Forcada and Francis M. Tyers. 2016. Apertium: a free/open source platform for machine translation and basic language technology. In *Proceedings of the 19th Annual Conference of the European Association for Machine Translation: Projects/Products*, Riga, Latvia. Baltic Journal of Modern Computing.

Barry Haddow, Rachel Bawden, Antonio Valerio Miceli Barone, Jindřich Helcl, and Alexandra Birch. 2022. Survey of low-resource machine translation. *Computational Linguistics*, 48(3):673–732.

Vu Cong Duy Hoang, Philipp Koehn, Gholamreza Haffari, and Trevor Cohn. 2018. Iterative back-translation for neural machine translation. In *Proceedings of the 2nd Workshop on Neural Machine Translation and Generation*, pages 18–24, Melbourne, Australia. Association for Computational Linguistics.

Thomas Kager. 2022. *Alto Adige: un'Europa in piccolo – I 50 anni del Secondo Statuto di autonomia*. Provincia autonoma di Bolzano – Alto Adige, Bolzano.

Tanmai Khanna, Jonathan N. Washington, Francis M. Tyers, Sevilay Bayatlı, Daniel G. Swanson, Tommi A. Pirinen, Irene Tang, and Hèctor Alòs i Font. 2021. Recent advances in Apertium, a free/open-source rule-based machine translation platform for low-resource languages. *Machine Translation*, 35(4):475–502.

Sara Moling, Ulrike Frenademetz, and Marlies Valentin. 2016. *Dizionario Italiano–Ladino Val Badia/Dizionar Ladin Val Badia–Talian*. Istitut Ladin Micurá de Rü, San Martin de Tor.

Yasmin Moslem, Rejwanul Haque, John D. Kelleher, and Andy Way. 2023. Adaptive machine translation with large language models. In *Proceedings of the 24th Annual Conference of the European Association for Machine Translation*, pages 227–237, Tampere, Finland. European Association for Machine Translation.

OpenAI. 2024. GPT-3.5 Turbo [gpt-3.5-turbo-0125]. Available at: `https://platform.openai.com`. Accessed on: February 2024.

Maja Popović. 2015. chrF: character n-gram F-score for automatic MT evaluation. In *Proceedings of the Tenth Workshop on Statistical Machine Translation*, pages 392–395, Lisbon, Portugal. Association for Computational Linguistics.

Matt Post. 2018. A call for clarity in reporting BLEU scores. In *Proceedings of the Third Conference on Machine Translation: Research Papers*, pages 186–191, Belgium, Brussels. Association for Computational Linguistics.

Alec Radford, Jeffrey Wu, Rewon Child, David Luan, Dario Amodei, Ilya Sutskever, et al. 2019. Language models are unsupervised multitask learners. *OpenAI blog*, 1(8):9.

Surangika Ranathunga, En-Shiun Annie Lee, Marjana Prifti Skenduli, Ravi Shekhar, Mehreen Alam, and Rishemjit Kaur. 2023. Neural machine translation for low-resource languages: A survey. *ACM Comput. Surv.*, 55(11).

Vipula Rawte, Swagata Chakraborty, Agnibh Pathak, Anubhav Sarkar, S.M Towhidul Islam Tonmoy, Aman Chadha, Amit Sheth, and Amitava Das. 2023. The troubling emergence of hallucination in large language models - an extensive definition, quantification, and prescriptive remediations. In *Proceedings of the 2023 Conference on Empirical Methods in Natural Language Processing*, pages 2541–2573, Singapore. Association for Computational Linguistics.

Nathaniel Robinson, Perez Ogayo, David R. Mortensen, and Graham Neubig. 2023. ChatGPT MT: Competitive for high- (but not low-) resource languages. In *Proceedings of the Eighth Conference on Machine Translation*, pages 392–418, Singapore. Association for Computational Linguistics.

Rico Sennrich, Barry Haddow, and Alexandra Birch. 2016. Improving Neural Machine Translation Models with Monolingual Data. In *Proceedings of the 54th Annual Meeting of the Association for Computational Linguistics (Volume 1: Long Papers)*, pages 86–96, Berlin, Germany. Association for Computational Linguistics.

Jiajun Shen, Peng-Jen Chen, Matthew Le, Junxian He, Jiatao Gu, Myle Ott, Michael Auli, and Marc'Aurelio Ranzato. 2021. The source-target domain mismatch problem in machine translation. In *Proceedings of the 16th Conference of the European Chapter of the Association for Computational Linguistics: Main Volume*, pages 1519–1533, Online. Association for Computational Linguistics.

Shumin Shi, Xing Wu, Rihai Su, and Heyan Huang. 2022. Low-resource neural machine translation: Methods and trends. *ACM Transactions on Asian and Low-Resource Language Information Processing*, 21(5):1–22.

Jörg Tiedemann. 2012. Parallel data, tools and interfaces in OPUS. In *Proceedings of the Eighth International Conference on Language Resources and Evaluation (LREC'12)*, pages 2214–2218, Istanbul, Turkey. European Language Resources Association (ELRA).

Jörg Tiedemann and Santhosh Thottingal. 2020. OPUS-MT – building open translation services for the world. In *Proceedings of the 22nd Annual Conference of the European Association for Machine Translation*, pages 479–480, Lisboa, Portugal. European Association for Machine Translation.

Thomas Wolf, Lysandre Debut, Victor Sanh, Julien Chaumond, Clement Delangue, Anthony Moi, Pierric Cistac, Tim Rault, Rémi Louf, Morgan Funtowicz, et al. 2020. Transformers: State-of-the-art natural language processing. In *Proceedings of the 2020 conference on empirical methods in natural language processing: system demonstrations*, pages 38–45.

Jiahao Xu, Yubin Ruan, Wei Bi, Guoping Huang, Shuming Shi, Lihui Chen, and Lemao Liu. 2022. On synthetic data for back translation. In *Proceedings of the 2022 Conference of the North American Chapter of the Association for Computational Linguistics: Human Language Technologies*, pages 419–430, Seattle, United States. Association for Computational Linguistics.

Biao Zhang, Barry Haddow, and Alexandra Birch. 2023. Prompting large language model for machine translation: a case study. In *Proceedings of the 40th International Conference on Machine Learning*, ICML'23. JMLR.org.

Terry Yue Zhuo, Qiongkai Xu, Xuanli He, and Trevor Cohn. 2023. Rethinking round-trip translation for machine translation evaluation. In *Findings of the Association for Computational Linguistics: ACL 2023*, pages 319–337, Toronto, Canada. Association for Computational Linguistics.

Barret Zoph, Deniz Yuret, Jonathan May, and Kevin Knight. 2016. Transfer Learning for Low-Resource Neural Machine Translation. *arXiv preprint*. ArXiv:1604.02201 [cs].

A Prompt template

```
I'll give you samples for the translation from Ladin to Italian:

{
    "translations": [
        {
          "Ladin": "scrí sües minunghes",
          "Italian": "scrivere le proprie opinioni"
        },
        {
          "Ladin": "mëte la secunda",
          "Italian": "mettere la seconda"
        },
        {
          "Ladin": '"zessa, i á prescia!"',
          "Italian": '"scansati, ho fretta!"'
        },
        {
          "Ladin": "passé ia le rü",
          "Italian": "oltrepassare il fiume"
        },
        ...
        {
          "Ladin": "chësc liber é to",
          "Italian": "questo libro è tuo"
        },
    ]
}

    Please generate the translation of each of the  16 entries in the given dictionary, where the
translations are empty. Return the same JSON dictionary where the values for Italian are filled:

{
    "translations": [
      {
        "Ladin": "Sperun da salvé almanco val', dijun:",
        "Italian": ""
      },
      {
        "Ladin": "Ince tröc toponims y cognoms ladins desmostra che l'identité ladina é coliada
ala natöra y ala cultura da munt",
        "Italian": ""
      },
      {
        "Ladin": "De profesciun este pech... co este pa rové pro chësc laur?",
        "Italian": ""
      },
      ...
      {
        "Ladin": "I dormi n pü' domisdé y spo ciamó val' ora dan mesanöt",
        "Italian": ""
      }
    ]
}
```

Listing 1: Prompt template used to obtain the Italian translations from the LLM.

AGE: Amharic, Ge'ez and English Parallel Dataset

Henok Biadglign Ademtew
Ethiopian AI Institute
henokb2124@gmail.com

Mikiyas Girma Birbo
Maharishi International University
mbirbo@miu.edu

Abstract

African languages are not well-represented in Natural Language Processing (NLP). The main reason is a lack of resources for training models. Low-resource languages, such as Amharic and Ge'ez, cannot benefit from modern NLP methods because of the lack of high-quality datasets. This paper presents AGE, an open-source tripartite alignment of Amharic, Ge'ez, and English parallel dataset. Additionally, we introduced a novel, 1,000 Ge'ez-centered sentences sourced from areas such as news and novels. Furthermore, we developed a model from a multilingual pre-trained language model, which brings 12.29 and 30.66 for English-Ge'ez and Ge'ez to English, respectively, and 9.39 and 12.29 for Amharic-Ge'ez and Ge'ez-Amharic respectively.

1 Introduction

Language is the foundation on which communication rests, allowing us to share ideas and interact with one another (Adebara and Abdul-Mageed, 2022). One of the NLP applications is machine translation (MT), which helps facilitate human-machine and human-human communications (Abate et al., 2019). Data availability is one of the criteria to categorize one language as a high or low-resource language (Ranathunga et al., 2021). Recently, interest in low-resource MT has been increasing both within the MT research community (Haddow et al., 2022), as well as in native speaker communities (Nekoto et al., 2020). Modern NLP technologies, however, have primarily been developed in Western societies (Adebara and Abdul-Mageed, 2022). The current state-of-the-art(SOTA) MT models were trained on enormous datasets, including sentences in a source language and their corresponding target language translations, which is the most effective of these systems(Tonja et al., 2023).

To date, there is no publicly available MT system for Ge'ez language and it's not represented in the commercial MT systems such as Lesan[1], Google Translate[2], Microsoft Translator[3], and Yandex Translate[4]. It is also not included in large-scale pre-trained multilingual models like NLLB(Team et al., 2022), MT5(Xue et al., 2021), ByT5(Xue et al., 2022), and M2M-100(Fan et al., 2020). This makes it harder for people to learn and use the language. So, by focusing on Ge'ez, an ancient language with profound cultural and religious significance in Ethiopia, alongside Amharic, the country's official working language, and English, a global lingua franca, this dataset aims to bridge the gap between historical linguistic treasures and modern technological advancements. Through this work, we aim to provide a dataset for researchers and technologists aiming to advance machine translation capabilities, linguistic studies, and cultural preservation efforts. Furthermore, by enriching the available resources for Ge'ez, we contribute to the broader goal of advancing low-resource languages.

2 Related work

One of the major challenges in developing MT models for Ge'ez is the lack of public data. There were attempts to compile parallel corpora for Ge'ez to English and Ge'ez to Amharic MT tasks, but the development was unsatisfactory. (Mulugeta, 2015) researched Ge'ez-Amharic MT using SMT. He used IRSTLM for language modeling. The research was conducted on a dataset comprising 12,840 parallel Amharic-Ge'ez sentences, achieving an average translation accuracy with a BLEU score of 8.26 based on 10-fold cross-validation. (Abate et al., 2019) is the only publicly available dataset that was part of an effort to train Statistical

[1]https://lesan.ai
[2]http://translate.google.com/
[3]https://www.microsoft.com/en-us/translator/
[4]https://translate.yandex.com

Proceedings of the The Seventh Workshop on Technologies for Machine Translation of Low-Resource Languages (LoResMT 2024), pages 139–145
August 15, 2024 ©2024 Association for Computational Linguistics

Machine Translation(SMT) for English-Ethiopian Languages and made 11,663 Ge'ez-English parallel sentences. They achieved English-Ge'ez and Ge'ez English translations with a BLEU score of 6.67 and 18.01, respectively. Using deep learning approaches, (Getachew and Yayeh, 2023) have explored bidirectional NMT from Ge'ez to English. The experiment was conducted by leveraging 16,569 parallel sentences from the Holy Bible and Battle of Saints and manually preparing daily conversational sentences. The results indicated that the transformer (**?**) model achieved BLEU scores of 27.19 for English to Ge'ez translation and 29.39 for Ge'ez to English translation. Another work by (Tegenaw et al., 2023) used NMT and transformers and attempted three experiments that used a pre-trained masked language model (MLM) utilizing a monolingual dataset of 33,004 sentences for each language. The experiments involved a parallel corpus for supervised learning without a pre-trained model and fine-tuning a pre-trained MLM with a bilingual dataset. The outcomes were evaluated using the BLEU score, achieving 31.65 in the second and 33.02 in the third experiment. Another recent work by (Wassie, 2023) improved translation by 4 BLEU using a new model but faced challenges with NLLB-200 for Ge'ez due to insufficient data. They also experimented with GPT-3.5's trial, which resulted in a 9.2 BLEU score, underperforming compared to their model's 15.2. They also highlighted the difficulties of training Ge'ez MT models.

A recurring issue noted in these experiments is the absence of data sharing with the public domain. As shown in Table 1, there is a lack of open-sourcing data and models, a significant obstacle to the representation of Ge'ez in NLP. This also indicates that despite extensive research in various studies, it's important for a unified effort among researchers to create and distribute resources open to the public. The collaborative effort would support further progress in expanding resources for the Ge'ez language.

3 Ge'ez Language

Ge'ez (ethiopge'ez), which is also known as Ethiopic, is one of the oldest Semitic languages (Tareke et al., 2002) and its alphabets is among the oldest alphabets still in use in the world of today. Furthermore, the Ge'ez language is among the four languages (Sabaean, Greek, and Arabic) that have been and continue to be used for ancient inscriptional arts. Ge'ez is currently not an actively spoken language nor a native tongue of any people. Its use is limited to the liturgical language of the Ethiopian Orthodox Tewahedo, Eritrean Orthodox Tewahedo, Ethiopian Catholic, and Eritrean Catholic Christians(Molla and Tabor, 2018). It is also used during prayer and at regularly scheduled public religious feast celebrations. The Bible dominates the literature, and it comprises the Deuterocanonical books. According to (Molla and Tabor, 2018), this language also has many medieval and early modern original texts. The majority of the essential works are correspondingly the literature of the Ethiopian Orthodox Tewahedo Church. These works include Christian Orthodox liturgy (service books, prayers, hymns), hagiographies, and a range of Patristic literature. Around 200 texts were written about home-grown Ethiopian saints from the fourteenth to the nineteenth century. The religious alignment of Ge'ez literature was due to traditional education being the obligation of priests and monks. More info about the alphabet on Ge'ez can be found in the appendix section.

4 Creation of the dataset

We introduce our newly Ge'ez-centered parallel dataset; **AGE** — Amharic, Ge'ez , English for machine translation.

4.1 Data Collection

Machine Translation (MT) necessitates using parallel sentences from source and target languages. We started by creating a novel parallel dataset comprising 1,000 sentence pairs. After cleaning, we extracted 17585 and 18676 sentence pairs for Amharic-Ge'ez and Ge'ez-English, respectively. The reason behind the number inconsistency is that some sources have either Amharic-Ge'ez or English-Ge'ez. For instance, with "Kufale" (The Book of Jubilees), our dataset comprised only sentence pairs in Ge'ez and English. The extracted pairs were collected from The Open Siddur Project[5], YouVersion[6], Ethiopic Bible[7], and Awde Mehret[8].

4.2 Data pre-processing

Our dataset, sourced from diverse sources, exhibited significant textual inconsistencies. We found

[5]https://opensiddur.org/

[6]https://www.bible.com/

[7]https://www.ethiopicbible.com/

[8]https://awdemehret.org/

Language	Author(s)	Sentences	Dataset	Model	Technique
Amharic, Ge'ez	(Mulugeta, 2015)	12, 840	✗	✗	SMT
Amharic, Ge'ez	(Kassa, 2018)	13,833	✗	✗	SMT
Amharic, Ge'ez	(Abel, 2018)	976	✗	✗	SMT
Ge'ez, English	(Abate et al., 2019)	11,663	✓	✗	SMT
Ge'ez, English	(Getachew and Yayeh, 2023)	16,569	✗	✗	NMT
Amharic, Ge'ez	(Tegenaw et al., 2023)	33,004	✗	✗	NMT
Amahric, Ge'ez	(Wassie, 2023)	4,000	✗	✗	MNMT

Table 1: Summary of related works for Ge'ez: Sentences show the number of sentences used during the experiment. Dataset and Model show the availability of datasets and models in publicly accessible repositories, and Technique shows the method used to build models.

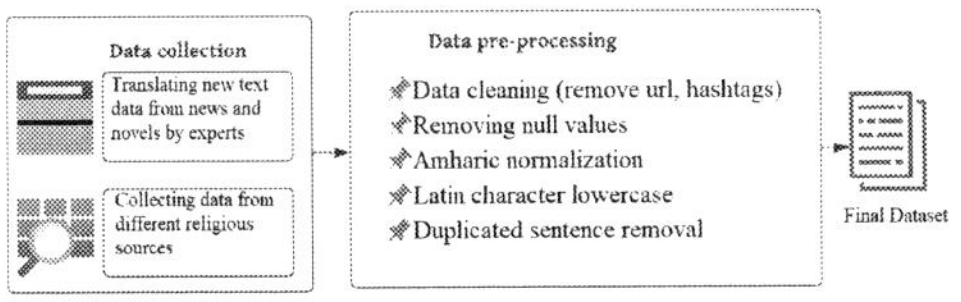

Figure 1: Data collection and pre-processing pipelines

Language Pair	Sentences	Token	Avg. Length
Amharic	17,584	17,585	13.35
Ge'ez		51,212	13.43
English	18,722	27,884	13.81
Ge'ez		54,160	13.43

Table 2: Overview of the Dataset Sizes and Characteristics

portions of the data excessively disordered and removed them from our collection. Figure 1 shows the general framework for the dataset development process. It had two primary tasks. The first task was data collection, which involved identifying the sources from which the tripartite parallel Amharic, Ge'ez, and English sentences were collected. The second task was translating a few collected sentences to Ge'ez. This task involved translators and reviewers. Three translators and three evaluators were assigned to handle a set of 1,000 sentences. We made an in-house tool to ease the translation and evaluation process, which significantly streamlined the entire workflow. We performed several preparatory actions to standardize all tokens in Amharic and English sentences gathered from multiple sources. These actions included cleaning the data (eliminating URLs, hashtags, and repeated sentences), normalizing Amharic homophone characters, and converting English characters to lowercase.

5 Baseline Experiments

As shown in table 1, prior research predominantly employed SMT(Josef and Ney, 2001), and a very few NMT using transformers (Vaswani et al., 2017). To extend these studies, we incorporated an approach by leveraging the NLLB-200 (Team et al., 2022), a pre-trained language model.

- **NLLB-200**: a sparsely gated 54B parameter Mixture-of-Experts(MoE) model. It has demonstrated SOTA results across many language pairs, improving the previous model's BLEU scores by 44%

Accessing the large NLLB-200 model requires a minimum of four 32GB GPUs just for inference, showcasing the need for significant computational resources. So, we used the NLLB-200 600M parameter variant, a dense transformer model distilled from NLLB-200 due to its much lower resource requirements, making it a more practical option for our computational constraints.

The work by (Adelani et al., 2022) to effectively adapt to large-scale pre-trained models and get improved performance suggests that these models have better capability for relatively smaller datasets. So, we split our dataset into TRAIN (80%), DEV (10%), and TEST split (10%). We fine-tune the model using the HuggingFace transformer tool(Wolf et al., 2020) with a learning rate 5e-5, a batch size of 4 per device, a maximum source length, and a maximum target length of 128, and a beam size of 10. All the experiments were performed on Google Colab Pro. Then, the quality of translation is assessed using the BLEU score(Papineni et al., 2002), a standard in the field for its objectivity and correlation with human judgment. Our baseline experiments focused on bidirectional translation tasks, Amharic-Ge'ez

Language pair	BLEU
Amharic-Ge'ez	9.39
Ge'ez-Amharic	12.29
English-Ge'ez	12.87
Ge'ez-English	30.66

Table 3: Baseline results of NLLB-200 600M

and English-Ge'ez translations, aiming to establish a foundational understanding of the NLLB-200 600M model's capabilities within the context of our dataset. Since our primary focus was developing machine translation for Ge'ez, we skipped training the model on bidirectional English-Amharic translation.

6 Results and Discussion

In this work, we adapted the NLLB-200 600M model to evaluate its performance in the Ge'ez language. Our results as shown in Table 3 reveal a clear gradient in BLEU score performance across various language pairs. For translations from Amharic to Ge'ez and vice versa, the model achieved BLEU scores of 9.03 and 12.26 for evaluation, with a slight increase in the prediction phase to 9.39 and 12.87, respectively. Our BLEU scores showed a dramatic increase in scores for the Ge'ez to English language pair. Notably, English translations demonstrated superior performance, with the Ge'ez to English pair achieving the highest scores of 30.35 in evaluation and 30.66 in prediction, indicating a robust model capability in this language direction.

The higher scores in recorded in translations involving English may be due to a combination of factors, including the richer linguistic resources available for English and the NLLB-200's pre-training, which includes 21.5 billion sentences in English (Team et al., 2022). The difference in scores between the language pairs involving Amharic and those involving English points to the challenges associated with being low-resource. The lower BLEU scores for Amharic to Ge'ez suggest inherent difficulties in capturing the nuances of Ge'ez, a Semitic language with complex morphology. (Tran et al., 2014) stated that translating into morphologically rich languages is a particularly difficult problem in machine translation due to the high degree of inflectional ambiguity in the target language, often only poorly captured by existing word translation models. On the other hand, better performance was registered for Ge'ez to English translation, which is an encouraging sign of the model's adaptability, especially considering that Ge'ez data wasn't included in NLLB-200's pretraining data. The model's success in this area showcases the potential of such systems when appropriately fine-tuned, even when working with languages traditionally underserved by NLP technologies. Finally, we will release our models and dataset for the public to use and expand on our work.

7 Conclusion and Future Works

This paper presents an attempt to prepare a standard parallel corpora for Ge'ez. One thousand newly translated sentences were gathered from nonreligious domains, and the rest text data was gathered from religious domains on the internet. Then, the data are further pre-processed and normalized to prepare a parallel dataset for the model training task. Using our dataset, we fintuned NLLB-200 model. The experimental results show that translating to and from English resulted in a better BLEU score than English to Ge'ez and Amharic to Ge'ez and vice versa. The abundance of English data in the pre-trained model and the morphological richness of Ethiopian languages significantly impact the model's performance during bidirectional training involving Ge'ez and Amharic and when these languages are target languages. To the best of our knowledge, this is the first ready-to-use Amharic, Ge'ez, English tripartite dataset. Our initiative to make the dataset and models open source will open doors for many researchers and developers. Future works include increasing both the quantity and diversity of the dataset. We also intend to incorporate the several Ge'ez data sources that are now absent from this dataset.

References

Solomon Teferra Abate, Michael Melese, Martha Yifiru Tachbelie, Million Meshesha, Solomon Atinafu, Wondwossen Mulugeta, Yaregal Assabie, Hafte Abera, Biniyam Ephrem, Tewodros Gebreselassie, et al. 2019. English-ethiopian languages statistical machine translation. In *Proceedings of the 2019 Workshop on Widening NLP*, pages 27–30.

Biruk Abel. 2018. Geez to amharic machine translation.

Ife Adebara and Muhammad Abdul-Mageed. 2022. Towards afrocentric nlp for african languages: Where we are and where we can go. *Preprint*, arXiv:2203.08351.

David Adelani, Jesujoba Alabi, Angela Fan, Julia Kreutzer, Xiaoyu Shen, Machel Reid, Dana Ruiter, Dietrich Klakow, Peter Nabende, Ernie Chang, Tajuddeen Gwadabe, Freshia Sackey, Bonaventure F. P. Dossou, Chris Emezue, Colin Leong, Michael Beukman, Shamsuddeen Muhammad, Guyo Jarso, Oreen Yousuf, Andre Niyongabo Rubungo, Gilles Hacheme, Eric Peter Wairagala, Muhammad Umair Nasir, Benjamin Ajibade, Tunde Ajayi, Yvonne Gitau, Jade Abbott, Mohamed Ahmed, Millicent Ochieng, Anuoluwapo Aremu, Perez Ogayo, Jonathan Mukiibi, Fatoumata Ouoba Kabore, Godson Kalipe, Derguene Mbaye, Allahsera Auguste Tapo, Victoire Memdjokam Koagne, Edwin Munkoh-Buabeng, Valencia Wagner, Idris Abdulmumin, Ayodele Awokoya, Happy Buzaaba, Blessing Sibanda, Andiswa Bukula, and Sam Manthalu. 2022. A few thousand translations go a long way! leveraging pre-trained models for African news translation. In *Proceedings of the 2022 Conference of the North American Chapter of the Association for Computational Linguistics: Human Language Technologies*, pages 3053–3070, Seattle, United States. Association for Computational Linguistics.

Angela Fan, Shruti Bhosale, Holger Schwenk, Zhiyi Ma, Ahmed El-Kishky, Siddharth Goyal, Mandeep Baines, Onur Celebi, Guillaume Wenzek, Vishrav Chaudhary, Naman Goyal, Tom Birch, Vitaliy Liptchinsky, Sergey Edunov, Edouard Grave, Michael Auli, and Armand Joulin. 2020. Beyond english-centric multilingual machine translation. *Preprint*, arXiv:2010.11125.

Sefineh Getachew and Yirga Yayeh. 2023. Gex'ez-english bi-directional neural machine translation using transformer. In *2023 International Conference on Information and Communication Technology for Development for Africa (ICT4DA)*, pages 160–164.

Barry Haddow, Rachel Bawden, Antonio Valerio Miceli Barone, Jindřich Helcl, and Alexandra Birch. 2022. Survey of low-resource machine translation. *Preprint*, arXiv:2109.00486.

Franz Josef and Hermann Ney. 2001. Statistical machine translation.

Tadesse Kassa. 2018. Morpheme-based bi-directional ge'ez -amharic machine translation.

Ertiban Demewoz Molla and Debre Tabor. 2018. An analysis of ge'ez language heritage potential: traditional church schools and the practices of ethiopian orthodox tewahido churches.

Dawit Mulugeta. 2015. Geez to amharic automatic machine translation: A statistical approach.

Wilhelmina Nekoto, Vukosi Marivate, Tshinondiwa Matsila, Timi Fasubaa, Taiwo Fagbohungbe, Solomon Oluwole Akinola, Shamsuddeen Muhammad, Salomon Kabongo Kabenamualu, Salomey Osei, Freshia Sackey, Rubungo Andre Niyongabo, Ricky Macharm, Perez Ogayo, Orevaoghene Ahia, Musie Meressa Berhe, Mofetoluwa Adeyemi, Masabata Mokgesi-Selinga, Lawrence Okegbemi, Laura Martinus, Kolawole Tajudeen, Kevin Degila, Kelechi Ogueji, Kathleen Siminyu, Julia Kreutzer, Jason Webster, Jamiil Toure Ali, Jade Abbott, Iroro Orife, Ignatius Ezeani, Idris Abdulkadir Dangana, Herman Kamper, Hady Elsahar, Goodness Duru, Ghollah Kioko, Murhabazi Espoir, Elan van Biljon, Daniel Whitenack, Christopher Onyefuluchi, Chris Chinenye Emezue, Bonaventure F. P. Dossou, Blessing Sibanda, Blessing Bassey, Ayodele Olabiyi, Arshath Ramkilowan, Alp Öktem, Adewale Akinfaderin, and Abdallah Bashir. 2020. Participatory research for low-resourced machine translation: A case study in African languages. In *Findings of the Association for Computational Linguistics: EMNLP 2020*, pages 2144–2160, Online. Association for Computational Linguistics.

Kishore Papineni, Salim Roukos, Todd Ward, and Wei-Jing Zhu. 2002. Bleu: a method for automatic evaluation of machine translation. In *Proceedings of the 40th Annual Meeting of the Association for Computational Linguistics*, pages 311–318, Philadelphia, Pennsylvania, USA. Association for Computational Linguistics.

Surangika Ranathunga, En-Shiun Annie Lee, Marjana Prifti Skenduli, Ravi Shekhar, Mehreen Alam, and Rishemjit Kaur. 2021. Neural machine translation for low-resource languages: A survey. *ACM Computing Surveys*.

Gebru Tareke, Bahru Zewde, and David Pool. 2002. A history of modern ethiopia 1855-1991. *The International Journal of African Historical Studies*, 35:587.

NLLB Team, Marta R. Costa-jussà, James Cross, Onur Çelebi, Maha Elbayad, Kenneth Heafield, Kevin Heffernan, Elahe Kalbassi, Janice Lam, Daniel Licht, Jean Maillard, Anna Sun, Skyler Wang, Guillaume Wenzek, Al Youngblood, Bapi Akula, Loic Barrault, Gabriel Mejia Gonzalez, Prangthip Hansanti, John Hoffman, Semarley Jarrett, Kaushik Ram Sadagopan, Dirk Rowe, Shannon Spruit, Chau Tran, Pierre Andrews, Necip Fazil Ayan, Shruti Bhosale, Sergey Edunov, Angela Fan, Cynthia Gao, Vedanuj Goswami, Francisco Guzmán, Philipp Koehn, Alexandre Mourachko, Christophe Ropers, Safiyyah Saleem, Holger Schwenk, and Jeff Wang. 2022. No language left behind: Scaling human-centered machine translation. *Preprint*, arXiv:2207.04672.

Ermias Tegenaw, Kris Calpotura, and Ashebir Dereje. 2023. Ge'ez to amharic translation with neural network-based technique.

Atnafu Lambebo Tonja, Tadesse Destaw Belay, Olga Kolesnikova, Seid Muhie Yimam, Abinew Ali Ayele, Grigori Sidorov, and Alexander Gelbukh. 2023. Amhen: Amharic-english large parallel corpus for machine translation.

Ke M. Tran, Arianna Bisazza, and Christof Monz. 2014. Word translation prediction for morphologically rich languages with bilingual neural networks. In *Conference on Empirical Methods in Natural Language Processing*.

Ashish Vaswani, Noam Shazeer, Niki Parmar, Jakob Uszkoreit, Llion Jones, Aidan N Gomez, Ł ukasz Kaiser, and Illia Polosukhin. 2017. Attention is all you need. In *Advances in Neural Information Processing Systems*, volume 30. Curran Associates, Inc.

Aman Kassahun Wassie. 2023. Machine translation for ge'ez language. *Preprint*, arXiv:2311.14530.

Thomas Wolf, Lysandre Debut, Victor Sanh, Julien Chaumond, Clement Delangue, Anthony Moi, Pierric Cistac, Tim Rault, Rémi Louf, Morgan Funtowicz, Joe Davison, Sam Shleifer, Patrick von Platen, Clara Ma, Yacine Jernite, Julien Plu, Canwen Xu, Teven Le Scao, Sylvain Gugger, Mariama Drame, Quentin Lhoest, and Alexander M. Rush. 2020. Huggingface's transformers: State-of-the-art natural language processing. *Preprint*, arXiv:1910.03771.

Linting Xue, Aditya Barua, Noah Constant, Rami Al-Rfou, Sharan Narang, Mihir Kale, Adam Roberts, and Colin Raffel. 2022. ByT5: Towards a token-free future with pre-trained byte-to-byte models. *Transactions of the Association for Computational Linguistics*, 10:291–306.

Linting Xue, Noah Constant, Adam Roberts, Mihir Kale, Rami Al-Rfou, Aditya Siddhant, Aditya Barua, and Colin Raffel. 2021. mT5: A massively multilingual pre-trained text-to-text transformer. In *Proceedings of the 2021 Conference of the North American Chapter of the Association for Computational Linguistics: Human Language Technologies*, pages 483–498, Online. Association for Computational Linguistics.

A Appendix

A.1 Loss Graph

Training loss curves for NLLB200 600M model between Amharic, Geez, and English, showing the progress of model learning over 10,000 steps. By the end of the 10,000 steps, the training loss for all models seems to converge, which means they may be approaching their optimal performance.

A.2 In-house tool web interface

Screenshot of a multilingual translation review interface showing sentence pairs in Amharic, Geez, and English, alongside user interaction options for approving or commenting on the translations for quality assurance and data curation purposes.

Figure 2: NLLB-200 Loss Graph

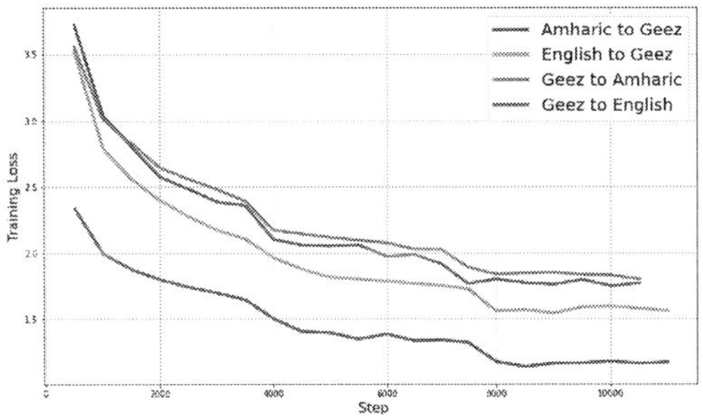

Figure 3: Reviewers interface of our in-house system.

Figure 4: Interface of our in-house system receiving all the data.

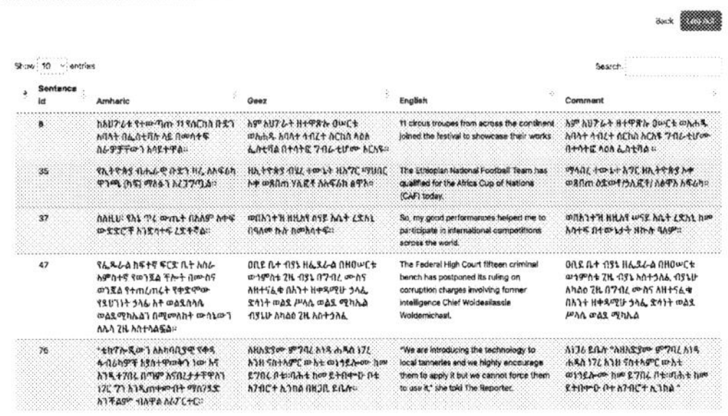

Learning-From-Mistakes Prompting for Indigenous Language Translation

You-Cheng Liao, Chen-Jui Yu, Chi-Yi Lin, He-Feng Yun,
Yen-Hsiang Wang, Hsiao-Min Li, Yao-Chung Fan*
Department of Computer Science and Engineering,
National Chung Hsing University, Taiwan
yfan@nchu.edu.tw

Abstract

Using large language models, this paper presents techniques to improve extremely low-resourced indigenous language translations. Our approaches are grounded in the use of (1) the presence of a datastore consisting of a limited number of parallel translation examples, (2) the inherent capabilities of LLMs like GPT-3.5, and (3) a word-level translation dictionary. We harness the potential of LLMs and in-context learning techniques in such a setting for using LLM as universal translators for extremely low-resourced languages. Our methodology hinge on utilizing LLMs as language compilers for selected language pairs, hypothesizing that they could internalize syntactic structures to facilitate accurate translation. We introduce three techniques: *KNN-Prompting with Retrieved Prompting Context, Chain-of-Thought Prompting, and Learning-from-Mistakes Prompting*, with the last method addressing past errors. The evaluation results suggest that, even with limited corpora, LLMs, when paired with proper prompting, can effectively translate extremely low-resource languages.

1 Introduction

In recent years, LLMs have showcased astonishing capabilities in the realm of natural language processing, particularly in tasks like language translation (Zhu et al., 2023), text generation (Yuan et al., 2022), and contextual understanding (Behnia et al., 2022). The robust functionality of these models has led us to reconsider their potential role in indigenous language translation.

In our pursuit to facilitate translations from Chinese to Taiwanese indigenous languages, we leverage the power of LLMs, buttressed by three foundational pillars: the presence of a datastore consisting of a limited number of parallel translation examples, the inherent capabilities of LLMs like GPT-3.5, and the integration of a word-level translation dictionary.

In this paper, we delineate three translation methodologies that build upon each other in a cumulative fashion. Each method represents a layer in our stratified approach, starting from leveraging contextual similarity in KNN-Prompting with Retrieved Prompting Context (RPC) to harnessing the didactic potential of Chain of Thought (CoT) Prompting, and culminating in the Learning-from-Mistakes (LFM) Prompting technique that incorporates feedback mechanisms for continuous improvement. Figure 1 provides an overview of our methodologies, illustrating a step-by-step translation enhancement process designed for the Taiwanese indigenous language context.

This paper is structured as follows: In Section 2, we review the literature and discuss the position of this study. In Section 3, we explore the CoT Prompting methodology, followed by an in-depth analysis of the LFM Prompting approach. In Section 4, we report the evaluation results. Through empirical evaluation and expert reviews, we demonstrate the effectiveness of the proposed methodologies.

2 Related Work

LLMs have exhibited excellent performance in language translation tasks, particularly evident in well-represented source languages like English and Chinese. Despite significant strides in translation performance for these languages, there remains a notable gap in the exploration of LLMs for low-resourced languages or those that have not been pre-trained. This aspect represents an under-explored area within the domain of research.

2.1 Low Resource Translation with LLM

LLMs' effectiveness on various task is primarily attributed to two main properties. Firstly, in-context learning (Brown et al., 2020; Lester et al., 2021) allows the model to learn to solve specific problems by providing a small number of exam-

Proceedings of the The Seventh Workshop on Technologies for Machine Translation of Low-Resource Languages (LoResMT 2024), pages 146–158
August 15, 2024 ©2024 Association for Computational Linguistics

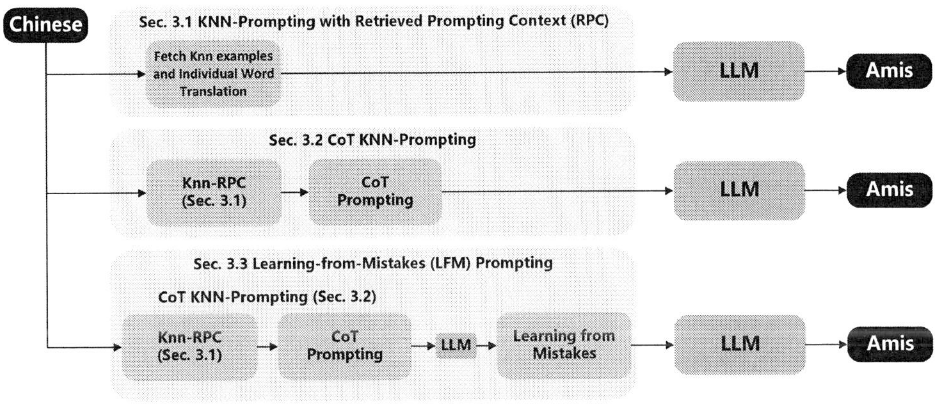

Figure 1: Methodology Overview

ples within the input context. The second one is the ability to follow the instruction (Ouyang et al., 2022; Mishra et al., 2021; Wei et al., 2021), instruction-tuned LLMs can be guiding to solve new task based on text instruction just as the scenario they were trained.

Recently, some research has focused on enhancing these instruction following LLMs through in-context learning, (Nguyen et al., 2023; Ahuja et al., 2023) explores the generation of unsupervised few-shot demonstrations to enhance translation effectiveness in low-resource scenarios. Additionally, (Yao et al., 2023) utilized cultural awareness to optimize alignment in different languages, further augmenting the translation performance of LLMs.

It is noteworthy that, the mentioned works above have focused on low-resource data for LLMs in languages that have been encountered during the pre-training phase. In contrast, our emphasis lies in a scenario where the model has not been previously trained in this specific language. In contrast to conventional approaches, we refrain from training parameters on limited parallel corpora (Gu et al., 2018; Lalrempuii and Soni, 2023). Instead, our goal is to leverage the understanding and reasoning capabilities of LLMs, coupled with the provided data, to accomplish translation tasks for previously unseen languages.

In summary, to the best of our knowledge, no study has delved into the challenges and applications of utilizing LLMs for languages that have not been encountered before.

2.2 Indigenous Language Translation

In the context of preserving and revitalizing indigenous languages, the work by (Zheng et al., 2022) stands as a notable contribution. Zheng and colleagues introduce the Amis-Mandarin dataset, which includes a parallel corpus comprising 5,751 Amis and Mandarin sentences. This dataset is of particular relevance to our research on translating Chinese sentences into Taiwanese indigenous languages. The Amis-Mandarin dataset provides a valuable resource for studying indigenous language translation. It aligns with the objectives of our study, as it offers a substantial parallel corpus, a fundamental component for training and evaluating translation models. Our research similarly leverages parallel corpora, although we focus on the translation of Chinese into various indigenous languages, including but not limited to Amis. In this study, we conduct experiments on six different indigenous languages.

Furthermore, (Zheng et al., 2022) compile a comprehensive dictionary containing 7,800 unique Amis words and phrases, each accompanied by its Mandarin definition. This lexical resource enhances the utility of their dataset for translation tasks. In our research, we assume the existence of a similar dictionary, emphasizing the importance of word-level translation between Chinese and Taiwanese indigenous languages.

Stap and Araabi (2023) evaluates the translation performance of different systems for Spanish to 11 indigenous languages from South America. The authors find that LLMs like ChatGPT are not yet good at translating into indigenous languages. This is likely due to a number of factors, including the lack of training data for indigenous languages, the complex grammar and sentence structure of indigenous languages, and the difficulty of capturing the nuances of indigenous culture in translation.

2.3 Unveiling LLMs' Proficiency in Tool Usage

In recent research, (Schick et al., 2023) discovered that LLMs exhibit the ability to discern how to employ tools provided by users, including external data. They adeptly combine this external information with their own knowledge to effectively address problem -solving tasks. These investigations delve into the mechanisms of CoT (Inaba et al., 2023) and Self-instruction (Yang et al., 2023) approaches, exploring how these methodologies assist LLMs in comprehending questions and utilizing the tools at their disposal. Additionally, there has been the development of question- answering datasets, such as ToolQA (Zhuang et al., 2023; Inaba et al., 2023), which aimed at faithfully evaluating the ability of LLMs to use external tools for question-answering.

Inspired by these explorations into the understanding and application capabilities of LLMs, we take a similar approach in our method design. We offer KNN examples and word-by-word translation as tools for LLMs to improve their language translation abilities.

2.4 Position of Our Paper

This research stands at the intersection of multiple areas, addressing the challenges of translating into low-resource indigenous languages using LLMs like ChatGPT. While prior works have explored low-resource translation and indigenous language preservation, our study distinguishes itself in two key aspects:

1. **Languages Unseen in Pre-training:** Unlike previous research that has primarily focused on low-resource data for LLMs in languages encountered during pre-training, our work emphasizes the scenario where the model has not been previously trained in the specific target language. We tackle the challenge of translating into languages that lack representation in the model's training data, making our approach more versatile and applicable to a broader range of indigenous languages.

2. **Few-Shot Prompting Techniques:** Our research pioneers the application of few-shot prompting techniques to enhance translation capabilities for indigenous languages. We introduce innovative methods, including *KNN-Prompting with RPC, CoT Prompting, and LFM Prompting*, tailored to leverage LLMs' inherent understanding and reasoning abilities. These techniques empower LLMs to effectively tackle low-resource language translation tasks, even when working with limited parallel corpora.

paper	In-context Learning	Fine-tune Parame.	Low-Resource Language	Unseen Language
(Yao et al., 2023)	✓			
(Nguyen et al., 2023)	✓		✓	
(Guerreiro et al., 2023)	✓		✓	
(Gu et al., 2018)		✓	✓	✓
(Lalrempuii and Soni, 2023)		✓	✓	✓
Our work	✓		✓	✓

Table 1: An overview of the existing language translation studies

In summary, our paper bridges the gap between LLMs and low-resource indigenous language translation, offering practical and innovative solutions for preserving and revitalizing endangered languages. By exploring the potential of these models in an uncharted linguistic landscape, we provide a fresh perspective and a promising direction for future research in this domain. For clarity, we also compare the related work in Table 1.

3 Methodology

Problem Setting and Assumptions The primary objective of this research is to enable the translation of Chinese sentences into Taiwanese indigenous languages through the utilization of LLMs. In pursuit of this goal, we make the following assumptions for the methods proposed in this study:

- **Datastore of Parallel Corpora:** Our first assumption centers on the availability of a datastore with limited translation examples. Within this datastore, each data entry comprises a pair of sentences: a source sentence in Chinese (the language intended for translation) and a corresponding target sentence in the specific Taiwanese indigenous language. This resource forms the backbone for our translation, facilitating the alignment of linguistic patterns and meanings.

- **Large Language Models:** The cornerstone of our translation methods is the utilization of large pre-trained language models, exemplified by GPT-3.5, as the primary translation engines.

- **Dictionary Existence:** In addition to the aforementioned resources, we introduce another assumption: the existence of a dictionary that spans word-level translations. This dictionary encompasses translations between indigenous language words and their corresponding Chinese counterparts.

Figure 1 outlines our study's methods for enhancing translation in a cumulative manner. The *KNN-Prompting with RPC* method forms the base, merging contextually similar sentences and word translations to inform the LLM's understanding of grammar and context. The *CoT Prompting* adds CoT demonstrations, showing RPC integration for effective translation. The *LFM Prompting* expands upon these with a feedback loop, leveraging previous translation errors to refine outcomes. This progressive strategy not only enhances LLM's translation proficiency but also promotes continual learning and accuracy improvement.

3.1 KNN-Prompting with Retrieved Prompting Context (RPC)

We investigate the application of few-shot learning through the KNN-Prompting concept, as discussed in the works of Shi et al. (Shi et al., 2022) and Xu et al. (Xu et al., 2023). Our approach not only leverages contextually similar examples but also incorporates individual translations for each word in the source language. The methodology unfolds in the following manner:

- When tasked with translating a sentence s, our method initiates by constructing a *Retrieved Prompting Context (RPC)* for s. This context includes:
  - k examples that are contextually analogous to s, selected based on their similarity.
  - Translations for each word in s, sourced from a comprehensive dictionary.
- For instances where direct word equivalents are unavailable, we employ the BERT-base-chinese model as an embedding tool. This model aids in computing similarities to identify the most appropriate substitute words.
- The core principle of our method is to enable the LLM to assimilate the grammatical norms and sentence constructs of the target language. It achieves this through the analysis of the k examples, thereby learning to organize the individually translated words into coherent and grammatically consistent sentences.

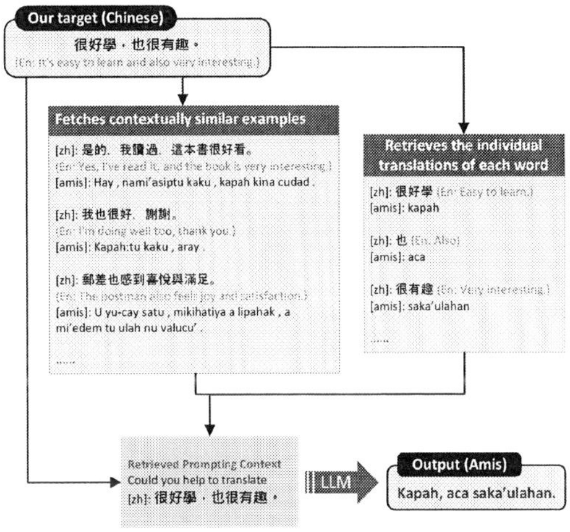

Figure 2: KNN-Prompting with RPC

For a practical illustration of this process, please see Figure 2, which provides a concrete example of the RPC in action. We also show an example for prompting in Table 5.

3.2 CoT Prompting

In this methodology, we harness the CoT strategy, as delineated by Wei et al. (Wei et al., 2022), to guide the LLM in effectively utilizing the RPC for translating a given sentence s. Specifically, this approach involves the following steps:

- When presented with a sentence s for translation, accompanied by KNN-RPC-prompting inputs (i.e., k contextually similar examples and individual word translations), we further augment the LLM's input with q CoT demonstrations. These demonstrations are designed to illustrate how to use the provided RPC to formulate the final translated sentences.
- An instance showcasing two CoT demonstrations is illustrated in Figure 3. It is important to note that these CoT demonstrations are integrated with the KNN-RPC-prompting inputs to serve as comprehensive prompting material for the LLM.
- For detailed examples of this prompting structure, please refer to Table 6 in the Appendix.

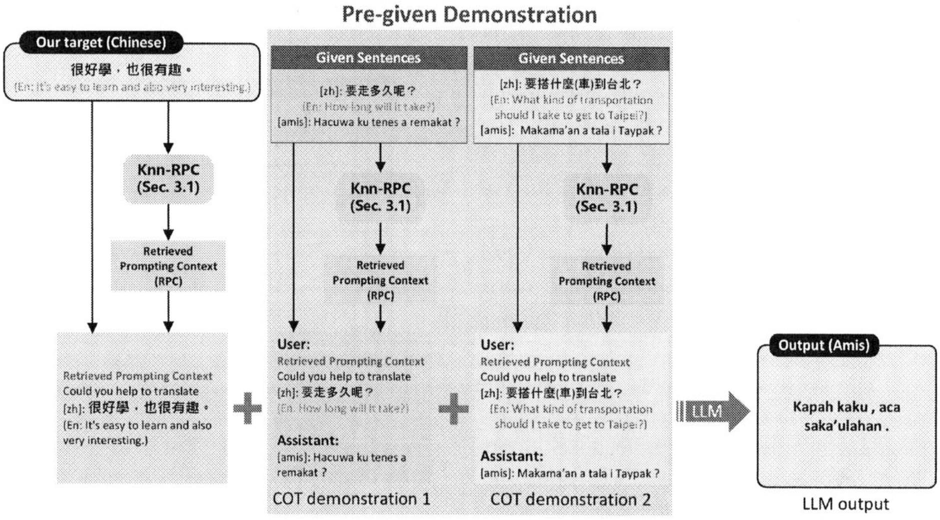

Figure 3: CoT KNN-Prompting: In this example, we have two CoT demonstrations. Note that each CoT demonstration comprises (1) A sample sentence, (2) RPC for the sentence, and (3) The ground-truth sentence. These CoT demonstrations are integrated with the KNN-RPC-prompting inputs to serve as comprehensive prompting material for the LLM.

The overarching aim of this methodology is to empower the LLM with an understanding of the grammatical rules and the proficiency to fully leverage the RPC, including both the retrieved sentences and individual word translations, for producing coherent and accurate translations.

3.3 Learning-from-Mistakes (LFM) Prompting

LFM Prompting is a two-stage approach aimed at enhancing the quality of translations. This method leverages the result from the CoT KNN-Prompting and incorporates a feedback mechanism by conducting trial translation to refine the translation based on past translation errors. The method works in the following phases:

- **Phase 1: Trial Translation with CoT Prompting** When given a sentence s to translate, we start by retrieving q contextually similar sentence pairs from the data store. Each pair (s_{q_i}, t_{q_i}) consists of a Chinese sentence s_{q_i} and its corresponding indigenous sentence t_{q_i}. For each s_{q_i}, we employ CoT KNN-Prompting (the method introduced in Section 3.2) to translate it, resulting in $\hat{t}_{q_i}$. At this stage, we have (s_{q_i}, t_{q_i}, $\hat{t}_{q_i}$). Our approach involves using these results as examples for the LLM to learn from its translation errors and make improvements.
- **Phase 2: Learning from Past Mistakes** The second phase of LFM Prompting introduces a crucial element: the incorporation of past translation errors. Specifically, we treat (s_{q_i}, t_{q_i}, $\hat{t}_{q_i}$) from the Phase 1 as LFM examples. In this phase, we present the LLM with a set of such examples, alongside the translation $\hat{t}$ generated by using CoT KNN-Prompting to translate s. The language model is tasked with refining $\hat{t}$ by considering the error examples in translation. It uses the provided examples of mistranslations to correct and improve the initial translation $\hat{t}$, aligning it more closely with the correct target language structure and meaning.

Furthermore, Figure 4 provides a visual representation of the entire architecture's workflow, illustrating the sequential processes outlined above. We also show a prompting example in Table 7.

4 Experiment

4.1 Model Usage

Utilizing the GPT-3.5-turbo-16k-0613 version with a temperature setting of 0, we employ Sentence BERT (Reimers and Gurevych, 2019) as the embedding model to retrieve k-nearest neighbor sentences. The similarity between sentences is computed using cosine similarity.

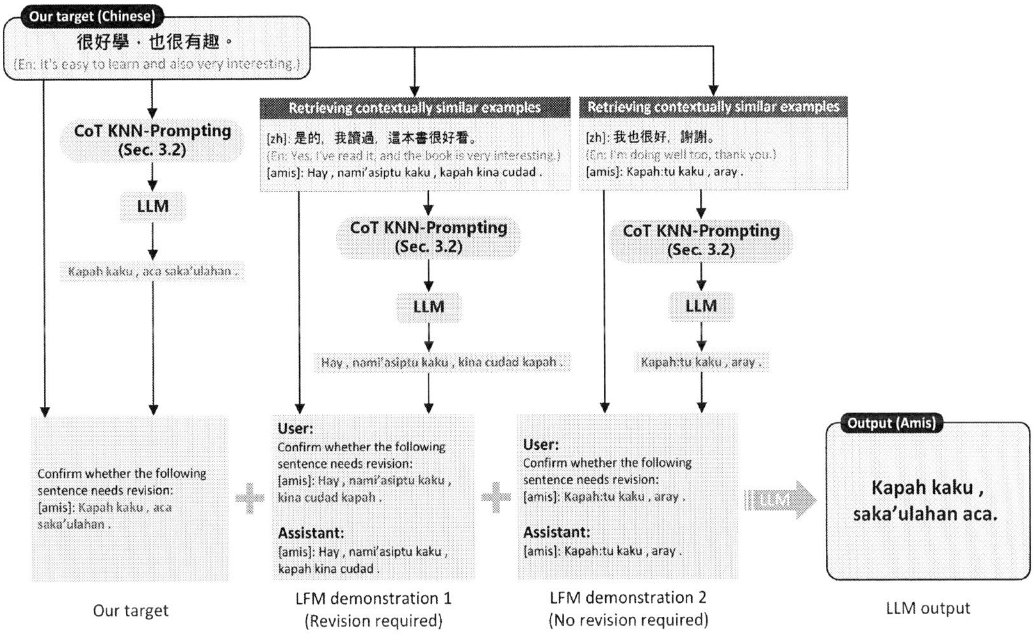

Figure 4: LFM Prompting

	Southern Amis			
Methods	**BLEU1**$_{STD}$	**BLEU2**$_{STD}$	**BLEU3**$_{STD}$	**chrF++**$_{STD}$
Zeroshot	1.0	0.0	0.0	3.9
20-shots	18.0	4.9	1.9	16.3
Knn-Prompting (k=5)	30.1	14.4	6.9	28.1
Knn-Prompting (k=10)	33.3	16.4	8.0	34.2
Knn-Prompting w. RPC (k=5)	$38.2_{2.2}$	$10.5_{1.8}$	$4.3_{1.1}$	$41.2_{1.1}$
Knn-Prompting w. RPC (k=10)	$37.8_{2.2}$	$12.5_{3.2}$	$5.2_{1.9}$	$41.5_{1.6}$
CoT Prompting	$44.4_{1.5}$	$14.3_{0.6}$	$5.9_{1.1}$	$43.5_{0.3}$
LFM Prompting	$44.4_{2.7}$	$17.5_{1.8}$	$8.2_{1.7}$	$44.9_{1.9}$

Table 2: The translation results for **Southern Amis**

4.2 Data Sets

We use the learning materials for various indigenous languages from the 'Klokah' website [1] provided by the Foundation for the Research and Development of Indigenous Languages in Taiwan as our evaluation corpora. Each indigenous group consists of 450 sentences with corresponding Chinese translations and a dictionary of 1000 words (single word translation). For each language, we divide this dataset into two parts:

- **Test Data -** A random selection of 100 sentences was used to evaluate the translation performance of various methods.
- **Reference Data -** The remaining 350 sentences and all dictionaries were used as reference materials for the LLM translation.

[1] `https://web.klokah.tw/`

4.3 Evaluation Results

4.3.1 Automatic Score

We've employed the GPT-3.5-turbo as our foundational language model for translation tests. Initially, we opted for Southern Amis, an indigenous language, as our primary focus, evaluating translation accuracy using the standard BLEU (Papineni et al., 2002) and chrF++ (Popović, 2017) metrics. As depicted in Table 2, the zero-shot translation results indicate the model's limitations in effectively translating this language in the absence of reference data, reflected in BLEU scores nearing zero. However, introducing 20-shot reference data prompts the model to engage in (Agrawal et al., 2022) in-context learning, resulting in a marginal improvement in BLEU scores. This highlights the potential of few-shot learning.

Furthermore, from the results in Table 2, we

Coastal Amis				
Methods	**BLEU1**$_{STD}$	**BLEU2**$_{STD}$	**BLEU3**$_{STD}$	**chrF++**$_{STD}$
Knn-Prompting w. RPC (k=5)	$42.9_{1.8}$	$11.8_{0.9}$	$4.7_{1.1}$	$45.4_{0.8}$
Knn-Prompting w. RPC (k=10)	$43.3_{1.2}$	$13.4_{0.6}$	$5.8_{0.8}$	$44.8_{1.1}$
CoT Prompting	$44.5_{2.8}$	$11.9_{3.0}$	$4.7_{2.3}$	$45.7_{1.6}$
LFM Prompting	$44.1_{2.0}$	$12.6_{2.9}$	$5.7_{2.5}$	$46.1_{1.8}$
Wanda Tayal				
Methods	**BLEU1**$_{STD}$	**BLEU2**$_{STD}$	**BLEU3**$_{STD}$	**chrF++**$_{STD}$
Knn-Prompting w. RPC (k=5)	$41.5_{2.5}$	$13.0_{2.1}$	$4.8_{1.6}$	$42.5_{2.4}$
Knn-Prompting w. RPC (k=10)	$42.1_{2.2}$	$13.6_{2.7}$	$5.7_{1.4}$	$42.8_{2.6}$
CoT Prompting	$46.3_{1.8}$	$14.4_{2.6}$	$5.8_{1.2}$	$44.7_{2.1}$
LFM Prompting	$45.2_{2.0}$	$14.0_{1.7}$	$5.8_{0.9}$	$43.9_{2.0}$
Siji Tayal				
Methods	**BLEU1**$_{STD}$	**BLEU2**$_{STD}$	**BLEU3**$_{STD}$	**chrF++**$_{STD}$
Knn-Prompting w. RPC (k=5)	$44.3_{3.2}$	$14.6_{2.1}$	$4.9_{1.7}$	$39.3_{2.0}$
Knn-Prompting w. RPC (k=10)	$44.4_{3.0}$	$14.5_{2.0}$	$5.4_{2.3}$	$40.9_{1.8}$
CoT Prompting	$47.5_{2.7}$	$16.0_{1.2}$	$5.9_{1.4}$	$41.2_{1.0}$
LFM Prompting	$50.0_{1.2}$	$20.0_{1.4}$	$9.3_{2.0}$	$43.4_{2.0}$
Duda Seediq				
Methods	**BLEU1**$_{STD}$	**BLEU2**$_{STD}$	**BLEU3**$_{STD}$	**chrF++**$_{STD}$
Knn-Prompting w. RPC (k=5)	$45.0_{1.2}$	$16.2_{1.5}$	$5.4_{0.8}$	$38.2_{0.8}$
Knn-Prompting w. RPC (k=10)	$45.7_{1.2}$	$17.1_{1.4}$	$6.7_{1.5}$	$39.3_{1.6}$
CoT Prompting	$46.1_{1.6}$	$17.5_{1.4}$	$6.9_{1.0}$	$38.9_{1.1}$
LFM Prompting	$46.3_{1.5}$	$17.3_{2.1}$	$6.9_{1.4}$	$39.3_{1.2}$

Table 3: The translation results for **Coastal Amis**, **Wanda Tayal**, **Siji Tayal**, and **Duda Seediq**

can observe that using KNN-Prompting by retrieving contextual-relevant examples improves translation quality. We can also observe that utilizing the Chain-of-Thought strategy to guide the LLM also brings an improvement in translation quality, with an increase in BLEU scores from 1 to 3. We also report experiment results with Coastal Amis, Wanda Tayal, Siji Tayal, and Duda Seediq languages. The results are shown in Tables 3.

When comparing models, we use BLEU3 as the main performance metric, as BLEU3 considers 3-gram matches, offering a more holistic view of the quality of translations, particularly in terms of fluency and coherence. In terms of BLEU3 scores, CoT Prompting consistently surpasses the base KNN-Prompting across all languages. This points towards the importance of capturing longer sequences and understanding the grammatical flow of the indigenous languages. We can also see the performance boost when we employ the LFM strategy with CoT in the compared languages.

4.3.2 Qualitive Review by Language Expert

In Table 4 in the appendix, we present the results of an evaluation by a Coastal Amis language expert, assessing translations from Chinese into Coastal Amis using various methods. This offers insights into the effectiveness of these translation strategies and helps us understand their impact on translation quality.

- Initially, the expert demonstrates a preference for translations produced by the LFM method, highlighting its contribution to linguistic precision and affirming the significant role of the LFM phase in enhancing translation quality.

- In the second dialogue, the expert's endorsement of the COT and LFM method suggests that its incorporation can refine the LLM's understanding and conveyance of the target language's nuances.

- There is an identified need for improvement in translating sentence structures, particularly with time adverbs such as " 非常" (very), " 很" (very), " 最" (most), and the placement of temporal terms like " 今天" (today), " 明天" (tomorrow) at the sentence's end. The LFM method is anticipated to guide the LLM in learning and internalizing these linguistic patterns, thereby refining the translations. Challenges such as dictionary absences are addressed by seeking synonyms, for instance, substituting " 專爲" (specially designed for) with " 最" (most), and " 南邊" (south) with " 藍色" (blue). We posit that expanding the dictionary will mitigate such issues, further enhancing translation fidelity.

Overall, the expert's reviews imply that the translation approach integrating the LFM strategy tends to yield more precise and culturally attuned translations. This suggests that for LLMs translating less-resourced languages, a strategy amalgamating error feedback with accumulative learning might prove more effective. These insights bolster the methodologies delineated in our paper, positing that a stratified and iterative enhancement approach can substantially uplift translation quality, particularly for languages with constrained structural and lexical resources.

5 Conclusion

This study delves into the capabilities of LLMs in translating indigenous languages. Despite a limited datastore of parallel translations, our introduced methodologies: *KNN-Prompting with RPC, CoT Prompting, and LFM Prompting* demonstrate effectiveness in harnessing LLMs for this task. Emphasizing our technical contribution, empirical results highlight the superior performance of the CoT Prompting and LFM strategy over the compared baseline, signifying its adeptness at capturing intricate linguistic nuances and offering an advanced approach to preserving linguistic diversity.

6 Limitations

The strength of this framework lies in its capacity to translate less common, niche languages with a limited number of examples. Nevertheless, several challenges were encountered during the experiments. For example, in the case of the Southern Amis language, the term 'we' can be translated as 'kami' or 'niyam,' among other options. Determining whether these terms carry subtle distinctions in meaning or are interchangeable necessitates the expertise of native speakers. Moreover, the use of the BLEU metric provides only one standardized answer, which may not consistently align with the actual context.

Furthermore, within the LFM context, structural or grammatical corrections are solely guided by prior examples, as the language model itself lacks the capability for independent reasoning and adjustment. Therefore, achieving significant breakthroughs in effectiveness remains a challenge. Finally, while our methods have demonstrated data-driven enhancements, they do not fully address the issue of insufficient few-shot data resulting in inconsistent translation outcomes. Further research and innovation are essential in addressing this matter.

Acknowledgement

This work is supported by NSTC 112-2634-F-005-002-project Smart Sustainable New Agriculture Research Center (SMARTer), NSTC Taiwan Project under grant 112-2221-E-005-075-MY3, and Ministry of Education, Taiwan.

References

Sweta Agrawal, Chunting Zhou, Mike Lewis, Luke Zettlemoyer, and Marjan Ghazvininejad. 2022. In-context examples selection for machine translation. *arXiv preprint arXiv:2212.02437*.

Kabir Ahuja, Rishav Hada, Millicent Ochieng, Prachi Jain, Harshita Diddee, Samuel Maina, Tanuja Ganu, Sameer Segal, Maxamed Axmed, Kalika Bali, et al. 2023. Mega: Multilingual evaluation of generative ai. *arXiv preprint arXiv:2303.12528*.

Rouzbeh Behnia, Mohammadreza Reza Ebrahimi, Jason Pacheco, and Balaji Padmanabhan. 2022. Ew-tune: A framework for privately fine-tuning large language models with differential privacy. In *2022 IEEE International Conference on Data Mining Workshops (ICDMW)*, pages 560–566. IEEE.

Tom Brown, Benjamin Mann, Nick Ryder, Melanie Subbiah, Jared D Kaplan, Prafulla Dhariwal, Arvind Neelakantan, Pranav Shyam, Girish Sastry, Amanda Askell, et al. 2020. Language models are few-shot learners. *Advances in neural information processing systems*, 33:1877–1901.

Jiatao Gu, Hany Hassan, Jacob Devlin, and Victor OK Li. 2018. Universal neural machine translation for extremely low resource languages. *arXiv preprint arXiv:1802.05368*.

Nuno M Guerreiro, Duarte Alves, Jonas Waldendorf, Barry Haddow, Alexandra Birch, Pierre Colombo, and André FT Martins. 2023. Hallucinations in large multilingual translation models. *arXiv preprint arXiv:2303.16104*.

Tatsuro Inaba, Hirokazu Kiyomaru, Fei Cheng, and Sadao Kurohashi. 2023. Multitool-cot: Gpt-3 can use multiple external tools with chain of thought prompting. *arXiv preprint arXiv:2305.16896*.

Candy Lalrempuii and Badal Soni. 2023. Investigating unsupervised neural machine translation for low-resource language pair english-mizo via lexically enhanced pre-trained language models. *ACM Transactions on Asian and Low-Resource Language Information Processing*, 22(8):1–18.

Brian Lester, Rami Al-Rfou, and Noah Constant. 2021. The power of scale for parameter-efficient prompt tuning. *arXiv preprint arXiv:2104.08691*.

Swaroop Mishra, Daniel Khashabi, Chitta Baral, and Hannaneh Hajishirzi. 2021. Cross-task generalization via natural language crowdsourcing instructions. *arXiv preprint arXiv:2104.08773*.

Xuan-Phi Nguyen, Sharifah Mahani Aljunied, Shafiq Joty, and Lidong Bing. 2023. Democratizing llms for low-resource languages by leveraging their english dominant abilities with linguistically-diverse prompts. *arXiv preprint arXiv:2306.11372*.

Long Ouyang, Jeffrey Wu, Xu Jiang, Diogo Almeida, Carroll Wainwright, Pamela Mishkin, Chong Zhang, Sandhini Agarwal, Katarina Slama, Alex Ray, et al. 2022. Training language models to follow instructions with human feedback. *Advances in Neural Information Processing Systems*, 35:27730–27744.

Kishore Papineni, Salim Roukos, Todd Ward, and Wei-Jing Zhu. 2002. Bleu: a method for automatic evaluation of machine translation. In *Proceedings of the 40th annual meeting of the Association for Computational Linguistics*, pages 311–318.

Maja Popović. 2017. chrf++: words helping character n-grams. In *Proceedings of the second conference on machine translation*, pages 612–618.

Nils Reimers and Iryna Gurevych. 2019. Sentence-bert: Sentence embeddings using siamese bert-networks. *arXiv preprint arXiv:1908.10084*.

Timo Schick, Jane Dwivedi-Yu, Roberto Dessì, Roberta Raileanu, Maria Lomeli, Luke Zettlemoyer, Nicola Cancedda, and Thomas Scialom. 2023. Toolformer: Language models can teach themselves to use tools. *arXiv preprint arXiv:2302.04761*.

Weijia Shi, Julian Michael, Suchin Gururangan, and Luke Zettlemoyer. 2022. Nearest neighbor zero-shot inference. In *Proceedings of the 2022 Conference on Empirical Methods in Natural Language Processing*, pages 3254–3265.

David Stap and Ali Araabi. 2023. Chatgpt is not a good indigenous translator. In *Proceedings of the Workshop on Natural Language Processing for Indigenous Languages of the Americas (AmericasNLP)*, pages 163–167.

Jason Wei, Maarten Bosma, Vincent Y Zhao, Kelvin Guu, Adams Wei Yu, Brian Lester, Nan Du, Andrew M Dai, and Quoc V Le. 2021. Finetuned language models are zero-shot learners. *arXiv preprint arXiv:2109.01652*.

Jason Wei, Xuezhi Wang, Dale Schuurmans, Maarten Bosma, Fei Xia, Ed Chi, Quoc V Le, Denny Zhou, et al. 2022. Chain-of-thought prompting elicits reasoning in large language models. *Advances in Neural Information Processing Systems*, 35:24824–24837.

Benfeng Xu, Quan Wang, Zhendong Mao, Yajuan Lyu, Qiaoqiao She, and Yongdong Zhang. 2023. k nn prompting: Beyond-context learning with calibration-free nearest neighbor inference. *arXiv preprint arXiv:2303.13824*.

Rui Yang, Lin Song, Yanwei Li, Sijie Zhao, Yixiao Ge, Xiu Li, and Ying Shan. 2023. Gpt4tools: Teaching large language model to use tools via self-instruction. *arXiv preprint arXiv:2305.18752*.

Binwei Yao, Ming Jiang, Diyi Yang, and Junjie Hu. 2023. Empowering llm-based machine translation with cultural awareness. *arXiv preprint arXiv:2305.14328*.

Xingdi Yuan, Tong Wang, Yen-Hsiang Wang, Emery Fine, Rania Abdelghani, Pauline Lucas, Hélène Sauzéon, and Pierre-Yves Oudeyer. 2022. Selecting better samples from pre-trained llms: A case study on question generation. *arXiv preprint arXiv:2209.11000*.

Francis Zheng, Edison Marrese-Taylor, and Yutaka Matsuko. 2022. A parallel corpus and dictionary for amis-mandarin translation. In *Proceedings of the 2nd International Workshop on Natural Language Processing for Digital Humanities*, pages 79–84.

Wenhao Zhu, Hongyi Liu, Qingxiu Dong, Jingjing Xu, Lingpeng Kong, Jiajun Chen, Lei Li, and Shujian Huang. 2023. Multilingual machine translation with large language models: Empirical results and analysis. *arXiv preprint arXiv:2304.04675*.

Yuchen Zhuang, Yue Yu, Kuan Wang, Haotian Sun, and Chao Zhang. 2023. Toolqa: A dataset for llm question answering with external tools. *arXiv preprint arXiv:2306.13304*.

Appendix

Coastal Amis language expert reviews translation results
[zh]: 你喜歡看書嗎？(En: Do you like reading books?) [CoT]: Kiso (你, you) maolah (喜歡, like) minengneng (看望, visit) a cudad (書, book) haw ? [LFM]: Kiso (你, you) maolah (喜歡, like) cudad (書, book) minengneng (看望, visit) haw ? [language expert]: Maolah (喜歡, like) kiso (你, you) minengneng (看望, visit) to codad (書, book) haw?
[zh]: 是的，我很喜歡。(En: Yes, I really like it.) [CoT]: Hai (是的, yes) , maolah (很喜歡, really like) to kako (我, I) . [LFM]: Hai (是的, yes) , maolah (很喜歡, really like) to kako (我, I) . [language expert]: Hai (是的, yes), ma'olah (很喜歡, really like) kako (我, I).
[zh]: 你會織布嗎？(En: Do you know how to weave?) [CoT]: Mafana' (會, know how to) kiso (你, you) a miteno'oy (織布, Weaving fabric) ? [LFM]: Mafana' (會, know how to) kiso (你, you) miteno'oy (織布, Weaving fabric) ? [language expert]: Mafana' (會, know how to) kiso (你, you) miteno'oy (織布, Weaving fabric) haw?
[zh]: 我最喜歡夏天。(En: I like summer the most.) [CoT]: Maolah (很喜歡, really like) kako (我, I) patodongan (專爲, Specially designed for) ko kaciherangan (夏天, summer) . [LFM]:Maolah (很喜歡, really like) kako (我, I) kaciherangan (夏天, summer) patodongan (專爲, Specially designed for) . [language expert]: O kaciherangan (夏天, summer) ko kaolahan (最喜愛的, favorite) ako(我, I).
[zh]: 我最喜歡藍色。(En: I like blue the most.) [CoT]: Maolah (喜歡, like) kako (我, I) patodongan (專爲, Specially designed for) satimolan (南邊, south) . [LFM]: Maolah (喜歡, like) kako (我, I) satimolan (南邊, south) patodongan (專爲, Specially designed for) . [language expert]: O langdaway (藍色, blue) a cengel (顏色, color) ko kaolahan (最喜歡, favorite) ako (我, I).
[zh]: 是的，天氣非常好。(En: Yes, the weather is very nice.) [CoT]: Hai (是的, yes) , romi'ad (天氣, weather) tada (非常, very) nga'ay (好, good) . [LFM]: Hai (是的, yes) , romi'ad (天氣, weather) tada (非常, very) nga'ay (好, good) . [language expert]: Hai (是的, yes), fangcal (很好, very good) ko romi'ad (天氣, weather) anini (今天, today).

Table 4: Result of Language Expert Review

Knn-Prompting with RPC
You are an Amis language translator. The followings are some [zh] to [amis] examples. Chinese: 是的，我讀過，這本書很好看。(English: Yes, I've read it, and the book is very interesting.) [Amis]: Hay, nami’ asiptu kaku, kapah kina cudad. [zh]: 我也很好，謝謝。(English: I'm doing well too, thank you.) [Amis]: Kapah:tu kaku, aray. [zh]: 郵差也感到喜悦與滿足。(English: The postman also feels joy and satisfaction.) [Amis]: U yu-cay satu, mikihatiya a lipahak, a mi’ edem tu ulah nu valucu’. : : [zh]: 很好學 (English: Easy to learn.) [Amis]: kapah [zh]: 也 (English: Also) [Amis]: aca [zh]: 很有趣 (English: Very interesting). [Amis]: saka’ ulahan Based on the above examples. Could you help to translate [zh]: 很好學，也很有趣. (English: It's easy to learn and interesting)

Table 5: Simplified Example for Knn-Prompting with RPC

CoT Demonstration 1

You are an Amis language translator. The followings some [zh] to [amis] examples.
[zh]: 現在幾點鐘？(En: What time is it now?)
[Amis]: Pina' ay ku tuki anini？
[zh]: 喔！她什麼時候回來呢？(En: Oh! When is she coming back?)
[Amis]: A, a hacuwa cira a taluma' ？
⋮
⋮
[zh]: 要 (En: Need)
[Amis]: aw
[zh]: 走 (En: Go)
[Amis]: rakat
[zh]: 幾天 (En: How many days.)
[Amis]: kapina a remi' ad
[zh]: 呢 (En: Question particle)
[Amis]: saw
Based on the above examples. Could you help to translate [zh]: 要走多久呢？
[Assistant:] Hacuwa ku tenes a remakat？

CoT Demonstration 2

You are an Amis language translator. The followings some [zh] to [amis] examples.
[zh]: 今年，我們伯伯全家人從台北搭車回來。(En: This year, our uncle's entire family came back from Taipei by car.)
[Amis]: Anini a miheca, makakarireng a taluma' ku vaki niyam atu wawa nira namaka Taypey.
[zh]: 火車比較快。(En: The train is faster.)
[Amis]: U silamalay ku kalamkamay.
⋮
⋮
[zh]: 要 (En: Need)
[Amis]: aw
[zh]: 搭什麼 (En: Take what.)
[Amis]: Makama' an
[zh]: 公車 (En: Bus)
[Amis]: vasu
[zh]: 到 (En: Arrive)
[Amis]: tangasa
[zh]: 台北 (En: Taipei)
[Amis]: Taypak
Based on the above examples. Could you help to translate [zh]: 要搭什麼（車）到台北？
[Assistant:] Makama' an a tala i Taypak？

CoT Prompting

You are an Amis language translator. The followings are some [zh] to [amis] examples.
Chinese: 是的，我讀過，這本書很好看。(English: Yes, I've read it, and the book is very interesting.)
[Amis]: Hay, nami' asiptu kaku, kapah kina cudad.
[zh]: 我也很好，謝謝。(English: I'm doing well too, thank you.)
[Amis]: Kapah:tu kaku, aray.
[zh]: 郵差也感到喜悅與滿足。(English: The postman also feels joy and satisfaction.)
[Amis]: U yu-cay satu, mikihatiya a lipahak, a mi' edem tu ulah nu valucu' .
[zh]: 很好學 (English: Easy to learn.)
[Amis]: kapah
[zh]: 也 (English: Also)
[Amis]: aca
[zh]: 很有趣 (English: Very interesting).
[Amis]: saka' ulahan
Based on the above examples. Could you help to translate [zh]: 很好學，也很有趣. (English: It's easy to learn and interesting)

Table 6: Example for Simplified CoT KNN-Prompting

LFM Prompting Example
Please analyze the differences between `[Your Answer]` and `[Correct Answer]` results. `[zh]`: 是的，我讀過，這本書很好看。(En: Yes, I've read it, and the book is very interesting.) `[Your Answer]`:Hay , nami' asiptu kaku , kina cudad kapah . `[Correct Answer]`: Hay , nami' asiptu kaku , kapah kina cudad . Please analyze the differences between `[Your Answer]` and `[Correct Answer]` results. `[zh]`: 我也很好，謝謝。(En: I'm doing well too, thank you.) `[Your Answer]`:Kapah:tu kaku , aray . `[Correct Answer]`: Kapah:tu kaku , aray .
You are an Amis language translator. The followings some [zh] to [amis] examples. `[zh]`: 是的，我讀過，這本書很好看。(En: Yes, I've read it, and the book is very interesting.) `[amis]`:Hay , nami' asiptu kaku , kapah kina cudad . `[zh]`: 我也很好，謝謝。(En: I'm doing well too, thank you.) `[amis]`:Kapah:tu kaku , aray . `[zh]`: 郵差也感到喜悅與滿足。(En: The postman also feels joy and satisfaction.) `[amis]`:U yu-cay satu , mikihatiya a lipahak , a mi' edem tu ulah nu valucu' . ... `[zh]`: 很好學 (En: Easy to learn.) `[amis]`: kapah `[zh]`: 也 (En: Also) `[amis]`: aca `[zh]`: 很有趣 (En: Very interesting.) `[amis]`: saka' ulahan Check whether the following sentence needs revision: `[zh]`: 很好學，也很有趣。(English: It's easy to learn and interesting) `[Your Answer]`:Kapah kaku , aca saka' ulahan . `[Correct Answer]`:

Table 7: Example for Simplified LFM Prompting. Note that as introduced in the LFM method, when given a sentence s (i.e., 很好學，也很有趣) to translate, we start by retrieving q contextually similar sentence pairs from the data store and use CoT KNN prompting to obtain trial translation results (the sentence followed `[Your Answer]`) and also the correct answer for enabling LFM.

Adopting Ensemble Learning for Cross-lingual Classification of Crisis-related Text On Social Media

Shareefa Al Amer[1,2], **Mark Lee**[1], **Phillip Smith**[1]
[1]*School of Computer Science*, University of Birmingham, United Kingdom
[2]*College of Computer Science & Information Technology*, King Faisal University, Saudi Arabia
alamersharifah@gmail.com, {m.g.lee,p.smith.7}@bham.ac.uk

Abstract

Cross-lingual classification poses a significant challenge in Natural Language Processing (NLP), especially when dealing with languages with scarce training data. This paper delves into the adaptation of ensemble learning to address this challenge, specifically for disaster-related social media texts. Initially, we employ Machine Translation to generate a parallel corpus in the target language to mitigate the issue of data scarcity and foster a robust training environment. Following this, we implement the bagging ensemble technique, integrating multiple classifiers into a cohesive model that demonstrates enhanced performance over individual classifiers. Our experimental results reveal significant improvements in adapting models for Arabic, utilising only English training data and markedly outperforming models intended for linguistically similar languages to English, with our ensemble model achieving an accuracy and F1 score of 0.78 when tested on original Arabic data. This research makes a substantial contribution to the field of cross-lingual classification, establishing a new benchmark for enhancing the effectiveness of language transfer in linguistically challenging scenarios.

1 Introduction

Cross-lingual transfer learning, which involves transferring models from one language to another or from one task to another, has gained significant attention in the field of natural language processing. This approach is particularly valuable in scenarios where task data in the target language is scarce, posing a limitation to training machine learning models for specific tasks such as classification. In such cases, machine translation has emerged as an effective solution to bridge the language gap, enabling acceptable performance in transfer learning (Ji et al., 2024; Huang et al., 2021).

Furthermore, the use of ensemble techniques in the context of cross-lingual classification has shown promise in achieving better performance and generalisation across multiple languages. Ensemble models, by combining multiple base models, can effectively capture diverse aspects of the data and mitigate the impact of language variations, thereby enhancing the robustness of cross-lingual classification systems.

The significance of transfer learning lies in its ability to utilise the wealth of data available in high-resource languages to benefit low-resource languages, thus enabling access to various NLP tasks. Data augmentation techniques, like Machine Translation, serve to amplify this effect by artificially expanding the dataset in the target language, which allows for a richer and more diverse linguistic feature set that models can learn from, leading to improved performance and reliability in cross-lingual applications.

The potential of ensemble learning in addressing the challenges of cross-lingual classification cannot be overstated. By leveraging the strengths of multiple learners, ensemble learning introduces a level of diversity that single models alone cannot achieve, significantly enhancing performance and generalisation capabilities across languages. This diversity is particularly crucial in cross-lingual scenarios, where linguistic and semantic disparities between languages can pose substantial barriers to effective model transfer. Ensemble methods can mitigate these barriers by combining predictions from multiple models, thereby reducing the risk of misclassification due to language-specific nuances or translation inaccuracies. Moreover, ensemble learning can adaptively focus on difficult-to-classify instances, ensuring that the aggregated model is not only more accurate but also more robust to the variability inherent in cross-lingual data. Consequently, the application of ensemble learning in cross-lingual classification opens up new avenues for building more resilient and adaptive NLP systems that can better serve the needs of a

Proceedings of the The Seventh Workshop on Technologies for Machine Translation of Low-Resource Languages (LoResMT 2024), pages 159–165
August 15, 2024

linguistically diverse world.

In addressing the challenge of cross-lingual transfer learning in situations where training data is non-existent, our work introduces an effective approach that significantly improves the efficacy of model transfer to the Arabic language, a language markedly different in structure and lexicon from English. A key aspect of our contribution is investigating viable strategies, including the integration of machine translation with a bagging ensemble approach, for classifying disaster-related social media posts in Arabic using solely English data. This technique demonstrates potential for broad application across various languages and domains, offering a solution for scenarios with limited data availability in the target language, provided there's access to extensive data in a resource-rich language.

2 Related Work

With growing interest in cross-lingual text classification, the challenge persists due to linguistic variations and data scarcity across languages. Ensemble classification models, employing multiple weak classifiers and combining their predictions through consistency functions like voting, have been widely used in monolingual tasks but less explored in cross-lingual contexts. Techniques such as bagging, AdaBoost, random forest, and gradient boosting have shown promise across various domains (Dong et al., 2020). Among the limited literature on cross-lingual applications, *Funnelling* and its advanced iteration, Generalised Funnelling (*GFun*), stand out for incorporating calibrated posterior probabilities and additional feature vectors to enhance classification performance on multilingual datasets. However, they assume the availability of training data in all target languages (Esuli et al., 2019; Moreo et al., 2021).

Earlier studies, such as those by (Kilimci and Akyokus, 2018) and (Bashmal and Alzeer, 2021), demonstrate the effectiveness of ensemble models in monolingual settings, suggesting potential for cross-lingual adaptation. Beyond ensemble models, research has explored leveraging linguistic similarities through character-based embeddings, joint training, and embedding alignment to address cross-lingual text classification. Techniques such as instance-weighting have also been employed to assign larger weights to source instances sharing common features with target samples during training. This approach aims to utilise resource-rich data while accommodating the specifics of the target language (Li et al., 2021).

While the foundation for cross-lingual text classification is robust, marked by a variety of methodologies from ensemble learning to linguistic feature exploitation, challenges remain in data availability, computational demands, and language diversity. Our work contributes to this ongoing effort by adapting an ensemble approach designed to enhance the effectiveness of cross-lingual classification, especially for under-resourced languages. This approach seeks to build on the existing body of research, pushing the boundaries of what is achievable in the realm of cross-lingual text classification.

3 Proposed Methodology

3.1 Problem Formulation

The challenge of accurately classifying disaster-related social media texts across multiple languages is paramount for effective emergency response, yet is significantly hindered by the lack of training data for various languages. This scarcity affects the development of effective cross-lingual classification models, especially for languages with minimal resources. We aim to tackle this issue by focusing on the cross-lingual classification of disaster-related texts within the context of languages that are underrepresented in training datasets.

Addressing the data disparity between high-resource and low-resource languages, which are often spoken by communities most affected by disasters, is crucial. The goal of this study is to utilise the abundant data from high-resource languages to improve the classification accuracy of texts in low-resource languages. In doing so, we aspire to enhance global disaster response efforts by ensuring that critical information reaches all linguistic groups, thereby overcoming language barriers that could potentially hinder timely and effective disaster management.

3.2 Model Overview

Our proposed model, depicted in Figures 1 and 2, addresses the challenge of cross-lingual classification of disaster-related social media texts through a structured methodology comprising four main components: Data Collection and Translation, Bootstrapping, Ensemble Model Learning, and Testing the Ensemble. The process begins with the acquisition of disaster-related texts from a high-resource language, namely English, followed by their translation into the target language, Arabic, to mitigate data scarcity. This is complemented by a bootstrapping phase that employs a bagging approach to split the dataset into separate subsets.

At the core of our methodology is the Ensemble Model Learning component, which utilises three classifiers to construct a robust model. This approach benefits from the diversity of data and significantly reduces the risks of overfitting. The ensemble model is subsequently tested with separate target language data to evaluate its effectiveness and applicability in real-world disaster scenarios. Through this integrated approach, which combines machine translation, iterative learning, and ensemble learning, we aim to enhance the classification of disaster-related texts across languages, thereby improving global disaster response capabilities.

4 Experiments

4.1 Data

We utilise the CrisisNLP dataset (Imran et al., 2016), with over 17,000 English X posts covering a range of disaster types such as earthquakes, floods, and diseases. This dataset was translated into Arabic using Google Translate to create a parallel corpus. To assess the model's performance in Arabic, we used the Kawarith dataset (Alharbi and Lee, 2021) which consists of 5,000 Arabic X posts with similar disaster classifications. This setup allows for effective cross-lingual model training and testing.

To prepare the data, we consolidated storm-related classes into a single "Storm" category to align both datasets and simplify classification. We ended up with three classes that are common to both the training and testing datasets, namely storm, disease, and irrelevant. Our preprocessing included removing non-ASCII characters, URLs, mentions, and normalising text (removing extra spaces, handling hashtags). This ensured clean, uniform datasets for our cross-lingual classification experiments.

4.2 Machine Translation Model Selection

To choose a suitable Machine Translation (MT) model for translating the data, we evaluated the performance of three open-source MT systems that support a wide range of languages, including Arabic, by calculating BLEU (Papineni et al., 2002) and METEOR (Banerjee and Lavie, 2005) scores. We sampled 1,000 posts from the English data and employed a human translator to obtain the reference translation. The same sample was then translated using three different MT models: Google Translate, Facebook's M2M, and MarianMT. While the differences in performance were not substantial, this evaluation assisted us in making the MT decision. We acknowledge that these metrics measure how closely the MT translations align with human translations, which is less critical in our case since the translation is for classifier consumption.

The results of this study are presented in Table 1. While the observed BLEU scores may appear low, they do not necessarily indicate poor model performance given the complexity of the task. Translating social media content is particularly challenging in machine translation, and achieving high BLEU scores in this domain is more difficult than in more formal types of text (Sabtan et al., 2021).

Notably, the observed METEOR scores are higher than the BLEU scores for the same models and languages. This could be attributed to METEOR's more comprehensive assessment of translation quality, including synonymy and sentence structure, which might be more forgiving than BLEU's strict n-gram matching approach, especially in the context of social media text.

4.3 Evaluation Metrics

For both the individual models and the ensemble model, these evaluation metrics are calculated based on their predictions on a separate test dataset. The evaluation includes calculating accuracy and F1 scores, including weighted, micro, and macro F1. The accuracy metric provides an overview of the model's overall performance, while the F1 scores give insights into the model's precision and recall for each class and their overall performance.

The ensemble model's evaluation involves combining the predictions of the individual classifiers using a voting mechanism. The predictions made by each individual classifier are considered, and the final prediction for each instance is determined by the class with the majority vote. The ensemble model's accuracy and F1 scores are then computed based on these aggregated predictions.

4.4 Experimental Settings

We employed the "xlm-roberta-base" (Conneau et al., 2020) as the base classifier for our ensembles with the same hyper-parameters, differing only in the data being handled. The tokenizer was configured with truncation enabled and a maximum to-

	BLEU	METEOR
Google Translate	**0.144**	**0.354**
Facebook M2M	0.097	0.283
MarianMT	0.081	0.236

Table 1: BLEU and METEOR scores calculated for each Machine Translation model translating the 1K sample to Arabic using human translation as the reference.

ken length set to the longest instance. Padding was also used to ensure uniform input lengths during training. The model architecture was loaded using the 'AutoModelFor-SequenceClassification.from-pretrained' method, which adapted the pre-trained XLM-RoBERTa to our specific task with three classes.

For our model training, we chose a batch size of 64 to balance computational efficiency and gradient stability, and we limited training to 10 epochs to optimise exposure to the dataset while preventing overfitting. The learning rate was set to 1e-5, chosen through experimentation to ensure fast convergence without overshooting, and weight decay was applied at a rate of 0.01 as a regularisation measure to enhance generalisation. To manage resources effectively, we saved the model at the end of each epoch but limited storage to only the latest model checkpoint, avoiding the resource strain of multiple checkpoints. This ensures training efficiency, model performance, and computational resource management.

4.5 Results

4.5.1 Experiment 1

In the first experiment, we fine-tuned two separate XLM-RoBERTa models for classifying parallel datasets (CrisisNLP and translated CrisisNLP), with each model being exposed to data in one language during training. These individual classifiers were then combined to create an ensemble model using a voting function to determine predictions for test instances. The best-performing model for each language was selected for predicting these instances. Subsequently, the ensemble model aggregated the predictions from the individual classifiers to generate the final prediction through a voting mechanism, as illustrated in Figure 1.

The performance of the individual models in the monolingual setting is presented in Table 2, where one XLM-RoBERTa model was fine-tuned on the original English data and another on the Arabic translation of the same data. Results are reported using accuracy, macro F1, and weighted F1 scores. The ensemble, combining predictions from both models and generating final predictions for the original Arabic test data through voting, achieved an accuracy of 0.75, with macro and weighted F1 scores of 0.63 and 0.74, respectively. This marks a significant improvement over our previous benchmark, achieving a 0.72 weighted average F1 score with machine-translated source data for training. These results underscore the effectiveness of the ensemble technique in a cross-lingual context, indicating the potential for further improvement by exploring alternative ensemble approaches.

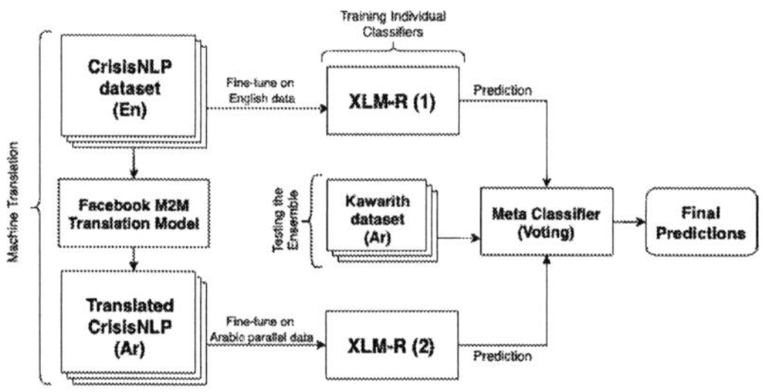

Figure 1: The approach of ensembling two individual classifiers trained on parallel (machine-translated) data in English and Arabic.

4.5.2 Experiment 2

Building on the successes of the first experiment, which already marked improvements over previous experiments and existing baselines as discussed in Section 4.5.1, our second experiment aimed at further enhancing performance by altering the architecture of the ensemble model. We introduced a joint training approach, leveraging an ensemble of three base classifiers. Each classifier was trained on a unique segment of the data, ensuring complete data separation among the models. This was achieved by initially merging the parallel datasets and then dividing this combined dataset into three segments using a bagging technique. The classifiers were then trained independently on

	Data	Accuracy	Macro F1	Micro F1	W Avg F1
Classifier 1	CrisisNLP (En)	0.96	0.96	0.95	0.96
Classifier 2	CrisisNLP (Ar)	0.94	0.94	0.94	0.94
Ensemble	Kawarith (test)	0.75	0.63	0.74	0.74

Table 2: Performance of individual XLM-R classifiers on monolingual data. The CrisisNLP (Ar) dataset represents the machine-translated Arabic data, while Kawarith is an original Arabic dataset used for testing the ensemble. The last set of results showcases the voting ensemble of both individual classifiers when evaluated on the Kawarith dataset.

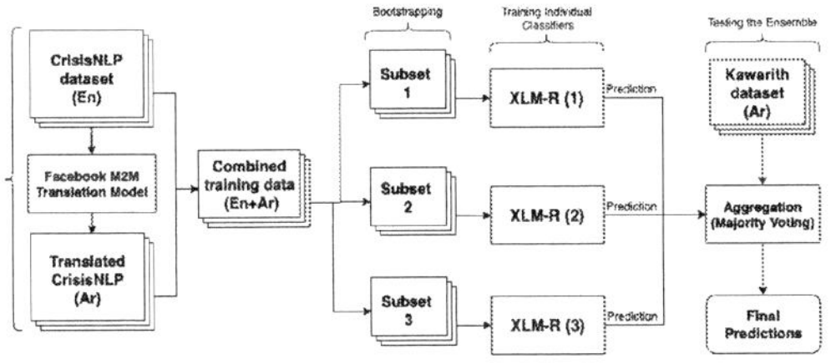

Figure 2: The bagging approach used in this experiment involves splitting the combined parallel data into three distinct subsets. Each subset is utilised to train a different instance of the XLM-R classifier.

these segments, with the best-performing model for each segment chosen for test sample prediction. A majority voting mechanism was subsequently employed for the final prediction, showcasing the ensemble's combined strength in making accurate cross-lingual classifications, as depicted in Figure 2.

This experiment aimed to maximise the ensemble's effectiveness by combining parallel training data, thereby exposing the models to both languages. The goal was to leverage the collective strength of the ensemble in adeptly handling the linguistic diversity presented by the datasets. The performance of the individual classifiers is presented in Table 3, with all three models achieving an accuracy and F1 score of approximately 0.93 on homogeneous data, underscoring their consistency. When evaluated on the original Arabic data (Kawarith), the ensemble of the three models demonstrated substantial improvement over the results of the first experiment, achieving an accuracy and F1 score of 0.78. Remarkably, this performance sets a new benchmark, surpassing existing efforts in similar cross-lingual classification challenges and underlining the potency of our ensemble approach in achieving state-of-the-art results in cross-lingual contexts.

4.5.3 Joint Training

To comprehensively assess the method's efficacy, we conducted benchmark comparisons by training a classifier on combined English and its Arabic translated datasets. This benchmark allowed a direct evaluation of the ensemble strategy's benefits over single-classifier approaches, crucial for understanding the impact of using multiple classifiers together in a cross-lingual context. Our findings show that while individual classifiers in the ensemble may perform less effectively than a singular classifier on homogeneous data, the ensemble as a whole surpasses the single classifier's performance on Arabic test data (zero-shot), highlighting the ensemble's superior handling of linguistic diversity. These results, summarised in Table 4, showcase the ensemble's ability to outperform despite the individual weaknesses of its components, demonstrating its strength in cross-lingual classification.

5 Discussion

The presence of data imbalance posed a significant challenge and had a noticeable impact on the model's performance. To address this issue, we made a trade-off between better classification and the potential loss of data. As a mitigation strategy, we introduced an additional layer to calculate class weights, accounting for the class imbalance. The class weight calculation function was designed to dynamically assign weights based on the distribution of instances in each class. If the data is already balanced, the function assigns equal weights to all classes. However, for classes with fewer instances, the function assigns higher weights, effectively prioritising those classes during training. By incorporating this mechanism, we aimed to balance the training process and alleviate the negative impact of data imbalance on the model's performance. This approach is particularly useful in scenarios where the dataset is heavily imbalanced, as it allows the model to focus more on the underrepre-

	Data	Accuracy	Macro F1	Micro F1	W Avg F1
Classifier 1	CrisisNLP (En+Ar*)	0.928	0.929	0.928	0.927
Classifier 2	CrisisNLP (En+Ar*)	0.933	0.934	0.933	0.932
Classifier 3	CrisisNLP (En+Ar*)	0.936	0.938	0.936	0.935
Ensemble	Kawarith (test)	0.78	0.70	0.78	0.78

Table 3: Performance of individual XLM-R classifiers on distinct subsets of the data. The last row showcases the voting ensemble of the three individual classifiers when evaluated on the Kawarith dataset. *The CrisisNLP (Ar) dataset represents the machine-translated Arabic data.

	Accuracy	Macro F1	Weighted Avg F1
Bagging Ensemble	0.78	0.70	0.78
Joint Training	0.69	0.70	0.70
Joint Training (homo)	0.95	0.95	0.95

Table 4: Performance comparison between bagging ensemble and an individual classifier trained on the same combined dataset. Last row shows the performance of the classifier when tested on the same training data (test portion).

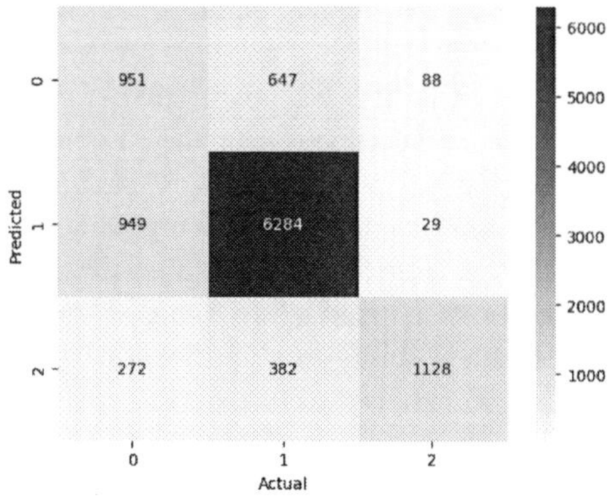

Figure 3: The confusion matrix of the ensemble classification results achieved through majority voting of three classifiers. 0, 1, and 2 correspond to irrelevant, storm, and disease classes, respectively.

sented classes, leading to improved generalisation and performance across all classes.

With a closer look at the individual scores, we notice that the mis-classification of class 0 (i.e., irrelevant) has affected the macro-average F1 resulting in a score of 0.70. However, the model performs relatively well in classifying other classes. The diverse nature of the irrelevant posts makes it challenging for the model to accurately classify them, and they are often mis-classified into other classes, mostly class 1 (storm). Figure 3 displays the confusion matrix, which provides a visualisation of the classification performance for each individual class.

6 Conclusion and future work

In this work, we have presented a practical solution for transferring models across languages when confronted with limited or nonexistent training data. Our experimentation involved the application of a bagging ensemble technique, with each experiment employing a distinct approach. By combining training data from both English and its Arabic translation, and partitioning (bagging) this combined dataset into separate splits, we observed a noteworthy enhancement in prediction performance compared to existing methodologies. Looking ahead, our future work will explore alternative ensemble approaches to tackle the same challenge. Additionally, extending the scope of our approach to a wider set of languages and tasks holds promising potential for further advancement.

References

Alaa Alharbi and Mark Lee. 2021. Kawarith: An Arabic Twitter Corpus for Crisis Events. *Proceedings of the Sixth Arabic Natural Language Processing Workshop*, pages 42–52.

Satanjeev Banerjee and Alon Lavie. 2005. METEOR: An Automatic Metric for MT Evaluation with Improved Correlation with Human Judgments. In *Intrinsic and Extrinsic Evaluation Measures for Machine Translation and/or Summarization, Proceedings of the Workshop ACL 2005.*

Laila Bashmal and Daliyah H. Alzeer. 2021. ArSarcasm Shared Task: An Ensemble BERT Model for Sarcasm Detection in Arabic Tweets. In *WANLP 2021 - 6th*

Arabic Natural Language Processing Workshop, Proceedings of the Workshop.

Alexis Conneau, Kartikay Khandelwal, Naman Goyal, Vishrav Chaudhary, Guillaume Wenzek, Francisco Guzmán, Edouard Grave, Myle Ott, Luke Zettlemoyer, and Veselin Stoyanov. 2020. Unsupervised Cross-lingual Representation Learning at Scale. *Proceedings of the 58th Annual Meeting of the Association for Computational Linguistics*, pages 8440–8451.

Xibin Dong, Zhiwen Yu, Wenming Cao, Yifan Shi, and Qianli Ma. 2020. A Survey on Ensemble Learning.

Andrea Esuli, Alejandro Moreo, and Fabrizio Sebastiani. 2019. Funnelling: A New Ensemble Method for Heterogeneous Transfer Learning and Its Application to Cross-lingual Text Classification. *ACM Transactions on Information Systems*, 37(3).

Kuan Hao Huang, Wasi Uddin Ahmad, Nanyun Peng, and Kai Wei Chang. 2021. Improving Zero-Shot Cross-Lingual Transfer Learning via Robust Training. In *EMNLP 2021 - 2021 Conference on Empirical Methods in Natural Language Processing, Proceedings.*

Muhammad Imran, Prasenjit Mitra, and Carlos Castillo. 2016. Twitter as a Lifeline: Human-Annotated Twitter Corpora for NLP of Crisis-Related Messages. *Proceedings of the 10th International Conference on Language Resources and Evaluation, LREC 2016.*

Shaoxiong Ji, Timothee Mickus, Vincent Segonne, and Jörg Tiedemann. 2024. Can Machine Translation Bridge Multilingual Pretraining and Cross-lingual Transfer Learning?

Zeynep H. Kilimci and Selim Akyokus. 2018. Deep Learning- and Word Embedding-based Heterogeneous Classifier Ensembles for Text Classification. *Complexity*, 2018.

Irene Li, Prithviraj Sen, Huaiyu Zhu, Yunyao Li, and Dragomir Radev. 2021. Improving Cross-lingual Text Classification with Zero-shot Instance-Weighting.

Alejandro Moreo, Andrea Pedrotti, and Fabrizio Sebastiani. 2021. Generalized Funnelling: Ensemble Learning and Heterogeneous Document Embeddings for Cross-lingual Text Classification. In *CEUR Workshop Proceedings*, volume 2947.

Kishore Papineni, Salim Roukos, Todd Ward, and Wei Jing Zhu. 2002. BLEU: A Method for Automatic Evaluation of Machine Translation. In *Proceedings of the Annual Meeting of the Association for Computational Linguistics*, volume 2002-July.

Yasser Muhammad Naguib Sabtan, Mohamed Saad Mahmoud Hussein, Hamza Ethelb, and Abdulfattah Omar. 2021. An Evaluation of the Accuracy of the Machine Translation Systems of Social Media Language. *International Journal of Advanced Computer Science and Applications*, 12(7).

Finetuning End-to-End Models for Estonian Conversational Spoken Language Translation

Tiia Sildam, Andra Velve, Tanel Alumäe
Department of Software Science
Tallinn University of Technology, Estonia

Abstract

This paper investigates the finetuning of end-to-end models for bidirectional Estonian-English and Estonian-Russian conversational speech-to-text translation. Due to the limited availability of speech translation data for Estonian, we created additional training data by web scraping and synthesizing data from speech recognition datasets using machine translation. We evaluated three publicly available end-to-end models: Whisper, OWSM 3.1, and SeamlessM4T. Our results indicate that fine-tuning with synthetic data enhances translation accuracy by a large margin, with SeamlessM4T matching or surpassing cascaded speech translation systems that use state-of-the-art speech recognition and machine translation models.

1 Introduction

Estonian language, spoken by around one million native speakers, has benefited significantly from the Estonian Language Technology Program in the last decades (Rehm et al., 2020). This initiative has fostered advancements in several key areas, such as automatic speech recognition (ASR) (Alumäe et al., 2023) and machine translation (MT) (Tättar et al., 2022). These improvements are largely due to investments in collecting relevant training data and the successful application of large multilingual pretrained models. Another crucial area of language technology is spoken language translation, which is essential for maintaining smaller languages like Estonian in today's digital world. This technology enables native speakers of a small language to access foreign language content more easily and allows for the broader dissemination of native language content. However, one of the significant challenges in developing these technologies is the lack of adequate training data for Estonian, particularly in conversational speech. This shortage hampers the ability to further enhance and refine speech translation tools.

In this study, we explore the finetuning of three publicly available end-to-end models for bidirectional Estonian-English and Estonian-Russian conversational speech translation tasks and evaluate their accuracy against the cascaded spoken language translation approach. Given the scarcity of speech translation datasets containing significant amounts of conversational speech for these translation directions, we explore two methods to generate additional data: synthesizing speech translation training data from ASR training data using machine translation, and scraping data (e.g., videos with subtitles) from the internet. We evaluate these models and finetuning approaches using automatic metrics (BLEU and BLEURT) on realistic conversational speech evaluation sets.

The main contribution of this paper is demonstrating that leading large publicly available end-to-end multilingual speech translation models can be fine-tuned to excel in translation tasks involving relatively low-resource languages by using synthetic data generated from diverse ASR training data. Another innovative aspect of the paper is showing that OpenAI's Whisper, originally trained only for translating into English, serves as an effective base model that can be finetuned for other speech translation directions. Additionally, we release an evaluation set for Estonian-English-Russian spoken language translation, which includes conversational speech recordings "from the wild", complete with manual transcripts and professionally produced translations[1]. The best-trained speech translation models are publicly available[2]. An example of an Estonian TV news broadcast with English and Russian subtitles generated by our finetuned Whisper model is available at `https://www.youtube.com/watch?v=rZPqauCYfXI`.

[1] `https://github.com/alumae/k6net6lke-benchmark`

[2] Finetuned Whisper: `https://huggingface.co/TalTechNLP/whisper-large-v3-et-en-ru.translate`

Proceedings of the The Seventh Workshop on Technologies for Machine Translation of Low-Resource Languages (LoResMT 2024), pages 166–174
August 15, 2024 ©2024 Association for Computational Linguistics

2 Available models

In this section, an overview of publicly accessible models suitable for speech translation in the targeted translation directions of our study will be provided.

2.1 Cascaded spoken language translation

The cascaded speech translation method involves initially using an ASR system to transcribe speech, followed by translating these transcriptions with a text-to-text MT system. Presently, one of the most widely used multilingual ASR model available to the public is OpenAI's Whisper (Radford et al., 2023). In our tests, we utilized the most effective *large-v3* model of Whisper to transcribe English and Russian speech. For Estonian, we used the same model, which was finetuned with 1334 hours of Estonian data available publicly from the TalTech Estonian Speech Dataset 1.0[3] (Alumäe et al., 2023). During the development of this paper, the leading publicly accessible text-to-text MT model for translations involving Estonian was Meta's NLLB-200 (NLLB Team et al., 2022). The NLLB model is available in various sizes, with the largest being the mixture-of-experts (MoE) version, which requires 350 GB of storage. For practical reasons, we opted for the largest dense model, which has 3.3 billion parameters. Machine translation to and from Estonian via text is also well supported by several proprietary vendors via API calls, such as Google and DeepL. The NLP research group at Tartu University offers a publicly accessible NMT system *Neurotõlge*[4] that is effective for Estonian MT tasks (Tättar et al., 2022), and it also provides a free web API for batch processing. OpenAI's GPT models are also capable of conducting machine translation through prompting.

2.2 End-to-end spoken language translation

Several publicly available multilingual end-to-end spoken language translation models have recently emerged. OpenAI's Whisper model can perform translation to English from all its supported speech recognition languages. Other translation directions are not supported by this model. The reported BLEU score for Estonian-to-English translation for the *large-v2* version of Whisper is 18.7, measured on the FLEURS dataset (Conneau et al., 2022) and 15.0, measured on the CoVoST 2 (Wang et al., 2020) dataset. Both of those datasets contain read speech. Whisper uses Transformer encoder-decoder architecture.

The Open Whisper-style Speech Model (OWSM) (Peng et al., 2023b) reproduces Whisper-style training using a diverse combination of publicly available datasets and the open-source toolkit ESPnet (Watanabe et al., 2018). It supports multilingual automatic speech recognition (ASR) and any-to-any speech translation (ST). The latest release of the model (3.1 EBF) uses the E-Branchformer (Kim et al., 2022) architecture in the encoder and Transformer in the decoder. The 1 billion parameter "base" version of OWSM 3.1 EBF has a reported BLEU score of 7.7 on the English-to-Estonian translation direction, measured on CoVoST 2.

The third publicly available multilingual speech translation model originates from Meta's SeamlessM4T project (Seamless Communication et al., 2023). SeamlessM4T translation models are capable of translating both speech and text modalities, and they can produce both text and speech output. Around 100 languages are supported, although speech output is supported for a much smaller subset of languages. While both Whisper and OWSM models are trained end-to-end from scratch, SeamlessM4T uses a more complicated process for training. First, a self-supervised speech encoder model w2v-BERT 2.0 is pretrained, using a corpus of 4.5M hours of unlabeled audio data covering more than 143 languages. This model is then bridged with the NLLB text-to-text translation model, using special adapter layers that map encoded and time-compressed speech features to the same semantic space as text tokens. This composed model is then finetuned for speech-to-text and speech-to-speech translation tasks, using paired text-text, speech-text and speech-speech data scraped from the web and aligned using a dedicated multimodal embedding and alignment model (Duquenne et al., 2023). The *SeamlessM4T-large-v2* reports a BLEU score of 29.3 on English-Estonian and 27.7 on Estonian-English test sets of CoVoST 2. On FLEURS, this model has a BLEU score of 22.4 on English-Estonian and 31.6 on Estonian-English speech-to-text test sets.

The out-of-the-box BLEU scores of the described models on Estonian-English speech translation tasks are reported in Table 1. Although the scores are measured on test sets containing only

[3] https://cs.taltech.ee/staff/tanel.alumae/data/est-pub-asr-data/

[4] https://neurotolge.ee/

		CoVoST 2		FLEURS	
Model	#Parameters	est-eng	eng-est	est-eng	eng-est
Whisper large-v3	1.55B	15.0	N/A	18.7	N/A
OWSM 3.1 EBF	1B	?	7.7	?	?
SeamlessM4T-v2 large	2.3B	27.7	29.3	31.6	22.4

Table 1: Speech translation BLEU scores of different publicly available models. N/A denotes that the model is not capable of translating in this direction, and question marks denote scores that are not reported.

read speech, the scores suggest that these models could be finetuned to perform well also on more conversational speech that is known to be more difficult to translate.

Whisper and OWSM models are designed to handle audio recordings of any length due to the integrated speech segmentation in their decoders. These models effectively generate time-stamped, subtitle-like transcripts, marking each decoded word block with start and end times. In the process of long-form decoding, the models work on 30-second segments of speech at a time, shifting the processing window by 30 seconds (or less) to start where the last decoded word block ended after each decoding step. On the other hand, SeamlessM4T models are limited to processing shorter, utterance-like speech segments, and their translation quality drops substantially with longer segments, often only translating the initial part of the segment. To address this, long recordings must be initially divided into shorter, speaker-consistent segments, typically no longer than 20 seconds, using voice activity detection and speaker segmentation technologies.

3 Methodology

The main focus of our work is finetuning publicly available speech translation models using additional data. Since there are no conversational speech translation datasets that include Estonian, we experiment with generating additional data on our own using two methods: web scraping and data synthesis. We compare the performance of all three existing speech translation models before and after finetuning with the same data.

Although Whisper is originally trained to perform only multilingual speech recognition and speech translation to English, it has been shown that it can perform speech translation to other directions with surprisingly high accuracy by changing only the prefix of the decoder. For example, Peng et al. (2023a) showed that by only modifying the prompt, Whisper can achieve 18.1 BLEU score on the English-German speech translation test set from the MuST-C corpus (Gangi et al., 2019). Therefore, we were relatively confident that Whisper can be finetuned for all translation directions that we were interested in.

The design of Whisper's prompt does not support the specification of alternative translation directions. Consequently, we finetuned Whisper using extra speech translation data by employing the "transcribe" prompt, where the language specified in the prompt matched the intended target language. At the inference stage, the expected target language was set in the prompt, but the source language remained unspecified to the model.

On all datasets, Whisper was finetuned[5] for three epochs over the additional translation datasets. A learning rate schedule with a peak rate of 1e-04 was used, with 500 warmup steps and a linearly decaying schedule towards 0 after the warmup. An effective batch size of 64 was used. Stochastic weight averaging (SWA) (Izmailov et al., 2018) with a learning rate of 1e-05 was applied during the last epoch. Adam optimizer was used.

The OWSM 3.1 EBF model underwent finetuning over five epochs, utilizing a batch size of 320 and a maximum learning rate of 2.0e-04, accompanied by a warmup phase of 600 steps. A label smoothing technique was employed with a smoothing factor of 0.1. During training, a multi-task encoder-decoder/CTC loss method was used (with source language transcript as supervision for the CTC head), setting the CTC loss weight at 0.3. The majority of these hyperparameters were adopted directly from the ESPnet's training recipe for the OWSM 3.1 EBF model without further adjustments.

The SeamlessM4T model was finetuned using a batch size of 48, peak learning rate of 1e-06 with 100 warmup steps. This finetuning setup integrated

[5]Finetuning code: `https://github.com/alumae/pl-whisper-finetuner`

Direction	Duration	#Files
Estonian to Eng/Rus	4.15h	7
English to Estonian	3.05h	5
Russian to Estonian	4.51h	6

Table 2: Amount of evaluation data per translaton direction.

Language	Model	WER
English	whisper-large-v3	24.5%
Russian	whisper-large-v3	21.1%
Estonian	whisper-large-v3	26.6%
Estonian	whisper-large-v3-est	9.7%

Table 3: Whisper's speech recognition WER on evaluation data.

automatic early stopping that measured the model's loss on heldout training data after every 1000 model updates and stopped training when the loss didn't improve during the last 10 evaluations. This usually happened during the second epoch.

For Whisper and OWSM, the training data was compiled to segments of maximally 30 seconds in length, which usually involved concatenating the transcripts of several adjacent utterances from the long-form training audio, together with the corresponding audio chunks (including the audio between transcription end and start times). The SeamlessM4T model was finetuned using the original utterances and/or subtitle segments.

All finetuning experiments were conducted using four Nvidia A100 (80GB) GPUs.

4 Experimental results

4.1 Evaluation data

A dedicated evaluation dataset was compiled for this project, using data from public sources (e.g. YouTube). When collecting evaluation data, we tried to ensure that it contains mostly long conversational speech recordings with different levels of spontaneousness, such as press conferences, TV talkshows, YouTube videos, and broadcast news with many interviews. Length of evaluation datasets for all directions varied between 3 and 4.6h. Evaluation data is described in Table 2.

Estonian evaluation data was manually transcribed. English and Russian data was all retrieved from YouTube and we relied on the manually created captions of the videos (after some manual post-editing). We took extra care to select such videos that have good quality verbatim captions. The translations for the evaluation data were created by professional translators in Estonia, using both audio transcriptions and audio files as source data.

Table 3 lists ASR word error rates (WER) of Whisper-based models on the evaluation data. The model *whisper-large-v3-est* stands for Whisper's *large-v3* model, finetuned using 1334 hours of Estonian ASR training data.

WERs were calculated using ASR hypotheses from Whisper's long-form decoding mechanism. Due to that, reference sentences are not aligned with hypotheses. WERs were calculated after removing punctuation, lowercasing both hypotheses and references, and aligning words in the hypotheses with references, using minimum WER segmentation (*mwerSegmenter*) (Matusov et al., 2005) via the SLTev toolkit (Ansari et al., 2021).

It must be noted that Whisper is generally very accurate on English and Russian evaluation data. The surprisingly high WER (compared to the results published by Radford et al. (2023)) is mostly caused by occasional hallucinations that repeat some segment transcripts many times.

4.2 Training data

In order to finetune the end-to-end speech translation models to perform better in translation directons involving Estonian conversational speech, we experimented with collecting additional data from the web, and synthesizing additional data from ASR training data using MT.

There are some publicly available speech translation datasets that include a relatively small amount of Estonian. The dataset with the largest amount of Estonian is CoVoST 2 with 364 hours of Estonian-English data and 3 hours of English-Estonian data. However, CoVoST 2 includes exclusively read speech and short sentences. The VoxPopuli corpus (Wang et al., 2021) also contains some Estonian speech, originating from the European Parliamant sessions, but only 3 hours of that are transcribed. Due to the small size or out-of-domain nature, we did not use those datasets for finetuning.

4.2.1 Scraping web data

Given the relatively small number of Estonian speakers, the amount of speech data available on the web for training speech translation models is limited. We aimed to find data featuring long-form conversational speech (rather than individual ut-

Source	est →		→ est	
	eng	rus	eng	rus
ETV+	-	-	-	182.7
TED	-	-	41.2	-
TV7	-	-	16.4	-
YouTube	39.6	18.2	-	433.9
	39.6	18.2	57.6	616.7

Table 4: Amount of training data in hours per translation direction, derived from subtitled online videos.

terances) since Whisper and OWSM require 30-second speech segments for training to develop models capable of transcribing long-form speech. We avoided sources with machine-generated subtitles.

We identified several good sources: ETV+ (a Russian-language TV channel of Estonian state media), TED talks with Estonian subtitles, TV7 (an international TV channel with Christian background), and various YouTube channels with consistently good subtitles.

Table 4 lists the amount of data we found for each translation direction. As can be seen, the sizes vary significantly across the four translation directions we target.

4.2.2 Synthetic data

There are two primary methods for generating synthetic data to train speech translation models: (1) using speech synthesis to create source speech data from existing MT training data, and (2) using MT to generate target text data from existing source language ASR training data. We chose the second method because we already had substantial amount of Estonian ASR training data from various conversational sources, and the current Estonian-to-English and Estonian-to-Russian MT systems produce relatively high-quality translations. The main drawback of the first method is the lack of MT training corpora that include transcribed conversational speech, making it challenging to achieve a wide variety of speakers and natural-sounding speech through speech synthesis.

As Estonian source speech data, we used the data available publicly from the TalTech Estonian Speech Dataset 1.0. It contains mostly speech from broadcast sources, with an emphasis on conversation speech, such as interviews and talk shows. In addition, it contains speech recordings from various conferences and seminars, and a relatively small amount of speech from the Estonian Parliament. All the speech data consists of long-form speech and has been manually transcribed and time-aligned with speech at an utterance level.

When searching for training data for English and Russian speech, we found it challenging to locate high-quality, long-form conversational speech data transcribed at the recording level with orthographic annotation, as needed for finetuning Whisper and OWSM models. For English, we used a subset of the Gigaspeech corpus (Chen et al., 2021), which includes long-form recordings (audiobooks, podcasts, and YouTube videos) transcribed at the utterance level. However, these utterances are uppercased, and only a limited set of punctuation marks (".,!?") are retained. To enhance the suitability of these transcripts as MT source data, we applied true-casing using a custom implementation. This implementation uses spaCy to split utterances into sentences and then uppercases sentence start tokens, proper nouns, and certain special words (such as *I*).

For Russian, we couldn't find any open datasets that contain sufficient amount of transcribed long-form speech data. A popular choice for training Russian ASR models is the Russian Open STT Dataset[6] which contains over 20 000 hours of transcribed Russian speech. However, this dataset contains exclusively relatively short utterances. Although most of the data in this dataset originates from long-form speech recordings, it is not possible to reconstruct homogeneous 30-second speech segments with the corresponding transcripts from this data, as the utterance IDs have been randomized. Therefore, we used two online sources as the Russian speech data, both of which come with good quality captions: Russian TEDx talks and the Russian language YouTube channel of the *Deutsche Welle* (DW) news broadcaster [7].

The total amounts of ASR datasets used as input for synthesizing MT-based speech translation data are listed in Table 5. For creating synthetic data for speech translation, the transcripts were machine-translated. We used Google Translate for translating Estonian and English language pair directions. Russian and Estonian language pair translations were done with University of Tartu's *Neurotõlge* MT system. Those choices were based on

[6] https://github.com/snakers4/open_stt

[7] https://www.youtube.com/dwrussianreporter

Language	Estonian	English	Russian
Sources	**TalTech Estonian Speech Dataset 1.0**	**Gigaspeech** (subset M): Audiobooks: 260h Podcasts: 350h YouTube: 390 h	**DW Russian**: 45h **TEDx talks:** 57h
Total	1334h	1000h	102h

Table 5: Amount of source-language ASR training data, used as input for creating synthetic speech translation data.

our budget, as well as on the reference transcript MT evaluation results in Table 6.

4.3 Evaluation metrics

We based our evaluation on two metrics: BLEU and BLEURT (Sellam et al., 2020). BLEURT is a learned metric, trained on subjective human evaluations scores of machine translation references and the corresponding MT candidates. BLEURT outputs scores that usually in the range of 0..1 (with 1 being a perfect match) and is found to be better correlated with human judgements in several languages. We used the multilingual BLEURT-20-D12 model introduced by Pu et al. (2021).

BLEU and BLEURT scores are calculated after aligning words in the translation candidates with references, using *mwerSegmenter* via the SLTev toolkit.

4.4 Results and discussion

Evaluation results, together with several baselines, are presented in Table 6.

The first section of rows in the table compares the performance of different MT systems on reference transcripts. It can be seen that while there are substantial differences between the proprietary systems among individual translation directions, the average scores in terms of both BLEU and BLEURT are surprisingly similar. The fully open source NLLB-200 model however doesn't reach the accuracy of the top proprietary systems.

The next section compares MT systems, when using automatically generated transcripts as input. For Russian and English, we used the Whisper *large-v3* model, while for Estonian, the finetuned Whisper model was used. All transcripts were generated using a beam size of 5, with speech activity detection activated in order to exclude non-speech segments from input. It can be seen that for Estonian source speech, using ASR instead of references transcripts deteriorates BLEU scores by around 3 points, while for Russian and English, the decrease in accuracy is larger, which is probably tied to the relatively low WER of Whisper on these datasets, as evident from Table 3.

The third section of rows compares the out-of-the-box performance of three publicly available end-to-end speech translation models. Whisper produced a segmented transcript directly from the long-form speech recordings, while for OWSM and SeamlessM4T, we segmented the speech into single-speaker chunks using pyannote 3.1 (Plaquet and Bredin, 2023). Decoding was performed using beam size of 5 for all models. The BLEU scores of SeamlessM4T demonstrate the complexity of translating automatically segmented conversational speech, compared to read speech consisting of single utterances: compared to the BLEU scores of the same model on CoVoST 2 and FLEURS test data shown in Table 1, the scores on our evaluation data are lower by a large margin. Contrary to the Estonian-English results on CoVoST 2, Whisper outperforms SeamlessM4T on our data, suggesting that Whisper is better suited for processing conversational speech. OWSM 3.1 EBF, which has a BLEU score of 7.7 on English-Estonian CoVoST 2 data, has close to zero scores on our data in all directions.

The last section of the table compares end-to-end speech translation models after finetuning with synthetic and/or web-scraped data. For Estonian-English and Estonian-Russian, finetuning on synthetic dataset outperforms web data by a large margin, which is expected based on the fact that the Estonian ASR comes from similar domains as evaluation data. In general, SeamlessM4T benefits more than Whisper from finetuning on properly segmented ASR data than from subtitles. This can be explained by the fact that subtitle start and end times are not always properly aligned with speech. For SeamlessM4T, which is finetuned on individual subtitle lines and the corresponding speech seg-

Model	Finetuned		BLEU					BLEURT				
	web	synt.	est →		→ est			est →		→ est		
			eng	rus	eng	rus	avg	eng	rus	eng	rus	avg
Text-to-text translation using reference transcripts												
Ref. + NLLB-200 3.3B	-	-	31.4	25.2	21.5	19.2	24.3	.652	.665	.529	.574	.605
Ref. + GPT3.5-turbo	-	-	36.1	28.3	21.3	23.8	27.4	.696	.703	.593	.665	.664
Ref. + GPT4	-	-	38.3	31.3	19.9	24.6	28.5	.702	.721	.609	.656	.672
Ref. + Google Translate	-	-	38.9	26.1	25.4	24.2	28.7	.690	.686	.576	.655	.652
Ref. + Neurotõlge	-	-	34.8	29.3	24.7	23.7	28.1	.656	.672	.558	.619	.626
Cascaded speech translation systems												
Whisper + NLLB-200 3.3B	-	-	28.8	23.1	15.4	13.2	20.1	.568	.568	.439	.537	.528
Whisper + GPT3.5-turbo	-	-	32.9	26.5	15.1	18.3	23.2	.649	.656	.470	.621	.599
Whisper + GPT4	-	-	35.1	29.8	16.3	18.3	24.9	.647	.687	.507	.625	.617
Whisper + Google Translate	-	-	35.2	23.8	17.4	16.1	22.9	.628	.617	.481	.585	.578
Whisper + Neurotõlge	-	-	31.9	26.6	16.1	16.0	22.7	.598	.612	.458	.566	.559
Public end-to-end speech translation models												
Whisper-large-v3	-	-	14.9	-	-	-	-	.451	-	-	-	-
OWSM 3.1 EBF	-	-	0.5	0.0	1.6	0.0	0.5	.176	.153	.147	.095	.143
SeamlessM4T v2 (large)	-	-	13.2	16.2	6.4	13.9	12.4	.348	.426	.227	.448	.362
Public end-to-end speech translation models after finetuning												
Whisper-large-v3	✓	-	17.9	11.7	13.1	14.3	14.2	.496	.413	.433	.523	.466
Whisper-large-v3	-	✓	33.2	26.1	14.5	14.8	22.2	.611	.605	.363	.500	.520
Whisper-large-v3	✓	✓	33.0	25.5	17.3	16.3	23.1	.614	.603	.458	.549	.560
OWSM 3.1 EBF	-	✓	25.8	18.7	11.9	8.5	16.2	.541	.463	.377	.360	.435
SeamlessM4T v2 (large)	✓	-	19.3	14.4	6.1	4.3	11.0	.468	.488	.234	.261	.363
SeamlessM4T v2 (large)	-	✓	35.4	26.8	18.8	16.4	24.4	.618	.603	.482	.494	.549
SeamlessM4T v2 (large)	✓	✓	34.7	25.9	19.1	12.9	23.1	.617	.605	.470	.426	.529

Table 6: Comparison of baseline scores, cascaded systems, off-the-shelf end-to-end models and finetuned end-to-end models.

ments, this causes the training data to be often corrupted. Whisper, on the other hand, is trained on 30-second chunks of speech that fit typically several lines of subtitles, and the proper subtitle timing is not as important.

Apart from a few outliers, the performance of SeamlessM4T and Whisper are similar, especially in terms of BLEURT scores. This confirms our speculation that Whisper can be finetuned to translate into other directions than it was originally trained for. The performance of OWSM 3.1 EBF is however noticeably lower than for other models after finetuning on synthetic data and in order to save compute time we didn't even finetune it on other datasets.

Since the differences between the BLEU scores from applying different models are relatively small, we used the Wilcoxon signed-rank test to assess whether the difference between the scores was statistically significant. We used BLEU scores of individual evaluation files as input to the paired test. Table 7 compares the difference between three systems: cascaded system involving Whisper and Google Translate and Whisper and SeamlessM4T end-to-end models, both finetuned using synthetic speech translation data. It can be seen that the best overall performance is achieved by the finetuned SeamlessM4T model, since no other model is significantly better in any of the directons, while it outperforms both the cascaded system and finetuned Whisper in the Estonian-Russian direction.

Although we haven't performed proper human

Model	Whisper + Google Translate				Whisper-large-v3 ft.				SeamlessM4T ft.			
	est-eng	est-rus	eng-est	rus-est	est-eng	est-rus	eng-est	rus-est	est-eng	est-rus	eng-est	rus-est
Whisper + Google Translate	-	-	-	-								
Whisper-large-v3 (finetuned)					-	-	-	-				
SeamlessM4T (finetuned)									-	-	-	-

Table 7: Statistically significant differences between systems, based on BLEU scores: if one of the models is significantly better than the other, the corresponding cell is colored using the corresponding color.

evaluation of the MT outputs, subjective evaluation by the authors suggests that our best Estonian-English and Estonian-Russian models produce translations that are accurate, fluent and therefore usable in many practical situations (see a translated TV news broadcast at `https://www.youtube.com/watch?v=rZPqauCYfXI`). For the opposite direction, the translations have a substantially lower quality by subjective evaluation. These findings correlate with BLEURT scores in Table 6.

5 Conclusion

In this study, we demonstrated the effectiveness of finetuning end-to-end models for Estonian conversational speech translation using synthetic and web-scraped data. Our experiments revealed that synthetic data derived from ASR training corpora significantly enhances model performance, especially for Whisper and SeamlessM4T models. While all three evaluated models benefited from additional training data, SeamlessM4T worked the most consistently in all directions, indicating its robustness in handling conversational speech translation tasks. The best finetuned models are already usable for Estonian-English and Estonian-English directions for real-world speech data.

The future direction of our research is experimenting with simultaneous speech translation where using end-to-end models is crucial.

References

Tanel Alumäe, Joonas Kalda, Külliki Bode, and Martin Kaitsa. 2023. Automatic closed captioning for Estonian live broadcasts. In *The 24th Nordic Conference on Computational Linguistics (NoDaLiDa)*, pages 492–499, Tórshavn, Faroe Islands.

Ebrahim Ansari, Ondrej Bojar, Barry Haddow, and Mohammad Mahmoudi. 2021. SLTEV: comprehensive evaluation of spoken language translation. In *Proceedings of the 16th Conference of the European Chapter of the Association for Computational Linguistics: System Demonstrations, EACL 2021*, pages 71–79, Online.

Guoguo Chen, Shuzhou Chai, Guan-Bo Wang, Jiayu Du, Wei-Qiang Zhang, Chao Weng, Dan Su, Daniel Povey, Jan Trmal, Junbo Zhang, Mingjie Jin, Sanjeev Khudanpur, Shinji Watanabe, Shuaijiang Zhao, Wei Zou, Xiangang Li, Xuchen Yao, Yongqing Wang, Zhao You, and Zhiyong Yan. 2021. GigaSpeech: An evolving, multi-domain ASR corpus with 10 000 hours of transcribed audio. In *Interspeech 2021, 22nd Annual Conference of the International Speech Communication Association*, pages 3670–3674, Brno, Czechia.

Alexis Conneau, Min Ma, Simran Khanuja, Yu Zhang, Vera Axelrod, Siddharth Dalmia, Jason Riesa, Clara Rivera, and Ankur Bapna. 2022. FLEURS: Few-shot learning evaluation of universal representations of speech. In *IEEE Spoken Language Technology Workshop, SLT 2022*, pages 798–805, Doha, Qatar.

Paul-Ambroise Duquenne, Holger Schwenk, and Benoît Sagot. 2023. SONAR: sentence-level multimodal and language-agnostic representations. *CoRR*, abs/2308.11466.

Mattia Antonino Di Gangi, Roldano Cattoni, Luisa Bentivogli, Matteo Negri, and Marco Turchi. 2019. MuST-C: a multilingual speech translation corpus. In *Proceedings of the 2019 Conference of the North American Chapter of the Association for Computational Linguistics: Human Language Technologies, NAACL-HLT 2019, Minneapolis, MN, Volume 1 (Long and Short Papers)*, pages 2012–2017, USA.

Pavel Izmailov, Dmitrii Podoprikhin, Timur Garipov, Dmitry P. Vetrov, and Andrew Gordon Wilson. 2018. Averaging weights leads to wider optima and better generalization. In *Proceedings of the Thirty-Fourth Conference on Uncertainty in Artificial Intelligence, UAI 2018*, pages 876–885, Monterey, California, USA.

Kwangyoun Kim, Felix Wu, Yifan Peng, Jing Pan, Prashant Sridhar, Kyu Jeong Han, and Shinji Watanabe. 2022. E-Branchformer: Branchformer with enhanced merging for speech recognition. In *IEEE Spoken Language Technology Workshop, SLT 2022*, pages 84–91, Doha, Qatar.

Evgeny Matusov, Gregor Leusch, Oliver Bender, and Hermann Ney. 2005. Evaluating machine translation output with automatic sentence segmentation. In *2005 International Workshop on Spoken Language Translation, IWSLT 2005*, pages 138–144, Pittsburgh, PA, USA.

NLLB Team, Marta R. Costa-jussà, James Cross, Onur Çelebi, Maha Elbayad, Kenneth Heafield, Kevin Heffernan, Elahe Kalbassi, Janice Lam, Daniel Licht, Jean Maillard, Anna Sun, Skyler Wang, Guillaume Wenzek, Al Youngblood, Bapi Akula, Loic Barrault, Gabriel Mejia Gonzalez, Prangthip Hansanti, John Hoffman, Semarley Jarrett, Kaushik Ram Sadagopan, Dirk Rowe, Shannon Spruit, Chau Tran, Pierre Andrews, Necip Fazil Ayan, Shruti Bhosale, Sergey Edunov, Angela Fan, Cynthia Gao, Vedanuj Goswami, Francisco Guzmán, Philipp Koehn, Alexandre Mourachko, Christophe Ropers, Safiyyah Saleem, Holger Schwenk, and Jeff Wang. 2022. No language left behind: Scaling human-centered machine translation. *Preprint*, arXiv:2207.04672.

Puyuan Peng, Brian Yan, Shinji Watanabe, and David Harwath. 2023a. Prompting the hidden talent of web-scale speech models for zero-shot task generalization. *CoRR*, abs/2305.11095.

Yifan Peng, Jinchuan Tian, Brian Yan, Dan Berrebbi, Xuankai Chang, Xinjian Li, Jiatong Shi, Siddhant Arora, William Chen, Roshan S. Sharma, Wangyou Zhang, Yui Sudo, Muhammad Shakeel, Jee-Weon Jung, Soumi Maiti, and Shinji Watanabe. 2023b. Reproducing Whisper-style training using an open-source toolkit and publicly available data. In *IEEE Automatic Speech Recognition and Understanding Workshop, ASRU 2023*, pages 1–8, Taipei, Taiwan.

Alexis Plaquet and Hervé Bredin. 2023. Powerset multi-class cross entropy loss for neural speaker diarization. *CoRR*, abs/2310.13025.

Amy Pu, Hyung Won Chung, Ankur P. Parikh, Sebastian Gehrmann, and Thibault Sellam. 2021. Learning compact metrics for MT. In *Proceedings of the 2021 Conference on Empirical Methods in Natural Language Processing, EMNLP 2021, Virtual Event /*, pages 751–762, Punta Cana, Dominican Republic.

Alec Radford, Jong Wook Kim, Tao Xu, Greg Brockman, Christine McLeavey, and Ilya Sutskever. 2023. Robust speech recognition via large-scale weak supervision. In *International Conference on Machine Learning, ICML 2023, 23-29 July 2023*, volume 202 of *Proceedings of Machine Learning Research*, pages 28492–28518, Honolulu, Hawaii, USA.

Georg Rehm, Katrin Marheinecke, Stefanie Hegele, Stelios Piperidis, Kalina Bontcheva, Jan Hajic, Khalid Choukri, Andrejs Vasiljevs, Gerhard Backfried, Christoph Prinz, José Manuél Gómez-Pérez, Luc Meertens, Paul Lukowicz, Josef van Genabith, Andrea Lösch, Philipp Slusallek, Morten Irgens, Patrick Gatellier, Joachim Köhler, Laure Le Bars, Dimitra Anastasiou, Albina Auksoriute, Núria Bel, António Branco, Gerhard Budin, Walter Daelemans, Koenraad De Smedt, Radovan Garabík, Maria Gavriilidou, Dagmar Gromann, Svetla Koeva, Simon Krek, Cvetana Krstev, Krister Lindén, Bernardo Magnini, Jan Odijk, Maciej Ogrodniczuk, Eiríkur Rögnvaldsson, Mike Rosner, Bolette S. Pedersen, Inguna Skadina, Marko Tadic, Dan Tufis, Tamás Váradi, Kadri Vider, Andy Way, and François Yvon. 2020. The European language technology landscape in 2020: Language-centric and human-centric AI for cross-cultural communication in multilingual Europe. In *Proceedings of The 12th Language Resources and Evaluation Conference, LREC 2020*, pages 3322–3332, Marseille, France.

Seamless Communication, Loïc Barrault, Yu-An Chung, Mariano Coria Meglioli, David Dale, Ning Dong, Mark Duppenthaler, Paul-Ambroise Duquenne, Brian Ellis, Hady Elsahar, Justin Haaheim, et al. 2023. Seamless: Multilingual expressive and streaming speech translation. *arXiv preprint arXiv:2312.05187*.

Thibault Sellam, Dipanjan Das, and Ankur P. Parikh. 2020. BLEURT: learning robust metrics for text generation. In *Proceedings of the 58th Annual Meeting of the Association for Computational Linguistics, ACL 2020*, pages 7881–7892, Online.

Andre Tättar, Taido Purason, Hele-Andra Kuulmets, Agnes Luhtaru, Liisa Rätsep, Maali Tars, Marcis Pinnis, Toms Bergmanis, and Mark Fishel. 2022. Open and competitive multilingual neural machine translation in production. *Balt. J. Mod. Comput.*, 10(3).

Changhan Wang, Morgane Rivière, Ann Lee, Anne Wu, Chaitanya Talnikar, Daniel Haziza, Mary Williamson, Juan Miguel Pino, and Emmanuel Dupoux. 2021. VoxPopuli: A large-scale multilingual speech corpus for representation learning, semi-supervised learning and interpretation. In *Proceedings of the 59th Annual Meeting of the Association for Computational Linguistics and the 11th International Joint Conference on Natural Language Processing, ACL/IJCNLP 2021, (Volume 1: Long Papers)*, pages 993–1003, Virtual Event.

Changhan Wang, Anne Wu, and Juan Miguel Pino. 2020. CoVoST 2: A massively multilingual speech-to-text translation corpus. *CoRR*, abs/2007.10310.

Shinji Watanabe, Takaaki Hori, Shigeki Karita, Tomoki Hayashi, Jiro Nishitoba, Yuya Unno, Nelson Enrique Yalta Soplin, Jahn Heymann, Matthew Wiesner, Nanxin Chen, Adithya Renduchintala, and Tsubasa Ochiai. 2018. ESPnet: End-to-end speech processing toolkit. In *Interspeech 2018, 19th Annual Conference of the International Speech Communication Association*, pages 2207–2211, Hyderabad, India.

Benchmarking Low-Resource Machine Translation Systems

Ana Alexandra Morim da Silva[1], Nikit Srivastava[1], Tatiana Moteu Ngoli[1], Michael Röder[1], Diego Moussallem[1,2], and Axel-Cyrille Ngonga Ngomo[1]

{ana.silva | michael.roeder | axel.ngonga}@upb.de
[1]DICE group, Department of Computer Science, Paderborn University, Germany
[2]Jusbrasil, Data Science Team, Rio de Janeiro, Brazil

Abstract

Assessing the performance of machine translation systems is of critical value, especially to languages with lower resource availability. Due to the large evaluation effort required by the translation task, studies often compare new systems against single systems or commercial solutions. Consequently, determining the best-performing system for specific languages is often unclear. This work benchmarks publicly available translation systems across 4 datasets and 26 languages, including low-resource languages. We consider both effectiveness and efficiency in our evaluation. Our results are made public through BENG—a FAIR benchmarking platform for Natural Language Generation tasks.

1 Introduction

The Machine Translation (MT) task is increasingly relevant in today's connected world as accessibility enables knowledge transfer. Hence, MT systems are recognized as prime tools in the Natural Language Processing (NLP) domain (Goyal et al., 2022). In recent years, Neural Machine Translation (NMT) (Bahdanau et al., 2015) has led the field as it achieves state-of-the-art performance for many language pairs (Gulcehre et al., 2017). However, NMT systems can become computationally demanding and the abundance of new systems also complicates a cross-system comparison. As a result, newly-released systems often compare their performance against single systems (NLLB Team et al., 2022; Tang et al., 2020). Furthermore, recent system analyses also focus on assessing the capability of commercial translation solutions (Zhu et al., 2023). To the best of our knowledge, no work exclusively considers open-source translation systems. Thus, leading to a lack of clarity when determining the best-performing and when identifying shortcomings among existing translation systems, an especially critical task for Low-Resource Languages (LRLs). While the translation task is vital to progress in general, it is still largely unfeasible to the $7,000+$ languages in the world.[1] From these, only close to $2,500$ are represented in the NLP field, with 88% considered to be low-resource. LRLs have a minimal resource availability that causes them to be largely untouched by the benefits of language technology (Joshi et al., 2020). With our work, we aim to contribute to a more complete picture of the current state of the art of machine translation with a focus on LRLs.

We compare four open-source NMT systems—LibreTranslate[2], Opus MT (Tiedemann and Thottingal, 2020), NLLB (NLLB Team et al., 2022), and mBART50 (Tang et al., 2020)—on four parallel machine-translation benchmark datasets—OPUS100 (Zhang et al., 2020), Europarl (Koehn, 2005), IWSLT2017 (Cettolo et al., 2017), and FLORES-200 (NLLB Team et al., 2022). Our evaluation comprises data from 26 different languages. Our results suggest that using languages with lower resource availability does not necessarily translate to lower system performance. However, we did observe more substantial variations in the systems' performance for these languages. Our analysis also showed that LibreTranslate had the highest token throughput among the evaluated systems. Some systems showed proficiency in certain languages, while others performed better according to a certain dataset. Our experiments are shared via BENG (Moussallem et al., 2020), an open-source benchmarking platform that improves the accessibility of experiment results according to the FAIR data principles (Wilkinson et al., 2016).[3]

[1]https://www.ethnologue.com/
[2]https://libretranslate.com/
[3]https://beng.dice-research.org/gerbil

Proceedings of the The Seventh Workshop on Technologies for Machine Translation of Low-Resource Languages (LoResMT 2024), pages 175–185
August 15, 2024

2 Preliminaries and Related Work

Machine Translation (MT) is the process of translating from a source language into a target language autonomously, i.e., without human intervention (Kenny, 2018; Bhattacharyya, 2015). This can be achieved through different approaches. Wang et al. (2022) divide MT techniques into rule- and corpus-based approaches. Corpus-based approaches can be further divided into example-based, statistical, and, more recently, neural approaches. In this work, we evaluate approaches of the latter category with a focus on low-resource languages. We describe both further within this section, along with relevant MT tools and platforms.

2.1 Low-Resource Languages

There are more than 7,000 human languages, with the vast majority being classified as low-resource languages (LRLs) (Magueresse et al., 2020). In contrast to high-resource languages (HRLs), LRLs have a low density of computational corpora (Cieri et al., 2016). However, it is often challenging to identify languages as low- or high-resource as the distinction is often difficult to quantify.

Joshi et al. (2020) propose a language taxonomy based on the quantities of labeled and unlabeled data available in each language. The labeled data is measured through the LDC catalog and the ELRA Map repositories, and the unlabeled data is based on Wikipedia articles.[4] The taxonomy separates languages into six types of languages: *The Left-Behinds* (0), *The Scraping-Bys* (1), *The Hopefuls* (2), *The Rising Stars* (3), *The Underdogs* (4), and *The Winners* (5). Simplified, class 0 languages have neither labeled nor unlabeled data; class 1-4 languages have unlabeled data available, but whose labeled data amount ranges from virtually non-existent to high; and class 5 languages have both high volumes of labeled and unlabeled data.

Hedderich et al. (2021) classify low-resource based on the availability of three data types: 1) task-specific labeled data that supports supervised NLP approaches, 2) unlabeled data that supports unsupervised learning, and 3) auxiliary data that supports learning by proxy. When both labeled and unlabeled data are insufficient in either quantity or quality, other methods can be used to bridge the gap, e.g., transfer learning, data augmentation techniques, distant supervision, and others (Burlot and Yvon, 2018; Gibadullin et al., 2019). Similar statistical studies revealed that more languages should benefit from the availability of NLP tools.

Simons et al. (2022) introduce an automatic approach to measure Digital Language Support for every language by measuring a language's presence across 143 digital tools. Digital support is measured by analyzing different categories of a language's digital presence, such as the level of content provision in a language, system encodings, surface-level tools for text processing, localized user interfaces, text meaning processing, speech processing, and the existence of virtual assistants. The languages are then classified as either still, emerging, ascending, vital, or thriving according to their level of digital support.

2.2 Neural Machine Translation Systems

In recent years, Neural Machine Translation (NMT) has transformed the MT task. By leveraging the currently available large parallel corpora, the MT task has been able to improve translation quality significantly thanks to recent developments in language models. However, large parallel corpora are not available for LRLs, making it difficult to tailor classic NMT models towards LRLs. Open-source translation toolkits like OpenNMT (Klein et al., 2017) and Marian NMT (Junczys-Dowmunt et al., 2018) also provide different neural architecture implementations, forming the backbone of many open-source systems. Below are some examples of open-source NMT systems that cater to LRLs.

LibreTranslate is an open-source NMT service that supports the translation across 46 languages including LRLs.[5] The tool relies on the open-source Argos Translate library to train a transformer-based model from OpenNMT (Klein et al., 2017).[6]

Fairseq (Ott et al., 2019) provides pre-trained convolutional and transformer-based MT models for the English, French, German, and Russian languages with English as source or target language. It is also a development toolkit for NMT tools.

Opus MT (Tiedemann and Thottingal, 2020) is an MT tool trained on the OPUS data (Zhang et al., 2020) based on Marian NMT (Junczys-Dowmunt et al., 2018). Opus MT is a transformer-based NMT system with 6 self-attention layers in the encoder

[4] LDC catalog: `https://catalog.ldc.upenn.edu/`; ELRA Map: `https://catalog.elra.info/en-us/`.

[5] `https://libretranslate.com/`

[6] Argos Translate: `https://github.com/argosopentech/argos-translate`

and the decoder network, with 8 attention heads in each layer.

mBART50 (Tang et al., 2020) is an extension of mBART (Liu et al., 2020) to demonstrate that multilingual translation models can be created through multilingual fine-tuning. mBART is a sequence-to-sequence generative pretraining model that incorporates languages by concatenating data. While mBART was trained on 25 mainly high-resource languages, Tang et al. (2020) enlarge the embedding layers and combine the monolingual data of the original 25 languages with additional languages to extend the model to more than 50 languages—including LRLs—without requiring to retrain from scratch.

NLLB (No Language Left Behind) (NLLB Team et al., 2022) is a collection of language models created to fill the void left in MT for LRLs. NLLB aims to narrow the performance gap between low and high-resource languages. The model is developed based on a sparsely gated mixture of experts trained on data obtained with novel data mining techniques tailored for LRLs. The model's performance was evaluated across $40,000$ translation directions on the human-translated benchmark dataset FLORES-200.

ALMA (Advanced Language Model-based Translator) (Xu et al., 2024) is a language model based on LLaMA-2 (Touvron et al., 2023) built specifically for machine translation. ALMA introduces a new fine-tuning scheme to improve translation in a zero-shot scenario. It first fine-tunes the model on monolingual data and then fine-tunes it on a parallel corpus. It currently supports 10 language pairs.

With the recent drive of using language models for machine translation, studies such as Zhu et al.'s have emerged to assess the machine translation quality of language models. Zhu et al. (2023) compared 10 different language models across 102 languages, with three languages, English, French, and Chinese, as either source or target language translations. The study provides a good reference point for translation for commercial solutions, as gate-kept models often performed better than open-source solutions. However, due to the large evaluation effort, and the cost of using commercial APIs, the study was only conducted on the first 100 sentences of one dataset: Flores-101 (Goyal et al., 2022). Furthermore, the language models are assessed in an in-context learning setting, where instructions are provided in addition to the translation as context. The authors also observed the influence of different instructions in 6 language pairs.

2.3 Translation Evaluation

The increasing demand for more and better MT tools led to the development of frameworks to simplify their usage. Multiple frameworks streamline the building and training process of language models for translation and offer efficiency. These tools standardize evaluation procedures and enable the user to either tune the models per their requirements or use them as-is. The user trades off fine-grained control over the models for simplicity of use.

2.3.1 Metrics

BLEU (Bilingual Evaluation Understudy) (Papineni et al., 2002) is an n-gram-based metric used to evaluate text generation systems, mostly chosen due to its low computational cost. In MT, BLEU correlates to human evaluation—the current gold standard—over the entire output. BLEU focuses on the precision between the n-grams in the generated text against those in a reference text. **BLEU NLTK** is an implementation of BLEU from the NLTK library[7] with smoothing applied to sentence-level BLEU scores.

METEOR (Banerjee and Lavie, 2005) is an MT metric that measures the harmonic mean between precision and recall of unigram matches, assigning a higher weight to recall. The word-to-word matching also considers synonyms via the WordNet synset. METEOR scores correlate to human evaluation at the sentence level, in contrast to BLEU.

chrF++ (Popović, 2015) is a variant of the chrF score where the F-score is calculated for both the character n-grams and the word n-grams with the default order being 6 and 2, respectively. chrF is a character-based n-gram F-score metric for MT. It also shows sentence and document-level correlation with human evaluation.

TER (Translation Edit Rate) (Snover et al., 2006) measures the minimum number of edits required to make an output match the corresponding reference. The edits include insertions, deletions, substitutions, word reordering, capitalization, and punctuation. Thus, making the method computationally expensive. The TER score is calculated by computing the number of edits divided by the average referenced words.

[7] https://www.nltk.org/

2.3.2 Benchmarking Frameworks

Systematic evaluations can be a key factor in a research field as they allow a clean comparison between the performance of different approaches over a set of tasks. Benchmarking frameworks support such evaluations and aim to standardize the evaluation for a specific task, including a common task definition, implementation of metrics, and the set of data that is used throughout the evaluation. In the past, different benchmarking frameworks have been proposed for the MT task. The majority of them are local frameworks, i.e., these frameworks compute a set of metrics over the system's output locally. sacreBLEU (Post, 2018) is such a framework and calls for reproducible BLEU scores in the community. Despite its name, it not only supports the BLEU metric, but also chrF, chrF++, and TER. COMET (Rei et al., 2020) trains multilingual MT evaluation models. It allows the user to either train a metric or use the available default models to score the translation output with its COMET-score. Appraise (Federmann, 2018) and HOPE (Gladkoff and Han, 2021) are local human-centric evaluation frameworks. They rely on human intervention due to the low agreement between human quality evaluation and automatic evaluation metrics for MT. Moussallem et al. (2020) propose BENG, an online benchmarking platform for natural language generation that abides by the FAIR data principles (Wilkinson et al., 2016).[8] BENG allows for the submission of multiple systems to be checked against a reference dataset and returns a unique experiment URI with the results. It computes the BLEU, METEOR, chrF++, and TER scores.

3 Evaluation

3.1 Experimental setup

We evaluated the performance of four NMT tools—LibreTranslate[9], Opus MT (Tiedemann and Thottingal, 2020), NLLB (NLLB Team et al., 2022), and mBART50 (Tang et al., 2020). We chose NMT approaches that are open-source, locally deployable, and support several languages, including LRLs. We executed our experiments using the Naïve Entity Aware Machine Translation (NEAMT) tool introduced by Srivastava et al. (2023). This framework was originally implemented as a step in a multilingual knowledge graph question-answering pipeline. It supports a combination of named entity recognition, entity linking, and MT systems. We've used NEAMT for the standard MT pipelines without any of the entity-awareness features as it allows modular and local deployments of new components and serves them through an API[10].

We measured both the quality of the systems' translation and the inherent time cost. Our first experiment compared the system performance across multiple languages. However, some datasets were small and offered limited support for LRLs. So in our second experiment, we compared the performance in languages across the largest datasets and considered 26 languages from all language classes of the taxonomy proposed by Joshi et al. (2020). All of our experiments consider the target language to be English.

3.2 Datasets

We considered four parallel machine-translation benchmark datasets OPUS100 (Zhang et al., 2020), Europarl (Koehn, 2005), IWSLT2017 (Cettolo et al., 2017), and FLORES-200 (NLLB Team et al., 2022). The statistics of the datasets are in Table 1 in the form of token and parallel pair counts. All the datasets have the same number of parallel pairs across languages, except for IWSLT2017. In this case, we averaged the number of pairs for the languages considered in this experiment.

OPUS100 (Zhang et al., 2020) is a parallel translation dataset randomly sampled from the OPUS corpus (Tiedemann, 2012) that covers 100 languages, focused on English. The represented domains in the dataset were not balanced, but sampling filters were applied to ensure no cross-lingual data leakage. This also means that the dataset is not sentence-aligned across languages, i.e., the test sets have different content w.r.t. the language, despite having the same document size.

Europarl (Koehn, 2005) is a parallel translation dataset from the Proceedings of the European Parliament that covers 11 languages. We used the *common-test-set*, a cross-lingual sentence-aligned split, as presented by Koehn (2005) in our experiments.

IWSLT2017 (Cettolo et al., 2017) is a parallel dataset based on TED talks introduced for the IWSLT 2017 multilingual translation task evaluation with language pairs from 5 languages. IWSLT

[8] https://beng.dice-research.org/gerbil/

[9] https://libretranslate.com/

[10] The MT models were deployed on a system with Intel(R) Xeon(R) CPU E5-2695 v3 @ 2.30GHz, 128 GB RAM, and Debian GNU/Linux 11.

		Datasets			
		OPUS100	Europarl	IWSLT2017	FLORES-200
LC	Language \ Parallel pairs	2 000	11 369	4 835	1 012
5	French (FR)	60 497	470 159	233 492	38 842
5	German (DE)	43 834	482 529	198 713	36 321
5	Japanese (JA)	24 617	–	244 772	44 660
4	Dutch (NL)	37 636	479 949	40 413	36 769
4	Finnish (FI)	34 806	540 970	–	41 844
4	Hindi (HI)	61 235	–	–	51 218
4	Italian (IT)	39 612	444 961	38 468	37 577
4	Korean (KO)	26 310	–	261 553	40 255
4	Russian (RU)	53 537	–	–	41 700
3	Bengali (BN)	63 760	–	–	56 407
3	Bulgarian (BG)	30 210	–	–	44 817
3	Estonian (ET)	44 883	–	–	41 940
3	Hebrew (HE)	28 239	–	–	40 810
3	Indonesian (ID)	23 755	–	–	33 015
3	Lithuanian (LT)	76 771	–	–	43 636
3	Romanian (RO)	31 144	–	47 187	43 676
3	Thai (TH)	48 232	–	–	78 226
3	Ukrainian (UK)	31 266	–	–	44 289
2	Irish (GA)	92 241	–	–	54 910
2	Xhosa (XH)	62 678	–	–	53 541
1	Macedonian (MK)	37 718	–	–	45 400
1	Malayalam (ML)	47 946	–	–	75 526
1	Nepali (NE)	25 228	–	–	54 488
1	Norwegian Bokmål (NB)	46 924	–	–	36 110
1	Telugu (TE)	26 491	–	–	61 108
0	Sinhala (SI)	15 369	–	–	23 886

(Vertical label on the LC column: Token count)

Table 1: Dataset statistics of the test corpora. The token counts were measured with the cased BERT multilingual base model tokenizer (Devlin et al., 2019).

also introduced an unofficial bilingual task to follow previous editions of the venue that extended the English-centric dataset to 4 other languages. The content and the document size of each test set differ for each language.

FLORES-200 (NLLB Team et al., 2022) is a manually curated dataset that covers 204 languages, based on Wikinews, Wikijunior, and Wikivoyage. The translations were done by professional translators and followed a series of automatic and manual quality review processes. All documents have the same content. As the test set of the dataset is kept blind, in our experiments we evaluated the performance on the *devtest* split.

3.3 Results

The results of the FLORES-200 and OPUS100 are listed in Table 2. NLLB performed better in the FLORES-200 dataset for 20 of the 26 languages with a statistically significant difference to the second-best system.[11] Likewise, Opus MT performed better in the OPUS100 for 19 of the 26 tested languages. The results of the Europarl and IWSLT2017 are in Table 3. LibreTranslate performed best in the Europarl dataset, while mBART50 performed better in IWSLT2017. Language-wise, LibreTranslate performed well in Russian and Estonian, mBART50 in Japanese,

[11]The significance tests were performed with paired bootstrap resampling (Post, 2018) with a 95% confidence interval.

LC	Language	FLORES-200					OPUS100				
		Libre	OPUS	NLLB	mBART		Libre	OPUS	NLLB	mBART	
5	FR	42.10	41.93	42.42	39.60	↗	34.45	**38.94**	32.84	36.04	↗
	DE	36.22	40.73	**41.49**	40.48	↗	33.63	**36.55**	27.01	35.22	↗
	JA	13.48	10.67	22.91	**23.93**	↗	03.93	**16.00**	13.33	10.72	↗
4	NL	29.51	29.67	**31.04**	25.89	↗	23.78	**34.92**	30.80	27.29	↗
	FI	24.71	29.55	**30.41**	26.04	↗	18.29	**28.58**	24.70	22.74	↗
	HI	26.97	09.90	**38.37**	32.46	↗	12.30	**33.78**	25.44	25.46	↗
	IT	28.70	29.94	**33.36**	27.35	↗	34.37	**38.20**	33.55	30.12	↗
	KO	14.31	15.80	**25.33**	20.70	↗	05.60	**21.12**	14.59	12.91	↗
	RU	**36.88**	30.15	33.29	31.78	↗	37.28	36.84	31.13	34.18	↗
3	BN	16.03	16.16	**32.85**	09.25	↗	22.42	**28.58**	20.96	07.33	↗
	BG	35.28	34.35	**38.11**	–	↗	34.25	34.52	32.03	–	↗
	ET	**38.83**	32.03	32.71	31.08	↗	**42.14**	39.83	28.63	33.80	↗
	HE	32.53	34.02	**38.19**	30.41	↗	26.69	**39.74**	35.74	29.70	↗
	ID	28.44	33.44	**40.56**	30.36	↗	21.26	**41.33**	34.59	26.99	↗
	LT	26.63	26.58	29.13	28.49	↗	49.43	**50.06**	37.83	37.74	↗
	RO	39.77	39.96	**42.39**	36.85	↗	39.11	**40.24**	36.51	30.65	↗
	TH	15.28	01.06	**25.69**	09.25	↗	**20.48**	08.55	20.35	07.44	↗
	UK	27.98	24.26	**36.79**	27.57	↗	11.11	**33.37**	26.31	21.73	↗
2	GA	30.52	12.11	**34.74**	–	↗	57.98	58.35	46.46	–	↗
	XH	–	02.28	**32.78**	12.21	↗	–	**25.41**	23.48	08.47	↗
1	MK	–	33.75	**39.49**	28.02	↗	–	**42.37**	30.55	24.62	↗
	ML	–	00.38	**32.87**	23.98	↗	–	02.86	18.21	**19.90**	↗
	NE	–	00.99	**37.32**	29.66	↗	–	**63.92**	15.20	49.14	↗
	NB	38.25	24.27	38.35	–	↗	35.36	**45.15**	35.37	–	↗
	TE	–	00.54	**36.40**	15.39	↗	–	59.13	25.88	60.98	↗
0	SI	–	06.52	**30.15**	23.50	↗	–	**33.89**	21.68	23.31	↗

Table 2: BLEU scores of the evaluation for the 17 LRLs and 9 HRLs of the FLORES-200 and OPUS100 datasets. The corresponding URIs are linked with the experiment's BLEU, METEOR, chrF++, and TER scores. The results in bold mark the system with the best BLEU value on a dataset and a statistically significant difference to the second-placed system. The underlined values are the best BLEU values without a significant difference to the next highest value on that dataset.

Opus MT in Romanian, and NLLB in French and German.

3.4 Discussion

We observe a tendency of NLLB and Opus MT towards achieving a better performance on the evaluation part of the dataset on which they have been trained on in comparison to their overall performance. Especially Opus MT seems to be overfitting to its training data, which is reflected by its performance on the FLORES-200 dataset. Opus MT achieves high BLEU scores for the languages Hindi, Irish, Xhosa, Nepali, Telugu, and Sinhala in the OPUS100, but very low scores for the same languages in the FLORES-200 dataset. For the NLLB system, this phenomenon was only observed for the Nepali language.

As expected, the results indicate that some languages are supported better than others. This is underlined by Figure 1, which summarizes the BLEU scores of all four systems on the FLORES-200 dataset. However, the diagram also shows that the evaluated systems do not always perform better on class 5 languages when compared to languages in lower classes. All four systems perform well when translating French and German to English. However, the translation of Japanese is not well supported by all four of them. Instead, all four

LC	Language	Europarl					IWSLT2017				
		Libre	OPUS	NLLB	mBART		Libre	OPUS	NLLB	mBART	
5	FR	**28.38**	25.95	23.43	25.97	↗	39.95	42.34	**43.06**	42.38	↗
	DE	**25.19**	22.18	20.33	22.15	↗	33.76	37.17	**38.49**	38.08	↗
	JA	-	-	-	-	-	6.39	8.50	15.60	**17.03**	↗
4	NL	14.16	**21.54**	19.14	18.93	↗	35.01	40.15	39.96	**43.13**	↗
	FI	19.78	**22.17**	18.48	21.89	↗	-	-	-	-	
	IT	**26.71**	24.52	21.47	20.93	↗	33.19	36.14	36.84	**39.48**	↗
	KO	-	-	-	-	-	9.38	23.44	20.91	**23.95**	↗
3	RO	-	-	-	-	-	37.98	**38.94**	37.87	34.59	↗

Table 3: BLEU scores of the evaluation of the Europarl and IWSLT2017 datasets. The experiment URIs are linked with the corresponding BLEU, METEOR, chrF++, and TER scores. The results in bold mark the system with the best BLEU value on a dataset and a statistically significant difference to the second-placed system. The underlined values are the best BLEU values without a significant difference to the next highest value on that dataset.

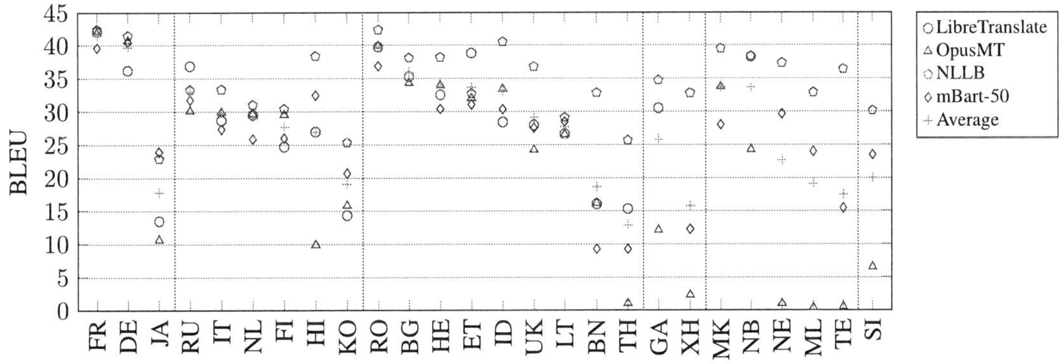

Figure 1: BLEU scores of all four systems and their average on the FLORES-200 dataset for 9 HRLs and 17 LRLs. The languages are sorted by their class from class 5 on the left to class 0 on the right. Within their class, the languages are sorted by the average system performance (orange).

systems perform better when translating the class 3 language Romanian than on Japanese or any class 4 language we look at in our evaluation. Similarly, LibreTranslate performs better on Estonian, Opus MT and NLLB better on Indonesian, Hebrew, and Ukrainian, when compared to Italian or Dutch. This even includes class 1 languages like Macedonian or Norwegian Bokmål for which the four systems achieve better performance than for most class 4 languages. As counter-examples, Thai, and Xhosa are not well supported by the majority of translation systems. Hence, our results suggest that freely available NMT systems can show a high BLEU score even on LRLs. At the same time, this result raises the question, which features of languages influence the performance of the NMT systems. It seems reasonable that an NMT system achieves a similar performance for similar languages, e.g., languages that originate from the same language family. However, although Romanian, French, and Italian belong to the group of Romance languages and the two latter even to the smaller group of Italo-Western languages, the performance of all four systems was significantly lower on Italian than on French or Romanian data. Similarly, German and Dutch belong to the group of languages but lead to quite different BLEU scores. Other language families like West Germanic (Dutch, German), Midlands Indo Aryan (Hindi, Nepali), and Neva (Estonian, Finnish) show similar results in our evaluation, while the languages of the families East Slavic (Russian, Ukrainian) and Macedo-Bulgarian (Bulgarian, Macedonian) let to similar BLEU scores within the families. Although our results point into this direction, the set of languages in our evaluation is too small to refute the hypothesis that families or groups of languages influence the performance of NMT systems. Hence, answering these questions remains future work.

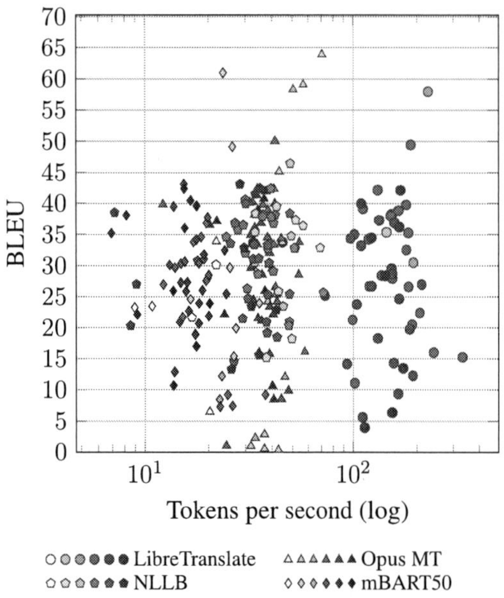

Figure 2: Comparison of the effectiveness (BLEU scores) and the efficiency (throughput). The latter is calculated as tokens per second. The filling of the marks represents the language class, i.e., unfilled marks represent a class 0 language while fully filled marks represent a class 5 language. Up and to the right is better.

Figure 2 shows a comparison of the effectiveness and efficiency of the single systems during all experiments that have been carried out within our evaluation. LibreTranslate shows the highest throughput in most experiments measured in tokens per second. Opus MT and NLLB achieve similar runtimes while mBART50 had the lowest throughput in most experiments. At the same time, we couldn't find a big difference between LRLs and HRLs concerning efficiency.

Figure 3 shows the average standard deviation per language sorted by language class. We observe increased deviations for LRLs when compared to HRLs. Despite the models being trained on LRLs-based data and the systems' language support for LRLs, the performance on these languages is still inconsistent. The Telugu, Malayalam, and Nepali languages are class 1 languages and show the highest deviation. While Bulgarian, a class 3 language, shows the lowest, followed by French and German, two class 5 languages. Hindi, a class 4 language, also shares an increased deviation following other Middle-Modern Indo-Aryan languages like Bengali and Nepali. Malayalam and Telugu are two South Dravidian languages with higher variations as well. This hints at systems having difficulties

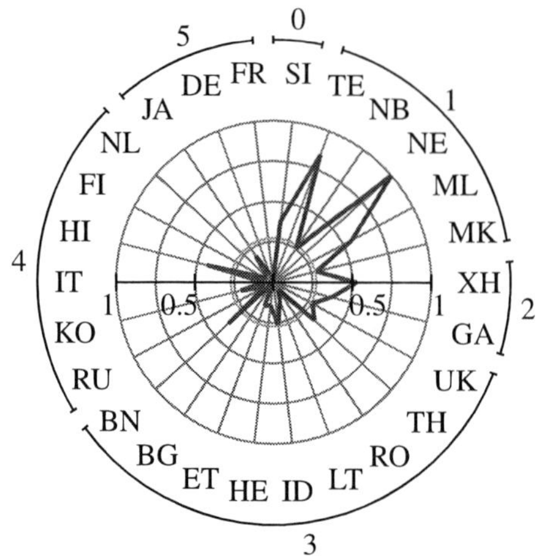

Figure 3: Average standard deviation of BLEU scores per language over all datasets sorted by language class. The values have been normalized using the highest standard deviation (22.06). The orange ring marks the average value over all languages.

processing languages from these families. No other family tree in this experiment presented higher deviations, e.g., Romance, Germanic, Slavic, or Finnic families.

4 Conclusion

We compared four open-source NMT systems on high and low-resource languages regarding their effectiveness and efficiency, filling a gap in the literature that focused on the evaluation of single systems or the comparison of commercial solutions. Our experiments show that open-source systems can perform well on LRLs, showcasing the NLP community's efforts in bridging the gap. However, the performance of the systems in these languages remains variable. Assessing the impact of the domain and genre of the training datasets on the translation quality remains a question for future work. Despite the existence of numerous evaluation frameworks for MT, we used BENG to share the evaluation data via a common space and hope that it boosts comparability across systems and datasets. The influence of language families and writing systems on the translation consistency of these systems requires further investigation.

Acknowledgements

This work has been supported by the Ministry of Culture and Science of North Rhine-Westphalia (MKW NRW) within the project SAIL under the grant no NW21-059D.

References

Dzmitry Bahdanau, Kyunghyun Cho, and Yoshua Bengio. 2015. Neural machine translation by jointly learning to align and translate. In *3rd International Conference on Learning Representations, ICLR 2015, San Diego, CA, USA, May 7-9, 2015, Conference Track Proceedings*.

Satanjeev Banerjee and Alon Lavie. 2005. METEOR: An automatic metric for MT evaluation with improved correlation with human judgments. In *Proceedings of the ACL Workshop on Intrinsic and Extrinsic Evaluation Measures for Machine Translation and/or Summarization*, pages 65–72, Ann Arbor, Michigan. Association for Computational Linguistics.

Pushpak Bhattacharyya. 2015. *Machine Translation*, 1st edition. Chapman and Hall/CRC.

Franck Burlot and François Yvon. 2018. Using monolingual data in neural machine translation: a systematic study. In *Proceedings of the Third Conference on Machine Translation: Research Papers*, pages 144–155, Brussels, Belgium. Association for Computational Linguistics.

Mauro Cettolo, Marcello Federico, Luisa Bentivogli, Jan Niehues, Sebastian Stüker, Katsuhito Sudoh, Koichiro Yoshino, and Christian Federmann. 2017. Overview of the IWSLT 2017 evaluation campaign. In *Proceedings of the 14th International Conference on Spoken Language Translation*, pages 2–14, Tokyo, Japan. International Workshop on Spoken Language Translation.

Christopher Cieri, Mike Maxwell, Stephanie Strassel, and Jennifer Tracey. 2016. Selection criteria for low resource language programs. In *Proceedings of the Tenth International Conference on Language Resources and Evaluation (LREC'16)*, pages 4543–4549, Portorož, Slovenia. European Language Resources Association (ELRA).

Jacob Devlin, Ming-Wei Chang, Kenton Lee, and Kristina Toutanova. 2019. BERT: Pre-training of deep bidirectional transformers for language understanding. In *Proceedings of the 2019 Conference of the North American Chapter of the Association for Computational Linguistics: Human Language Technologies, Volume 1 (Long and Short Papers)*, pages 4171–4186, Minneapolis, Minnesota. Association for Computational Linguistics.

Christian Federmann. 2018. Appraise evaluation framework for machine translation. In *Proceedings of the 27th International Conference on Computational Linguistics: System Demonstrations*, pages 86–88, Santa Fe, New Mexico. Association for Computational Linguistics.

Ilshat Gibadullin, Aidar Valeev, Albina Khusainova, and Adil Khan. 2019. A survey of methods to leverage monolingual data in low-resource neural machine translation. *CoRR*, abs/1910.00373.

Serge Gladkoff and Lifeng Han. 2021. Hope: A task-oriented and human-centric evaluation framework using professional post-editing towards more effective MT evaluation.

Naman Goyal, Cynthia Gao, Vishrav Chaudhary, Peng-Jen Chen, Guillaume Wenzek, Da Ju, Sanjana Krishnan, Marc'Aurelio Ranzato, Francisco Guzmán, and Angela Fan. 2022. The Flores-101 evaluation benchmark for low-resource and multilingual machine translation. *Transactions of the Association for Computational Linguistics*, 10:522–538.

Caglar Gulcehre, Orhan Firat, Kelvin Xu, Kyunghyun Cho, and Yoshua Bengio. 2017. On integrating a language model into neural machine translation. *Computer Speech & Language*, 45:137–148.

Michael A. Hedderich, Lukas Lange, Heike Adel, Jannik Strötgen, and Dietrich Klakow. 2021. A survey on recent approaches for natural language processing in low-resource scenarios. In *Proceedings of the 2021 Conference of the North American Chapter of the Association for Computational Linguistics: Human Language Technologies*, pages 2545–2568, Online. Association for Computational Linguistics.

Pratik Joshi, Sebastin Santy, Amar Budhiraja, Kalika Bali, and Monojit Choudhury. 2020. The state and fate of linguistic diversity and inclusion in the NLP world. In *Proceedings of the 58th Annual Meeting of the Association for Computational Linguistics*.

Marcin Junczys-Dowmunt, Roman Grundkiewicz, Tomasz Dwojak, Hieu Hoang, Kenneth Heafield, Tom Neckermann, Frank Seide, Ulrich Germann, Alham Fikri Aji, Nikolay Bogoychev, André F. T. Martins, and Alexandra Birch. 2018. Marian: Fast neural machine translation in C++. In *Proceedings of ACL 2018, System Demonstrations*, pages 116–121, Melbourne, Australia. Association for Computational Linguistics.

Dorothy Kenny. 2018. Machine translation. In J.P. Rawling and P. Wilson, editors, *The Routledge Handbook of Translation and Philosophy*, 1st edition. Routledge.

Guillaume Klein, Yoon Kim, Yuntian Deng, Jean Senellart, and Alexander Rush. 2017. OpenNMT: Open-source toolkit for neural machine translation. In *Proceedings of ACL 2017, System Demonstrations*, pages 67–72, Vancouver, Canada. Association for Computational Linguistics.

Philipp Koehn. 2005. Europarl: A parallel corpus for statistical machine translation. In *Proceedings of Machine Translation Summit X: Papers*, pages 79–86, Phuket, Thailand.

Yinhan Liu, Jiatao Gu, Naman Goyal, Xian Li, Sergey Edunov, Marjan Ghazvininejad, Mike Lewis, and Luke Zettlemoyer. 2020. Multilingual denoising pre-training for neural machine translation.

Alexandre Magueresse, Vincent Carles, and Evan Heetderks. 2020. Low-resource languages: A review of past work and future challenges. *CoRR*, abs/2006.07264.

Diego Moussallem, Paramjot Kaur, Thiago Ferreira, Chris van der Lee, Anastasia Shimorina, Felix Conrads, Michael Röder, René Speck, Claire Gardent, Simon Mille, Nikolai Ilinykh, and Axel-Cyrille Ngonga Ngomo. 2020. A general benchmarking framework for text generation. In *Proceedings of the 3rd International Workshop on Natural Language Generation from the Semantic Web (WebNLG+)*, pages 27–33, Dublin, Ireland (Virtual). Association for Computational Linguistics.

NLLB Team, Marta R. Costa-jussà, James Cross, Onur Çelebi, Maha Elbayad, Kenneth Heafield, Kevin Heffernan, Elahe Kalbassi, Janice Lam, Daniel Licht, Jean Maillard, Anna Sun, Skyler Wang, Guillaume Wenzek, Al Youngblood, Bapi Akula, Loic Barrault, Gabriel Mejia-Gonzalez, Prangthip Hansanti, John Hoffman, Semarley Jarrett, Kaushik Ram Sadagopan, Dirk Rowe, Shannon Spruit, Chau Tran, Pierre Andrews, Necip Fazil Ayan, Shruti Bhosale, Sergey Edunov, Angela Fan, Cynthia Gao, Vedanuj Goswami, Francisco Guzmán, Philipp Koehn, Alexandre Mourachko, Christophe Ropers, Safiyyah Saleem, Holger Schwenk, and Jeff Wang. 2022. No language left behind: Scaling human-centered machine translation.

Myle Ott, Sergey Edunov, Alexei Baevski, Angela Fan, Sam Gross, Nathan Ng, David Grangier, and Michael Auli. 2019. fairseq: A fast, extensible toolkit for sequence modeling. In *Proceedings of NAACL-HLT 2019: Demonstrations*.

Kishore Papineni, Salim Roukos, Todd Ward, and Wei jing Zhu. 2002. Bleu: a method for automatic evaluation of machine translation. pages 311–318.

Maja Popović. 2015. chrF: character n-gram F-score for automatic MT evaluation. In *Proceedings of the Tenth Workshop on Statistical Machine Translation*, pages 392–395, Lisbon, Portugal. Association for Computational Linguistics.

Matt Post. 2018. A call for clarity in reporting BLEU scores. In *Proceedings of the Third Conference on Machine Translation: Research Papers*, pages 186–191, Belgium, Brussels. Association for Computational Linguistics.

Ricardo Rei, Craig Stewart, Ana C Farinha, and Alon Lavie. 2020. COMET: A neural framework for MT evaluation. In *Proceedings of the 2020 Conference on Empirical Methods in Natural Language Processing (EMNLP)*, pages 2685–2702, Online. Association for Computational Linguistics.

Gary F. Simons, Abbey L. L. Thomas, and Chad K. K. White. 2022. Assessing digital language support on a global scale. In *Proceedings of the 29th International Conference on Computational Linguistics*, pages 4299–4305, Gyeongju, Republic of Korea. International Committee on Computational Linguistics.

Matthew Snover, Bonnie Dorr, Rich Schwartz, Linnea Micciulla, and John Makhoul. 2006. A study of translation edit rate with targeted human annotation. In *Proceedings of the 7th Conference of the Association for Machine Translation in the Americas: Technical Papers*, pages 223–231, Cambridge, Massachusetts, USA. Association for Machine Translation in the Americas.

Nikit Srivastava, Aleksandr Perevalov, Denis Kuchelev, Diego Moussallem, Axel-Cyrille Ngonga Ngomo, and Andreas Both. 2023. Lingua franca – entity-aware machine translation approach for question answering over knowledge graphs. In *Proceedings of the 12th Knowledge Capture Conference 2023*, K-CAP '23, page 122–130, New York, NY, USA. Association for Computing Machinery.

Yuqing Tang, Chau Tran, Xian Li, Peng-Jen Chen, Naman Goyal, Vishrav Chaudhary, Jiatao Gu, and Angela Fan. 2020. Multilingual translation with extensible multilingual pretraining and finetuning. *CoRR*, abs/2008.00401.

Jörg Tiedemann. 2012. Parallel data, tools and interfaces in OPUS. In *Proceedings of the Eighth International Conference on Language Resources and Evaluation (LREC'12)*, pages 2214–2218, Istanbul, Turkey. European Language Resources Association (ELRA).

Jörg Tiedemann and Santhosh Thottingal. 2020. OPUS-MT – building open translation services for the world. In *Proceedings of the 22nd Annual Conference of the European Association for Machine Translation*, pages 479–480, Lisboa, Portugal. European Association for Machine Translation.

Hugo Touvron, Louis Martin, Kevin Stone, Peter Albert, Amjad Almahairi, Yasmine Babaei, Nikolay Bashlykov, Soumya Batra, Prajjwal Bhargava, Shruti Bhosale, Dan Bikel, Lukas Blecher, Cristian Canton Ferrer, Moya Chen, Guillem Cucurull, David Esiobu, Jude Fernandes, Jeremy Fu, Wenyin Fu, Brian Fuller, Cynthia Gao, Vedanuj Goswami, Naman Goyal, Anthony Hartshorn, Saghar Hosseini, Rui Hou, Hakan Inan, Marcin Kardas, Viktor Kerkez, Madian Khabsa, Isabel Kloumann, Artem Korenev, Punit Singh Koura, Marie-Anne Lachaux, Thibaut Lavril, Jenya Lee, Diana Liskovich, Yinghai Lu, Yuning Mao, Xavier Martinet, Todor Mihaylov, Pushkar Mishra, Igor Molybog, Yixin Nie, Andrew Poulton, Jeremy Reizenstein, Rashi Rungta, Kalyan Saladi, Alan Schelten, Ruan Silva, Eric Michael Smith, Ranjan Subramanian, Xiaoqing Ellen Tan, Binh Tang, Ross Taylor, Adina Williams, Jian Xiang Kuan, Puxin Xu, Zheng Yan, Iliyan Zarov, Yuchen Zhang, Angela Fan, Melanie Kambadur, Sharan Narang, Aurelien Rodriguez, Robert Stojnic, Sergey Edunov, and Thomas Scialom. 2023. Llama 2: Open foundation and fine-tuned chat models.

Haifeng Wang, Hua Wu, Zhongjun He, Liang Huang, and Kenneth Ward Church. 2022. Progress in machine translation. *Engineering*, 18:143–153.

Mark D. Wilkinson, Michel Dumontier, Jan I. Aalbersberg, Gabrielle Appleton, Myles Axton, Arie Baak, Niklas Blomberg, Jan-Willem Boiten, Luiz Bonino da Silva Santos, Philip E. Bourne, Jildau Bouwman, Anthony J. Brookes, Tim Clark, Mercè Crosas, Ingrid Dillo, Olivier Dumon, Scott Edmunds, Chris T. Evelo, Richard Finkers, Alejandra Gonzalez-Beltran, Alasdair J.G. Gray, Paul Groth, Carole Goble, Jeffrey S. Grethe, Jaap Heringa, Peter A.C. Hoen, Rob Hooft, Tobias Kuhn, Ruben Kok, Joost Kok, Scott J. Lusher, Maryann E. Martone, Albert Mons, Abel L. Packer, Bengt Persson, Philippe Rocca-Serra, Marco Roos, Rene van Schaik, Susanna-Assunta Sansone, Erik Schultes, Thierry Sengstag, Ted Slater, George Strawn, Morris A. Swertz, Mark Thompson, Johan van der Lei, Erik van Mulligen, Jan Velterop, Andra Waagmeester, Peter Wittenburg, Katherine Wolstencroft, Jun Zhao, and Barend Mons. 2016. The FAIR Guiding Principles for scientific data management and stewardship. *Scientific data*, 3.

Haoran Xu, Young Jin Kim, Amr Sharaf, and Hany Hassan Awadalla. 2024. A paradigm shift in machine translation: Boosting translation performance of large language models. In *The Twelfth International Conference on Learning Representations*.

Biao Zhang, Philip Williams, Ivan Titov, and Rico Sennrich. 2020. Improving massively multilingual neural machine translation and zero-shot translation. In *Proceedings of the 58th Annual Meeting of the Association for Computational Linguistics*, pages 1628–1639, Online. Association for Computational Linguistics.

Wenhao Zhu, Hongyi Liu, Qingxiu Dong, Jingjing Xu, Shujian Huang, Lingpeng Kong, Jiajun Chen, and Lei Li. 2023. Multilingual machine translation with large language models: Empirical results and analysis.

Rosetta Balcanica: Deriving a "Gold Standard" Neural Machine Translation (NMT) Parallel Dataset for Western Balkan Languages

Edmon Begoli
Oak Ridge National Laboratory
begolie@ornl.gov

Maria Mahbub
Oak Ridge National Laboratory
mahbubm@ornl.gov

Sudarshan Srinivasan
Oak Ridge National Laboratory
srinivasans@ornl.gov

Abstract

The *Rosetta Balcanica* is an ongoing effort to expand the resources for low-resource western Balkan languages. This effort focuses on discovering and using accurately translated, officially mapped, and curated parallel language resources and their preparation and use as neural machine translation (NMT) datasets. Some of the guiding principles, practices, and methods employed by *Rosetta Balcanica* are generalizable and could apply to other low-resource language resource expansion efforts. With this goal in mind, we present our rationale and approach to discovering and using meticulously translated and officially curated low-resource language resources and our use of these resources to develop a parallel "gold standard" translation training resource. Secondly, we describe our specific methodology for NMT dataset development from these resources and its publication to a widely-used and accessible repository for natural language processing (*Hugging Face Hub*). Finally, we discuss the trade-offs and limitations of our current approach and the roadmap for future development and expansion of the current *Rosetta Balcanica* language resource.

[1]

1 Introduction

Many underresourced languages are spoken by ethnic groups residing in regions affected by economic, social, or other crises. These circumstances frequently necessitate the involvement of international institutions focused on economic assistance, the promotion of human rights, the advancement of democratic structures and processes, humanitarian aid, peacekeeping, and regional economic and political stabilization. As part of these activities, these institutions issue reports and studies that support their missions and goals.

The documents produced by international organizations operating in regions affected by these factors require precise translation to: a) preserve the original meaning of the master communique, and b) accurately convey that meaning across the languages of the regional groups. Such documents constitute a "golden standard" for any downstream cross-lingual computational linguistics tasks, particularly machine translation training. For a data set to fit such a standard, it must map across parallel data sets at the phrase and paragraph levels with high accuracy, be produced by professional translators, and be issued by an authoritative publication body.

Neural machine translation (NMT) (Bahdanau et al., 2014) is a state-of-the-art approach to machine translation that uses an end-to-end encoder-decoder architecture with attention mechanisms (Vaswani et al., 2017), to translate source language sentences into target language sentences. Attention-based models are particularly well-suited for translation tasks as they support the training of models that can maintain attention on complex relationships and dependencies between two related sequences. For example, attention-based models excel at learning relationships between words and phrases in two languages, even when the languages do not have a one-to-one mapping.

Accurate and complete sentence-to-sentence alignment between the source and target languages in a training dataset is particularly important for effectively training neural machine translation models because it helps the NMT model form accurate patterns of attention. Therefore, a "golden"

Proceedings of the The Seventh Workshop on Technologies for Machine Translation of Low-Resource Languages (LoResMT 2024), pages 186–192
August 15, 2024 ©2024 Association for Computational Linguistics

training set in low-resource languages is of great value for effective low-resource NMT model development, as the training content is meticulously translated and aligned at the phrase, sentence, and paragraph levels.

This effort focuses on the Western Balkan languages, a region in South Central Europe comprising countries formed by the breakup of former Yugoslavia and Albania. The languages spoken in this region include dialects of Southern Slavic languages (Serbian, Croatian, Bosnian, Macedonian, Slovenian, etc.), Albanian, and others (Friedman, 2011). These languages and resources were selected due to our familiarity with the region's cultural, historical, and ethnic circumstances, and our fluency in several of these language groups (including Croatian, Bosnian, Serbian, and to some degree, Macedonian).

Furthermore, given the significant similarity between Croatian, Serbian, and Bosnian languages (Ljubesic et al., 2007), some of these parallel resources, with translations from English, Shqip, and Macedonian to either Serbian, Croatian, or Bosnian, can potentially be used to cross-map the translations between all three languages. This significantly boosts these three language resources and their use for other multilingual tasks (Pourdamghani and Knight, 2017).

The development of high-quality, meticulously translated parallel datasets for low-resource languages such as those in the Western Balkans is crucial for advancing neural machine translation. In this paper, we outline the methodology, challenges, and future directions for creating these datasets, which serve as foundational resources for enhancing multilingual and cross-lingual computational linguistics.

2 Background

Many of the languages of the Western Balkans are spoken by small national groups or ethnic minorities and are considered low-resource languages (Tyers and Alperen, 2010; Mati et al., 2021; Kunchukuttan and Bhattacharyya, 2021). Albanian, or Shqip, is spoken by 7.5 million people worldwide, with approximately 4.5 million speakers in the region. Although an Indo-European language, it is unique and is not closely related to any other Indo-European language. Macedonian (Masson and Davies, 2016), an east-south Slavic language, is spoken by approximately two million people.

Furthermore, the region has been severely affected by a series of regional wars, which, in addition to causing significant population losses, have been followed by economic depopulation (Lukic et al., 2012), a trend that continues today (Lutz and Gailey, 2020). It is estimated that 4.4 million people have emigrated from the region (World Bank Group and WIIW, 2018, p.42).

2.1 Related Work

A number of parallel language resources for the languages of the Western Balkans. Many of these resources are the results of volunteer or officially sanctioned projects where news sites and individual works of well-known literature or other resources were collected into a corpus.

META-SHARE is the web site that curates and maintains most of these of parallel language resources for Western Balkan languages. Macedonian-Croatian Parallel Corpus (**mk-hr_pcorp**) (Cebović and Tadić, 2016) is a parallel corpus consisting of fictional synchronic prose texts with over 500,000 tokens in each language and 39,735 aligned sentences. South-East European Parallel Corpus (Tyers and Alperen, 2010) is a corpus of South-East European languages derived from The South-East European Times website. The website is a collection of regional news that was sponsored by the United States European Command, dedicated to coverage of Southeast Europe (it ended publication in March 2015). The South-East European Parallel Corpus includes, among others, resources in Albanian (41,741,782 tokens), Macedonian (37,623,521 tokens) and Croatian (34,968,453 tokens).

A parallel corpus for the tourism domain focusing on English and Croatian languages was created by leveraging automatic data crawlers to collect parallel data from the web (Toral et al., 2017). The dataset was used to train machine translation (MT) systems for the tourism domain, aiming to optimize translation tasks relevant to this specific field.

Parallel Global Voices (PGV) (Prokopidis et al., 2016) is a parallel language dataset, derived from the Global Voices multilingual group of websites, where volunteers publish and translate news stories in more than 40 languages.

Parallel Data, Tools and Interfaces in OPUS is a growing resource of freely accessible parallel corpora. It also provides tools for processing parallel and monolingual data, as well as several interfaces to search the data, making it a unique resource for various research activities (Tiedemann, 2012). Albanian from Taoteba, a collection of volunteer contributed sentences and translations that has 2,532 Albanian, 77,988 Macedonian, 5,301 Croatian, 45,786 Serbian and 619 Bosnian sentences. A recent survey of resources and methods for Serbian Language was presented in (Marovac et al., 2023).

However, most of the available resources such as Common Crawl[2] or Internet Archive[3] that are commonly used by the research community to build parallel datasets (Banón et al., 2022; El-Kishky et al., 2019) suffer from limitations. They often comprise language structures that are either inadequately translated or lack meticulous alignment across languages. In contrast, the resources utilized in *Rosetta Balcanica* stand out for their rigorous curation process. They have been curated from texts translated by official sources and meticulously mapped to multiple languages, ensuring high-quality and accurate representations to serve as resources for a wide range of applications.

2.2 Data Source

The Organization for Security and Cooperation in Europe (OSCE) (Galbreath, 2007) is the world's largest intergovernmental security-oriented organization. Its mission includes conflict prevention, arms control, the promotion of democratic values and processes, and the protection and promotion of human rights, among other objectives. The OSCE has several missions in the Western Balkans, specifically in Albania, Bosnia and Herzegovina, Kosovo, and Serbia. As part of its mission, the OSCE publishes and curates multilingual official documents relevant to its activities in the region. Their website [4] hosts an extensive resource library of reports and white papers, with a significant section dedicated to the Western Balkans.

For its translators, the OSCE requires a university degree in interpretation or a related field, with a requisite perfect command of the languages of interest and professional proficiency in English (preferably as a mother tongue). Pertinent to the region and languages of interest, the OSCE publishes reports, studies, and white papers on human rights, democratic elections, hate crime statistics, and other topics within the OSCE's scope and mission. Given the scarcity of language resources and the high quality of multilingual translations, we have included all these resources.

[2]`https://commoncrawl.org/`

[3]`https://archive.org/`

[4]`https://www.osce.org/resources/documents`

3 Approach

Our overall approach to the development of Rosetta Balcanica was to identify the specific, officially translated multilanguage resources amenable to raw language processing and then convert them into a general and neutrally formatted parallel language resource. From there, we chose to post-format this neutral resource into a specific format (e.g. Hugging Face Hub format), with the intention of making it accessible to a large group of NLP practitioners.

We started the collection process by attempting to automate the search, retrieval, and preprocessing of downloaded resources. We encountered a number of errors related to standard document formatting (page numbers, header/footer dividers) that made automation complex, uncertain and error prone, so we delayed the entire automation process in favor of manual collection and preprocessing to make initial progress in corpus development (first stage/release in a roadmap (see Figure 4). We intend to develop and proceed with a more robust automation starting with the second stage.

3.1 Selection and Preparation

We selected OSCE resources by language, starting with Shqip, assuming that there will be at least one translation (English) for the Shqip resources. In most cases, we found parallel translations between English, Shqip and the combination of Macedonian and Serbian, and in some instances, such as regional publications or annual OSCE reports, the documents were translated into multiple languages.

3.2 Parallel Dataset Creation

Following best practices for the development of parallel datasets, we create a folder for each document and then convert each PDF into a plain text representation. In particular, all document folders reside in a *language combination* directory named corresponding to the language of the documents it contains. For example, if a directory contains folders for documents that involve the three languages English, Macedonian, and Shqip, our language combination directory would be named *english-macedonian-shqip*. This folder structure allows us to add more documents to an already existing directory or to add new language combinations with new documents in the future.

We applied minimal formatting to remove page numbers and other non-linguistic features such as header artifacts. Then, we made sure that language files are aligned with each other at the paragraph and sentence level. The resulting structure is a folder named after each document, with each file entry representing a translation of the same content as seen in figure 1.

Figure 1: A folder structure and sample content for parallel language document.

This shows the structure for the content extracted from the document titled "Conclusions and Recommendations" from the 5th Annual South East Media Conference[5]. Table 1 shows some random samples extracted from this document for the three languages.

3.3 Validation

Given that the sources covered under Rosetta Balcanica are officially translated materials, we only performed spot validation to ensure alignment between the texts. Specifically, we validated the translations by randomly sampling parallel sentences and verifying their translations in Google Translate.

3.4 *Hugging Face Hub*

Hugging Face is the largest online NLP community engaged around the use and sharing of state-of-the-art models. A part of this community is a Hugging Face Hub where NLP researchers can upload, share, and access data sets and models. At the time of the writing of this manuscript, there are over 900 datasets and more than 25 metrics available. Data on Hugging Face hub follows a *Dataset* convention. *Datasets* is a library to easily access and share data sets and evaluation metrics for Natural Language Processing (NLP), computer vision, and audio tasks. Once part of the hub, the data sets can be loaded into a Hugging Face pipeline with a single line of code and used to train neural machine translation models (NMT).

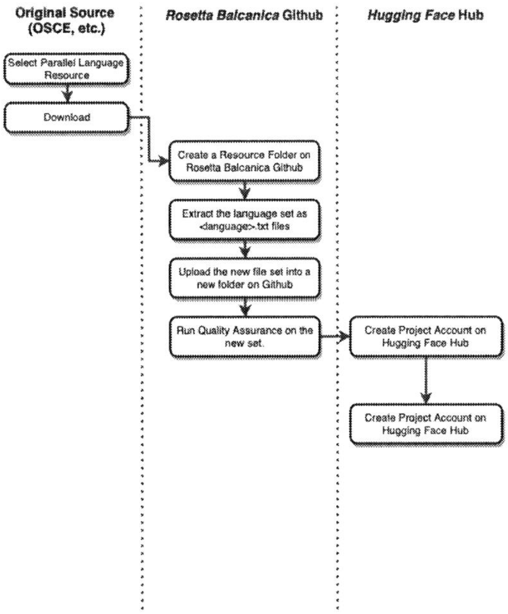

Figure 2: Rosetta Balcanica dataset development and registration workflow (Release 1).

We use a script that automatically scrapes all the document folders within a language combination directory and then extracts and aggregates all the sentences in each language text file to create a single text file corresponding to each language. This script then parses these language files to create a Hugging Face compliant dataset. Specifically, we create a temporary folder, which contains language-pair folders for each language. For example, the language combination directory *english-macedonian-shqip* containing documents from the three languages would result in two language pair folders *en-ma* and *en-sh*. We followed the convention of using the first two letters of the language to name the folder. Each language-pair directory contains 4 files corresponding to training and testing files for each language in the language pair following Hugging Face's machine translation dataset convention. These are then zipped up into

[5]`https://www.osce.org/representative-on-freedom-of-media/384549`

English	Macedonian	Shqip
OSCE SOUTH EAST EUROPE MEDIA CONFERENCE CONCLUSIONS AND RECOMMENDATIONS	КОНФЕРЕНЦИЈА НА ОБСЕ ЗА МЕДИУМИ ВО ЈУГОИСТОЧНА ЕВРОПА ЗАКЛУЧОЦИ И ПРЕПОРАКИ	KONFERENCA E OSBE-SË PËR MEDIA NË EVROPËN JUGLINDORE KONKLUZIONE DHE REKOMANDIME
Trade unions need to be recognized as legitimate representatives of journalists.	Синдикатите треба да се признаат како легитимни претставници на новинарите.	Sindikatat duhet të njihen si përfaqësues legjitim të gazetarëve.
Encourage investigative pieces and journalism also in PSM in line with best practices of the sector.	Поттикнување истражувачки стории и новинарство и во ЈМС, согласно најдобрите практики во секторот	Inkurajim i reportazheve dhe gazetarisë hulumtuese edhe në transmetuesit publikë në pajtim me praktikat më të mira.

Table 1: Sample parallel language document content from the OSCE 5th Annual South East Media Conference

rosetta_balcanica.tar.gz which is saved at the root of the repository.

All these files are currently hosted on Github at our repository[6]. The data sets are made accessible via the compressed zip file through the Hugging Face Hub by directly accessing the Github repository. Finally, we upload the dataset to Hugging-Face Hub [7] for easy access.

4 Dataset Statistics

The first release of the *Rosetta Balcanica* focuses on the parallel documents in Shqip and Macedonian. For this release, we used only Shqip resources available through OSCE.

4.1 Corpus Statistics

Counts	English	Macedonian	Shqip
# of Sentences	8567	8567	8567
# of Tokens	137620	148459	168202
# of Unique Tokens	7839	14565	18911

Table 2: Parallel English-Macedonian-Shqip Corpus Statistics

4.2 Topics Represented

As expected, there is an obvious and deliberate bias in the topics presented in the OSCE corpus figure 3. These topics reflect the subjects of the publications and reports that are within the scope of OSCE's mission in the Western Balkan countries - human rights watch (and related violations), elections, conflicts and incidents, and overall socio-cultural and economic development. These topics are expected to dominate the corpus for the first two to three releases of the dataset while we are focusing on OSCE and Hague Tribunal original sources. We plan to diversify the topics over time, but, overall, we are deliberately choosing a narrowly focused dataset that is of a highest quality, and the tradeoff of that approach will be lower topic diversity.

5 Challenges and Limitations

Maceodonian and Serbian entries are written in Cyrillic script. To compare the entries between Serbian, and, for example, Croatian and Bosnian, which are otherwise very similar languages, an additional transliteration step is required. OSCE is a trusted dataset so we did not perform transliteration of all the data. We checked 1% of randomly selected samples and found those accurately translated.

6 Future Work

The scope of the work presented in this encompasses the work on the OSCE dataset, which is topically narrow, and primarily performing manual preprocessing to minimize "debugging" time. Future work will encompass a) inclusion of other, similarly structured parallel language datasets, and b) automation of dataset retrieval and preprocessing.

Once we process OSCE resources for all Western languages, we will work to process Hague tribunal documents which are, like OSCE, profes-

[6]https://github.com/ebegoli/rosetta-balcanica

[7]https://huggingface.co/datasets/sudarshan85/rosetta_balcanica

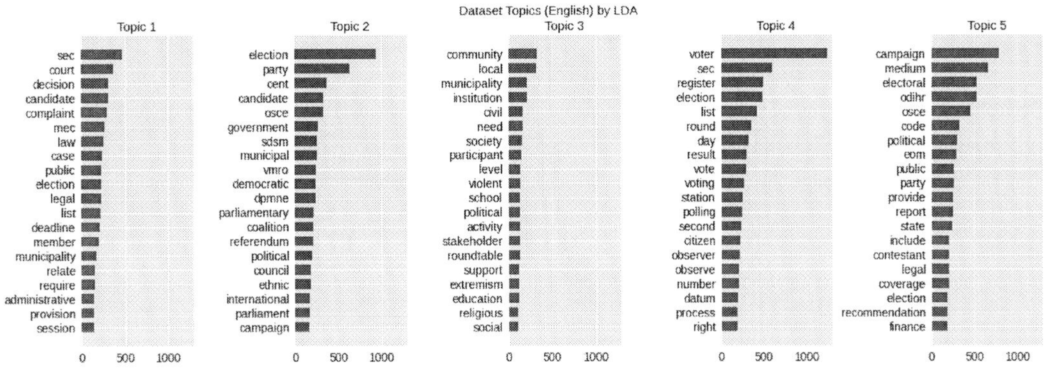

Figure 3: A representation of topics in the corpus.

sionally translated and available in most Western Balkan languages. After that, we will focus on the general multi-lingual resources from official media sources. We will focus on the latter mostly to diversify the topics and balance out representation.

Rosetta Balcanica is on an ongoing project, and the development of new resources continues. Although it is an ongoing process, we have identified releases and milestones (Figure 4) in a roadmap that maps to the inclusion of specific language resources and the dataset development tools (e.g. resource retrieval and pre-processing automation, quality assurance, dataset registration, etc.).

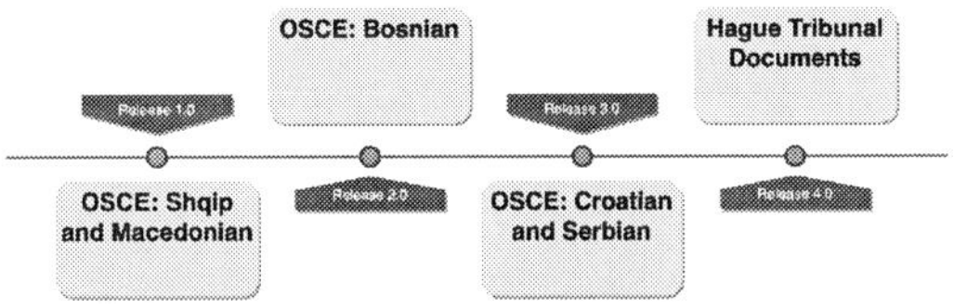

Figure 4: Roadmap of releases for 2021-2023 for Rosetta Balcanica.

We mentioned earlier that we attempted to automate the dataset collection/retrieval and preprocessing step. We found that the complexities and error-proneness of automation attempts, at that time, were slowing us down in the process of dataset development more than they were helping us. It is evident, though, that this process needs to be automated in order to be scalable and easily re-usable, and it is on our roadmap to automate the process. In fact, we are in the process of improving the automation process, and we expect that the automation scripts will be available by the time this paper is published (mid-2022).

7 Conclusion

There are three takeaways from the *Rosetta Balcanica* effort of that are, we presume, of interest to the natural language processing community:

1. Similar organizations, with a perhaps different mission, are likely sources of the similar "golden set" materials that can be used for the development of similar parallel datasets for low-resource languages. We recommend exploring similar resources for other low-resource languages. These could be UNESCO, UNICEF, United Nations, and other international organizations.
2. The workflow presented in this paper is a practice that we recommend as well. The approach we have taken, where we curate a single, raw corpus in parallel languages and then use it to create a training library or modality-specific dataset (Hugging Face Hub) is an approach that makes the dataset readily available to a broad community that uses state-of-the-art NLP methods (neural machine translation, etc.). This approach also scales well because the original, raw source can be used for the development of other library and modality-specific datasets.
3. While we found automated retrieval and preparation of data sources to be challenging and error-prone, we still intend to pursue this route in the future, and we encourage other similar efforts to attempt the same.

8 Acknowledgements

This manuscript has been in part co-authored by UT-Battelle, LLC under Contract No. DE-AC05-

00OR22725 with the U.S. Department of Energy.

References

Dzmitry Bahdanau, Kyunghyun Cho, and Yoshua Bengio. 2014. Neural machine translation by jointly learning to align and translate. *arXiv preprint arXiv:1409.0473*.

Marta Banón, Miquel Espla-Gomis, Mikel L Forcada, Cristian García-Romero, Taja Kuzman, Nikola Ljubešić, Rik van Noord, Leopoldo Pla Sempere, Gema Ramírez-Sánchez, Peter Rupnik, et al. 2022. Macocu: Massive collection and curation of monolingual and bilingual data: focus on under-resourced languages. In *23rd Annual Conference of the European Association for Machine Translation, EAMT 2022*, pages 303–304. European Association for Machine Translation.

Ines Cebović and Marko Tadić. 2016. Building the macedonian-croatian parallel corpus. In *Proceedings of the Tenth International Conference on Language Resources and Evaluation (LREC'16)*, pages 4241–4244.

Ahmed El-Kishky, Vishrav Chaudhary, Francisco Guzmán, and Philipp Koehn. 2019. Ccaligned: A massive collection of cross-lingual web-document pairs. *arXiv preprint arXiv:1911.06154*.

Victor A Friedman. 2011. The balkan languages and balkan linguistics. *Annual Review of Anthropology*, 40:275–291.

David J Galbreath. 2007. *The organization for security and co-operation in Europe (OSCE)*. Routledge.

Anoop Kunchukuttan and Pushpak Bhattacharyya. 2021. Machine translation and transliteration involving related and low-resource languages.

Nikola Ljubesic, Nives Mikelic, and Damir Boras. 2007. Language indentification: How to distinguish similar languages? In *2007 29th International Conference on Information Technology Interfaces*, pages 541–546. IEEE.

Tamara Lukic, Rastislav Stojsavljevic, Branislav Durdev, Imre Nagy, and Bojan Dercan. 2012. Depopulation in the western balkan countries. *European Journal of Geography*, 3(2):6–23.

Wolfgang Lutz and Nicholas Gailey. 2020. Depopulation as a policy challenge in the context of global demographic trends.

Ulfeta A Marovac, Aldina R Avdić, and Nikola Lj Milošević. 2023. A survey of resources and methods for natural language processing of serbian language. *arXiv preprint arXiv:2304.05468*.

Olivier Masson and Anna Morpurgo Davies. 2016. Macedonian language. In *Oxford Research Encyclopedia of Classics*.

Diellza Nagavci Mati, Mentor Hamiti, Arsim Susuri, Besnik Selimi, and Jaumin Ajdari. 2021. Building dictionaries for low resource languages: Challenges of unsupervised learning. *Annals of Emerging Technologies in Computing (AETiC)*, 5(3):52–58.

Nima Pourdamghani and Kevin Knight. 2017. Deciphering related languages. In *Proceedings of the 2017 Conference on Empirical Methods in Natural Language Processing*, pages 2513–2518.

Prokopis Prokopidis, Vassilis Papavassiliou, and Stelios Piperidis. 2016. Parallel global voices: a collection of multilingual corpora with citizen media stories. In *Proceedings of the Tenth International Conference on Language Resources and Evaluation (LREC'16)*, pages 900–905.

Jörg Tiedemann. 2012. Parallel data, tools and interfaces in opus. In *Lrec*, volume 2012, pages 2214–2218. Citeseer.

Antonio Toral, Miquel Esplá-Gomis, Filip Klubička, Nikola Ljubešić, Vassilis Papavassiliou, Prokopis Prokopidis, Raphael Rubino, and Andy Way. 2017. Crawl and crowd to bring machine translation to under-resourced languages. *Language resources and evaluation*, 51:1019–1051.

Francis M Tyers and Murat Serdar Alperen. 2010. South-east european times: A parallel corpus of balkan languages. In *Proceedings of the LREC workshop on exploitation of multilingual resources and tools for Central and (South-) Eastern European Languages*, pages 49–53. Citeseer.

Ashish Vaswani, Noam Shazeer, Niki Parmar, Jakob Uszkoreit, Llion Jones, Aidan N Gomez, Łukasz Kaiser, and Illia Polosukhin. 2017. Attention is all you need. In *Advances in neural information processing systems*, pages 5998–6008.

World Bank Group and WIIW. 2018. Western balkans labor market trends 2018.

Irish-based Large Language Model with Extreme Low-Resource Settings in Machine Translation

Khanh-Tung Tran
University College Cork
Ireland
123128577@umail.ucc.ie

Barry O'Sullivan*
University College Cork
Ireland
b.osullivan@cs.ucc.ie

Hoang D. Nguyen
University College Cork
Ireland
hn@cs.ucc.ie

Abstract

Large Language Models (LLMs) have demonstrated exceptional performances in a wide range of natural language processing tasks. However, their success does not always extend to machine translation, particularly in challenging scenarios such as translating low-resource languages. This study investigates the multilingual capability of LLMs, with a case study on Irish, an extremely low-resource language, focusing on translation tasks between English and Irish. We propose a dynamic, efficient language adaptation framework for English-centric LLMs, which involves layer-specific adjustments and subsequent fine-tuning for machine translation. Our findings highlight several key insights: (1) different layers in the LLM serve distinct functions such as language understanding and task reasoning, (2) effective translation requires extensive pre-training on both source and target languages, and (3) targeted fine-tuning for machine translation leads to significant improvements of 36.7% for English to Irish and 133.4% for Irish to English compared to the previous state-of-the-art.

1 Introduction

Large Language Models (LLMs) have recently revolutionized the field of Natural Language Processing (NLP), demonstrating remarkable performance across a wide range of tasks. These models, built on the transformer architecture, leverage vast amounts of data to achieve exceptional levels of linguistic understanding. However, significant challenges remain, particularly in the domain of machine translation for low-resource languages (Bawden and Yvon, 2023). Traditional approaches for Neural Machine Translation (NMT) are often data-inefficient and rely on large numbers of parallel data pairs to obtain reliable performance, limiting their applicability in low-resource tasks (Ranathunga et al., 2023; Lamar and Kaya, 2023).

This paper seeks to explore the multilingual capabilities of LLMs, specifically focusing on Irish, an extremely low-resource language, and the translation tasks between English and Irish. Irish, classified as an endangered language, poses unique challenges for machine translation. The limited availability of parallel corpora (Lankford et al., 2022; Ojha et al., 2021) and the sparse representation in pre-training datasets (Barry et al., 2022; Tran et al., 2024) make it a vital candidate for investigating the potential of LLMs in low-resource settings. LLMs, such as ChatGPT (OpenAI, 2022, 2024), BLOOM (Workshop et al., 2023), and the Llama series (Touvron et al., 2023a,b), are predominantly English-centric, although pre-trained on multilingual datasets. The extent to which these models can effectively translate between low-resource languages remains an open question.

Our research identifies several key insights to successfully apply LLM to the low-resource scenario, such as the requirement for the LLMs to be bilingual through extensive pre-training on both languages. We propose a novel framework for efficiently adapting English-centric LLMs to a novel unseen language, and further fine-tuning for the task of machine translation. Our approach involves a two-stage training process: dynamic continued pre-training, where we selectively train layers of the LLM based on their language capability, indicated by retrieval scores, and additional fine-tuning on specific machine translation datasets. By focusing on the layers responsible for language understanding and reasoning, we aim to enhance the bilingual capabilities of the LLM while being efficient, requiring only a fraction of the model's total parameters for effective language adaptation. Specifically, we achieve an improvement of up to 46.14 BLEU score for Irish to English translation and 13.22 BLEU score for English to Irish transla-

*Corresponding Author

Proceedings of the The Seventh Workshop on Technologies for Machine Translation of Low-Resource Languages (LoResMT 2024), pages 193–202
August 15, 2024 ©2024 Association for Computational Linguistics

tion compared to previous state-of-the-art methods on the LoResMT-2021 dataset (Ojha et al., 2021).

Our source code and model weights are made publicly available at `https://github.com/ReML-AI/UCCIX` for future research and benchmarking purposes.

2 Related Work

2.1 Neural Machine Translation

Neural Machine Translation (NMT) has become the dominant approach in the field of machine translation, largely due to the success of sequence-to-sequence models and the introduction of attention mechanisms. The advent of the Transformer model (Vaswani et al., 2017) offers a more efficient and scalable architecture that relies entirely on attention mechanisms. Transformers have become the backbone for most state-of-the-art (SoTA) NMT systems (Lankford et al., 2021; Team et al., 2022). Despite these advancements, NMT systems still struggle with translating low-resource languages due to the lack of sufficient training data. Various approaches have been proposed to mitigate this issue, such as transfer learning (Zoph et al., 2016; Chen and Abdul-mageed, 2023) and multilingual NMT (Johnson et al., 2017; Dabre et al., 2020). These methods leverage information from high-resource languages or use monolingual data to further improve translation quality for low-resource languages, but significant challenges remain. One of the main challenges is the dependence on parallel data, which is notably deficient for low-resource languages.

In this work, we explore a recent paradigm (Workshop et al., 2023; Bawden and Yvon, 2023), by applying LLMs to the domain of NMT. We leverage the vast amount of pre-training conducted for LLMs and investigate whether their capabilities can be transferred to NMT tasks, particularly for low-resource languages. However, it should be noted that while LLMs can be pre-trained on multiple languages, their pre-training data is mostly monolingual per sample, making it uncertain how well the models can translate across languages.

2.2 Large Language Models

LLMs have garnered attention for their impressive text generation capabilities and versatility across various NLP tasks. However, most of these models, either closed-source ones such as ChatGPT, or open-source models like BLOOM (Workshop et al., 2023), and the Llama series (Touvron et al., 2023a,b) have demonstrated significant proficiency in handling a variety of languages and tasks. However, these models predominantly focus on widely spoken languages like English, leading to a performance disparity when applied to low-resource languages. Recent surveys (Bawden and Yvon, 2023; Hendy et al., 2023) have investigated the capability of LLMs for machine translation tasks, reporting that LLMs can perform well in these scenarios, especially for high-resource languages. However, their effectiveness in low-resource settings, such as in Irish, remains limited due to the lack of adequate training data.

UCCIX (Tran et al., 2024) is a recent LLM developed with a focus on Irish, a Definitely Endangered language as recognized by UNESCO (UNESCO, 2010). Given the limited availability of Irish data, the authors proposed a framework for language adaptation of an English-centric LLM to make it bilingual. Despite this, issues such as catastrophic forgetting of English have been observed, as a consequence of continued pre-training on Irish data.

With the case study on Irish, we investigate the potential usages of such models for the translation tasks between Irish and English, as part of the effort to preserve the Irish language and prevent its loss. We analyze the bilingual capabilities of the LLM and propose an adaptive language adaptation strategy to balance the model's performance between the two languages. This approach aims to enhance the efficiency of adapting LLMs in low-resource settings, ensuring robust performance in both high-resource and low-resource languages.

2.3 Low-Resource Settings

Research on the challenges of addressing low-resource languages in NLP is essential given the diversity of languages and the demand for inclusive technology. Since large annotated datasets are necessary for training strong models, low-resource languages frequently lack them, making it challenging to achieve good performance using traditional techniques. As pointed out in recent survey (Ranathunga et al., 2023), if there are less than 0.5 million parallel sentences in the parallel corpora, a language pair is deemed "low-resource" in an MT scenario, and if there are less than 0.1 million parallel sentences, it is deemed "extremely low-resource".

Irish, an endangered language, fits into the 'extremely low-resource' category. Recent works report a composite dataset from different sources amounting to only 25,000 (Lankford et al., 2022) or 52,000 (Lankford et al., 2021) parallel sentences. Given this limited amount of data, we investigate whether the large amount of available monolingual data can aid in improving performance through the use of LLMs. Our findings highlight the effectiveness of further fine-tuning LLMs for the machine translation task, even with such sparse data.

3 Method

3.1 Preliminary Explorations

Large Language Models (LLMs) are typically built using the transformer decoder-only architecture, consisting of multiple stacked transformer layers. While LLMs are often trained on large-scale English-dominant text corpora, they often also include a small percentage of texts in multiple languages due to the vast size of the training data. This raises the question of whether LLMs can understand underpresented languages effectively. For instance, in the Llama series of models, the Irish language constitutes less than 0.005% of the training corpus. To explore this, we conduct few-shot prompting experiments with the machine translation task between English (dominant language) and Irish (extremely low-resource language). Few-shot prompting allows LLMs to follow specific input patterns and leverage their pre-trained knowledge for the translation task. We investigate the performance in both directions: Irish to English (assessing LLM's understanding of the low-resource language) and English to Irish (analyzing its capability to generate text in the target language). Table 1 shows examples of the prompts used. The results, presented in Table 2 and Figure 1, highlight the following insights:

- English-centric LLMs may have some understanding of low-resource languages but struggle with text generation in those languages. This is evident by the strong performance of the Irish to English direction, with gpt-3.5-turbo and Llama 2-70B able to outperform the previous task-specific SoTA (Lankford et al., 2021), up to 7.97 BLEU score.
- Efficient translation requires extensive pre-training on both languages, as evidenced by UCCIX outperforming English-centric LLMs, beating the much larger gpt-3.5-turbo model.
- Generally, providing examples (few-shot prompting) helps LLMs follow the task format better (Figure 1), aligning with previous findings (Brown et al., 2020).

To further investigate LLM behavior without relying on few-shot prompting and the variants it created, we analyze the sentence retrieval task. The sentence retrieval task (Artetxe and Schwenk, 2019; Dufter and Schütze, 2020; Yong et al., 2023), aims to identify the closest sentence in English given a representation of a sentence in a new language (Irish). We compute sentence retrieval accuracy at each layer of different pretrained models to understand where and how language understanding capabilities emerge. For this analysis, we focus on the Llama 2 model, a popular and widely-used open-sourced LLM.

Prompt English->Irish	Prompt Irish->English
Aistrigh Béarla go Gaeilge: Béarla: When needed, EMA and the other European regulators take action. Gaeilge: Gníomhaíonn EMA agus rialtóirí Eorpacha eile nuair is gá. Béarla: mumps Gaeilge: na leicní Béarla: woman holding a phone Gaeilge: bean a bhfuil fón aici Béarla: 17 June 2020 - EU COVID-19 vaccines strategy unveiled Gaeilge: 17 Meitheamh 2020 - Straitéis an Aontais um vacsaíní in aghaidh COVID-19 curtha i láthair Béarla: 31 August 2020 - Coronavirus Global Response: The Commission joins the COVID-19 Vaccine Global Access Facility Gaeilge: 31 Lúnasa 2020 - An Fhreagairt Dhomhanda ar an gCoróinvíreas: An Coimisiún páirteach sa tSaoráid Rochtana Domhanda ar Vacsaíní in aghaidh COVID-19 Béarla: {input} Gaeilge:	Aistrigh Gaeilge go Béarla: Gaeilge: Gníomhaíonn EMA agus rialtóirí Eorpacha eile nuair is gá. Béarla: When needed, EMA and the other European regulators take action. Gaeilge: na leicní Béarla: mumps Gaeilge: bean a bhfuil fón aici Béarla: woman holding a phone Gaeilge: 17 Meitheamh 2020 - Straitéis an Aontais um vacsaíní in aghaidh COVID-19 curtha i láthair Béarla: 17 June 2020 - EU COVID-19 vaccines strategy unveiled Gaeilge: 31 Lúnasa 2020 - An Fhreagairt Dhomhanda ar an gCoróinvíreas: An Coimisiún páirteach sa tSaoráid Rochtana Domhanda ar Vacsaíní in aghaidh COVID-19 Béarla: 31 August 2020 - Coronavirus Global Response: The Commission joins the COVID-19 Vaccine Global Access Facility Gaeilge: {input} Béarla:

Table 1: 5-shot prompts used to evaluate pre-trained LLMs on machine translation tasks.

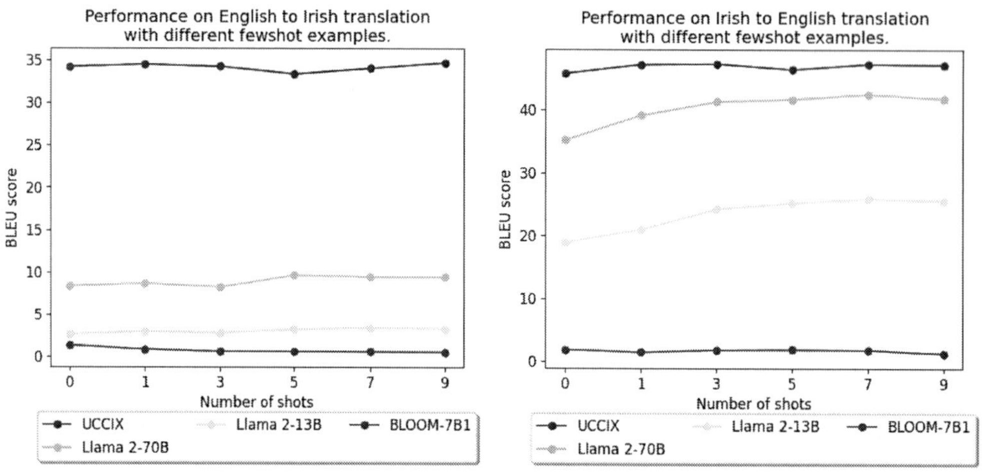

(a) English to Irish translation

(b) Irish to English translation

Figure 1: Effects of a number of fewshot examples during prompting for different models on a) English to Irish translation, and b) Irish to English translation on the LoResMT-2021 dataset.

Model	BLEU on English->Irish	BLEU on Irish->English
SoTA from LoResMT2021 (Lankford et al., 2021)	**36.0**	34.6
gpt-3.5-turbo	18.64	42.57
Llama 2-70B	9.63	41.66
Llama 2-13B	3.25	25.60
BLOOM-7B1	0.61	1.84
UCCIX	33.34	**46.36**

Table 2: BLEU scores on machine translation tasks for baseline NMT model (Lankford et al., 2021), English-Irish bilingual LLMs (UCCIX (Tran et al., 2024)), and other LLMs.

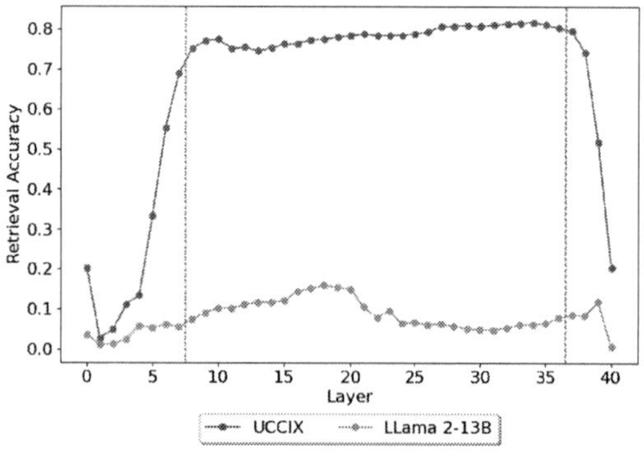

Figure 2: Sentence retrieval accuracy score across layers of UCCIX, English-Irish bilingual LLM and Llama 2-13B, English-centric LLM.

Formally, given $D = \{(s_0^{ga}, s_0^{en}), \ldots, (s_i^{ga}, s_i^{en}), \ldots, (s_{N-1}^{ga}, s_{N-1}^{en}), \}$ a dataset of parallel sentences in Irish (denoted s^{ga}) and English (denoted s^{en}), the sentence retrieval task involves finding the closest English sentence given an Irish sentence representation. A generative (decoder-only) LLM processes the input textual data autoregressively through each transformer layer. The text is first tokenized into subword units and mapped into embeddings through a learned embedding matrix. The embeddings are input to transformer layers, maintaining their dimensions throughout the forward pass. Given the initial input embedding at position j as h_0^j, the corresponding output latent embedding at layer l is computed as:

$$h_l^j = f_l(h_{l-1}^0, \ldots, h_{l-1}^j) \quad (1)$$

with f_l as the transformer block at layer l, $l \in [0, L)$ for an LLM with L layers. For instance, Llama 2-13B and the finetuned version UCCIX have $L = 41$ layers. The sentence representation at each layer is calculated as the average over embeddings at all positions:

$$e_l = \frac{1}{K} \sum_{k=0}^{K-1} h_l^k \quad (2)$$

Thus, the retrieval accuracy for sentence i at

layer l is determined by:

$$\text{accuracy}_{l,i} = \begin{cases} 1 & \text{if } \underset{i \in [0,N)}{\text{argmax}} \cos(e_{l,i}^{ga}, e_{l,i}^{en}) = i \\ 0 & \text{otherwise} \end{cases} \quad (3)$$

where cos is the cosine similarity between embeddings.

As observed in Figure 2, intermediate layers of UCCIX (visualized as between the 2 horizontal lines) achieve almost perfect retrieval score, a trend that can also be noticed in the base LLaMA 2 model, although to a lesser extent. This leads us to hypothesize that there are two types of layers in the architecture of LLMs: (1) *interface layers*, which consist of the input layer (the first few layers) that analyze the language of the input text, extracting information such as syntax, lexical structure, and the output layer (the last few layers) that map back to the token space of the target languages, and (2) *reasoning layers*, which are the intermediate layers capable of reasoning and performing the task at hand. As the interface layers contain information about the unique characteristics of each language, they fail in retrieving sentences with the same meaning but written in different languages, hence the low retrieval scores.

3.2 Proposed Framework for Dynamic and Efficient Language Adaptation

Building on our insights, we propose a framework for efficiently adapting LLMs to understand additional languages and to the machine translation task. This framework, as depicted in Figure 3, involves two main stages: dynamic continued pre-training for language adaptation and additional fine-tuning on machine translation data.

Based on our preliminary experiments, we hypothesize that certain layers of the LLM function as interface and reasoning layers for bilingual understanding. Thus, we dynamically identify and train only the relevant layers. Specifically, we use the retrieval score accuracy_l for each layer l of the original English-centric LLM to guide this process.

For the input layers, which are part of the interface layers, we select layers from 0 to the first layer that has a retrieval score larger than α_s:

$$l_{input} = \{l \mid 0 \leq l \leq \underset{l}{\text{argmin}}(\text{accuracy}_l > \alpha_s)\} \quad (4)$$

Similarly, for the output interface layers, we select from the last layer and move backward to the first layer that has a retrieval score smaller than α_e:

$$l_{output} = \{l \mid \underset{l}{\text{argmax}}(\text{accuracy}_l < \alpha_e) \leq l < L\} \quad (5)$$

By focusing training on these identified layers, we aim to enhance the LLM's bilingual capabilities by targeting the layers in charge of language understanding while maintaining the reasoning capabilities of the LLM. Moreover, the proposed training strategy is efficient, as it reduces number of layers that require training.

After the dynamic continued pre-training stage, we further fine-tune the LLM on specific machine translation datasets. This step ensures that the model not only understands both languages but also effectively translates between them. The additional training is performed on both directions: English to Irish and Irish to English with full fine-tuning, as both interface layers and reasoning layers are vital to adapt the LLM to this specific task. During this stage, we compute the training loss solely on the target language sentence, and ignore prediction loss on the task prompt and input sentence.

4 Experiments

4.1 Datasets

For language adaptation with continued pre-training, we utilize the monolingual corpus introduced in UCCIX (Tran et al., 2024). The monolingual dataset includes data from various sources such as CulturaX(Nguyen et al., 2023), Glot500 (ImaniGooghari et al., 2023), Irish Wikipedia, providing valuable content from Irish sites and pages. To ensures a fair comparison, we also choose the base pre-trained LLM to be Llama 2-13B, same as UCCIX. The dataset in total has approximately 500M Irish tokens, significantly smaller than the original 2T tokens used to train Llama 2.

For the fine-tuning phase, we combine the corpus of LoResMT (Ojha et al., 2021) and ga-Health (Lankford et al., 2022), both in-domain datasets for the health domain, resulting in a total of 17k samples for the training set.

For MT evaluation, we report the BLEU score, a common metric in the literature, for both translation directions: English to Irish and Irish to English. The evaluation set from LoResMT comprises 500 samples for English to Irish and 250 samples for Irish to English. For the fine-tuning MT data, we

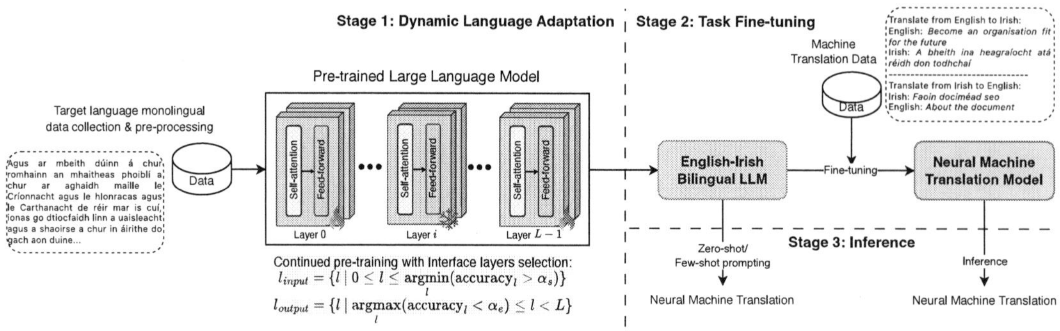

Figure 3: Our main pipeline, including two training stages: 1) dynamic language adaptation of base English-centric to the target language, and 2) further fine-tuning using parallel data for the neural machine translation task.

directly use the corpus from previous works, adhering to the training split of LoResMT to avoid any data contamination issues. Additionally, the pre-training corpus from UCCIX is monolingual, while the evaluation data is parallel between the two languages. Consequently, the problem of data contamination is further mitigated.

4.2 Experimental Setup

For language adaptation with continued pre-training, we start with the base Llama 2-13B model, pre-trained on an English-dominant corpus of 2T tokens. This ensures a fair comparison with the English-Irish bilingual LLM, UCCIX, which also based on Llama 2-13B. In this foundational work, for simplicity, we set both α_s and α_e to 0.075 selecting 11 layers as interface layers for training out of 41 layers in total in Llama 2-13B. This means we train approximately 25% of the total model parameters, ensuring the technique to be efficient, compared to full fine-tuning. Following UCCIX, we also expand the tokenizer to include 10k native Irish tokens before continued pre-training. During this phase, we train the model with the AdamW optimizer for a total of 2 epochs, with a learning rate of $1e-4$, a batch size of 96 samples, each 4096 tokens long. Training is distributed across 6 NVIDIA H100 GPUs with a gradient accumulation step of 8. We leverage DeepSpeed (Rasley et al., 2020) for the training process. The pre-trained LLMs can be used for the machine translation task through few-shot prompting. By default, we design a prompt in Irish, with a description of the task and 5 examples (5-shot prompting), as illustrated in Table 1. The 5 examples are initially randomly chosen from the development subset.

For fine-tuning the machine translation task, we train the model for at most 10 epochs on the training set. We use the AdamW optimizer, setting the learning rate to $1e-4$ for full fine-tuning, and to $1e-3$ for training with parameter efficient methods. These values are chosen through grid search. We also leverage DeepSpeed in this stage, with a batch size of 96 samples, each 4096 token long distributed across 6 H100 GPUs. Each experiment is repeated 3 times across random seeds, and we report the average results for robust evaluation. The model is prompted as illustrated in the right part of Figure 3 for inference.

Model	BLEU on English → Irish	BLEU on Irish → English
Llama 2-13B	3.25	25.60
UCCIX	**33.34**	**46.36**
$\text{UCCIX}_{(IA)^3}$	19.53	39.48
UCCIX_{LoRA}	26.14	43.65
$\text{UCCIX}_{reasoning\_layer}$	29.27	42.71
$\text{UCCIX}_{interface\_layer}$	30.69	46.07

Table 3: Comparison between our framework with other language adaptation techniques: full fine-tuning (UCCIX), parameter-efficient (UCCIX_{LoRA}, $\text{UCCIX}_{(IA)^3}$) and the ablation study with the training of reasoning layers ($\text{UCCIX}_{reasoning\_layer}$).

5 Results and Discussion

5.1 Langugage Adaptation Effectiveness

Table 3 demonstrates the efficiency and performance of our proposed dynamic language adaptation approach, $\text{UCCIX}_{interface\_layer}$. Despite training only 25% of the parameters, our method remains competitive with UCCIX, which employs full fine-tuning. For instance, the performance drop

Model	Acc. on Cloze Test (0-shot)	Acc. on SIB-200 (Irish subset) (10-shot)	Exact-match on IrishQA (ga) (5-shot)	Exact-match on Natural Question (5-shot)	Exact-match on IrishQA (en) (5-shot)	Acc. on Wino-grande (5-shot)	Acc. norm on HellaSwag (10-shot)	Average
gpt-3.5-turbo	N/A	N/A	0.2222	**0.4660**	0.3333	N/A	N/A	N/A
Llama 2-70B	0.63	0.7059	0.2963	0.3806	0.4074	**0.8374**	**0.8701**	0.5897
Llama 2-13B	0.54	0.5343	0.3148	0.3069	0.4444	0.7609	0.8223	0.5319
BLOOM-7B1	0.45	0.1471	0.0000	0.0806	0.1667	0.6519	0.6202	0.3024
UCCIX	**0.75**	0.7794	**0.3889**	0.1668	0.3704	0.7135	0.7758	0.5635
UCCIX$_{(IA)^3}$	0.45	0.7353	0.2222	0.2490	0.4815	0.7435	0.7883	0.5242
UCCIX$_{LoRA}$	0.67	0.7792	0.2963	0.2704	**0.5370**	0.7474	0.7851	0.5836
UCCIX$_{reasoning_layer}$	0.64	0.7304	0.2222	0.1950	0.3889	0.7167	0.7903	0.5262
UCCIX$_{interface_layer}$	0.69	**0.7892**	**0.3889**	0.2404	**0.5370**	0.7451	0.7971	**0.5982**

Table 4: Evaluation results of pre-trained models on curated set of Irish (first 3 columns) and English (the following 4 columns) benchmarking datasets (Tran et al., 2024). We compute *Average* as the mean across all metrics.

is minimal, only 0.29%, for the Irish to English translation task. Compared to other parameter efficient fine-tuning techniques, including LoRA (Hu et al., 2022) and (IA)^3 (Liu et al., 2022), our dynamic interface layers training approach achieves the strongest performance. Additionally, unlike other methods that require injecting additional parameters during training and merging with the original model for efficient inference, our method does not introduce any additional parameters, allowing the model to be ready for use directly after training.

We conduct an ablation study where we train the reasoning layers instead of the interface layers selected in Equation 2 and Equation 3. We denote this as UCCIX$_{reasoning_layer}$. Our approach outperforms this method in both English to Irish and Irish to English translation directions, with a gap of 1.42 and 3.36 BLEU scores, respectively.

To further analyze the bilingual capability of models trained with our proposed approach, both learning the new language and preserving the capability in the original language, we benchmark on the curated set of Irish and English benchmarking datasets introduced in (Tran et al., 2024). This curated set includes diverse tasks such as topic classification and open-ended question answering. The results, as illustrated in Table 4, highlight the balanced performance between the two languages for UCCIX$_{interface_layer}$, where we achieve top-1 average score of 0.5982, surpassing the much larger model Llama 2-70B (0.5897). Our model also achieves SoTA results on 3 out of 7 datasets, namely SIB-200, IrishQA (Irish version), and IrishQA (English version). Furthermore, in benchmarking with Irish tasks, our model performs comparably to UCCIX, which was fully fine-tuned

Model	BLEU on English → Irish	BLEU on Irish → English
Llama 2-13B-*mt*	31.74	62.52
UCCIX-*mt*	**49.22**	76.44
UCCIX$_{interface_layer}$-*mt*	39.10	**80.74**

Table 5: Fine-tuning results on machine translation tasks for baseline English-centric LLM (Llama 2-13B) and English-Irish bilingual LLMs (UCCIX). Here *-mt* denotes further finetuning for the machine translation task.

to focus on Irish, while being efficient, as we only trained 25% of the parameters compared to UCCIX. This validates our hypothesis on interface and reasoning layers: fine-tuning interface layers allows the model to understand additional languages without catastrophic forgetting, and freezing the reasoning layers helps maintain the model's usefulness and effectiveness.

5.2 Machine Translation Fine-tuning Result

We carry out further fine-tuning experiments to investigate whether LLMs can be further adapted to this specific task. As shown in the preliminary experiment in Section 3.1, prompting pre-trained LLMs seem to be effective only when they are extensively trained on both source and target languages. In addition to fine-tuning UCCIX and UCCIX$_{interface_layer}$, we also fine-tuned the English-centric LLM Llama 2-13B to investigate whether exposure to a small amount of parallel data can enhance its performance. Results in Table 5 indicate that further fine-tuning helps significantly, with a substantial performance jump for Llama 2-13B, from 3.25 to 34.16 BLEU score for English to Irish, and from 25.60 to 62.52 for Irish to English.

Nevertheless, having a base bilingual pre-trained LLM is important. Fine-tuning results with both UCCIX and UCCIX$_{interface_layer}$ showcase impressive performance gaps. UCCIX-*mt* achieves a new SoTA result for Irish to English translation, with a gap of 13.22 (49.22 compared to 36.0), and on English to Irish task, and UCCIX$_{interface_layer}$-*mt* surpasses the SoTA with a gap of 46.14 BLEU score.

In general, the results convincingly demonstrate the effectiveness of leveraging large-scale pretrained LLMs for machine translation tasks involving extremely low-resource languages. By further fine-tuning on the limited available parallel data, we can significantly enhance translation performance, even in resource-constrained scenarios.

6 Conclusion

In this work, we investigate the application of LLMs to the domain of neural machine translation, particularly focusing on Irish, an extremely low-resource language. We analyze the bilingual capabilities of LLMs and propose a dynamic language adaptation strategy aimed at balancing the model's performance across multiple languages. We hypothesize that certain layers of the LLM serve as interface layers for language understanding, and reasoning layers, and we develop a novel, efficient training approach that dynamically identifies and trains only the relevant layers. Our experimental results demonstrate the effectiveness of our approach, achieving balanced performance between languages. Moreover, we show that leveraging large-scale pre-trained LLMs and further finetuning them on machine translation tasks with limited parallel data can significantly enhance translation performance in resource-constrained scenarios, with performance enhancement up to 46.14 BLEU score. This highlights the potential of our method to improve machine translation tasks involving extremely low-resource languages.

Acknowledgements

We would like to acknowledge CloudCIX Limited for the generous collaborative support of computing resources on their NVIDIA HGX/H100 GPU cluster. This research work has emanated from research conducted with financial support from Science Foundation Ireland under Grant 12/RC/2289-P2 and 18/CRT/6223.

Limitations

In this work, we focus specifically on the Irish language and a bilingual translation scenario. Our experiments are primarily conducted using the LoResMT-2021 dataset for the translation task. While our proposed framework can theoretically be applied to other languages and multilingual scenarios, further experiments are beneficial to verify its generalizability across different languages and diverse datasets.

Ethics Statement

Our work contributes to language technologies that support the digitalization and preservation of low-resource languages, with a particular focus on Irish. We aim to promote linguistic diversity and inclusivity by enhancing the accessibility and usability of endangered languages through advanced machine translation techniques.

References

Mikel Artetxe and Holger Schwenk. 2019. Massively Multilingual Sentence Embeddings for Zero-Shot Cross-Lingual Transfer and Beyond. *Transactions of the Association for Computational Linguistics*, 7:597–610.

James Barry, Joachim Wagner, Lauren Cassidy, Alan Cowap, Teresa Lynn, Abigail Walsh, Mícheál J. Ó Meachair, and Jennifer Foster. 2022. gaBERT — an Irish language model. In *Proceedings of the Thirteenth Language Resources and Evaluation Conference*, pages 4774–4788, Marseille, France. European Language Resources Association.

Rachel Bawden and François Yvon. 2023. Investigating the translation performance of a large multilingual language model: the case of BLOOM. In *Proceedings of the 24th Annual Conference of the European Association for Machine Translation*, pages 157–170, Tampere, Finland. European Association for Machine Translation.

Tom Brown, Benjamin Mann, Nick Ryder, Melanie Subbiah, Jared D Kaplan, Prafulla Dhariwal, Arvind Neelakantan, Pranav Shyam, Girish Sastry, Amanda Askell, et al. 2020. Language models are few-shot learners. *Advances in neural information processing systems*, 33:1877–1901.

Wei-rui Chen and Muhammad Abdul-mageed. 2023. Improving neural machine translation of indigenous languages with multilingual transfer learning. In *Proceedings of the Sixth Workshop on Technologies for Machine Translation of Low-Resource Languages (LoResMT 2023)*, pages 73–85, Dubrovnik, Croatia. Association for Computational Linguistics.

Raj Dabre, Chenhui Chu, and Anoop Kunchukuttan. 2020. A survey of multilingual neural machine translation. *ACM Comput. Surv.*, 53(5).

Philipp Dufter and Hinrich Schütze. 2020. Identifying elements essential for BERT's multilinguality. In *Proceedings of the 2020 Conference on Empirical Methods in Natural Language Processing (EMNLP)*, pages 4423–4437, Online. Association for Computational Linguistics.

Amr Hendy, Mohamed Abdelrehim, Amr Sharaf, Vikas Raunak, Mohamed Gabr, Hitokazu Matsushita, Young Jin Kim, Mohamed Afify, and Hany Hassan Awadalla. 2023. How good are gpt models at machine translation? a comprehensive evaluation.

Edward J Hu, yelong shen, Phillip Wallis, Zeyuan Allen-Zhu, Yuanzhi Li, Shean Wang, Lu Wang, and Weizhu Chen. 2022. LoRA: Low-rank adaptation of large language models. In *International Conference on Learning Representations*.

Ayyoob ImaniGooghari, Peiqin Lin, Amir Hossein Kargaran, Silvia Severini, Masoud Jalili Sabet, Nora Kassner, Chunlan Ma, Helmut Schmid, André Martins, François Yvon, and Hinrich Schütze. 2023. Glot500: Scaling multilingual corpora and language models to 500 languages. In *Proceedings of the 61st Annual Meeting of the Association for Computational Linguistics (Volume 1: Long Papers)*, pages 1082–1117, Toronto, Canada. Association for Computational Linguistics.

Melvin Johnson, Mike Schuster, Quoc V. Le, Maxim Krikun, Yonghui Wu, Zhifeng Chen, Nikhil Thorat, Fernanda Viégas, Martin Wattenberg, Greg Corrado, Macduff Hughes, and Jeffrey Dean. 2017. Google's multilingual neural machine translation system: Enabling zero-shot translation. *Transactions of the Association for Computational Linguistics*, 5:339–351.

Annie Lamar and Zeyneb Kaya. 2023. Measuring the impact of data augmentation methods for extremely low-resource NMT. In *Proceedings of the Sixth Workshop on Technologies for Machine Translation of Low-Resource Languages (LoResMT 2023)*, pages 101–109, Dubrovnik, Croatia. Association for Computational Linguistics.

Séamus Lankford, Haithem Afli, Órla Ní Loinsigh, and Andy Way. 2022. gaHealth: An English–Irish bilingual corpus of health data. In *Proceedings of the Thirteenth Language Resources and Evaluation Conference*, pages 6753–6758, Marseille, France. European Language Resources Association.

Seamus Lankford, Haithem Afli, and Andy Way. 2021. Machine translation in the covid domain: an English-Irish case study for LoResMT 2021. In *Proceedings of the 4th Workshop on Technologies for MT of Low Resource Languages (LoResMT2021)*, pages 144–150, Virtual. Association for Machine Translation in the Americas.

Haokun Liu, Derek Tam, Mohammed Muqeeth, Jay Mohta, Tenghao Huang, Mohit Bansal, and Colin A Raffel. 2022. Few-shot parameter-efficient fine-tuning is better and cheaper than in-context learning. *Advances in Neural Information Processing Systems*, 35:1950–1965.

Thuat Nguyen, Chien Van Nguyen, Viet Dac Lai, Hieu Man, Nghia Trung Ngo, Franck Dernoncourt, Ryan A. Rossi, and Thien Huu Nguyen. 2023. Culturax: A cleaned, enormous, and multilingual dataset for large language models in 167 languages.

Atul Kr. Ojha, Chao-Hong Liu, Katharina Kann, John Ortega, Sheetal Shatam, and Theodorus Fransen. 2021. Findings of the LoResMT 2021 shared task on COVID and sign language for low-resource languages. In *Proceedings of the 4th Workshop on Technologies for MT of Low Resource Languages (LoResMT2021)*, pages 114–123, Virtual. Association for Machine Translation in the Americas.

OpenAI. 2022. Introducing chatgpt.

OpenAI. 2024. Gpt-4 technical report.

Surangika Ranathunga, En-Shiun Annie Lee, Marjana Prifti Skenduli, Ravi Shekhar, Mehreen Alam, and Rishemjit Kaur. 2023. Neural machine translation for low-resource languages: A survey. *ACM Comput. Surv.*, 55(11).

Jeff Rasley, Samyam Rajbhandari, Olatunji Ruwase, and Yuxiong He. 2020. Deepspeed: System optimizations enable training deep learning models with over 100 billion parameters. In *Proceedings of the 26th ACM SIGKDD International Conference on Knowledge Discovery & Data Mining*, KDD '20, page 3505–3506, New York, NY, USA. Association for Computing Machinery.

NLLB Team, Marta R. Costa-jussà, James Cross, Onur Çelebi, Maha Elbayad, Kenneth Heafield, Kevin Heffernan, Elahe Kalbassi, Janice Lam, Daniel Licht, Jean Maillard, Anna Sun, Skyler Wang, Guillaume Wenzek, Al Youngblood, Bapi Akula, Loic Barrault, Gabriel Mejia Gonzalez, Prangthip Hansanti, John Hoffman, Semarley Jarrett, Kaushik Ram Sadagopan, Dirk Rowe, Shannon Spruit, Chau Tran, Pierre Andrews, Necip Fazil Ayan, Shruti Bhosale, Sergey Edunov, Angela Fan, Cynthia Gao, Vedanuj Goswami, Francisco Guzmán, Philipp Koehn, Alexandre Mourachko, Christophe Ropers, Safiyyah Saleem, Holger Schwenk, and Jeff Wang. 2022. No language left behind: Scaling human-centered machine translation.

Hugo Touvron, Thibaut Lavril, Gautier Izacard, Xavier Martinet, Marie-Anne Lachaux, Timothée Lacroix, Baptiste Rozière, Naman Goyal, Eric Hambro, Faisal Azhar, et al. 2023a. Llama: Open and efficient foundation language models. *arXiv preprint arXiv:2302.13971*.

Hugo Touvron, Louis Martin, Kevin Stone, Peter Albert, Amjad Almahairi, Yasmine Babaei, Nikolay Bashlykov, Soumya Batra, Prajjwal Bhargava, Shruti Bhosale, et al. 2023b. Llama 2: Open foundation and fine-tuned chat models. *arXiv preprint arXiv:2307.09288*.

Khanh-Tung Tran, Barry O'Sullivan, and Hoang D. Nguyen. 2024. UCCIX: Irish-eXcellence Large Language Model.

UNESCO, editor. 2010. *Atlas of the world's languages in danger*, 3 edition. Memory of Peoples Series. UNESCO.

Ashish Vaswani, Noam Shazeer, Niki Parmar, Jakob Uszkoreit, Llion Jones, Aidan N Gomez, Łukasz Kaiser, and Illia Polosukhin. 2017. Attention is all you need. *Advances in neural information processing systems*, 30.

BigScience Workshop et al. 2023. BLOOM: A 176b-parameter open-access multilingual language model.

Zheng Xin Yong, Hailey Schoelkopf, Niklas Muennighoff, Alham Fikri Aji, David Ifeoluwa Adelani, Khalid Almubarak, M Saiful Bari, Lintang Sutawika, Jungo Kasai, Ahmed Baruwa, Genta Winata, Stella Biderman, Edward Raff, Dragomir Radev, and Vassilina Nikoulina. 2023. BLOOM+1: Adding language support to BLOOM for zero-shot prompting. In *Proceedings of the 61st Annual Meeting of the Association for Computational Linguistics (Volume 1: Long Papers)*, pages 11682–11703, Toronto, Canada. Association for Computational Linguistics.

Barret Zoph, Deniz Yuret, Jonathan May, and Kevin Knight. 2016. Transfer learning for low-resource neural machine translation. In *Proceedings of the 2016 Conference on Empirical Methods in Natural Language Processing*, pages 1568–1575, Austin, Texas. Association for Computational Linguistics.

Author Index

Association for Computational Linguistics
209 N. Eighth Street
Stroudsburg, Pennsylvania 18360

ISBN 979-8-3313-0169-9

CURRAN ASSOCIATES INC.
proceedings.com